A Convenient Country House

*A Historical Sketch of the Edwards family and
the development of Ed*

GW00598966

Hazel McCay

ISBN 10: 0-9554584-0-4
ISBN 13: 978-0-9554584-0-8
© Published by Edwards Primary School, Castlederg.

Printed by Browne Printers Ltd.
Letterkenny, Co. Donegal.
tel.: +353 74 9121387
e-mail: reception@browneprinters.com

Year 4 Children admire their finished mural.   Year 4 : 2004 - 2005

Back row. L - R: Kyle Duncan. Martin Baird. Emily Maxwell. Olivia Kealley. Scott Gordon. Alan Boyd. Alex Harpur. Adam Bustard.

Front Left: Shirley Love. Shirley Harpur. Shannon Watson. Lynsay Glenn. Front Right: Hannah Hawkes. Chloe Hall. Leah Lowry. Jane Condy.

Contents

Foreword.

It is a great pleasure and privilege to have been asked to write a short foreword for this book "A Convenient Country House."

I have been associated with Edwards Primary School for the past thirty years. My three children all received their excellent primary school education at Edwards and I was pleased to have been elected to serve as a school Governor for 27 years and as Chairman of the Board of Governors for 5 years during the construction of the "state of the art" new school building, which was completed in January 2005.

This book sets out a detailed history of the Edwards family from 1600 to the late 1800's. It also traces the development of the school from 1737 right up to a wonderful modern day facility in January 2005.

Teaching and education are not just about bricks and mortar and hi-tech equipment but have much more to do with the quality and dedication of all staff, who are and have been associated with Edwards Primary School.

The book gives us many interesting snapshots of some of the more influential members of staff, both past and present, but it is important to recognise that all staff make a valuable contribution to the school. The book also mentions many of the achievements, both academic and sporting, of the pupils.

I am fully aware of the amount of research that went into the preparation of this book and our sincere thanks must go to Mrs Hazel McCay, who not only carried out the research but also was responsible for writing the book.

It is my privilege to commend it to you and hope that contributors and readers alike enjoy the contents.

Dr Morris Brown. January 2006.

Acknowledgements.

This historical sketch of the Edwards family and the development of Edwards School would not have been possible but for the help of so many people, both known and unknown, whose assistance was invaluable in the preparation of this book.

Thanks to Mr A. S. Orr who had the vision of recording the history of the school at this important point in its development. I also express my sincere thanks to the Western Education and Library Board who provided funding through Development and Dissemination of Good Practice and who made this venture possible. Grateful thanks to Mr Tom Doherty and Mrs Sheila McCaul whose belief in the project led to an extension of the funding. To Mrs Lesley Marriott and Mr Seamus Bradley, thank you for your help in the evaluation process. I am also very grateful to the Principal, Mr A.S. Orr and the Board of Governors, who placed at my disposal the Management Committee Minutes and any available information held in school and have been most supportive and encouraging. My grateful thanks to Mrs Anne Hunter who gave freely of her time and so ably assisted with research in the P.R.O.N.I. Thanks also to Mrs Julie Ann Warnock and Miss Dianne Barratt, who taught Year 5 in my absence.

I am also deeply indebted to many organisations and individuals who have helped with archival material:

- The Deputy Keeper of Records, Public Records Office of Northern Ireland for permission to use the material related to the Edwards family and Edwards Primary School.
- Dr Ann McVeigh, P.R.O.N.I. for her help and advice and to all the other members of staff who gave assistance, dealt with queries and provided photocopies of material.
- The Right Honourable Earl of Castlestewart for permission to use extracts from the Castlestewart Papers and for sending me extracts from "The Stuarts of the House of Castlestuart in Ireland."
- The staff in Castlederg Library, Omagh Library, The Centre for Migration

Studies and The Linenhall Library, Belfast.

- Mr Michéal O'Comain in the Office of the Chief Herald in Dublin for his time, research and advice.
- Mr Anthony Kirby from the Environment and Heritage Service.
- Mr Aubrey Fielding in St. Columb's Cathedral, Londonderry.
- Councillor Jim Emery who freely gave his time to contribute so many items, offer sound advice and answer so many questions.
- Mr Willie Douglas, J.P. Burnfoot, Dungiven, for all his help with the history in Bovevagh Parish.
- Mr Wesley Atchison, Editor, Tyrone Constitution, for permission to use extracts from past papers and for continual publicity of Edwards' events.
- Mr Alan Neill, Photographer, Tyrone Constitution, who kindly supplied many photographs.
- To Mary Lafferty from The News Letter for her help with publicity.
- Mr Adam Shaw in the Archival Department of Glasgow University for help with the Matriculation Albums.
- Canon W. Quill for the use of Derg Parish Church Burial Records.

I am hugely grateful to all the wonderful people that I have only met through the Internet but have generously provided so much useful information:

- Mr Simon Elliott who made such an effort to provide many pointers to the Edwards family.
- Gordon and Gayle Perkins, in Queensland, Australia, who have taken the trouble to send so much relative material, both by email and by post.
- Mr Mark Meredith from London, who provided a vast amount of his personal records of the Holmes family.
- Mrs Virginia Miller in Victoria, Canada for her interest and help with the Semple connection.
- Dr. Linde Lunney in U.C.D. for help with the Cairnes family.
- Mr George Speer, Brentwood, California, U.S.A.
  for sharing the Edwards gedcom file.

Many former pupils and members of staff, both past and present and their friends and families, have donated photographs and proffered a wealth of information. I thank them most sincerely:

Mrs P. Bratton, Mr T. Bratton, Mrs M. Buchanan, Mr R. Clarke, Mr R. Clarke, Mr S. Clarke, Mr A. Crawford, Mr J. Emery, Mrs S. Emery, Mr E. Faulkner, Mrs C. Ferry, Mr T. Forsythe, Mr A. Gant, Mr I. Gowdy, Mrs H. Graham, Mrs J. Hamilton (deceased), Mr G. Huey, Mrs J. Huey, Mrs F. Irwin, Mrs E. Kissick, Mrs I. Lambert, Mrs A. Leitch, Mr D. Leitch, Mr A. Lyons, Miss J. Lyons, Mrs A. Millar, Mr W. Millar, Mrs P. Murray, Miss L. McCay, Miss S. McCay, Mrs V. MacDougall, Mr S. McFarland, Mr and Mrs M. McHale, Mrs O. McKean (deceased), Mrs G. McKinley, Mrs A. McNutt, Miss C. Noble, Mrs P. Quigley, Mr S. Reid, Mrs J. Riddall, Miss M. Robinson, Miss C. Roke, Mrs E. Ryan, Mrs S. Sproule, Mrs P. Stewart, Mr T. Sturdee, Mrs B. Waibel, Mrs E. Walls, Mr J. Walls, Mr A. Watt, Mrs M. Watt, Mr R. Watt, Mrs A. Waugh, Mr R. Waugh, Mr W. Waugh, Mrs M. West, Mr D. Williamson and Mrs D. Wilson.

Thanks are also due to Mrs E. Walls, Mrs H. Kerrigan and Miss J. Moore, the office staff of Edwards P.S. and Miss E McKane, Classroom Assistant, who helped with many queries, phone calls and typing, Mrs P. Bratton, Miss M. Kinloch and Miss M. Young from the Nursery for photographs and information, Mr Thomas Kerrigan for help with the family tree, Mr Alan Coulter for staff and class photographs and to Miss A. M. Hodge and Mrs P. Bratton for taking time to proof read the history.
I extend my grateful thanks to all members of staff for their interest and support.

A special word of thanks and appreciation to Mr Seamus Browne and the staff of Browne Printers of Letterkenny for their patience, expertise and advice, particularly Mrs Adrienne Randles and Mr Igor Kruk for all their dedicated work in the design.

Introduction.

Locally everyone in the Castlederg area knows of Edwards Primary School and in a tenuous manner most might know that it was called after someone who lived in the area many years ago. But apart from that brief pointer to history, very little, if anything, is known of the Edwards family. Where they came from, what they did and where they went, seemed to be buried in the secrets of the dim and distant past.

I was given the task to uncover the family history and its link with the development of Edwards School and here I apologise for my inadequacies—I am not a researcher, nor a historian or a writer, but I have tried my best in the limited time available to me to find out as much as I can and to record it as best I can. If there are gaps, I am sorry and perhaps someday, someone else with greater knowledge and expertise will fill them in.

Meantime, I hope that what I have found out and am now about to share with you will be of interest and fill the void in a fascinating part of the history of the local area. I also hope it will be useful for the staff and pupils of Edwards Primary School to have an understanding and awareness of the school's past history and that they will enjoy the various stories as they are incorporated into the curriculum.

In the quest to acquire information I have searched limitless web-sites and dusty library shelves, read countless books, scoured old newspapers dissipated by the ravages of time, asked interminable questions, made many phone calls, delighted in numerous email messages, talked to knowledgeable historians and representatives of various bodies, wandered through sadly overgrown and disused graveyards and derelict churches and immersed myself in the wealth of enchanting documents held in the Public Records Office of Northern Ireland. (P.R.O.N.I.) Along the way I have encountered the most helpful people and I am grateful for so much assistance so freely given. I have had contributions from all over the world and in this way I have been able to travel through uncharted territory and reveal hitherto unknown and forgotten facts.

Of all the avenues I travelled down, the P.R.O.N.I. was certainly the most productive. The wonderful wealth of precious documents deposited there has revealed the rich tapestry of the life and times of a truly fascinating family with a remarkable history and many tales to tell.

I have tried to relate the history of the Edwards' in chronicles, following each family on the Genealogical Table in descending order and hope that you will have as much pleasure in reading the historical anecdotes as I have had in researching them.

I have traced the history of the school since it was just a seed in the mind of Hugh Edwards, up until the opening of the new building in 2005, and as I travelled through the many changes in situation, buildings, staff, curriculum and teaching methods, as well as the memories and achievements of past pupils, I hope the reader will gain an insight into what has been the core of the community for almost two hundred years.

The school has come a long way since its inception as "a convenient country house" and I am sure that all associated with it can look upon it with a great deal of pride and confidence in its future.

A

HISTORICAL

SKETCH

OF

THE

EDWARDS

FAMILY.

Origins of The Edwards Family.

Family historical records dating back to the sixteenth and seventeenth century are sketchy but by all accounts the Edwards family appeared to be of Welsh origin, with an estate in Flintshire, North Wales. It is also thought that they had London connections. As was the case with many leading seventeenth century families, they were engaged in military affairs and were staunch supporters of the crown.

King James I(1603-1625) and his successor, Charles I(1625-1649) ruled by the Divine Right of Kings – the doctrine under which Kings were appointed by God and so were not answerable to men. Charles' behaviour led Parliament to revolution and from 1629 he ruled without any Parliament, after the M.P.'s made him accept a petition of right, guaranteeing them powers such as approval of taxation. The King's apparent support for Catholics also made him deeply unpopular with Protestant parliamentarians. Desperate for funds to quell a Scottish revolt in 1640, Charles recalled Parliament and in 1642 tried to arrest five M.P.'s. This sparked off a civil war, which Charles lost and he was imprisoned in 1648 by the army. A High Court was appointed and Charles was condemned to death. He was executed in 1649 in London, after which Britain became a commonwealth or republic under Oliver Cromwell.

Under the creation of the commonwealth Hugh Edwards lost the Flintshire estate and prudently retired to Ireland. The exact date in which the family arrived in Ireland is unknown, but the first of the name noted in Ulster was that of Edward Edwards at the funeral of Sir Arthur Chichester, in October 1625. Chichester had been the Deputy of Ireland and Edwards was "in charge of his leader's horse, suitably plumed and draped in black, in the long procession honouring a great soldier."[1]

During the Roundheads' ascendancy and control by Cromwell as Lord Protector, nothing is known of Edwards' activities. But after Cromwell died, King Charles II assumed the throne and he remembered the loyalty of the Edwards'. A Royal Charter granted Hugh Edwards five townlands in the parish of Bovevagh, Londonderry, in lieu of the estate he had lost in Wales.[2] Londonderry was chiefly the territory of the O'Cahans or O'Kanes and the lands given to Edwards were part of the confiscated lands of Manus O'Cahan who had rebelled in 1641. They were namely the townlands of Bonnanaboigh, Glenconway, Leeke, Straw and Templemoyle and amounted to almost three thousand acres. These were fertile lands in the beautiful Roe valley and as townlands are still in existence today, although the Edwards name has now died out in the region. The name Straw has variations and may be written as "Strews" or "Strath", the latter being the Scottish version and means a level place beside a river. Wills and other documents relating to the family use all three spellings.

The "Census of Ireland in 1659 for Londonderry Citty and County" cites Hugh Edwards as being a merchant in "ye Diamond" along with fourteen English and Scots and six Irish people.[3]

Minutes of the First Corporation after the Restoration indicate that Hugh Edwards was an active participant in the affairs of the City. He was an Alderman and Mayor of the City four years before his death in 1672. He was M.P. for the City in 1661 in the Dublin Parliament and in 1669 he acted as High Sheriff of Tyrone.

His elevated status in Tyrone resulted from his purchase of a large landed estate known as the Manor of Hastings, which extended from near Omagh to the shores of Lough Derg on one side and in another direction nearly to the Gap of Barnesmore. This was an estate that had been forfeited by the Earl of Tyrone and granted in 1609 at the time of the Plantation of Ulster, to Sir John Davys, Attorney General for Ireland. Sir John Davys' daughter, Lucy, married Ferdinand, Lord Hastings, later known as the Earl of Huntingdon, and he inherited the estate on the death of Davys in 1626. [4]

An interesting account of the transactions that took place at the time is recorded in a letter written by Elizabeth Lowther, (nee Jack, of Ardstraw) the great grandmother of Gordon Perkins. She wrote, *"The Seige of Derry was in the year 1688 and my history begins a few years earlier. The country was in a state of civil war. The Manor of Hastings was the largest estate in the north of Ireland and the owner was the Countess of Huntingdon, but she was so much alarmed at the state of the country that she decided to sell it. The estate lies in County Tyrone, between Castlederg and Omagh. It is now owned by four landlords, the Earl of*

Castlestewart being the largest proprietor. The family residence, a fine old building within a mile of Castlederg, is called Castlegore. One of my first ancestors, a Mr Edwards, came over from London. He was the son of a London merchant. He brought the money over in gold, bought the estate and paid the Countess of Huntingdon." [5]

I have not managed to locate any official documents regarding the purchase of the estate but the above details and many others in the letter, correlate with other accounts and in the absence of confirmation, may be accepted as a fairly accurate description of the events. Genealogical notes on the family also endorse the purchase and suggest that Hugh Edwards lived in the Manor of Hastings, "when not attending to his duties as M.P. for the City of Londonderry in the Dublin Parliament".

Except for his involvement in politics not a lot is known about Hugh on a personal level. He had a sister Margaret who was married to a man named Grot, possibly of French Huguenot origin, but nothing further is known of them. Edward Edwards, who played an important role in the funeral of Arthur Chichester, may or may not have been related; the only known facts are that both were alive around the same period and both were involved in affairs of state.[6]

Hugh's wife was also named Margaret, but her maiden name is unknown and they had eight children, six sons and two daughters; **Hugh, Edward, Robert, Thomas, William, Margaret, Lyle and Alice.** The latter child died in infancy, Lyle died aged eight and William died aged twenty-five. All were buried at St. Columb's Cathedral, Londonderry. Hugh, the eldest son, is not named first in his father's will, and it is thought that he may have been of a delicate constitution. He died on 9th of October 1667 and is also buried at Londonderry. Robert was married and left one son, Edward, but nothing is known about them except that acquittance of his father's goods was granted to him in 1684.

More is known about Hugh's second son Edward, who was born in 1640, the only survivor of the six sons, and he married Mary Moncrieff. She was the daughter of Thomas Moncrieff, (or Muncrieffe, as it is sometimes spelt), Captain in Command of the Sixth Company of Foot, raised during the Siege for the defence of Derry, and afterwards Alderman of the Corporation and Sheriff of Derry in 1690. Edward inherited from his father, the estates of "Strath" (Straw), which included the townlands of Straw, Bonnanaboigh, Leek, Templemoyle and Glenconway in County Londonderry and The Manor of Hastings in County Tyrone. In early life he resided partly in Londonderry, but mainly in "Strath House", the ancestral home, beautifully situated on the western bank of the River Roe, and which has been since then and up to the late 1800's, continuously in the occupancy of his lineage and name.[7]

In 1675 it is said that he came to reside in the Castle of Derg, a fortified stronghold, suited to the exigencies of the time, and built by Sir John Davys in 1615. But this is a matter of speculation as other accounts suggest that the castle was destroyed when Sir Phelim O'Neill besieged it in 1641. Edward held the title of High Sheriff of Tyrone in the years 1674, 1675 and 1685 and was Sheriff of the City and County of Derry in 1671.[8]

The story of Edward and his descendants is recounted in a later chapter.

1. Genealogical notes on the Edwards Family. PRONI: D2547/30

2. Ibid.

3. A Census of Ireland c. 1659, Seamus Pender, P123

4. Details of the townlands in the Manor of Hastings are included in Appendix 1.

5. This letter, written by Elizabeth Lowther, came from the collection of Gordon and Gayle Perkins, Queensland, Australia. Gordon's grandparents were Francis George Perkins and Moina Phyllis Osterlund. Moina's mother was Elizabeth Lowther, (nee Jack), from Ardstraw. Her mother was Eliza Jack (nee Welsh) whose mother was Elizabeth Welsh (nee Stewart), who had eloped from Castlegore, (where she had been under the protection of Olivia, Countess Rosse, daughter of Hugh Edwards), and had married James Welsh, son of Rev. Andrew Welsh, Dissenting Minister in Ardstraw.

6.   The printed notes on the descendants of Hugh Edwards.
     PRONI: D/245/15

7.   Ibid.

8.   The Plantation in Ulster 1608-1620. Rev. George Hill. Appendix U, High
     Sheriffs of Tyrone, P444.

The Last will and Testament of Hugh Edwards

26th June 1662.

In the name of god Amen I
Hugh Edwards of y[e] City of London-
Derry Merch[t]: being in p[er]fect health &
memory (bleſsed bee y[e] god of heaben) at
y[e] time at y[e] writeing hereof, but being
senſible that I muſt dye, and leave
this world when y[e] lord seeth my time, / therfore
bequeath my soule to god that gave it
and hope that through y[e] m[er]ritts of his
sonne Jesus Chriſt I shall bee saved and
live w[th] him in heaben and as for
my worldly goods I leaue them as
followeth. /
ffirſt I leaue my Wife Margarett
Edwards

Edward's father, Hugh, drew up his will, written in large flourishing handwriting, on 26th of June 1662. The original document, written on thick yellow paper, and held in the P.R.O.N.I., is in fine condition and with patience, is legible. (See the copy included.) It is thirteen pages long and uses the language of the time—"ye" for "the" and "s" written as "f" would be in script today.

Wills often reveal much about a person and from Hugh's we can tell that he was a thoughtful and generous husband and father. He made provision for his wife and family and made alternative arrangements if his first wishes could not be carried out. He did not name individual items but left all his estate "both real and personal", "money, goods or land" to his wife and family. He mentions sums of five hundred pounds and in 1662 that was a lot of money!

He wished that his wife Margaret, who had been " a most dutifull and respective yoakfellow to me and to my children" should be the sole executor and administrator of his estate. He also stated that he wanted his sons to "assist her in all things for her good and ye good of my children". A third of all his possessions was bequeathed to Margaret, provided she would not marry after his death and the remainder was to be divided equally between his six sons, all of whom were alive at that time, and whom he hoped would be "happie and fruitfull on ye earth", (although Hugh and Lyle actually died before their father.) His wish also was that his wife would, during all her life, "enjoy one of those two houses I now live in and ye other house I leave to my son Edward". He did not name the houses but it may be assumed that he referred to the house in Strath or Straw and Castlegore in the Manor of Hastings. To his daughter Margaret he bequeathed "five hundred pounds to be paid to her after the birth of her first borne, according to ye lawes of Scotland provided she marry by and with ye consent of her mother and brother and friends." He then left it to the disposal of her brothers, Edward and Hugh, and Robert Houston "to give her what they think fitt" but "if it shall please god to remove her I desire only the sum of five hundred pounds to be divided betwixt ye whole children."

Through the years the Edwards family have shown their staunch support for the church and the community in which they lived. Hugh set a fine example; he instructed Edward and Hugh to pay "yearly into ye church of Londonderry for ye space of twenty years after my decease for ye poor of this parish ye sum of fiftie shillings a year during ye time of twenty years and that to begin immediately after my death".

Hugh died on the 24th of February 1672 and was buried in St. Columb's Cathedral. His family erected what is now recognised as the oldest memorial in the Cathedral, in his honour in 1674. It is situated in the north aisle and has been described as "barbaric". The inscription in Latin is flanked on either side by colonettes (with spiral flutes and bands). At the top is a Coat of Arms, featuring four birds and underneath the inscription is a panel showing mortuary symbols such as skulls, bones, hourglasses, a tolling bell, mattocks and a coffin. The monument was originally overlaid with a coating of black, white and red paste and despite the ravages of time; remnants of the paste remain visible. (See photographs)

Margaret, Hugh's wife, died on the 20th November 1679, in the same month as their son William, and preceded by six of their family. She too is buried in the Cathedral grounds.

The information in this chapter is based on the Last Will and Testament of Hugh Edwards 1662. PRONI: D/847/27/7

The memorial to Hugh Edwards in St. Columb's Cathedral, Londonderry.

The Cairnes Connection.

The Genealogical Table of the Cairnes Family. PRONI D/1618/14/11

Anyone familiar with the Siege of Derry or the memorials in St Columb's Cathedral will be aware of the name "Cairnes" and its connotations with the historical events of the seventeenth century.

There is some debate as to the first name of the earliest member of the Cairnes family to settle in Ireland. The printed notes of the Edwards descendants refer to Thomas Cairnes of Orchardstown, Scotland, while the genealogical notes of Rev Alexander Fleming, written to Lord Castlestewart, refer to Alexander Cairnes, who was born in 1580 at Cults, Wigtownshire, Scotland. Henry Cairnes Lawlor's book "The History of the Family of Cairns or Cairnes" also details the early ancestor as Alexander of Cults and since Lawlor was a descendant and an authority on the Cairnes family his version may be accepted.[1]

In any case, he came to Ireland with his uncle, Murray, Earl of Annandale, having received grants of land of the confiscated estates in Monaghan, Tyrone and Donegal. He settled in Donoughmore, Co. Donegal, in 1610. He married Jane, daughter of John Scott of Colefad, of the house of Bucclugh or Buecleuch, and his wife, Mary Anne, daughter of the Earl of Annandale. They had three sons, John, David and Robert and a daughter Mary.

The Cairnes family settled in the Clogher area around 1638; John lived in the Manor of Cecil and Robert and David at Knockmany. Estates were often known by dual names and Parsonstown was an early name for the Cecil estate, as the first patentee was Sir William Parsons, the King's Surveyor-General.

Cecil Manor, Clogher, home of John Cairnes. Might the Manor of Hastings or Castlegore, home of Edwards family, have been like this?

David eventually became Lord of the Manors of Killyfaddy and Cecil. The name Killyfaddy was also known as "Raveagh" and people are frequently referred to in the Edwards genealogical table as "of Raveagh."

The family played an important role in the siege of Derry in 1689. David Cairnes of Knockmany was a merchant in the city and Lawlor states that he "was the first gentleman of position in the surrounding counties to reach the city" some time before the Jacobite forces besieged the city. "Cairnes at once addressed the citizens in the Diamond, strongly approved of what had been done and in glowing terms commended the bravery of those who had shut the gates." (His nephew, Captain William Cairnes, was one of the original apprentice boys who closed the Ferry Quay Gate and later served in King William's army at the Battle of the Boyne.)

An efficient organiser, David set to work, assessing the position. He "summoned a meeting of the prominent citizens, and the magazine having been seized, caused an inventory to be made of the arms and ammunition available, and of the provisions to be counted upon in case of a siege."

These were thought to be too meagre and Cairnes was despatched to London to request assistance from King William. He had his own boat in the Foyle and set sail. Although hampered by bad weather he eventually arrived in London and as law agent for the Irish Society, promptly obtained a meeting with the King who ordered immediate measures to be taken for the forwarding of military supplies to the city. Captain James Hamilton was despatched with "arms and accoutrements for 2000 men" in the "Deliverance" and he brought with him a despatch to Governor Lundy, "one of the ablest officers in the army and a staunch supporter of His Majesty," assuring him of the King's support and giving detailed instructions as to the strengthening of the fortifications. But when Cairnes arrived in the city he found nothing had been done and he suspected treachery. However he assured the Council and the citizens of the King's support and encouraged everyone to stay in the city and support the cause.

The outcome after a supreme defensive effort, lasting one hundred and five days, enduring hardship, hunger and death, was victory for the Williamite supporters and the tireless Cairnes who had done much to encourage the people of the city. David, who was born on 16th November 1645, was a much admired and respected personality. He was a Councillor at Law and Recorder of Derry in 1691. He served as a Lieutenant Colonel in Murray's Dragoons and he was a very loyal supporter of the Derry Garrison. It is also said that he represented Derry's interest at King William's Court in London with outstanding ability. As a lawyer, he had wholeheartedly supported the shutting of the gates during the siege, unlike many other professional men. He was elected as M.P. for Derry from 1692 – 1722 in appreciation of his great leadership.

In 1676 David married Margaret Edwards, the only daughter of Hugh and his wife Margaret. They had five children, two sons and three daughters. The first born, Robert, known as "little son" died young, as did their two daughters, Elizabeth and Margaret. These infants were buried in St. Michan's Church Of Ireland in Dublin, close to Cairnes' lodgings in Capel Street.[2] Details of their sad deaths are scarce and the cause of death is unknown but infant mortality was high in those days. Their son John survived to become an

David Cairnes.

Army Captain but was unfortunately killed in a duel in Newcastle-on-Tyne on 28th of March 1719. Duels at this time were an everyday occurrence and unfortunately the results were often fatal. Unmarried, John left no issue.

The memorial to David Cairnes in St. Columb's Cathedral

This left their only remaining daughter Jane, who was born in 1680. She was also known as Joanna and she married her first cousin, Thomas Edwards, of Castlegore, Castlederg, the second son of Edward Edwards and his wife Mary (Moncrieff). Their story will be related in the next chapter.

Many accounts written about the siege of

Derry record the heroic efforts of David Cairnes and a memorial tablet in St. Columb's Cathedral, erected by The Honourable, the Irish Society, (which was the body set up to supervise and manage the Plantation of Ulster) describes David as "A pious Christian, An intelligent lawyer and an heroic defender of his RELIGION and his COUNTRY".

David Cairnes died in 1722, aged seventy-seven, and his remains were interred in the grounds of St. Columb's Cathedral, in his beloved city of Londonderry.

1. Much of information in this chapter has been derived from "A History of the Family of Cairnes or Cairns," by Henry Cairns Lawlor, now a very rare book, which may be found in the Linenhall Library, Belfast.

2. See the Chapter entitled The Family of Thomas Edwards and Jane Cairnes for more information on St Michan's Church, Dublin.

The Family of Edward Edwards and Mary Moncrieff.

When Hugh Edwards died in 1672, having made careful arrangements through his last will and testament, for the disposal of his property and assets, little did he realise that his greatest legacy was to leave the family a surviving son who ensured the continuation of the lineage and name Edwards.

Son Edward, who was born in 1640, continued his father's contribution to the political and administrative life of the country, acting three times as High Sheriff of Tyrone, (1674, 1675, 1685) and once as High Sheriff of Londonderry.

The High Sheriff was appointed either by the Crown or by the Irish Treasurer, mostly from the largest property owners in the County or prominent townspeople. It was the responsibility of the High Sheriff to select twenty-three members of the Grand Jury, which was the most important local body in the late eighteenth and early nineteenth century and was empowered to raise money by means of county rates. The Crown's judges visited each county twice yearly and held assizes for the hearing and adjudication of cases, with the assistance of the Grand Jury. Its responsibilities also included the upkeep of local institutions such as hospitals and lunatic asylums as well as the construction and maintenance of roads and bridges. In fact, "Old Grand Jury Road" outside Crossgar in County Down, today still bears testament to the fact that roads were sometimes named after their early caretakers. Members of the Grand Jury were usually leading property owners in the county and the order in which they stood on the list gave a good indication of their social standing.

It would therefore be safe to accept that Edward Edwards, as the High Sheriff of Tyrone, was regarded as an important landowner and was prominent in the administration of the area. He married Mary Moncrieff on the 16th of January 1667 and together they had ten children: **Hugh, Thomas, Edward, Robert, Robert, William, Matthew, Elizabeth, Mary and Edward.**

They came to live in Castlederg in 1675 and it is thought that the family was born and raised here. Unfortunately six of the ten children died young. Hugh, born in 1668, only lived until the age of fourteen and was buried at Londonderry in April 1682, while a succession of children died in infancy. Edward died in January 1675, Robert lived only fourteen months, from April 1674 until July

26

1675, William, born in 1677 and Matthew who was born in December 1678, died as infants, while Elizabeth died in October 1681.

This sad chain of mortalities serves to underline the difficulties of life in the seventeenth century, despite the family being one of means. Women of all classes married young and had large families, sadly however it was expected that at least half would die in infancy.

The surviving members of the family, Edward, Mary, Robert and Thomas, lived to reasonable ages and all had interesting stories.

Recalling the fact that Edward and Mary Edwards had two sons, Robert and Edward, who both died in 1675, it is somewhat strange and bizarre to note that they called two later sons by the same first names, but apparently this practice was not uncommon.

This second surviving son, Robert, was probably born in 1676 and had Kilcroagh, part of the Manor of Hastings, for life and for the lives of his sons Edward and Matthew. He too was a Captain in King William's Army.

Various sources, including references in the letter written by Gordon Perkins' great grandmother and alluded to earlier, tell the amazing love story behind Robert's marriage to Martha la Vie on the 4th of November 1700.

The Cairnes family, as we know, were great followers of King William of Orange. Sir Alexander Cairnes of Knockmany, Clogher, was sent on a mission to France and whilst there was introduced to Henry, Count la Vie, a French nobleman and a Colonel in the Army. His wife was dead but he had three beautiful daughters. Sir Alexander fell in love with the eldest daughter and married her, bringing her back to Ireland to live. The la Vie family were Huguenot or Protestant and shortly after this event, there was widespread torture and a massacre of Protestants in France. Count la Vie and his daughters fled from France to the safety of the Cairnes' home in Londonderry. It is said that they were brought to Ireland by a sympathetic boat Captain, amazingly concealed in barrels of apples. In Londonderry Robert Edwards was introduced to Martha, the younger daughter, fell in love with her and eventually married her in 1700.[1]

Count Henry la Vie was described as a very fine soldier and fought through the kingdom with William's army; the last battle in which he fought was Aughrim in 1690.

Edward, probably born in 1680, is the surviving son of Edward and Mary, of whom least is known. He married and had children as he is mentioned in the 1721 will of his brother Thomas, as "brother Edward and his children," but beyond that nothing is known, as no details have been recorded in the genealogical notes or on the family tree nor do any of his documents remain.

Edward and Mary's daughter, also called Mary, was born on March 6th 1681 and she survived until she was fifty. Her marriage, recorded on the family tree, was to Stephen Ash, son of another well-connected Londonderry family. He was born on Christmas Day 1675, the fifth son of Captain John Ash, of Ashbrook, Sheriff of Londonderry, 1676, and his third wife Elizabeth Holland, daughter of Captain William Holland. Stephen took the name of Holland with an estate granted him by his mother. His brother, Captain Thomas Ash, was a well-noted historian of the siege. Mary and Stephen went on to have four sons and two daughters, of whom only one daughter married and had children. Two of their sons died in 1736, nothing further is known of the other two sons and one daughter died unmarried so whether the Ash-Holland name died out in that family line is unclear.

Perhaps the most pertinent member of the family of Edward and Mary, for those with an interest in Edwards School, has to be Thomas, the father of the school benefactor, Hugh. Thomas was born in January 1670 and is called the "eldest" (surviving) son in his father's will of 1688. His story, which will be related in another chapter, is long and interesting, as he did much to perpetuate the Edwards family name.

The lives of Edward Edwards and his wife Mary were remarkable for their brevity. Although we know little of their overall health, both died young, maybe due to the stresses of having such a large family and suffering multiple bereavements. Mary died in January 1682, less than a year after giving birth to her youngest daughter Mary, and followed by son Hugh in April. Edward died in 1688, aged forty-eight, an age that would be considered youthful by today's standards and leaving very young orphans. How the children were reared is unclear, but as Thomas was the eldest survivor at eighteen when his father died, perhaps he shouldered the responsibility. However, it is good to report that the family line remained strong and continued through Robert and Thomas.

1. This description of the Cairnes family and the La Vie connection is recorded in The Printed Notes on the Descendants of Hugh Edwards. PRONI : D/2547/15

The Family and Descendants of Robert Edwards and Martha la Vie.

Research into the Edwards family has uncovered a tangled web of inter-marriage and compelling anecdotes. In this chapter I have attempted to trace the family and descendants of Robert and Martha but it is easy to become lost in the profusion of similar names, which are repeated time and time again.

Robert of Kilcroagh, second surviving son of Edward and Mary, was a landowner and Captain in King William's army. This brought him into contact with gentry and military personnel, therefore it was not surprising that he was introduced to Mademoiselle Martha la Vie, daughter of Count Henry la Vie, following their remarkable escape from France concealed in barrels of apples. Like the Edwards,' the la Vie family were strong Protestants and they had fled from France, rather than denounce their faith.

Robert and Martha were married on the 4th of November 1700 and they lived at Kilcroagh, part of the Manor of Hastings, and a short distance from the town of Castlederg.

Local people still associate the Edwards family with Kilcroagh and a fine farmhouse remains on the site, with an enclosed yard surrounded by sturdy, well-maintained outbuildings. It is quite possible that this is the original house. The present owners, Mr and Mrs Michael McHale, confirm that it is a rambling old house that the McHale family have owned since 1912. To the best of their knowledge, many of the original features such as the shape of the house, the outhouses and the courtyard, the garden and the trees, still remain as they were in past centuries.

Kilcroagh House, Castlederg, home of Robert Edwards and Martha la Vie and their family from 1700.

Original outbuildings in the enclosed yard of Kilcroagh House.

A minor road linking Kilcroagh and Dartans is still called the carriage road and indeed a legend abounds that on a clear moonlit night about the hour of midnight a coach and four black horses can be seen clattering past on its ghostly way!

For Robert and Martha Edwards, the rambling hills and peaceful countryside of Tyrone provided an ideal setting in which to raise a family. Together they had two sons and four or five daughters---- the exact details of the minor family members are not known. Their sons, **Henry-Edward** and **Matthew,** and their daughter **Mary**, are named on the family tree but the other daughters are referred to in vague terms.

While there is little evidence to suggest how the children of the early Edwards families were educated, there is no doubt that they had some form of schooling, as in many cases they went into the army, the church, were involved in affairs of state or assumed professional occupations. In the seventeenth and early eighteenth centuries there was a number of different types of school available. Hedge schools provided some opportunities for elementary learning as wandering scholars traversed the countryside setting up "schools" on the sunny side of a hedge in good weather, giving holidays when it rained and visiting in farmhouses in the wintertime. There were also Diocesan or Parish schools that promoted English culture, although there were actually very few of them. However, as the Edwards families were wealthy it is possible that the children received private education and then progressed to one of the Royal Schools, which were established by James I following the Plantation in 1608. Foyle College was established in 1617, (although it was not known by that name until 1814), the Charter establishing Armagh Royal was dated 1627, while the schools in Dungannon, Raphoe, Cavan, Bannagher and Enniskillen were well established by 1662. These institutions educated a large proportion of the sons of the nobility and the gentry and prepared them for entry to university, which for the most part was Trinity College Dublin, although improved means of travelling meant access to English and Scottish Universities such as Oxford, Cambridge and Glasgow.

Henry-Edward Edwards and Mary Osborne.

The present Straw House, Bovevagh, home of Henry Edward Edwards and Jean Ross in 1739.

Henry-Edward, later called Edward, the first-born son of Robert and Martha, was well educated, as he grew up to become a Physician, but unfortunately there are no details of how he achieved this. He lived in Straw House on the Bovevagh estate and as he was not involved in farming he sold his interest in Kilcroagh to his brother Matthew.

Edward firstly married Jean Ross of Newtownlimavady (later Limavady) on May 5th 1739 and both parties drew up an elaborate marriage settlement. It is beautifully written on thick parchment paper and is held in the P.R.O.N.I. Jean was born on March 2nd 1716 and sadly died at the age of twenty four, within a year of her marriage to Edward. They had no children, but Edward married secondly, Mary Osborne, (nee Caskey) and they had a family of seven children, four boys and three girls---**Robert, Matthew, James, Frederick, Martha, Mary and Ann.**

Turning to these grandchildren of Robert and Martha enlarges the family circle to encompass many members of the Bovevagh community, as Edward and his wife Mary reared their seven children in County Londonderry. Their first son Robert grew up and married his cousin Elizabeth Edwards, the fourth child of Matthew and his wife Ann Donaldson, and they continued to live at Straw. Details of their family are included in the next section.

Their second son Matthew, who was a Colonel in the local Volunteers, inherited half of the townland of Leek. At that time there were three groups of Yeomanry or Volunteers in the area. They were based at Leek, Myroe and Bovevagh. Matthew married a widow, Sarah Haslett, and had one son **Francis.** He in turn married and also had one son, whose address on the family tree is given as Sauchiehall Street, Glasgow, and although he had three offspring they have not been traced.

The other half of the townland of Leek was bequeathed to Edward and Mary's third son, James, who was born in 1761. Interestingly, he married into an important and well-off local family whose name is still associated with Bovevagh today. His chosen bride was Nancy Douglas, (she was sometimes called Ann), detailed on the family tree as the sister of James Douglas and aunt of James Douglas of Ardenarive. This townland name exists today but the locals spell it "Ardinariff " and the name Douglas remains prominent. James and Nancy had a large family of four sons and six daughters, **Edward, James, Samuel, Frederick, Margaret, Rebecca, Ann, Elizabeth, Mary Jane and Martha** and as some of them have interesting stories, they will be related later in another chapter.

Frederick, Edward and Mary's fourth son, who inherited Templemoyle, and Ann, their last child, appear to have died unmarried while Martha grew up to marry Rev. Francis Gray, who was the Minister in Camnish Presbyterian Church.

When visiting the village of Burnfoot in the Parish of Bovevagh, near Dungiven, to carry out research, I met Mr Willie Douglas J.P., from Ardinariff, a wonderful gentleman in his eighties, who, as an ardent lover of music, teaches the local flute band and claims to have the largest collection of flute band music in the world! Although from Ardinariff, Willie does not claim to be related to Nancy Douglas who married James Edwards, but it is rather romantic to imagine there is a connection!

Bovevagh Presbyterian Church (Camnish), Dungiven.

Mr Willie Douglas J.P. Clerk of Session of Bovevagh Presbyterian Church.

However, as a knowledgeable and articulate gentleman, he related a lot of interesting stories and had an awareness of the Edwards family, although the name has now died out in the Dungiven area.

Mr Douglas and I visited Bovevagh Presbyterian Church at Camnish, where he is the Clerk of Session, and we viewed the Douglas graves in the churchyard and the plaque on the wall in the church that commemorates Edward Gray, son of the

Rev. Francis Gray, Minister of Camnish for many years, and his wife, Martha Edwards, (Edward and Mary's fifth child). Their descendants emigrated to America, but family members returned to Bovevagh and erected the memorial in the church.

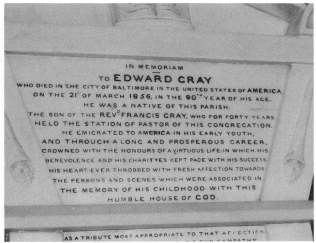

IN MEMORIAM
To E DWARD GRAY
WHO DIED IN THE CITY OF BALTIMORE IN THE UNITED STATES OF AMERICA
ON THE 21ˢ OF MARCH 1856, IN THE 90ᵀᴴ YEAR OF HIS AGE.
HE WAS A NATIVE OF THIS PARISH:
THE SON OF THE REVᵈ FRANCIS GRAY, WHO FOR FORTY YEARS
HELD THE STATION OF PASTOR OF THIS CONGREGATION.
HE EMIGRATED TO AMERICA IN HIS EARLY YOUTH,
AND THROUGH A LONG AND PROSPEROUS CAREER,
CROWNED WITH THE HONOURS OF A VIRTUOUS LIFE-IN WHICH HIS
BENEVOLENCE AND HIS CHARITIES KEPT PACE WITH HIS SUCCESS
HIS HEART EVER THROBBED WITH FRESH AFFECTION TOWARDS
THE PERSONS AND SCENES WHICH WERE ASSOCIATED IN
THE MEMORY OF HIS CHILDHOOD WITH THIS
HUMBLE HOUSE OF GOD.

AS A TRIBUTE MOST APPROPRIATE TO THAT AFFECTION

The Douglas family grave in Bovevagh Presbyterian Churchyard.

The memorial to Edward Gray, son of Rev. Francis Gray and Martha Edwards.

As these families continued to live in the area up until the late nineteenth century the Ordnance Survey Memoirs of Ireland for the Parishes of County Londonderry, 1834-1835, make reference to them, their homes and the churches. The Presbyterian Meeting House at Camnish had been built about seventy years and was described as "devoid of architectural beauty", but was well whitewashed. The inside was "not well finished: no ceiling covers the rafters, the pews are all of different dates, some only are painted."[1] Today, it is an attractive, well-maintained, stone building, and although still plain inside, is comfortable and pleasantly functional.

The O.S. Memoirs detail the "Gentlemen's Seats" as the "Glebe House, Straw House, and Ballyharigan House." "Straw House, so called from the townland in which it is situated, is the residence of Mrs Sarah Edwards, the widow of the late Edward Augustus Edwards Esquire. It is a comfortable and substantial family mansion."

Describing the woods in the area it states, "There are a few fine old trees about Mrs Edward's residence in Straw."

The richness and fertility of the parish were also commented upon and it is hardly surprising that there were many corn and flax mills; those in Straw being the property of Mrs Edwards, while the corn mill in Ardinariff, and the flax mill in Bovevagh, were owned by Mr James Douglas.

It is also interesting to note that the schoolhouse in Bonnanaboigh is mentioned; "The schoolhouse in Bonnanaboigh is situated near the church and is well finished, being built of freestone and ornamented. It is of the same date as the church (1820) and cost 100 pounds, one half of which was contributed by the Society for Discountenancing Vice and the other, with half an acre of land, by the late Edward Edwards Esq."

So Edwards Primary School, Castlederg, was not the only one to have benefited from the generosity of the Edwards family!

The penultimate member of Edward and Mary's family, also called Mary, married Samuel Osborne, son of Revd. Osborne and they had a family of three sons and three daughters. The family tree gives neither dates for their births nor any other information about them but some intriguing stories of the Osbornes are still told in Dungiven to this day! There is nothing that confirms the veracity of the tales, but they are worth telling!

The Osbornes lived at Ballyharigan House and the story goes that a nephew was entitled to inherit the property, but two of his uncles did not want this to happen. Rumour has it that they killed the nephew and buried his body in the end of a drain and now his ghost haunts the house!! Speculating on why the murder was never investigated and confirmed, or the murderers brought to justice, only ruins the romanticism of the story!

Another story is told of an Osborne lady who married a man named Ford, who was a drunkard. She alleged that he was in a home but he disappeared and she wanted him presumed dead. However the assumption locally was that she had killed him and disposed of the body. She was an eccentric character and was supposed to go around at night toting a Colt .45 revolver, so the locals knew to keep their distance!

Of course gossip loses nothing in the telling and the truth may never be known!

Matthew Edwards and Ann Donaldson.

Matthew, the second son of Robert and Martha, lived also at Kilcroagh. In November 1743 he married Ann Donaldson, said to be of "a good family in Belfast." [2] H. C. Lawlor states that the Donaldsons were at one time a most influential family in County Antrim, whose lands were all on the Earl of Antrim's estate. They also held influential positions in County Armagh, having been described as having " a lease for three lives renewable of these lands" of Castle Dillon.

Matthew and Ann went on to have eleven children; **Robert, Edward, Thomas, Elizabeth, Hugh, Matthew, Nehemiah, John, Henry, Ann and Cairns.** This family was born in the second half of the eighteenth century and were reared at Kilcroagh. The first-born son was named Robert but few details have been discovered about him so he remains a colourless character who died intestate before June 1805.

The Edwards' interest in the church was perpetuated through Edward who was the second son of Matthew and Ann. He was a clerk in holy orders and lived at Mount Bernard and is known to have used as his seal, a bird with the letters E.E. He married Mary Hunter and their daughter **Olivia** was described as an heiress. She grew up to marry John Bagot, who was the Rector of Fontstown, Kildare, and in turn they had three sons and two daughters; one son was a Canon and interestingly one of their daughters, Annie Olivia, married Thomas Lindsay Stack D.D. who was a Canon of Derry Cathedral and both are buried in Cappagh Church of Ireland Parish Burial Ground, near Omagh. [3]

Details are scarce for many of Matthew and Ann's children. Son Thomas had his will proved in November 1787, Hugh married a girl called Knilans and had a son and a daughter, John died before December 1785, Henry was a solicitor and married Prudence Taggart and had a daughter called **Catherine,** while Ann and Cairnes died unmarried in the 1820's. The sixth child was named Matthew after his father and he was Pro-Collector of Strabane and he inherited part of Kilcroagh. He married Rosa Araminata Campbell and they had a daughter **Catherine** who married Captain Edmund Boys and they had two sons.

Elizabeth married her cousin Robert, (Edward and Mary's elder son) and they had a family of five daughters and one son: **Ann, Harriet, Martha, Elizabeth, Edward-Augustus and Eleanor.**

The first-born daughter, Ann, took as her husband John Sproule, (whose grandparents were also Robert and Martha Edwards!) They had several sons and daughters who all emigrated to America.

Harriet and Eleanor died unmarried as far as the details on the family tree indicate. Martha married George Semple, nephew of John Semple of Mullenabrien (now spelt Mullanabreen), a townland near Castlederg, and his wife Sara Given, (whose brother, James Given, married Mary Jane, daughter of Robert Stuart and Mary Edwards.) Martha and George had four children, **William, John, George and Robert,** although only John and George are recorded on the genealogical table. William became a Physician and lived at Pettigo and reared three daughters, **Matilda, Ann and Hannah.** Martha and George's second son, John, who was born in 1803 and died on 19th of June 1890, came into possession of Straw House in Bovevagh after the death of Augustus Edwards. John firstly married Catherine Acheson of Grouse Lodge, Co Donegal, near the Fermanagh border, but had no issue. Secondly he married Anna Wright on 11th of October 1851 in Ardstraw.

Just recently I had a very interesting email from Virginia Miller in Victoria, British Columbia, Canada, who had discovered that her great-great-great grandmother was Martha Edwards. Sifting through the genealogical notes that she sent, I found that her mother was Marjorie Boyd, born in Montana in 1910. Marjorie's father was John Boyd, born in Drumneechy, Co. Londonderry, in 1870 and he had married Jane Smyth of Limavady on 22nd of July 1902. They had emigrated to America, travelling on the ship "Columbia", sailing from Glasgow and are recorded on the Ellis Island Passenger Arrival List of July 18th 1904. John's father was also named John, and in Bovevagh Presbyterian Church in 1863 he had married Matilda Semple who was the third daughter of Dr William Semple of Pettigo, whose mother was Martha Edwards!

Elizabeth, the fourth daughter of Robert and Elizabeth, also married her cousin Robert, son of Hugh, the fifth child of Matthew and Ann. Their only offspring was a son Hugh, who was educated for Trinity College Dublin, but died a young man.

Nehemiah Edwards, seventh child of Matthew and Ann, was born in 1758 and it is at this point that we note that as a grandchild of Robert and Martha, he married another grandchild, Elizabeth Sproule, in other words we have cousins marrying again. They had a family of three sons and a daughter, **John, Thomas, Edward and Elizabeth,** and it is with great sadness that I have to report that this was the last generation of Edwards in Castlederg!

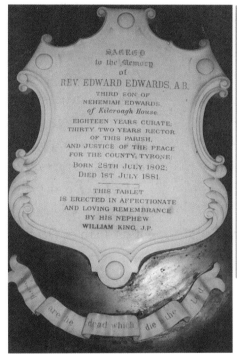

Memorial tablets to Rev. Edward Edwards A.B. and William King-Edwards D.L. in Derg Parish Church

John, of Kilcroagh, was born in 1803 and died unmarried in 1880. Thomas died unmarried in America. Edward, born in 1808, was Rector of Castlederg from 1848—1880. He was J.P. for County Tyrone and died at his residence, Mount Bernard in July 1881. A memorial plaque in Derg Parish Church records his contribution as Rector and was erected by his nephew; William King J.P. Unfortunately his death also marked the end of the Edwards name in Castlederg. Elizabeth was the only daughter of Nehemiah and Elizabeth, and surely aware of the imminent demise of the family name assumed the name King-Edwards when she married Bethel King and went to live at Dartans House. They had one son **William** who married Sarah Ramsey. Their descendants, who assumed the King-

Edwards surname, were; **Jane Elizabeth, John Edward Edwards, William Bethel and Thomas Ramsay.** The names are all recorded on the large headstone of the King-Edwards grave, which is situated in a prominent position adjacent to the

Dartans House, the home of Elizabeth Edwards and her husband William King-Edwards. It was later the home of the Lyons family.

doorway of Derg Parish Church, but the name has died out and there are no King-Edwards family members remaining in the locality.

KING – EDWARDS

Nehemiah Edwards Kilcroagh
Died 5ᵗʰ April 1846 aged 85 years
His wife Elizabeth
Died 24ᵗʰ November 1859 aged 84 years
Their son Rev. Edward Edwards B.A. J.P.
For 50 years Minister of this Parish
Died 1ˢᵗ July 1881 aged 79 years
Their son John
Died 31ˢᵗ March 1887 aged 89 years
Their only Daughter Elizabeth
Widow of Bether King
Died 14ᵗʰ march 1895 aged 90 years
Also William Bether son of W King Edwards
died 13ᵗʰ Nov 1895 aged 23 years
John Edward Edwards King – Edwards
Born 8ᵗʰ January 1871 died 9ᵗʰ October 1901
Sarah Ester wife of W King-Edwards
Born 1840 died 6ᵗʰ November 1906
Also William King Edwards
Died 23ʳᵈ December 1912 aged 69 years
D.L. and J.P. for County Tyrone
Thomas Ramsay King–Edwards M.D.
M.B.E.
Died at Watlington Oxfordshire
March 18ᵗʰ 1933 aged 58 years

"Blessed are dead which

The inscription on the King-Edwards gravestone in Derg Parish graveyard.

Edward Augustus Edwards, fifth child of Robert and Elizabeth, who was born in 1786, married Sarah Boyle, daughter of a solicitor in Dungiven. He died on 23rd January 1830, having had no issue.

On a visit to Dungiven I discovered the grave of Edward Augustus Edwards in Bovevagh Old Churchyard. Many of the family are buried there but the graveyard is very overgrown and the headstones are flat on the ground, hence are very difficult to find. It is also very hard to read the inscriptions that have suffered at the hands of the elements and time.

The gravestone of Edward Augustus Edwards in Bovevagh Old Churchyard.

Edward Augustus Edwards was accorded the right of an important person of the area, in that his tombstone is to be found within the crumbling walls of the old church, which is rurally situated on a hillside, above the rambling River Roe. Only one other indecipherable gravestone is situated within the church.

The following is the inscription on the tombstone:

"Sacred to the memory of Edward Augustus Edwards Esq, aged 44 years, who on the morning of the 23rd day of January 1830, after a short but painful illness, calmly resigned his spirit to the God who gave it, in a sure and certain hope of a glorious resurrection to eternal life through the merits of a crucified Saviour, by whose grace alone he was enabled with his dying breath to declare his humble yet confident trust of seeing him arise as the Sun of Righteousness with healing on his wings. Beneath this stone is also the remains of his mother Elizabeth Edwards who departed this life, the 5th day of June 1826, aged 76 years. Also the remains of Sarah Maria Edwards otherwise Boyle, wife of the said Edward Augustus Edwards who departed this life on the first day of July 1836, aged 44 years."

What a wonderful inscription, so carefully and neatly hewn on the plain headstone, resting in the peaceful church with the sky as its roof.

Then, following the death of Edward Augustus the house at Straw was left to his nephew, John Semple, third son of George Semple and Martha Edwards.

Mary Edwards and Robert Roe Stewart.

Of Robert and Martha's numerous daughters, Mary is the only one whose husband and details of their subsequent family, are recorded. Perhaps this is because he was of a noteworthy family. On 9th September 1726, Mary married Robert Roe Stewart, eldest son of George Stewart of Termon near Omagh. He was the third son of Colonel Robert Stewart who was great grandson of Andrew, second Lord Ochiltree, direct descendants of the Royal House of Stuart.

Robert was born in 1687 and went on to become a distinguished preacher. He served as a Presbyterian minister in Carland, near Dungannon, and was able to conduct his pulpit services in the native Irish tongue. His brother William was married to Mary O'Neil, granddaughter of the Earl of Tyrone. He died on 12th of April 1746 and is buried in Newmills Churchyard.

1. The Ordnance Survey Memoirs of Ireland, Parishes of Londonderry, VII, 1834-35, Volume 25.

2. From The Genealogical Table of the Edwards Family. PRONI : D/3000/114/1

3. Tombstones of the Omey, William J. McGrew, P43.

The Will of Doctor Henry Edward Edwards.
(D. 1778)

Edward, as he was commonly known, the first born son of Robert and Martha of Kilcroagh, sold his interest in Kilcroagh to his older brother Matthew on 18th November 1747 and continued to live and work as a physician at Straw.

His interesting will was dated 17th March 1777 and is neatly and legibly written in his own hand.[1] It helps paint a picture of a by-gone way of life and gives an insight into the considerable wealth that was enjoyed by the Edwards family in Straw.

In it he left his four sons, Robert, Matthew, Frederick and James equal portions of his estate. He indicated that a settlement had been drawn up with his wife Mary in 1769 in Dungiven, which gave her forty pounds a year out of the lands of Leek but that she had often promised to resign and give it up. In case she should decide to make a formal resignation of the agreement it was Edward's wish "to give and bequeath to the said Mary my beloved wife twenty pounds a year out of Leek aforesaid also bed board and entertainment in my house as formerly during her life provided she lives single and performs the above conditions." Unfortunately the particular lines concerning his wishes if Mary refused or "marries and parts from her children" are illegible due to the fold in the paper! No reason was given as to why there was to be a fifty per cent reduction in the amount she was to receive after his death but perhaps the forty pounds was an amount which covered the living allowance for both of them.

To Robert, his eldest son he left "the townland of Straw with all the houses and implements thereon" as well as the corn mill "and also the townland of Bunonaboigh with all the rights members and appurtenances in as full and ample a manner as I possess them myself to him and his heirs male forever."

To Matthew and James and their heirs male forever he bequeathed "the townland of Leek with its appurtenances share and share alike."

Frederick and Robert were given the "bog and turf leave in the mountain thereof with liberty to draw home by the usual roads trespass free," while Frederick was given the south half of the townland of Templemoyle."

In many wills the details of smaller items are not given but in Edward's will it is

43

interesting to note that he left his eldest daughter Martha "my old diamond ring", which is thought to have come from his mother Martha. Strangely his second daughter Mary, was to receive one hundred pounds while the younger daughter, Anne was to be given two hundred pounds. He also left his executors discretionary powers to award them an addition of one hundred pounds if they behaved "with prudence and discretion and marry to the liking and approbation of their relations."

Edward also referred to the will of his cousin Hugh who died in 1737 and who had bequeathed his estate to his daughter, Olivia, Countess Rosse. Being aware that there were no "heirs male" and unlikely to be so, as last in remainder he thought there was "not only a chance but a probability" that the Manor of Hastings would descend to him and his heirs. With that in mind he bequeathed the Castlederg estate to be equally divided among his four sons, Robert, Matthew, Frederick and James. Regarding the "Demesne and Mansion House of Castlegore" he wished that it should be "annexed and be apart of that share which should be allotted to my son Robert Edwards and my will is that my personal estate consisting of cows – horses- sheep- grain-and household furniture should remain as they now are and be the property of my son Robert Edwards." His goods and chattels he wanted judiciously valued in case they needed to be shared equally among the four children. He also hoped that the children " should live and keep together in my Mansion House and be accommodated with diet and lodging at the expense of my son Robert until such time as the value of their several lodgings should be deemed and equivalent to their respective shares of my said personal estate."

However we now know that the estate did not fall to him. Instead, on the death of Olivia, Hugh's last surviving daughter in 1820, (who had no heirs), the house and demesne, being an entailed estate passed over to the eldest son of Hugh's sister Margaret, Andrew Thomas Stuart, 9th Baron Castlestuart. Thus it passed out of the hands of the Edwards family.

Edward appointed his trusted friends, Mr James Douglas of Ardenariff, Mr James Hamilton of Londonderry, his nephew Rev. Edward Edwards, John Kyle of Camnish and Alexander Calhoun of Dungiven as the executors of his will dated the 17th day of March 1777.

I Edward Edwards of the parish of Boovah and
County of _____ being ___ ___ in ___
and ___ in the natural Infirmities incident to Age and
a dangerous disease afflicting me at present have had
certain and sufficient warning of my approaching
Dissolution do in the name of Almighty God in whom
I trust Make and Ordain this my last Will and Testa=
ment in manner and form following ___ First I commit
my Soul unto God who gave it, and my body to be
buried in a decent and Christian but ___ ___ manner
___ nothing doubting that it shall be ___ again at the
general Resurrection by the Almighty power of God and our
Saviour Jesus Christ ___ And as for my Estate real and personal
and such Worldly Goods as it has pleased ___ to ___ me
in this life I dispose of them in the following manner (vizt)
First I do Appoint and ___ that all my ___ Debts
be discharged out of the ___ of ___ due in my Estate
and the Debts due to me by Bond or otherwise with the
___ of the ___ ___ Rent of the ___ and Whatever
remains unpaid of the said Debts together with the
Legacies hereafter named should be equally and propor=
=tionably applied by my Executors to my Four Sons Robert,
Mathew, Theodrick and James according to the Rent roll of
such Shares as they shall ___ ___ ___ in the year
One Thousand Seven Hundred and Sixty nine in the Town of
Dungiven there was a Settlement made on my Wife Mary
Edwards otherwise ___ of Thirty pounds a year during
___ of the

1. The will of Doctor Henry Edward Edwards (1777), PRONI : D/2547/1

45

The Family of Thomas Edwards and Jane Cairnes.

Thomas Edwards, of Castlegore, eldest surviving son of Edward and Mary (Muncriffe), born in January 1670, was bequeathed the family estate in Tyrone. Families who had received plantation estates bore the legacy of their remit to develop the area in which they lived by planting woods, cultivating land, growing crops and keeping animals as well as providing housing, employment, schools and churches. Thomas lived at Castlegore and was long remembered in the area as a developer of its resources. He was said to be a man of pleasing and upright manners.

But perhaps the most interesting feature of Thomas' life was his marriage to his cousin Jane (Joanna) Cairnes on 13th of July 1699 and the raising of their family of ten children. Jane, daughter of David Cairnes and Margaret Edwards, was born in 1680.

The first of their family was **Elizabeth** who died in infancy and was buried at Castlederg. Sadly their second child, a son called **David,** also died in infancy and he too was buried at Castlederg. **Margaret** was born next, followed by **Hugh,** (the benefactor of Edwards School), then **Mary, Jane, Arabella, Edward, Thomas and Cairnes.**

Details of their childhood, upbringing and education do not seem to exist and we have to rely on the family tree to provide later particulars. However, like their cousins, the family of Robert and Martha, who lived at Kilcroagh, they were also educated. Again it is most likely that they had private home education. In the cases of the male members in particular, it is possible that they went to the Royal School in Londonderry and furthered their education at University or in the Army. Noting the families into which they married gives us some insight into the circles in which the Edwards' moved. These included those with particular military connections, landed gentry, statesmen and professional people such as legal and church representatives.

Margaret was married on June 1st 1722 to Robert Stuart, eldest son of Andrew Stuart of Stuart Hall, Co. Tyrone.[1]

This family of Stuart are representatives of the ancient family of Ochiltree. The last Stuart, Lord Ochiltree, by Royal permission, surrendered the lands and the barony to James I, receiving the extensive estates in County Tyrone, which are still held by the family at Stewartstown. The Earls of Castlestuart claim to be the head representatives in the pure male line of the Royal house of Stuart.

In the "Genealogical and Historical Sketch of the Stuarts of Castlestuart" by Rev. Andrew Godfrey Stuart, M.A., Margaret is described as the sister of Hugh Edwards Esq. of Castlegore, "a person of very considerable estate." However, he made no attempt to give any further information about her, which underlined the greater importance that was then attached to males! (For further details see the chapters on the Stuarts and the Edwards and Stuart links.)

Hugh, the fourth son of Thomas and Jane, has quite a long and detailed story and it is dealt with in a separate chapter.

Mary was the fifth child in the family and it is known that she married twice, firstly to Hugh Liston, by whom she had three sons, **William, Thomas and Hugh.** Left a widow at an early age, she went on to marry Dalway Stuart, second son of Andrew Stuart of Stuart Hall and they had a son **Andrew** and a daughter **Ann.**

Jane and Arabella came next in succession in the family of Thomas and Jane. Jane or Jean, the sixth child was born in 1705 and died unmarried on August 12th 1730. She was buried at Castlederg and was described as "the darling of her relations and intimate acquaintances, lamented indeed by all." [2]

Arabella was sometimes known as Isabella, as mentioned in Burkes' pedigree of the Cairnes family, and she married James Richardson of Springtown, who after her demise actually went on to marry secondly, Ann, widow of his brother-in-law, Hugh.

Edward was the eighth child in this large family. He had a military background and was known as "the Old Major." He lived at Loughmuck, Dungannon. Interestingly his wedding took place in the billiards room at Castlegore around 1737. He married Isabella, daughter of James Hamilton of Strabane, of the Abercorn family. They had a family of three girls and one son, **Ann, Mary, Margaret and Edward Cairnes.** The girls died unmarried while Edward Cairnes, who was probably born in 1742, and was known as "the Young Major" married Ann Bailie, a widow and daughter of Sir L. Mannix, of Glanmire, Co. Cork. They had two daughters, **Ann** and **Elizabeth** and a son, **Hugh Gore,** born in 1789, who was the only survivor.

Third surviving son and ninth child of Thomas and Jane, was also named Thomas. He was a Lieutenant and lived in The Fig Tree, Bachelor's Walk, Dublin, and while not a lot is known of his activities, a tattered certificate remains to prove that he received Holy Communion in St Michan's Church in Dublin on 3rd June 1744.[3] Under the terms of the Test Act, as a descendant of a "plantation family," he was obliged to partake several times a year of the Sacrament of Holy Communion, according to the rites of the Church of Ireland, and if this had not been certified he would have been deprived of public offices.

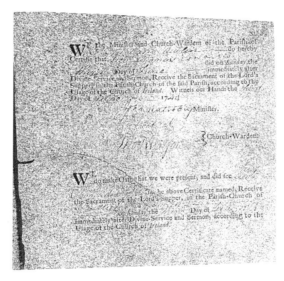

A Certificate proving that Lt. Thomas Edwards, Hugh's brother, received the Sacrament of the Lord's Supper in 1744 in St. Michan's Church, Dublin.

It is also the church that was attended by the Cairnes family and where some of their infants are buried.

Incidentally, the ancient church of St. Michan is named after a Danish Bishop and has one of the oldest organs still in use. It is believed that George F. Handel visited Dublin in 1742 and played it while composing the Messiah. The church also has unique vaults in which you can view macabre open caskets containing mummified bodies. More details are available on the website www.irelandforvisitors.com

Thomas married on 14th February 1743, Elizabeth, daughter of William

Thwaites, also of Dublin. They had two daughters, **Elizabeth and Esther** or **Essy** and a son **Cairnes.** Esther married James Brabazon of the Earls of Meath and they resided at Mornington House near Drogheda, Esther assuming the title "Lady of Drogheda."

An intriguing story is told concerning Esther's second cousin, previously mentioned Hugh Gore Edwards, who was a Lieutenant Colonel in the 32nd Regiment. About 1810, he had set off on a sea voyage. The vessel encountered bad weather in the Irish Sea and became a wreck off the coast of Meath, at the mouth of the Boyne. On presenting himself at a house in the hope of help, Hugh discovered that he was at the door of his father's cousin, Esther Brabazon. She recognized him and the story goes that, as she had no children of her own, she called the household together and in front of all present she declared the shipwrecked soldier her heir. He duly succeeded to David Cairnes' estate.[4]

 H. C. Lawlor suggests that although this story is "doubtless founded on fact, a reference to the terms of David Cairnes' will discloses the fact that Mrs Brabazon had no right to the Raveagh estate. It was strictly limited to the male heirs of the sons of Jane Edwards, and on the death of Mrs Brabazon's father, Thomas, without male issue, it passed by right, not to Mrs Brabazon, but to young Edwards' father, (the Old Major), who was abroad and probably ignorant of the terms of his ancestor's will."

Thomas and Jane's tenth son was named Cairnes and he lived at Rathmelton, Co. Donegal. The P.R.O.N.I. holds an interesting bundle of letters belonging to Cairnes, but unfortunately they are so badly burned it is impossible to make coherent sense of the contents.

Of interest too is a legal document asking for an opinion on the legitimacy of a Heads of a will that had been drawn up by "Cairnes Edwards of Rathmelton in the County Dunygall" in October or November 1746 and which lay in the custody of an Attorney, Mr Hamilton, in Londonderry and had not been "put into form." Thomas Edwards as the executor for Cairnes Edwards presented the case.[5] Cairnes had made a will on 4th of August 1747 in Strabane, and said that he had made no other will nor did he intend to alter the will. But in July 1748 "Cairnes was seized with a pluretick fever of which he died." Some days before his death, Mr Hamilton from Londonderry, brought up the Heads of a Will that had been drawn up in 1746. After reading some paragraphs to the very ill Cairnes, Hamilton asked him if he remembered and approved of what he had written. The reply, "in a very low tone of voice, (being extremely ill), was Aye" and when Hamilton suggested some additions which would need Cairnes' approval, he declined and said he would think of the other things the next day. He then lapsed into a delirious state and a Physician was called. He felt it necessary "to apply a Blystering plaister to bring him a little to his reason in order to execute the will."

Meantime Hamilton was despatched to draw up a will as far as Cairnes had agreed, "to have so much of it perfected when he came to himself, which some time after happened but not so thoroughly that the Physician or the Attorney thought him in a proper condition to execute a will."

When he had improved somewhat and was further asked about the execution of his will, Cairnes then recalled that he had a will lying in Strabane and suggested that there was no need for any trouble about the matter. Shortly afterwards Cairnes passed away "without any farther execution of another will or the Heads of a Will."

Thomas' request concerning the legitimacy of the Heads of a Will document was met with the opinion "that it can't be now deemed as a will or a codicil to the will of August 1747, or take away from Thomas any part of the personal estate given him by the will of 1747."

This curious document gives us an intriguing and informative insight into both the medical and legal aspects of life in the eighteenth century. How difficult and intricate the twists and turns of life and death.

1.   The present Earl of Castlestewart kindly passed on this information from his personal copy of A Genealogical and Historical Sketch of the Stuarts of the House of Castlestuart in Ireland by Rev. Andrew Godfrey Stuart, M.A., but a copy of this rare volume is available in the Linenhall Library, Belfast.

2.   Notes on the Holmes, Edwards and Stuart Families by Mark Meredith.

3.   Certificate of Receipt of Lord's Supper, St Michan's Church of Ireland, Dublin, 1744 for Lieut. Thomas Edwards. PRONI: D/1618/15/5

4.   From the details on Brabazon in the Printed Notes On the Descendants of Hugh Edwards. PRONI: D/2547/15

5.   The Case and Opinion on the Administration of Cairnes Edwards, PRONI: D/1618/1

The Hugh Edwards Story.

For anyone with an interest in, or a connection with Edwards Primary School, no matter how slight, the name of Hugh Edwards must surely ring a bell! Hugh is our reason for being and although it was slow in getting off the ground in the first place, the school has been flourishing for over one hundred and eighty years. Hugh Edwards was an educated gentleman and in keeping with the tradition of the landlords of the day, tried to improve the lives of those less fortunate than himself.

6ᵗᵒ Martii 1719.

Nomina discipulorum primae classis qui hoc Anno Academiam intrarunt sub praesidio Magistri Gershomi Carmichall.

Alexander Lecky Scoto-Hibernus

Carolus Baxter Scoto-Hibernus

Willielmus Brown Scoto-Hibernus

Willielmus Fariss Scoto-Hibernus

Henricus Killpatrick Scoto-Hibernus

Jacobus Neilson Scoto-Hibernus

Jacobus Ross Scoto-Hibernus

Johannes England Anglus

Joannes Macky Scoto-Hibernus

Josephus Dawson Anglus

Thomas Moore Scoto-Hibernus

Nomina discipulorum secundae classis qui hoc Anno Academiam intrarunt sub praesidio Magistri Joannis Lowdoun.

Gulielmus Pardew Anglus

Hugo Edwards Anglo–Hibernus filius primogenitus Thomae Edwards de Hastings Armigeri

Robertus Kilsall Anglus

Thomas Burges Anglus

Joannes Dallowe Anglus

Nomina discipulorum tertiae classis qui hoc Anno Academiam intrarunt sub praesidio Magistri Roberti Dick.

Carolus Cochrane filius Joannis Cochrane de Watersyde

David Harvey Scoto-Hibernus

Edwardus Boyd

Gulielmus Anigus

Henricus Eliott Scotus

Gulielmus Orr

Jacobus Stirling

Joannes Alexander

Joannes Anderson

Joannes Campbell

Joannes Hutton

Joannes McAlpin

Joannes Miller

Nigellus Campbell filius Johannis Campbell filii Archiobaldi quondam Comitis de Argyle

An extract from Munimenta Alme Universitatis Glasgugenisis: records of the University of Glasgow, showing in Latin, Hugh Edwards's attendance.

Glasgow University was highly regarded as a seat of learning in the early eighteenth century and the Matriculation Albums of 6th of March 1719 describe Hugh Edwards as a student of second class of John Lowden.[1] It appears that Hugh did not actually graduate, but that was not uncommon during this period. To have attended university was enough to enter a profession and a certificate of graduation was unnecessary.

Students of this period did not specialise in a specific subject. They were allocated a regent who taught them for their entire university life. In Hugh's case this was John Lowden. The classes taught were Latin, Greek, Logic, Ethics and Physics, usually over five years.

He was also described as "filius primogenitus" ---the first-born son and "heir of Thomas Edwards of Hastings" but we know that he was indeed the fourth child of Thomas and Jane of Castlegore in the Manor of Hastings and born around 1700.

In 1728 he married Anne Mervyn, daughter of Audley Mervyn of Castle Mervyn, Trillick, M.P. for Strabane 1695 and Tyrone 1703-1717. Anne's brother Henry was also an M.P. for Augher and Tyrone.[2]

Hugh and Anne had four daughters; **Olivia, Jane, Elizabeth and Arabella.** They lived at Castlegore and were actively involved in the life of the area.

Lewis in his Topographical Dictionary of Ireland 1837, writing about Castlederg, states that "There was anciently a church in the town, which was in ruins in 1619, when it was rebuilt by Sir John Davys; but being destroyed by Sir Phelim O'Nial in 1641, there was no church until 1731, when the neat present edifice was built by Hugh Edwards Esq., of Castlegore." This was surely proof that the local landlord did much to help improve the area in which he lived.

Of the four daughters of Hugh and Anne, the only one to marry was Olivia, who wed Richard Gore, Earl of Rosse, on 16th of February 1754.

The Earls of Rosse and Arran descended directly from Richard Gore, Lord Mayor of London, who died in 1607, aged 90. His son, Sir Paul Gore, Bart., came to Ireland in charge of a troop of horse, and got large grants of land in Fermanagh, Tyrone and Donegal, which he collected into a Manor, called Manor Gore and resided at Bellisle and Castle Gore, (County Donegal) which he defended in the Irish rebellion in 1641. The family home, (Belle Isle, Lisbellaw, Co. Fermanagh) is

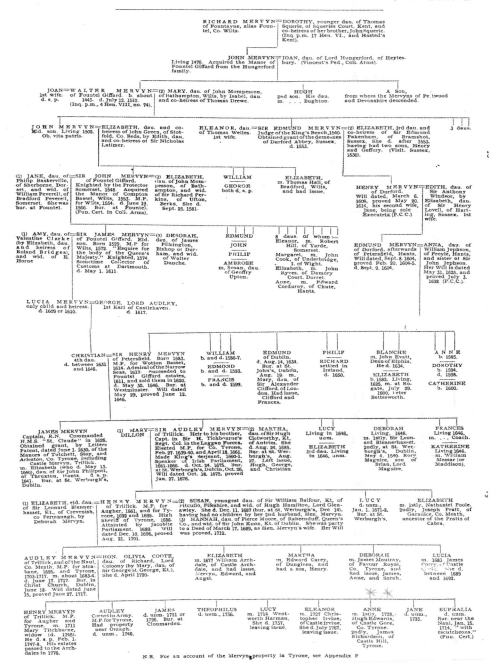

beautifully situated on an island in Lough Erne.[3]

6. MERVYN, OF FOUNTEL GIFFARD, WILTS, AND CASTLE MERVYN, CO. TYRONE.

The family tree of Mervyn of Fountel Giffard, Wilts and Castle Mervyn, Co. Tyrone, showing Hugh Edwards' wife, Anne.

N.B. For an account of the Mervyn property in Tyrone, see Appendix F

The name Gore comes from the Medieval English system of crop rotation when fields were divided into strips. Inevitably they did not divide equally and sometimes, triangular bits were left over and these were known as gores, from the Anglo-Saxon word for a triangular-shaped spearhead.

Sir Paul Gore had two sons—Sir Ralph Gore, Bart., from whom descended the Earls of Rosse and Sir Arthur Gore Bart., ancestor of the Earls of Arran. Sir Ralph, the fourth Bart., was a distinguished lawyer, was Attorney General, Chancellor of the Exchequer, Chief Justice and raised to the peerage as Viscount Bellisle and Earl of Rosse and served as chairman to the House of Lords..

Olivia Edwards' husband, Richard, the second Earl of Rosse, distinguished in military service, was Commander of the Forces in Ireland. Unfortunately they did not have a happy marriage and after less than three years together, they agreed to live apart.

She married secondly Captain John Bateman, third son of Rowland Bateman, Oak Park, Co. Kerry, but left no issue by either marriage.

Olivia, with two of her sisters, were co-heiresses of their father's estate and as the last remaining member of the family line Olivia resided in the family seat at Castlegore.

One of the best descriptions of it and of its last occupant has to be that of John Gamble in his "View of Society and Manners in the North of Ireland, 1819." He wrote, **" We walked up the rugged hill that leads to Castle Gore. Though, not many years ago, the seat of grandeur and magnificence, Castle Gore is now almost as absolute a picture of desolation as I ever beheld. Yet it is interesting even in decay; elevated on a high hill, it is seen in every direction, and the antique avenue of old trees has further effect of beauty in this land of mountains and floods."**

It is said that Castlegore was situated at the junction of the main Ederney and Killeter roads and was on the farm that now belongs to Mr Oliver Sproule. Sadly, there is no trace left of what was obviously in its day a wonderful mansion. What a beautiful picture Gamble painted and what a shame it is that Castlegore is no longer there for us to see in all its splendour.

However a different image is portrayed of Olivia. While she was responsible for the simple plaque erected in her father's memory which still stands in Derg Parish

Church, (see photograph) and which praises his benevolence and generosity, the same could not be said of her. Here is what Gamble said, "Until lately, it (Castlegore) was the residence of Lady Ross, a woman who has long outlived her generation, her eyesight and all her passions, except that one which increases with age. She lingered in this her ancient castle, until the floors cracking under her feet, and the ceilings tumbling on her head, admonished her to tardy and reluctant flight; for the trifle it would have taken to avert this calamity, she could not bear to part with. She would perhaps have been a wonder in any country, but she has an

The memorial tablet to Hugh Edwards in Derg Parish Church.

especial wonder in this one, where profusion is the defect of the gentry, and parsimony the only fault which the poor do not forgive. Her garb, it is said, was that of a beggar woman; she lived on the coarsest food, and shivered over the miserable faggot which she herself picked up, though her yard was filled with poultry, and her huge turf stacks were the nightly, and even daily prey of robbers. Many other stories are told of her, which, if true, indicate a degree of avarice that may well be called disease."

A vision that speaks volumes and requires no further explanation!

Her father Hugh, in his will of 1737, which will be detailed in the next chapter, entailed his estate upon the eldest son of his sister Margaret, in case his four daughters should die without male issue, as indeed was the case. This meant that after Olivia died the property of Castlegore was carried over to the Earls of Castlestuart.

1. This information was derived from Munimenta Alme Universitatis Glasguensis: Records of the University of Glasgow from its foundation until 1727 [Maitland Club], 1854

2. The family tree of Mervyn, of Fountell Giffard, Wilts, and Castle Mervyn, Co. Tyrone, from The Memoirs of the Archdales with the Descents of some Allied Families by Henry Blackwood Archdale.

3. From Richard Gore, Earl of Ross, in the Printed Notes on the Descendants of Hugh Edwards. PRONI: D/2547/15

The Will of Hugh Edwards 1737.

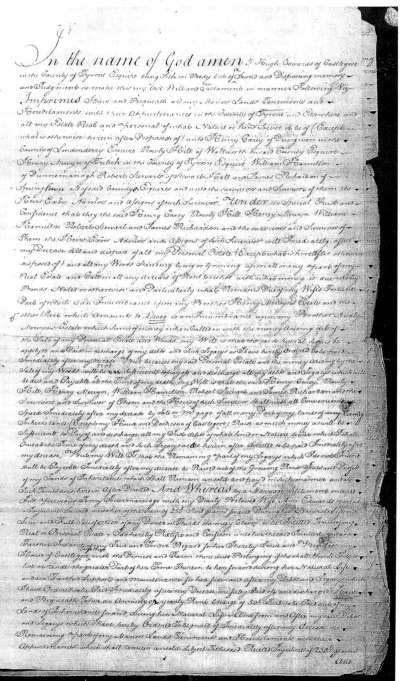

An extract from the will of Hugh Edwards 1737.

The "Big House" was certainly a feature of the landscape and the social system in Ireland in the late seventeenth and eighteenth centuries. To the ordinary mortals both the houses and their inhabitants were the subjects of intrigue and open curiosity. The lives of the inmates were in sharp contrast for the most part with the humble poor and their cabin dwellings. The image of the country gentleman was one of an educated, swashbuckling type; entertaining, hunting, shooting and fishing, supervising the work being carried out on the estates and travelling to the city to pursue business commitments. The ladies of the upper classes would have enjoyed a sedate and pleasant life style, with servants doing the manual work and nothing more strenuous for them to do than sewing and embroidery or making preserves and cordials.

The last will and testament of Hugh Edwards does much to confirm these sentiments and the picture it impresses on our minds is most interesting and revealing. He appointed as executors the landed squires of the day; Henry Carey of Dungiven,(a cousin of his wife, Anne), Rowley Hill of Walworth, Henry Mervyn of Trillick, (his brother-in-law), William Hamilton of Dunnamannagh, Robert Stuart of Stuart Hall and James Richardson of Springtown, (both also brothers-in-law). They were charged with disposing of all his estate immediately after his decease, by "sale or mortgage" all or part of his lands or inheritance, except for the House and Demesne of Castlegore, calling in arrears of rent, collecting Bonds Notes and the remainder due from his wife's fortune and using these sums to settle debts and legacies. However they were only to raise as much money as they needed at the time of his death to satisfy the debts while future legacies would be raised out of rents "Issues and Profits" of the inherited land.

He referred to a marriage settlement that had been drawn up for his wife Ann, giving her an annual entitlement of £250 sterling, which he wished her to continue to have along with the House of Castlegore and the Demesne and Farm. But in the case of her death, the House and Demesne were bequeathed to his eldest daughter, Olivia, and entailed to her male heirs or the male heirs of her sisters in succession. In the event of his daughters dying without any heirs (as indeed was the case), the estate was to go to his brother Thomas and his male heirs or his brother Cairnes and his male heirs in order of seniority. If there were no living male heirs, then the estate was destined to pass on to Andrew Thomas

Stuart, eldest son of Hugh's sister Margaret. With the benefit of hindsight we know that due to failure of male heirs this is exactly what happened and thus the Edwards estate passed over to the Castlestuarts.

Impressive sums of money were mentioned in Hugh Edward's will, indicating the extent of his personal fortune. His daughters Jane and Elizabeth, were bequeathed £4000 each, to be received "at their respective days of marriage," providing of course that the marriage met with the consent of the executors. Marriage without such consent reduced the sum to £500!

However we know they died unmarried, so they missed their chances!

For some strange reason, Hugh's fourth daughter, Arabella, noted on the family tree as being unmarried in 1737, and therefore still alive, is not mentioned in the will. Hugh refers to the "said three daughters" and following reference to them by name; he goes on to refer to his brothers. We could speculate on the reason why Arabella was not mentioned; maybe she suffered from some mental or physical disorder or illness, in which instance one might have expected some provision to be made for her, but nothing confirms this conjecture.

The sum of £120 per annum was bequeathed by Hugh for the "education and maintenance" of his three daughters; again Arabella was not mentioned, and his executors were instructed to increase the sum if it wasn't sufficient.

The upkeep of his buildings and the improvements of Castlegore were seen as important by Hugh. He left £30 yearly for that purpose in a Draft in the hands of "George Dewart, my Chief Gardiner." Unfortunately we know that Olivia failed to carry out the necessary maintenance and Castlegore fell into an irreversible state of decay.

Smaller amounts of money and specific interesting items are now enumerated as follows:

- £50 to his wife Ann and three daughters to buy mourning.
- To his wife and family: his coach, four wheeled chair and harness and everything belonging to them.
- To his wife and family: eight of the best draft cattle, servants, horses, Household furniture and plate.
- £10 to brother Edward to buy mourning, plus another addition of £30 for his child or children, providing he created no disturbance or opposition to

the will, in which case, he was to receive nothing!

- To brother Thomas £10 to buy him mourning along with "my Padd Blew Betty, (a horse), the saddle and furniture scarlet trimmed with gold lace, also my small case of pistols, my plate handled gilt sword, my gold watch with the chain and seal" and £500.
- To brother Cairnes £10 "and also my Padd Gelding Grew Forster" and £1200. Part of this money had come from a £500 settlement in their father's will, plus £700 that had originally been intended for him from his grandfather- David Cairnes' will. In order to prevent any further disputes Hugh allocated the said £1200.
- To his brother and sister Stuart the sum of £20 to buy them mourning.
- To brother Stuart "my young grey mare together with my Blue Velvet Saddle and Blue Velvet furniture laced and fringed with gold with the silver mounting thereunto belonging."
- To his brother and sister Stuart "my largest case of silver mounted pistols and the sum of £200 sterling to be distributed in such shares and proportions among their children as they shall think fit."
- To his sister Mary Liston £10 to buy her and her two sons mourning. Also the sum of £100 for herself.
- To Mary's two sons, Thomas and Hugh, a total of £1200, with the interest from the sum to go towards their education, (which was left in the hands of Mr John Ferguson of Strabane.)
- To brother Edward's children £300.
- To Thomas Edward's children £500.
- To sister Stuart's children £200.
- To James Richardson of Springtown "£10 sterling to buy him mourning, my silver mounted cutlash and my Blue Velvet laced Belt and also my set of stone buckles and the further sum of £200 sterling to be applied as directed in a Paper of Instructions sealed up and directed for him, which paper may not be opened by any person till it be carefully delivered to himself."
- To William Cairnes of Killyfaddy "£10 sterling to buy him mourning together with my Grey stoned horse and my set of Blue Cloath furniture

laced with silver."

- To cousin Edward of Kilcroagh "£10 to buy him mourning, my Cane and all my books that treat of Physick, Anatomy, Surgery and Poetry of all kinds and I recommend to him the care of all my other Books and when he happens to be out of the country he may entrust them with such persons as will take good care of them."
- To cousin Matthew Edwards of Kilcroagh "£10 sterling to buy him mourning, my small fowling piece, the Powder Flask and pouche thereunto belonging."
- To "my friend Patrick Orr of Londonderry Merchant £30 together with my pair of silver spurs and my little Grey Mare Boswell with the saddle cloth and bridle."
- To Mr John Ferguson, Strabane, £10 to buy mourning.
- To Mr Nehemiah Donaldson of Dirge, £10 to buy mourning.
- To Rev. Mr John Browne of Dirge, £10 to buy mourning. Also £40 sterling.
- Cancellation of a debt of arrears of rent for the widow of James Grimstone.
- To William Ashe of Londonderry £50 to discharge debts and accounts.
- To Mr William Boyd of Londonderry £16 sterling.
- To "my Nurse a Suit of Mourning and the benefit of the farm she now lives in during her natural life."
- To his old servant Hugh Grimstone "£20 sterling."
- To his sister the sum of "£10 sterling."
- To the "poor of the City of Londonderry £10 sterling."
- To the "poor of the Manor of Hastings £10 sterling."
- The sum of "£20 to be given among such of my servants as my wife shall judge most deserving."
- £40 sterling for the use of the Dissenting Protestant Congregation (Presbyterian), (which had been bequeathed by his sister Jane, but was still in his hands), and the £10 interest from it was for the use of the Dissenting Minister and Congregation of Dirge.
- To John Ferguson, Edward Edwards, John Semple and Thomas Sproule and

their Survivors and heirs, the "Meeting House together with the lands upon which it stands and the little house and park thereunto belonging free of all rent for the use of the Congregation."

- £6 sterling to be paid to Robert Downes, John Browne, and Nehemiah Donaldson and their successors "to be distributed annually among six of the old decayed inhabitants of the Manor of Hastings."

- Hugh acknowledged that his papers were in a confused state and accounts, receipts and Bonds were intermingled with other papers "in my Closet Old Escrutore and two Writing Desks which are all at Castlegore" so he requested his friends Patrick Orr, Rev John Browne and Rev Nehemiah Donaldson to "help his dear wife in carefully sorting said papers."

- To James Funston and George Dewar "leases of their several holdings which join Dirge Bridge at both ends," with Renewal Clauses, whereby they would pay a half year's rent at each renewal. Yearly rent was to stand at £5 per annum with a 12d per pound Receivers fee. This was on condition that neither of them would sell the property, in which case they would be fined £4.10.

- Also to James Funston and George Dewar a suit of mourning.

- The lease granted to James and Charles Caldwell of the lands of Killen and Edenasopp to be renewed on the former terms if they so desired.

- £40 to be equally divided between the two sons and two daughters of his late Aunt, Mrs Mary Holland of Liffog.

- To Mr John Lennon, of the City of Londonderry, the sum of £10 to buy mourning.

- To Alderman Alexander Knox £10 sterling to buy him mourning.

- To his executors, (the landed gentry mentioned at the beginning), and his wife, he granted the responsibility for the "fortunes and education" of his three daughters.

- To any of the executors not already mentioned, £10 each.

Finally, Hugh brought his will to a close in the customary manner, recommending his soul to God and asking pardon for his sins. He requested that his body should be interred in Derg Chapel in an "orderly decent manner" and that the place of his interment should be "under the Funeral Inscription to the North East of the pulpit."

The original will, beautifully scripted on thin, yellowed paper and very legible, is available in the P.R.O.N.I. A copy is held in Edwards Primary School but it loses a lot in the photocopying process and one does not gain the sense of history and age that emanates from the original document.

This wonderful conglomeration of wishes reveals much about the unquestionable wealth and fortune of Hugh Edwards. It also tells us much about his character and his values, particularly his regard for education. It is worth noting that he specifically left his books in care of his cousin Edward, with the special instruction to leave them in the care of another trustworthy person, should he be away for any reason. The subject matter of his books is also interesting—Physick, Anatomy, Surgery, Poetry----did Hugh become a Physician like his cousin Henry Edward Edwards of Straw?

While we don't have answers for many questions, we do know that Hugh wished to see education, which was then solely the prerogative of the rich, extended to the poorer classes.

This chapter is based on The Will of Hugh Edwards, 1737, PRONI : D/847/21/1/2

A Convenient Country House.

I Devise and Bequeath to Mr John Ferguson of Strabane my Cousin Edward Edwards of [illegible] John Semple of [illegible] and Thomas [illegible] of Clare [illegible] To the Survivors and Survivor of them and the Heirs of such Survivor forever [illegible] for the use of the said Dissenting Minister and Congregation of Derg as they shall Think proper and I Devise and Bequeath unto the said John Ferguson Edward Edwards John Semple and Thomas [illegible] and the Survivors and Survivor of them and the heirs of such Survivor the Meeting House together with the Lands upon which it stands and the little House and park thereunto belonging [illegible] Congregation [illegible] I Will [illegible] my said Trustees Henry Cary, Dudley Hill, Henry Mervyn, William Hamilton, Robert Stewart, and James Richardson and the Survivors and Survivor of them and the Heirs of such Survivor shall within one year next after my Decease Build a Convenient Country House for Entertaining a Master and Six poor Boys on the Road leading from Derg Bridge to Frighlagh Houses and that they also lay out about One Acre of land for a Garden to said House which House and Garden is to be Free of Rent for ever and that they pay the sum of 24£ Sterling per annum to the Revd Mr Robert Downs Rector of Urney & the Revd John Brown Curate of Derge Chappell and the Revd Nehemiah Donaldson Dissenting Minister of Derg Congregation and to their Successors Rectors of Urney Curates of Derg Chappell and Ministers of the Dissenting Congregation of Derg which said Sum of 24£ is to be by them laid out to teach Six Poor Protestant Boys to read Write and [illegible] and Sing Psalms and to supply them with Meat Drink Washing and lodging and also to Furnish them with Cloathing their Coats and [illegible] to be of Course Blew Cloath and their Linnen Suitable and as soon as they are Well Instructed [illegible] they may be put out [illegible] Trades but more particularly to the Weaver Trade [illegible] Each of them [illegible] Apprentice Fee which sum I Expect will be saved out of the 24£ [illegible] after paying all manner of Charges which they were at in teaching them [illegible] the sum of 6£ [illegible] to the said Robert Downs John Brown and Nehemiah Donaldson [illegible] to be by them distributed annually among [illegible] Inhabitants of the Manor of Castlings And Whereas [illegible]

Hugh's wish was that his executors and their survivors and heirs would "**within one year next after my decease build a convenient Country House for entertaining a Master and six poor Boys on the Road leading from Dirge Bridge to Frighlagh Houses and that they also lay out about one Acre of land for a garden to said House which House and Garden is to be free of rent for ever and that they pay the sum of £24 sterling per annum to The Reverend Robert Downes Rector of Urney and the Reverend John Browne Curate of Derg Chapel and the Reverend Nehemiah Donaldson Dissenting Minister of Derge Congregation.................. to teach six poor Protestant boys to**

Read Write Cypher and sing Psalms and to supply them with Meat Drink Washing and Lodging and also to furnish them in Cloathing, their coats and caps to be of course blue Cloth and their Linnen suitable and as soon as they are well instructed as above then I desire that they may be put out to several Trades but more particularly to the Weaver trade of different kinds and to give each of them £2 sterling as an apprentice fee which sum I expect will be saved out of the £24 per annum after paying all manner of charges which they were at in teaching them." [1]

The lack of punctuation is very apparent in this sort of lengthy prose, transcribed straight from the Will, but when you add in the appropriate commas and full stops, it begins to be comprehensible.

So this is where it all began!! Pupils and teachers of Edwards Primary School take note! How things have changed over the years! Firstly the school was to be for boys only, very much in keeping with the ethos of the eighteenth century and the subjects were the basic three R's with the singing of psalms thrown in to provide the spiritual element.

It could perhaps be suggested that this was to be an early sort of Boarding School, in that board and lodging were to be provided. The discipline of uniform is also striking and one wonders whether Hugh based his ideas on the Bluecoat School that was established in Dublin.

Edward McLysaght in his book "Irish Life in the Seventeenth Century" refers to the Bluecoat School at the King's Hospital;

"an hospital for about sixty boys who have a chaplain, and schoolmaster, they are clad in blue coats lined with yellow and as they grow up they are put to trades."

A drawing of the uniform worn by the boys in The Blue Coat School, the Royal Hospital, Kilmainham, Dublin.
The Blue-coat School Uniform. A blue frieze coat over yellow petticoats and yellow stockings.

This was a foundation dating from the reign of King Charles II and it is interesting to note the similarities with the ideas expressed by Hugh.

It may also be coincidental, but the Edwards seal in Derg Parish Church is blue and yellow and the present uniform of the pupils of Edwards Primary School contains the same colours.

In any case, the wishes of Hugh were indeed visionary and in succeeding chapters I will relate how the school has evolved from this embryonic form.

This chapter is based on the Will of Hugh Edwards, 1737, PRONI : D/847/21/1

The Castlestuart Connection.
Who were the Castlestuarts?

Rev. George Hill writing in his book "An Historical Account of the Plantation in Ulster, 1608-1620," states that the Stewart family were amongst the earliest patentees of land in Tyrone during the Plantation.

The Stewarts or Stuarts, representatives of the Lords Ochiltree, were Scottish in origin. They belonged to an old noble family whose surname derived from Walter, the High Steward of Scotland in the twelfth century, whose son Robert, (died 1290), was the first of the Stuart Kings and whose descendants were the direct line of the Stuart Kings of Scotland. [1]

Andrew Stewart was described as "a young nobleman of impeccable background and proven military ability" and on the death of his father he became the third Lord Ochiltree and had estates in the Galloway and Strathclyde regions. In 1608 he was sent by King James I to help quell feuds in the Western Isles, taking with him his uncle, John Knox, the well-known Scottish reformer. He was successful in this but the King had no money to give him to reward his services, so in 1609 he instead offered him land in County Tyrone, including the Manor of Castlestewart and later Manor Forward, which included the areas around Farlough and Roughan, all in the barony of Dungannon. [2]

In 1619 King James I created "Andrew Stewart, (1560-1629) Lord Stewart, Baron of Castle Stewart in the county of Tyrone, to hold said honour to him and the heirs male of his body." Andrew settled at Stuart Hall and his son, also named Andrew, made his home at Roughan, where there were the remains of an Elizabethan castle. This unique building is unfortunately now in ruins, but had a small central block and four wide towers at the corners.

In common with many Protestant Planters, Andrew built houses, farmed the land, constructed a castle and provided employment and housing for the local populace. It is said that the younger Andrew was responsible for the planning and building of the village of Stewartstown.

While the family name of the Earls Castle Stewart is Stuart, there is a confusing mix up in the spelling of the name. It may be spelt either way--- Stewart or Stuart.

There is also some orthographic confusion over the seat from which the Earls come. In some cases it is called Eary, Eyerie, Errie, Irry or Try and was christened Stuart Hall in the early 18th century, a name by which it is still known.

STUART HALL

Postcards showing front and rear views of Stuart Hall Stewartstown, Co. Tyrone, ancestral home of the Castlestewarts.

It is situated near Stewartstown, Co. Tyrone and it is described in Mark Bence-Jones' book "a Guide to Irish Country Houses" (1988) as a "three storey Georgian block with a pillared porch, joined to an old tower house by a C19 Gothic wing. In recent years the top two stories of the main block were removed, giving it the appearance of a Georgian bungalow. The house was bombed c.1974 and subsequently demolished."

However the house was rebuilt and remains the family home of the present Earl of Castlestewart.

1.   This information can be traced on a family tree kindly provided by Gordon and Gayle Perkins, Queensland, Australia. It shows the descendants up to the Rev Andrew Welsh, Minister in Ardstraw, Gordon's ggggrandparent.

2.   A History of the Parish of Tullanisken, Newmills, Co Tyrone. E.E. Donnelly M.Sc. B.A. Dip. Ed.

For further information see Castle Stewart in Burke's Peerage and Baronetage, P.514.

The Genealogical and Historical Sketch of the Stuarts of Catlestewart by Rev. Andrew Godfrey Stuart, M.A. provides an interesting and detailed insight into the family.

The Castle Stewart Papers consist of 950 individually numbered documents, 42 volumes, 41 bundles and 10 PRONI boxes. PRONI : D/1618

The Stuart and Edwards Family Links.

Succeeding generations of Stuarts enjoyed the title granted by James I and the Edwards family married into the Stuart family on no less than five known occasions.

The first marriage took place on June 1st 1722, between Margaret Edwards, sister of school benefactor, Hugh, and Robert, (born 3rd March 1700), de jure 8th Baron Castlestewart.

The marriage settlement drawn up between Robert Stewart and Margaret Edwards in 1722.

Robert Stuart "was in command of a troop of dragoons, holding a Royal Commission and he lived for the most part the quiet life of a country gentleman at Stuart Hall," presumably accompanied by his wife and family. He and Margaret had six children, two sons and four daughters.

The Edwards and Stuart families firmly believed in the continuance of family names and it is very easy to become mixed up in the generations!

Robert and Margaret Stuart's first born was **Cairnes** who died of a fever at the age of fourteen. Their second son, **Andrew Thomas,** who succeeded his father as 9th Baron and First Earl Castlestuart, was born on 29th of August 1725. He was High Sheriff of Tyrone in 1755. He married and had male issue and so the title was passed on.

Daughters **Jane and Olivia** died unmarried and without issue while daughter **Harriet** married James Hamilton Esq. of Strabane, a cadet of the family of Abercorn, having been descended from Sir Claud, first Baron of Paisley. They had five children.

Daughter **Eleanor** was described as "an elder child" and in 1758 she married Rev. Peter Pelissier, perhaps of French Huguenot connection. He was the son of Abel Pelissier and was educated at Trinity College Dublin. He was the Curate of Laragh Bryan in the Parish of Maynooth in 1765.

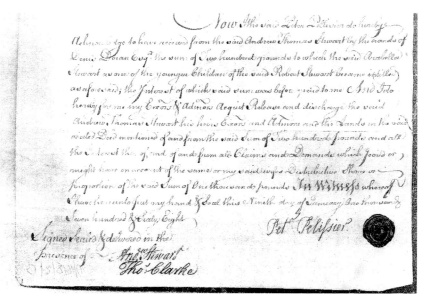

A receipt for £200, received by Peter Pelissier, from Andrew Thomas Stewart, his brother in law.

According to Canon John H. Gebbie in his book "Ardstraw—Historical Survey of a Parish 1600—1900," the Church of Ireland rector in Ardstraw from 1753 until 1781 was John Pelissier, D.D. Vice Provost of T.C.D., and whether he was related is a matter of speculation, but it is rather coincidental to find two men with this unusual name, having connections with the area around the same time. Four years after the marriage of Margaret Edwards and Robert Stuart, Margaret's cousin, Mary Edwards, daughter of Robert and Martha (la Vie), also married into the Stuart family, taking as her husband on 9th of September 1726,

Robert Stewart, eldest son of George Roe Stewart of Termon, who was a great grandson of Andrew, 2nd Lord Ochiltree.

Mary and Robert had a large family of ten children, six sons and four daughters **Samuel, George E., Martha, Elizabeth, Robert, Andrew, Edward, Alexander, Mary Jane, unnamed.** Their first son, Samuel, was born about 1728 and he married his step cousin, Magdalene Bruce. She was the daughter of a Colonel Bruce, of a fine old Scottish family, and his wife Elizabeth, who was the third daughter of George Roe Stuart of Termon and his second wife Magdalene Sanderson. Samuel and Magdalene had two daughters, (their story later), but no male issue and Samuel died, it is thought before 1774. His widow remarried a Mr Caldwell of Ballybryan and had one daughter, Mary. Interestingly, she married The Rev. Robert Alexander, father of William Alexander, Lord Bishop of Derry who was the husband of the well-known hymn writer Cecil Frances Alexander.

George E. Stewart, second son, was born about 1730 and very little is known about him. He served on the Grand Jury in 1774 and 1776 and inherited Strews or Strath. He sold property at Tattiesallagh to Lord Belmore in May 1779 and although it is said that he married "a lady of property" nothing further is known and they died without issue.

A daughter, Martha, was born in 1732 and she went on to marry William Holmes of Donaghmore, Dungannon, in 1750. Their descendants will be recounted later in the next chapter.

The next daughter Elizabeth was born in 1734. Whether she had a long or short life in unknown and apart from a brief mention on the family tree, her existence was unremarkable.

More details are usually found on the males in a family. We are told that Robert was born about 1736. He did not marry and had no issue but he was described as "a gifted singer and a wonderfully neat penman". His death took place in April 1818 and he was buried at Drumragh. His grave is inside the walls of the old ruined church and the gravestone has the mortuary symbols of skull and crossbones at the top.

Andrew Stewart was the next son born about 1738. In 1755, aged seventeen, he entered Trinity College, Dublin and was elected a scholar in 1762. He became Curate of Pubble, near Enniskillen, until 1776. He was obviously something of a diplomat as he was said to have been "distinguished in controversy" and was said to have written an eloquent interceding letter to Alexander Stuart of Drumnasple, Dungannon, on behalf of Alexander's younger brother, George, a surgeon.[1] He also married an Edwards but her name or descent is not known; however he had a son Robert and two daughters, of whom there are no further known details.

While the family seemed to support the established and dissenting churches, Edward, who was born about 1740, was alleged to have spent his fortune in propagating Methodism. Where he lived and worked or where he died has unfortunately not been recorded.

The Edwards and Stuart families were quite noteworthy for the number of members who served in the forces or were involved in the church. It was not often that one of them could be described as a writer, but Alexander Stuart, born about 1742, was distinguished in that field.

He printed and published various works of great accuracy, including "fine volume in folio of Burkett on the New Testament by and for A. Stuart at St Audoen's Arch," "The Hibernian Gazetteer," "The Law of Elections," "The Irish Merlin or Gentleman's Almanack," and "The West Briton Calendar."[2] He lived and worked at 86, Bride Street in Dublin and was admitted a Freeman in 1774. He was married and had one son Robert, who was supposedly musically talented and went to live in Birmingham. Alexander was buried in St. Brigid's Churchyard, Dublin on 27th January 1819.

Mary and Robert's daughter Mary Jane, born in 1744, has an interesting and romantic story. Apparently she was staying in Castlegore, under the care and protection of her second cousin, Olivia, Countess Rosse, when a romance blossomed between her and James Given of Langfield! This may have been a rather clandestine affair as it is recorded that she eloped from Castlegore and married her sweetheart! The circumstances are uncertain but one might suspect that she was underage, however this has not been confirmed.

The final child of Mary and Robert was a daughter, born in 1746 and she may have died very young, as there are no further details on her life.

The marriage of two brothers to two sisters is quite common and this happened in the case of the Edwards and Stuart families. Margaret Edwards' sister Mary was married firstly to Hugh Liston and secondly to Dalway Stuart, second son of

Andrew Stuart of Stuart Hall, brother of Margaret's husband Robert. They had two children, **Andrew,** who died at sixteen years of age and a daughter **Ann.**

Finally the last documented marriage between the Edwards and Stuarts took place between Lieutenant Colonel Hugh Gore Edwards, (who was earlier mentioned as inheriting his great Aunt Esther Brabazon's property-Raveagh-following his shipwreck off Drogheda) and Elizabeth Stuart, second daughter of Rev. Alexander George Stuart, Rector of Tullaniskin, near Dungannon, and his wife Mary, (daughter of Rev. George Evans, Rector of Killyman Parish).

They had three sons and six daughters and as one of the last Edwards families listed on the genealogical table it is sad to report that the Edwards lineage did not continue through them. The eldest son **Edward** was born in 1818 and served as a Lieutenant in the 21st Fusiliers and in the 32nd Regiment. He died on 9th of August 1844, in India, aged twenty-six and unmarried, and is buried in Castlederg.

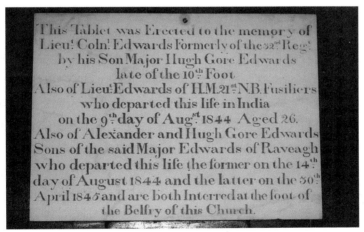

A memorial tablet to members of the Edwards family in Derg Parish Church.

The family tree simply notes that daughters **Priscilla, Mary, Isabella, and Emmeline** were born and died, while in the cases of Mary and Isabella, they married and died. Doubtless there was much more to all of their lives but it has not been recorded, hence we know nothing of where or how they lived or died. Daughter **Ann** married Edward Thomas Litton who was a nephew of Edward Litton, Master of Chancery and cousin of Edward Falconer Litton, Q.C., who was elected as M.P. for Tyrone in 1880. She died before 1851 and they had no issue.

Sons **Alexander and Hugh Gore,** whose names are also recorded on the memorial plaque in Derg Parish Church, died unmarried and aged eighteen and sixteen. Again we see that this Edwards family suffered multiple bereavements in successive years and indeed as far as is known these deaths represent the end of the Edwards lineage.

The last surviving daughter, **Elizabeth,** born on 1st September 1819, married on August 16th 1852, Robert Gore, fourth son of the Honourable and Very Rev. George Gore, Dean of Killala, and grandson of Arthur Saunders, 2nd Earl of Arran. Their family of five sons and three daughters, **Hugh, Thomas, Robert, Arthur, John, Emily and twins, Frances Sophia and Mary Elizabeth** are last to be named on the Edwards genealogical table but their descendants up to the present day are listed in Burke's Peerage.

This concludes the known links between the Stewart and Edwards families and although it is sad to document the Edwards decline, on a happier note it is good to say the Stewart family still continue to live in Stuart Hall, Stewartstown!

1.   An interesting account of the life and times of Rev. Alexander Stewart, who was rector of Tullanisken Parish Church, Dungannon from 1807-1819, is contained in "A History of the Parish of Tullanisken, Newmills, Co Tyrone, by Eileen Elizabeth Donnelly. M.Sc. B.A. Dip. Ed.

2.   The Genealogical Table of the Edwards Family. PRONI ; D/3000/114/1

The Holmes Connection.

In an attempt to find any living descendants of the Edwards families I spent a long time trawling genealogical websites with varied degrees of success. While I did not discover any living Edwards personnel it was with much pleasure that I received an email from Mr Mark Meredith of London, who was a fountain of knowledge on the Holmes family and indeed a direct descendant of that lineage. Mark shared a great deal of interesting and valuable history with me and I will try to impart some of it in this work as it brings the history of the Edwards family up to the present day.

Martha Stewart, mentioned previously, first daughter of Rev. Robert and Mary (Edwards) Stewart, was born in 1732 at Carland, Dungannon, and married in 1750, William Holmes, a gentleman of "Bray Island" and Donoughmore, Dungannon, Co. Tyrone. He was known as William Holmes, the younger, and was an officer in the army. After his brother's death he inherited the family lands at Donoughmore and the money left to him by his father was held in trust by James Moore Hamilton, of Desertcreat, Co. Tyrone, a member of the family of the Dukes of Hamilton.

William and Martha had four children, **Elizabeth Stewart, Robert, William and Arabella.** Elizabeth Stewart Holmes (1751-1776) was born at Donoughmore and married on 4th May 1768, James Boyle, a Colonel in Limavady Volunteers and a member of the Earls of Glasgow. They had no issue and after Elizabeth died at the early age of twenty-five he went on to marry three more times leaving at the time of his death a total of eleven children!

Major Robert Holmes (1758-1838), first son of William and Martha, was also born at Donoughmore and served in India as an officer before returning to Ireland where he became a barrister in 1795. He bought the lands of Bray or Brigh from his brother Stewart on 13th March 1804. On 13th February he married Margaret Macartney of Stone Park, Co. Fermanagh. He died at Caroline Row, Dublin, on 21st December 1838 and was buried with his wife at Tullyniskin Parish Church, Newmills, Dungannon, leaving three children, **Arabella Sophia, William and Francis,** both of whom were solicitors. (William was Sessional Crown

Attorney for Tyrone). It may be useful to remind us that these are the great grandchildren of Mary Edwards and Rev. Robert Stewart and that by this stage the name Edwards was in decline.

Perhaps the most interesting member of the family of William and Martha Holmes is William, who was born in 1762. He acquired an education as a surgeon before 31st March 1787, when he purchased a commission in the medical department of the British Army. He said, *"as was customary in those days, I paid 400 guineas for it."* As surgeon to the 5th Foot he was immediately sent to and stationed in Quebec.

He tended Indians in Detroit, acted as Senior Medical Officer in Upper and Lower Canada and had a civil practice in Quebec. He was involved in the Free Masons and the Baron's Club, a convivial meeting made up of twenty-one members who were the principal merchants in the colony.

William Holmes married firstly on 3rd January 1789, Mary Ann Jacobs, daughter of Seigneur Samuel Jacobs, of St Denis-sur-Richlieu. They lived in Upper Town, Quebec, where they had a family of six children; **William Edward, Matilda,** who married General James Fogo of Duchray Castle, Stirlingshire, **Maria,** who married Major-General William Furneaux, of Swilly House, Devonshire, **Sophia,** who married Arthur Luce Trelauney Collins of Ham House, Devonshire, **Theresa,** who married Captain Montgomery Cairnes, a descendant of David Cairnes and lastly, **Robert,** who was born and died in 1802. At that time the Duke of Kent was stationed in Quebec and he became good friends with William and acted as godfather to their son William Edward Holmes. (1789-1825).

After the death of his first wife in 1803 William married again on 12th of May 1807 at the English Cathedral, Quebec, Margaret MacNider (1764-1838), widow of Colonel James Johnston. This marriage brought him property and financial security and he lived in the St Lewis Ward amongst many other notorieties of the day. He retired from the army and became a keen farmer and an active member of the Agriculture Society. He continued his work as a physician and was also an examiner of candidates for medical licences. He became a Justice of the Peace in 1821 and for many years worked with mentally ill patients. He was known familiarly as the "Insane Physician" and he worked tirelessly for the improvement of conditions for his patients. By 1825 most of his work was being undertaken by younger staff and in 1824 his son in law, Sydney Bellingham, of Castle Bellingham, Co. Louth, (who had married daughter Arabella), described him as "a tall grey-headed sixty year old gentleman with small eyes and a slight north of Ireland brogue." By 1832, two years before his death, "the old doctor wore a loose dressing gown and slippers, and spent the greater part of his day at the Garrison Library, not a stone's throw from his residence, where he provoked much fun amongst the officers by his free and easy costume." According to Bellingham he had been generous and kind to his patients, was well liked in the religious hospitals and had frequently "declined payment for his advice and his medicines." On the other hand a rival and political opponent, Painchaud, asserted that he had overcharged for country calls and that he was hampered in his practice by a poor facility in French. Nonetheless, he was highly regarded as a successful practitioner and had represented well the medical establishment and British Military authority in a period of professional and political conflict and change. He died on 24th February 1834 at Quebec, leaving five children.

William Edward Holmes (1789-1825)

William's son **William Edward** (1789-1825) also became a doctor and he was described as "popular and well-known" in Quebec. He was a member of the Royal College of Surgeons, London and was granted a licence to practice, (signed by his father), to "practise in physic, surgery, midwifery, etc. in the province of Quebec", as of 31st of October 1816. He was married on 8th of December 1817. The amazing coincidence of this union was that the marriage took place at his father's home, (which was also his bride's mother's home), to Ann, daughter of Colonel James Johnston, by his wife and William's step-mother, Margaret MacNider. Sadly, William Edward died after a long illness at Quebec on 27th March 1825, at the young age of twenty-nine. Shortly after his death his widow moved to Montreal with her six children.

One of these children was Sophia Naiters Holmes who was born on March 16th 1820. She grew up to marry Chief Justice The Honourable Sir William Collis Meredith Q.C., D.C.L. (1812-1894), in Christ Church Cathedral, Montreal. He was the second son of Rev. Thomas Meredith, (1777-1819), a former fellow of Trinity College, Dublin, who for six years had been a rector in the Parish Church of Ardtrea, near Cookstown, Co. Tyrone. An interesting story is told of his death on 2nd May 1819, which according to the wording of his memorial in the church, was due to "a sudden and awful visitation." A local legend explains that a ghost haunted the rectory and greatly disturbed his family and servants, causing them to leave. The rector, Rev. Thomas Meredith, was told to use a silver bullet to shoot the ghost. He tried and failed in the attempt and next morning was found dead at his hall door, while an object like a devil made horrid noises out of the windows! It was suggested by some Roman Catholic neighbours that a priest should be brought along to "lay" the thing. The priest arrived and with the help of a jar of whiskey managed to calm the ghost. When the priest was about to pour the last glass for himself the ghost made himself as thin and long as "a Lough Neagh eel" and slipped into the jar to get the last drops, whereupon the priest hammered the cork into place, capturing the evil thing. It was buried in the cellar of the rectory and it still can be heard calling to be released!!

Sophia and William had a family of ten children, one of whom, Frederick Edmund, also became a K.C. and led an illustrious life among the legal profession in Montreal.

Frederick Edmund Meredith was Mr Mark Meredith's great grandfather and I am deeply indebted to him for furnishing me with all the details on the Holmes family and their connections with the Edwards'. Some of the details of the Holmes family members are included on the Edwards family tree but it is not complete and further information will be held in Edwards Primary School.

The information for this chapter was kindly sent by Mr Mark Meredith of London.

The descendants of James and Nancy (Ann) Edwards.
Migration, Murder and Mystery.

Two thin, tattered and torn pages from a family Bible, deposited in the P.R.O.N.I. are all that are left to tell us about the issue of James and Nancy (or Ann) Edwards, who lived in Straw House. James was the third son of Doctor Henry Edward Edwards and Mary Caskey and was a grandson of Robert Edwards and Martha le Vie.

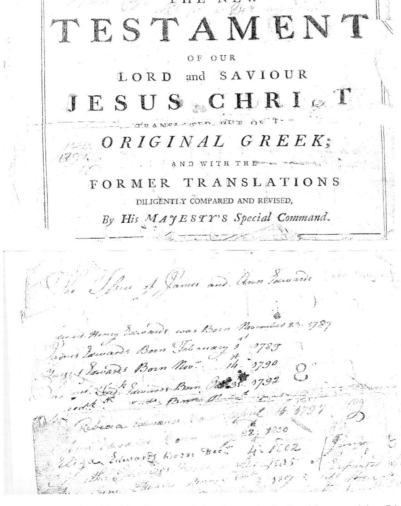

Two pages from The New Testament belonging to the family of James and Ann Edwards.

James and Nancy had the following children, **Edward, James, Samuel, Frederick, Margaret, Rebecca, Ann, Elizabeth, Mary-Jane and Martha,** and although the writing is faded and in some places illegible due to the fold in the paper, it is for the most part quite clear and the dates of birth are definite. 1792 is the scribbled date on the first page along with what looks like the name of "Samuel Edwards of Bov" and other words that are indecipherable. The names of all the children and their birth dates are written in a neat script on the second page, while the deaths of Mary Jane and James are also included. (See copy)

For the first time in the study of the Edwards family it is only now that we record the emigration of its members. The outbreak of war between Britain and the United States of America in 1812 had stopped the flow of emigration but once the war ended emigration began strongly during 1815. By 1816 it was estimated that 6,000 people had left Ireland for America and this rose to 20,000 by 1818. The factors behind the emigration are those that could still be used today---collapse in the market for agricultural produce, a series of wet summers, a decline in the standard of living and a general depression. These, coupled with the stories of a better life style on "the other side of the sheugh" led many to embark on the long and perilous journey to America.

The Ulster American Folk Park tells in its own inimitable fashion, and much better than the mere written word can, the stories of those who emigrated from Tyrone at that time---John Joseph Hughes, Hugh Campbell and Thomas Mellon to name but a few!

Like Mellon and Hughes, who began a family chain of emigration, we find no less than four members of the family of James and Nancy Edwards immigrated to America. They were Edward, Samuel, Frederick and Margaret who went to Chilicothe, Ohio. Edward was aged thirty and the others were in their twenties when they emigrated.

A very interesting, well written and most informative letter from Edward H. Edwards, composed in Baltimore, to his uncle James Douglas, tells of the twelve-week "tedious but pleasant" journey, which was mostly calm and without serious incidents. The most dangerous episodes he reported were "when a squall struck us and turned the sails all black" and a change of wind caused "an awful spectacle two seas met coming different directions and rose to the air perhaps as thick as a hogshead."[1]   While he refers in the letter to "we" and talks of Samuel and Frederick, it is not clear whether Margaret was present or if she came out at a different time.

A Letter written by Edward H. Edwards from Baltimore, to his Uncle James Douglas, describing his epic twelve-week journey from Ireland to America.

marks Aunt & Ned Join one in love to Grandmother Rebecca Aunt mother James

and the children Aunt Gray James & Mill please tell her she may expect a letter

from Francis Shortly with an inclosure You ever affectionate

Edw H Edwards

please write me on receipt of this I am anxious to hear from you Direct it

To Edw H Edwards
　　　Care
Edward Gray Baltimore

Mrs James Dorca(?)
Roseborough
Fartrush[imperf] ...
... land

P.R.O. (N.I.)

Acc. No. 2547

class D2547

No.

Sub. No.

N.13 I had a letter from my uncle Bateman two days ago with an

invitation to go and spend some time there which one will decline as it would

be expensive the are all well there remember to aunt and uncle Osborne and

all particular friends that I may omit mentioning tell Letty Hesson I remember

her Kindness to me

E.H.E

Letters were folded and sealed in 1817 and envelopes were not used.

The port of departure was Lough Swilly, and he says they foresaw a long passage due to the very light winds. Food was reasonably plentiful and they had twice secured supplies of bread and flour from vessels they met at sea. They had a hearty breakfast of "stirrabout and porter" and later in the morning and in the middle of the day, "coffee or tea with ham bread and butter." Not a bad diet but perhaps somewhat monotonous for twelve weeks! Obviously they brought ample supplies, as he wrote that in sight of land he still had " about three score of meal some biscuit one and a half hams some beef with sugar tea and coffee in proportion", and he was sorry that he had brought any spirits as some of the passengers were "out of provisions at seven weeks and depended on the generosity of others who dare risk to divide their stock as self preservation is certainly the first law of nature."

Edward arrived on the eighth of October 1817 and penned his letter in Baltimore on November 2nd, the reason for the delay being the wish to provide more information. He also had brought with him many goods to sell--- linen, "which appears to pay but poorly", shirts that sold at about "17 shillings Irish", glue, on which he had eight pounds profit and "shoe thread which I have not disposed of yet." He received assistance from "our worthy friend Edward Grey" (who may have been his cousin), and he was purchasing goods to take to St Louis, Mississippi, 300 miles from Chilicothe, Ohio, " a place you say is almost out of the world." Mr Grey introduced him to "gentlemen of this city" and gave him credit for any amount of goods, which would suggest that he was well off and influential.

Lack of money was not a problem for Edward as he revealed he had brought with him 12,000 dollars from which he hoped he could raise a fortune. He intended to take Samuel with him, as he was afraid "to commit him to a stranger who would not take care to instruct him and turn the Leek habits from him." (Edward was determined to leave Ireland behind!)

As for Frederick, he was trying to find him "a situation here" and later in the letter he said that Frederick was employed at the cotton factory "for which he receives one and a half dollars per day."

Edward expressed concern for the people at home who were "in the grip of a fatal and malignant fever" and shock at the sudden death of his uncle. He concluded his letter by sending love to Grandmother, Rebecca, (sister) Aunt, mother, James and the children, (brother in law and family), Aunt Grey, (Martha, wife of Rev. Grey), James and Frederick, (possibly uncles).

Unfortunately this letter was the only one that was kept and the progress and lives of the immigrants after that is unknown. The family tree records the deaths of Edward, Samuel and Margaret in America and both men were unmarried. Sadly it is here that I have to record again the demise of the Edwards name, descending from James, as there was no male issue. Margaret, born in November 1990, in Leeke married her fourth cousin, John Dickson, of Whitefort, near Tubbermore, had four sons and three daughters in Carrolton, Missouris, U.S.A.

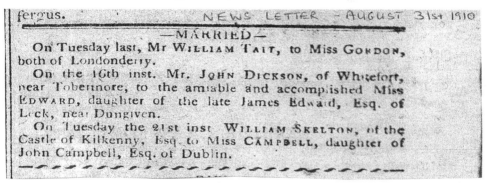

fergus. NEWS LETTER - AUGUST 31st 1910

—MARRIED—

On Tuesday last, Mr WILLIAM TAIT, to Miss GORDON, both of Londonderry.

On the 16th inst. Mr. JOHN DICKSON, of Whitefort, near Tobermore, to the amiable and accomplished Miss EDWARD, daughter of the late James Edward, Esq. of Leck, near Dungiven.

On Tuesday the 21st inst WILLIAM SKELTON, of the Castle of Kilkenny, Esq. to Miss CAMPBELL, daughter of John Campbell, Esq. of Dublin.

An extract from the News Letter - August 31st 1810, giving notice of the marriage of John Dickson and Margaret Edwards. They emigrated to America and died there.

Five of the Edwards sisters remained in Ireland. The entry on the family Bible tells us that "Mary Jane Edwards departed this life on July 10th 1808," aged just eight months. Elizabeth and Martha both died unmarried and are buried in Bovevagh Meeting House Yard.

Rebecca married James Dickson, brother of Margaret's husband John. They had four sons and four daughters but I was unable to find any trace of them.

Ann, who was born in 1800, married her cousin on her mother's side, Andrew Smythe, and they had a family of two sons and one daughter. They lived at Rose Cottage, Bovevagh and the owner of the present house thinks it dates from the mid 1800's and that the original cottage is one of the disused outbuildings. Although their surname should have been Smythe, Ann and Andrew's son James took in the name Douglas, after his grandmother, and son Samuel called himself

Smythe –Edwards, thus retaining his mother's name. In any case one can see that efforts were being made to retain the Edwards name.

Samuel Smythe—Edwards is still remembered in the Dungiven area today. He was an eminent Unionist, a member of the Ulster Unionist Council, was on the Executive of the North Derry Unionist Association, President of Bovevagh Branch, formed Ardinariff and Bovevagh Unionist Clubs, supported the Orange Institution and was involved in the Ulster Volunteer Force. He was also a faithful member of Bovevagh Presbyterian Church and his obituary notice, dated 1914, reflected the esteem in which he was held in the community. (See newspaper extract.)[2]

1. A letter from Edward Edwards of Baltimore to his uncle, James Douglas. PRONI: D/2547/3. The letter illustrates the way in which letters were sent without envelopes. They were folded and sealed and the address written on the outer side of the writing paper.
A transcript of the letter is also available in the library of the Centre for Migration Studies, The Ulster American Folk Park, Omagh

2. Newsletter obituary notice 1914. PRONI D/2547/25

A newspaper obituary notice for Samuel Smythe Edwards.

Rosebrook Cottage Bovevagh, in 1920, home of the Edwards and Douglas families.

Rosebrook Cottage as it is today.

The Tragic Death of Frederick Edwards 1844

When one thinks of those who emigrated in the past, images of Revolutionaries, pioneers, Presidents, wealthy businessmen and rich bankers spring to mind, but it must not be forgotten that there were also lesser mortals and not every story was one of success.

Turning now to the story of Frederick brings an element of tragic realism into the Edwards history. Frederick, who had emigrated in 1817 with his brothers Edward and Samuel, settled in Bourneville, Ross County, Ohio. In 1844 he was working in the grocery store belonging to his cousin Douglas Smythe. He slept in a room that was divided from the store by a partition. On the night of the 19th of November 1844, a man, later known to be Henry Thomas, a serial burglar, and an accomplice, Leroy Maxon, burgled the store. Frederick was alerted by the activity and leaping from his bed, threw himself upon Thomas, who proceeded to draw a knife, wounding him in the temple, the lungs, the left side and the abdomen and after a final frantic scuffle, fatally stabbing his victim.

This tragedy is revealed in minute detail in a booklet, deposited in the P.R.O.N.I., (a copy of which is held in Edwards P.S.) entitled "The Trial and Confession of Henry Thomas, Sentenced to be hung on Friday the 6th day of March 1846, for the murder of Frederick Edwards."[1] His picture is shown on the front cover (See copy) and the trial is recorded in the book in the form of a drama, with each person stating their case in front of Judges Read and Hitchcock and a Jury of twelve men.

A doctor stated that he had examined the victim and found the first wound between the ribs was about five inches deep, there was another wound in the back, which went into the liver, five wounds in the chest and a very deep wound in the abdomen. Death, he thought was not instantaneous. Some witnesses recorded their last sightings of Frederick while others recalled seeing the defendants.

The booklet details Judge Read's Charge to the Jury to look at the circumstances and the evidence, and to decide whether the defendant was guilty of murder in the first degree or whether it was unintentional and therefore – manslaughter.

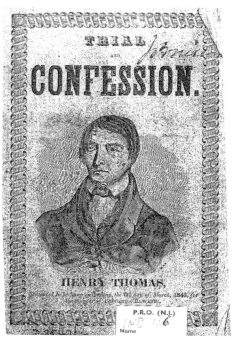

The front page of the booklet covering the Trial and Confession of Henry Thomas who murdered Frederick Edwards.

The Confession to the Murder of Frederick Edwards by Henry Thomas.

The Jury was then directed to deliver their verdict at nine o'clock next morning. When the prisoner was brought into court next day he was asked if he had anything to say and he took the unusual step of thanking the Court for the able counsel, the officers for their kindness to him, and stating that he had no unfriendly feelings towards the Jury. He commented upon the testimony of some of the witnesses, "delivering his remarks in a firm voice and without any more embarrassment than one would naturally have who was not in the habit of public speaking."

The Jury then rendered their verdict, which was "**GUILTY OF MURDER IN THE FIRST DEGREE**," whereupon the Judge declared the sentence, saying, "**The Court sentence you, Henry Thomas, to be taken hence to the jail of Ross County from whence you came, there to be safely kept until Friday, the 6th day of March 1846, then on said day, between the hours of eleven o'clock in the forenoon and 3 o'clock in the afternoon of said day, to be hanged by the neck until you are dead and may God have mercy upon your soul.**"

"The Confession" by Thomas was made to Spencer Lusk while he was confined to prison, charged with being an accomplice in the murder of Edwards. In it he details his shady dealings before the murder and then he tells of the burglary and the subsequent attack on Edwards and how Maxon assisted him in the killing. An accompanying black and white drawing illustrates the tragedy. [2]

The Murder of Frederick Edwards.

91

While it would appear that Thomas did not intend to kill his victim, there is no doubt that he was an armed serial burglar with a chequered history and he was intent on robbery. How unfortunate for poor Frederick and the members of his family who had emigrated in such good faith.

1. The Trial and Confession of Henry Thomas. PRONI: D/2547/6

2. The Admission to Murder by Henry Thomas. PRONI: D/2547/5

From Ardstraw To Australia.

It is often said that fact is stranger than fiction and I surely felt that this maxim was so true after encountering Mrs Gayle Perkins "while surfing the net." I first came across Gayle's name on a genealogical web site message board when I noticed that she had been corresponding with a researcher in Dublin who was working on David Cairnes. After corresponding with her and reading her amazing family history and coming to terms with the fact that someone from the other side of the world was able to tell me facts about local people mentioned on the Edwards family tree, I eventually began to comprehend her story as I fitted the parts of the jigsaw together!

Elizabeth Lowther of (Drumnaboy), Drumnabey, Castlederg.

Gayle too, was trying to figure out exactly who Cairnes was, and in her letter explaining where she was coming from, she quoted extracts from a letter written by her husband's great grandmother, Elizabeth Lowther, who was originally Elizabeth Jack from Magheracolton.

It was very exciting to read that this old lady had written so many years ago of a Mr Edwards coming from London to buy the Manor of Hastings (referred to earlier) and she went on to describe the flight from France of the la Vie family, she detailed the family of Robert Stewart and Mary Edwards and stated that their daughter Elizabeth Stewart was her grandmother.

This was really a coincidental and totally amazing find for me as the names were all on the family tree and it was incredible that I could get in touch with a living Edwards descendant!

I immediately despatched an email to Gayle and after ascertaining that we were indeed researching the same line, she was most helpful in sending so much information, family trees and a C.D. of her research. I am humbly indebted to her for all her kind assistance and I will now try to share some of her amazing information with you.

I will begin the story with the fascinating tale of Elizabeth Stewart, daughter of Samuel Stewart and Magdalene Bruce and granddaughter of Mary Edwards and Robert Stewart. She was born in 1759, and for some strange reason was committed to the somewhat dubious care of her second cousin once removed, Olivia, Countess of Rosse, who was living in the old Edwards mansion house of Castlegore.

It is said that history often repeats itself and indeed we find it happening in this case. Like her aunt, Mary Jane Stewart, who had eloped from Castlegore and married James Given some years earlier, Elizabeth also eloped and at the tender age of sixteen married James Welsh, eldest son of Rev. Andrew Welsh of Ardstraw and his wife Jane Maxwell, (who incidentally was the daughter of Rev. James Maxwell of Omagh.)

James was a Lieutenant in the Volunteers and the account written by Gordon Perkins's great grandmother, Elizabeth Lowther, and their family trees, indicate that James' father, Andrew Welsh, was a great grandson of John Knox, the Scottish Reformer. Knox had married secondly Margaret Stewart, a cousin of Mary Queen of Scots and a daughter of Andrew Stewart, Lord Ochiltree. Their daughter Elizabeth married Rev. John Welsh, Minister of Ayr and in turn their great-great grandson was Andrew Welsh of Ardstraw.

James Welsh and Elizabeth Stewart had four sons and three daughters, **Andrew, John, William, Stewart, Eliza, Deborah and Grace.** Eliza went on to marry Andrew Jack of Magheracolton and in turn their daughter Elizabeth married Walter Lowther of Drumnaboy, (Drumnabey) near Castlederg. (See photograph.) The Lowthers emigrated to Australia where their daughter Moina married Francis George Perkins. (They were the grandparents of Gayle's husband Gordon.)

In his book "The Genealogical and Historical Sketch of the Stuarts of Castlestuart," Rev Andrew Godfrey Stuart documents in great detail many stories of the Welsh clergymen and the difficulties that they encountered in their ministries. His accounts concur with what Elizabeth Lowther wrote and the following is part of her description:

"I will begin my paper with John Knox the great Scottish Reformer who was born in Edinburgh nearly three centuries ago. His wife was a Miss Ochiltree: she was of Royal descent. John Knox got an estate with his wife called Ranfurly, somewhere near Edinburgh. The Knox's have it still. John Knox had three daughters who all married clergymen. The eldest married the Refd. John Walsh, minister of Ayre, about fifty miles down the Clyde from Glasgow.

After James I went to reign in England, he wished to compel all men to embrace the Church of England. He would not tolerate Presbyterian clergymen and had them imprisoned if they did not conform to his rules. He imprisoned the Revd. John Walsh of Ayre. When he had been some time in prison his health began to fail and his wife undertook the journey to London to see the King. She told him that her husband had been a year in prison and was in a poor state of health and she hoped the King would liberate him. The King said there was nothing easier. He gave her a piece of paper and told her that he must sign that. She had a big white apron on, and she held it out to the King saying she would hold his head there first. The King asked her how many children John Knox had; she said three. And were they lads or lasses. "Oh," she said, "They are all lasses." Then the King thanked God, for he said, "Had they been lads I could scarce have hoped to hold my kingdom against them." So she came back to Scotland and they made a vow that they would never bring up a child to the ministry.

As soon as the eldest child was old enough they secured him a commission in the army and after he rose to be captain of his regiment he was called to Londonderry for civil war was in progress at the time. He married a Miss Dean somewhere in the vicinity. He and his wife had a family and they made up their minds to bring up one son to the ministry. Sometime after Captain Walsh was called to active service at the siege of Gibraltar and fell there fighting for his country. But his wife kept her promise and brought up the eldest boy to the ministry for he gave promise to be clever and after going about for sometime he got a call to Ardstraw Parish. He got a splendid farm at Magheracolton and a fine house. It was often said that neither rich nor poor ever left his house either hungry or dry. His hospitality was unbounded. There were three clergymen in the big parish. Fitzgerald the Rector, Father Maguire the priest and the Revd. Andrew Walsh who was the great grandson of John Knox. He preached forty-seven years in the parish of Ardstraw. These three clergymen dined weekly with the old Marquis of Hamilton at Baronscourt.

My great grandfather married Miss Jane Maxwell of Omagh. Her father the Revd. James Maxwell preached sixty years in Omagh. There has been a new church built and in it there was erected a marble tablet to his memory, in which it says he was the direct ancestor of the present Lord Farnham.

The Revd. Andrew Walsh had two sons and three daughters. The eldest son sold the place and married a Miss Irvine of Strabane and went to live in Sligo so we know very little about him, but my grandfather James Walsh lived on a small farm and seemed quite happy."

What a historical treasure this letter is and it is wonderful that it has survived over the years and that we have been given the privileged opportunity to peruse it. In Elizabeth's letter she spells Welsh as Walsh but her facts appear to be accurate and indeed are confirmed by Rev Andrew Godfrey Stuart in his book on the Castlestuarts. He spells the family name as Welsh and it also appears in this way on the Edwards family tree.

As she stated Rev. James Maxwell was indeed the Minister in the Presbyterian Church in Omagh for over fifty years and the new church was built in 1721.

It is most interesting and amusing to compare Elizabeth Lowther's account of Mrs Welsh's visit to the King with that written by Stuart who offers greater detail. He claimed that the King asked her who her father was and when she replied "John Knox" he exclaimed, "Knox and Welsh, the devil never made such a match as that!" Then when she requested that he give her husband his native air he replied "Give him his native air....give him the devil!" "Give that to your hungry courtiers," said she, offended at his profaneness."

To complete the story, the King at last reluctantly complied with Mrs Welsh's wishes and Mr Welsh was given permission to preach in London, but only when his hours were numbered. According to Stuart "he ascended the pulpit once, and preached long and fervently; and thence returning to his chamber, within two hours he calmly, and without pain, expired."

James and Elizabeth Welsh both died in 1839 and their obituary notices in the Londonderry Journal pay tribute to their virtues. James was recognised as "an affectionate husband, a tender parent and a kind friend" while the accolade to his wife reported "she was of ancient descent but with only a small share of the property of her ancestors, inherited the nobleness of spirit. She disdained to court the fame of the great; her maxim being that esteem was due only to the good and the just........She had been educated a member of the Established Church but on her marriage became a Presbyterian. She was very partial to the Methodists and read their magazine."

In the historical information that I received from Gayle Perkins, she includes further letters and details on the Lowther and Jack families, which were also recorded by Elizabeth Lowther, and for historical interest these will be retained in Edwards Primary School.

1. This letter, written by Elizabeth Lowther, is part of the information sent by Gordon and Gayle Perkins, Queensland, Australia.

The Edwards Coat of Arms and Family Crest.

In carrying out the research into the Edwards family, more questions were often raised than were answered. One such area that remains an enigma is that of the existence of a coat or coats of arms or a family crest.

There are many laws governing the bearing of arms. During the Middle Ages the practice of bearing personal symbols, colours and designs on shields was adopted. This was furthered in the fourteenth century when personal insignia were embroidered on suits of armour and mail, hence the origin of the term "coat of arms." In the fifteenth century laws were passed governing the designing and bearing of personal coats of arms and many of them remain in place today.

In 1552 the office of "Ulster, King of Arms" was instituted in Ireland to regulate the use of heraldic arms and was an extension of the English College of Arms and English Heraldry. This marked a significant change in Gaelic Irish custom. English heraldry was asserted on primogenacy, or the rule whereby real estate is passed on to the first-born while the Gaelic Irish based inheritance on kinship.

One of the main rules as far as inheritance goes was that the first born male could inherit his father's coat of arms unchanged but any subsequent sons had to make some sort of change or adopt an entirely new coat of arms.

With this in mind I went on to study the Edwards coats of arms.

The Edwards memorial in St Columb's Cathedral, Londonderry, clearly shows a rectangular coat of arms bearing a cross, engraved between four birds with a helmet and another bird at the top.

The top part of the memorial to Hugh Edwards in St Columb's Cathedral, showing the coat of arms.

The Edwards motif above the entrance door of Derg Parish Church and that of the gravestone against the belfry wall show a coat of arms of circular design, surrounded by leaves and curved shapes. There is a helmet at the top and a bird with a sword in its beak. Inside the circle, which is divided in half, one side shows a fretted chevron, with two birds at the top and one underneath, while the other half is blank except for a plain chevron.

The Edwards gravestone that is placed against the belfry wall in Derg Parish Church.

A copy of the gravestone over the door of Derg Parish Church.

On the wall inside the church there is another plaque showing the circular coat of arms with the three birds and the helmet while above the memorial to Rev Edward Edwards is a bird bearing a sword and the motto below states PRO PATRIA SEMPER (always for my country). We also know that he used a bird as his seal along with the letters E.E.

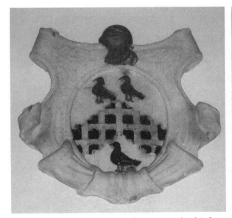

An Edwards wall plaque featuring the birds.

The Edwards motto on the wall in Derg Parish Church.

Many documents in the P.R.O.N.I. relating to the Edwards family bear the seals of the family members concerned and although they are often very indistinct it is sometimes possible to distinguish the birds.

The question of the existence of the Edwards arms must have cropped up in the past as I discovered two pages in the P.R.O.N.I. entitled "Edwards Armory Notes."[1] It is not clear who wrote the notes but they were obviously written in answer to a query about the possibility of a coat of arms.

Here is a transcript of the document, which is written in heraldic shorthand:

"The General Armory states

"Edwards of Rhyl North Wales Ar. across flory engr. between four Cornish Choughs sa. armed gu.

Ulster at Dublin Castle has no Irish records in connection with name of Edwards.

Mention that you have been with Mr Vicars, Ulster King at Arms and Dublin Herald who stated he would mention your enquiry to Lt. Farnham Bourke, Esq. Somerset Herald in the College of Arms, Queen Victoria Street, London, whom he said you should see and to whom show photo and pedigree. He will be able to tell you what coats of arms have been granted allowed or recognised in connection with the families or name Edwards."

The second page details different Edwards coats of arms according to the lineage, all of them bearing Cornish choughs, (the chough is a type of crow with red legs and a red beak, found commonly in coastal areas of England and Ireland), but does not confirm any of them as belonging to the members of this particular branch of Edwards.

In an attempt to clarify the issue I contacted the Office of the Chief Herald in Dublin and was given a lot of assistance by Mr Mícheál O'Comain, who explained that many families who exhibit a coat of arms often simply adopt arms that are not rightfully theirs. He went on to say that one can not simply produce and display a coat of arms without first of all being able to prove one's pedigree and then applying to the appropriate Heraldic authority for a grant of arms. The grant of arms creates a form of property, which is vested in the grantee, who may display the arms on a "shield or banner or otherwise according to the laws of arms." The grant of arms is recorded in the Register of Arms and is a matter of public record.

He then instructed me to search the "Hayes Manuscript Sources for the History of Irish Civilisation" to ascertain if the Edwards family had any manuscripts lodged in the Genealogical Office and I found out that Manuscript 170, pages 61-62, gave the pedigree of Edwards of Castlegore, Co. Tyrone, c.1680- c.1780.

On returning with what I thought was a positive lead, he then checked his records and informed me that although the manuscript existed, an application by any member of the Edwards family for a licence to bear arms had not been given in Ireland, but that it could have been granted in England or Wales.

Despite following up those lines I still unfortunately did not manage to verify the definite existence of the Edwards arms.

We can only conclude that they used coats of arms and there is a continued employment of the bird or chough in memorials and seals, as is evident in Derg Parish Church.

Former Edwards P.S. Principal, the late Mr T. F. Riddall, designed the badge for the uniform of the pupils of the school and he incorporated the symbols of the bridge, turrets of the castle and the Edwards symbol, the bird, which he insisted was a chough, but it is not known if he had any further knowledge of the use of that particular symbol.

1. Edwards Armory Notes, a hand written letter, describes the Arms of Edwards of Rhyl. PRONI: D/2547/28

IS YOUR NAME EDWARDS?

IS YOUR NAME EDWARDS?

£100,000,000 Awaiting the Rightful Heir.

Yet another enormous fortune is awaiting a rightful heir. It is common knowledge that about forty acres of land in New York was originally owned by a Mr. Edwards, who migrated to America from Londonderry in the eighteenth century, and who died about the time of the War of Independence. The land is controlled by the American Government, and it has increased in value until it is now worth close upon £100,000,000, the real owners being the descendants or relatives of the man Edwards.

Naturally there have been many claims to this enormous fortune, and there is little doubt that an immense amount of money would have to be spent in litigation before the American Government handed over this valuable piece of land. It has been suggested that the whole of the claimants should form themselves into a syndicate, says the 'Standard,' and that together they should seek to establish the claim of the one who appears to be the most nearly related. Then, if the money is won, the nearest relative could have half, and there would still be plenty left to divide among the others.

In the meantime, much interest has been aroused by a family Bible which is in the possession of an umbrella-maker, Mr. Robert Williams, who lives in a quaint little shop at the back of the Edgware Road, which Bible contains many particulars of the original owner of the land and his family.

From the point of view of a claimant of this gigantic fortune, the Bible, of course, is invaluable, and Mr. Williams almost every day receives communications from members of the Edwards family asking for particulars of the entries.

From what these claimants have told Mr. Williams, there must be at least a hundred relatives of the original

An article from Tit-Bits magazine, 1912, seeking the Edwards heir to a fortune in New York. PRONI : D/2547/24

If your name is **Edwards** then I have some great news for you!! But you'd better hurry as you need to **promptly** get in touch with the American Government about your rights to some property in New York!!

However I am sorry to inform you that you may already be too late as this was the subject of an article, which appeared in the "Tit-Bits" magazine on March 12th 1916.[1]

The extract is a copy of the article and as you can read, the American Government was searching for the rightful owners of about forty acres of prime land in New York, which had originally been owned by a Mr Edwards who had emigrated from Londonderry in the eighteenth century, but who had since died about the time of the War of Independence. The subsequent owners would then have been the closest descendants of Mr Edwards and I do not know if they were ever traced but if your name is Edwards it might just be worth asking some questions!!!

1. Article from "Tit-Bits" magazine, PRONI: D/2547/24

And Finally.....

It is often said that after the words "and finally" comes the second half, but in this instance, I have little more to write on the Edwards family history. The subject has been very much like a jigsaw and my purpose was to try to put together as many pieces as I could. I have done as much as possible, within the constraints of time and my own inadequacies as a researcher and historian. There are still many missing pieces but I sincerely hope my findings will be of interest and will answer some, if not all, of the questions about this wonderful family whose lives have touched us in Londonderry, Dungiven, Castlederg, or further afield in one way or another.

There are still more avenues that could be explored. Time did not allow me to look into Civil Registration Records but in cases where these are available, more information might be gleaned.

I have been disappointed that I did not manage to find any family portraits or photographs or any trace at all of the wonderful mansion of Castlegore. What a pity! Maybe...just maybe..... someone, somewhere, will turn up a print or picture!

The whereabouts of all the family heirlooms is also an enigma. Maybe someone has Hugh Edwards' pistols, his plate handled gilt sword or his gold watch with the chain and seal, or articles of furniture from Castlegore, and doesn't realise the significance of the artefacts, or maybe they no longer exist.

There may also still be living Edwards descendants and it would be wonderful to hear from any descendants or anyone who knows of a connection with the past. This might help with bringing the family tree up to date. The links with the Holmes, Perkins, Miller and Speer families were most interesting and invaluable and helped to add links in the chain.

In the meantime the appeals posted on the message boards of various genealogical websites might generate further response and maybe someday we could be surprised and find an Edwards descendant knocking on the door!

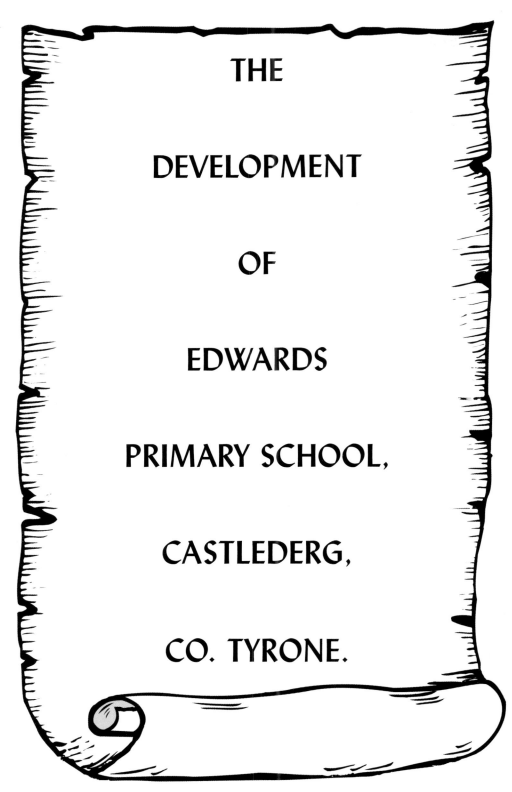

THE

DEVELOPMENT

OF

EDWARDS

PRIMARY SCHOOL,

CASTLEDERG,

CO. TYRONE.

The Establishment of the Hugh Edwards Charity School.

I now turn from the family history to unravel the details of the establishment and development of Edwards Primary School.

Bearing in mind the unsavoury picture of Olivia, Countess of Ross, which was painted by John Gamble in 1819, it is hardly surprising to record that she did not carry out her father's generous and visionary wish, declared in his will of 1737, to provide "a school and a master to educate six poor boys."

Gamble hinted that stories told about her indicated "a degree of avarice that may well be called a disease" and these sentiments are confirmed in a Chancery Suit, which was presented on the ninth of December 1808, by the Plaintiffs, the Commissioners of Charitable Donations and Bequests against the Defendant, John Bateman, Esq., second husband of Olivia.[1]

A previous complaint had been exhibited in the Court in June 1808, probably in response to a request from the "the Rector of Urney, the Curate of the Perpetual Cure of Castlederg and the Presbyterian Minister of Castlederg," stating that they had "written to Lord Castlestuart, the present proprietor of the property of Mr Edwards, stating the bequest and requesting him to fulfil the intentions of the Testator and in the case of non-compliance," asking the Commissioners for Charitable Bequests to "take legal measures for the recovery of the same."

In December 1808 the Court found that Olivia, Countess of Rosse, and John Bateman, although separated, "are and have been in possession and receipt of the rents and profits of the said estate since the death of the said testator" but within a year of Hugh's death in 1737, they had not "caused such house to be built and such quantity of land allotted as a garden thereto for the entertainment of a Master and six poor boys as directed by the will," nor had any of the allocated £24 been paid to the Ministers of the various churches or their successors. It was evident that all or most of the other debts, legacies and bequests had been satisfied and that "a large sum" arising from the sale of the woods had been lodged but had not been applied to the provision of the house and garden in the townland of Sessiagh, as directed by Hugh.[2]

Repeated applications had been made to the Countess of Ross and Bateman but the Defendants "sometimes give out and pretend that the said Hugh Edwards the Testator did not die seized or possessed of any estate real or personal sufficient to answer the Bequests in the said will." In other words, the Defendants tried to suggest that there was neither money nor property to satisfy the bequest.

However it was recognised that Bateman and Olivia still had "a very considerable amount" left after payment of all debts and legacies and that they had the deeds and papers relating to the said property and that they showed a clear yearly profit rent of two thousand pounds and upwards. Still they pretended that the estates were subject to such incumbrances and charges that they did not realise this amount or sometimes they pleaded that the lands of Sessiagh were not freehold or in their possession.

To counter this the Court ordered all relevant papers to be brought in for examination by the Plaintiffs and that a Receiver would be appointed to receive the rents and profits of the lands. Sir John Charles Hamilton, the surviving trustee, was asked to ensure that the arrears of several yearly rents or sums should be applied to the charitable purposes mentioned.

As John Bateman did not appear to answer the bill he was finally charged with Contempt of Court and ordered to pay the full costs of the Decree.

Following the Decree it is unclear when the first school was actually established as no early records exist, but the Ordnance Survey Memoirs for the Parish of Skirts of Urney and Ardstraw, County Tyrone, by J. Rodrigo Ward in 1836, indicate that a National School was established in Castlederg in 1822 and at the

lished 1822; income: patronage 2 pounds per annum, from pupils 1s 6d each per quarter; intellectual education: books of all kinds furnished by the National Board; moral education: Scriptures are read and catechisms heard by the master; number of pupils: males, 32 under 10 years of age, 26 from 10 to 15, 1 above 15, 59 total males; females, 7 under 10 years of age, 6 from 10 to 15, 13 total females; 72 total number of pupils, 15 Protestants, 30 Presbyterians, 27 Roman Catholics; master Alexander Eglington, Protestant.

An extract from the Ordnance Survey Memoirs for the Parish of Skirts of Urney and Ardstraw, by J. Rodrigo Ward, 1836.

time of the survey was serving 72 children under the master, Alexander Eglinton. It is also notable that there were only 13 females as opposed to 59 males in attendance, and rather amusing to read the religious breakdown as "15 Protestants, 30 Presbyterians and 27 Roman Catholics."

Although Ward refers to the school as a "National School," these as such did not come into being until after the introduction of the National System of Education in 1832, so at its inception in 1822 the school may have been any one of a number of different types of school in vogue then.

1.   A transcript of the Chancery Suit is held in Edwards P.S. Castlederg.

2.   Ibid.

Schools In Ireland in the 19th Century.

At the beginning of the nineteenth century there were numerous schools in Ireland but many were in poor condition and badly conducted. Three societies of an educational character were in receipt of Government money to provide education. These were the Incorporated Society for promoting English Protestant Schools in Ireland, the Association incorporated for discountenancing Vice and promoting the Knowledge and Practice of the Christian Religion, and thirdly, The Hibernian Society. These schools based their teaching on the Bible, prayer books and proselytism, and many were found by the Royal Commission on Irish Education in 1824 to be mere hovels, with teachers who were mainly men of very little education, while their pupils attained a very low standard in reading, writing and arithmetic.

Another society which was also recognised and its work appreciated by the Government, was the Society for promoting the Education of the Poor of Ireland, later known as the Kildare Place Society, due to the situation of its offices in Dublin. It had been established in 1811 and appeared to have had a well-organized system of education of the poor. Attention was paid to economy of time and money, cleanliness and discipline, and there was no interference with religion. The Society also published and sold books, helped to build schools, trained teachers and provided inspectors to oversee standards.

In 1828, a select committee of the House of Commons studied the reports of the Commissioners of Irish Education Enquiry of 1825-1827, and as a result passed a series of resolutions favouring the establishment of a National system of education, encouraging the idea of integrated schooling and allowing for religious instruction to be given separately by the clergy of each denomination. Parliament was to provide grants for education supplemented with local contributions, build and support schools, train teachers and have an inspection system. The curriculum was to comprise spelling, reading, writing (on slates and on paper), geography, grammar, arithmetic, geometry, bookkeeping and needlework for girls only.

School textbooks were issued by the Commissioners and for the time, were well printed, illustrated and bound. Except in "necessitous cases," when they were provided free, the books were sold to pupils for a few pence and were passed from older family members to the younger and indeed passed along generations. Readers were of a high standard and had little subject matter of interest to children, however they were well thought of and educated many children to appreciate valuable literary material.

In 1831, under the direction of the Chief Secretary, E.G. Stanley, the House of Commons set up the National School system by voting £30,000 for Primary education in Ireland, which was not actually new money; instead they withdrew their financial support for the Kildare Place Society and the other groups involved in promoting education.

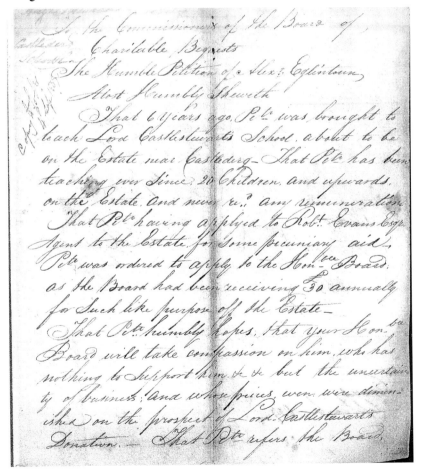

A copy of the plea from Alexander Eglintoun to the Commissioners of Charitable Bequests, requesting payment for his services. PRONI: A/633/25

Whether the early school in Castlederg was assisted by one of the societies is unknown but there is the likelihood that Lord Castlestuart, the landlord, who would have been aware of the Hugh Edwards Bequest, organized the first school. He may have provided a converted building on the estate, as a letter written in 1839, on behalf of the Master, Alexander Eglinton, (his name is also spelt "Eglintoun"), stated that six years earlier "he had been brought to teach Lord Castlestewart's School." The letter was sent to the Commissioners of the Board of Charitable Bequests, in September 1839, appealing for payment for teaching "twenty children and upwards" in what was referred to as the "Hugh Edwards Charity Castlederg School." The following is a transcript of the letter:

"To the Commissioners of the Board of Charitable Bequests
The Humble Petition of Alexander Eglintoun, Most Humbly Sheweth That six years ago Petitioner was brought to teach Lord Castlestewart's School, about to be on the estate near Castlederg—That Petitioner has been teaching ever since 20 children and upwards on the estate and never received any remuneration. That Petitioner having applied to Robert Evans Esq. Agent to the estate for some pecuniary aid, Petitioner was ordered to apply to the Honourable Board, as the Board had been receiving about £30 annually for such like purpose off the estate. That Petitioner humbly hopes that our Honourable Board will take compassion on him who has nothing to support him but the uncertainty of business; and whose prices, even were diminished on the prospect of Lord Castlestewart's Donation. That the Petitioner refers the Board to Revd. A. Hamilton, Mt. Bernard or Revd. John Crockett, Castlederg or Robert Evans Esq, all or any of them can inform the Board the certainty of the Petition.
By a due consideration of this your Petitioner is ever bound in duty to pray- ---Alexander Eglintoun, Castlederg, August 26th 1839."

In a subsequent letter, dated 5th September 1839, the Commissioners asked the Trustees of the Hugh Edwards Charity to report upon the application and statement of Eglinton. Their answer was as follows:

"We beg to inform in reply that Alexander Eglinton has been teaching school for many years past in the town of Castlederg, that it is possible his design in coming here as a teacher was that he might be appointed master of the school about to be established in compliance with the will of the late Mr Edwards, that he teaches many of the children of the tenants on the Castlegore estate for which he receives little or no remuneration, that he does not receive any remuneration from Lord Castlestewart as do the other

schoolmasters on his Lordship's estate for the reason that we believe that his Lordship pays annually a large sum for this purpose of promoting education in the neighbourhood of Castlederg, and that he has a large family and is miserably poor. If some pounds were granted to him we conceive it would not be a misapplication of the fund."

Three trustees, Archie Hamilton, John Crockett and Robert Evans, signed the letter.

A further letter was sent by them on 21st November 1839 to the Board of Charitable Bequests, stating that Lord Castlestewart's agent was willing to pay whatever the Board would reasonably allow as an award for Eglinton's service and that they hoped he would receive a "gratuity as soon as possible" as "he had contracted some debt to raise his family" and had raised his hopes in expectation of payment.

At this point correspondence on the matter either ceased or was not retained and it is not known if Master Eglinton received his dues, however the National Board continued to record six-monthly payments of four pounds.

This meagre payment by the Board of National Education was often supplemented by local subscriptions and fees paid by the pupils. Very often teachers also took on other work to add to their meagre income, such as tutoring private pupils, farming, acting as parish clerks and sextons, surveying land or drawing up leases and wills.

Copies of the letters from Alexander Eglinton and the replies from the Commissioners are held in Edwards P.S. Castlederg.

The National Education System.

One of the aims of the National Education system was to provide training for teachers, so Marlborough Street Training College was set up in Dublin in 1838. Their Inspectors selected candidates. Young men who had some experience of teaching in a National School were given a short period of five months training but this system was criticised as it was thought that there was little difference between trained and untrained teachers! Subjects studied were agriculture and horticulture, principles of teaching and practice in the classrooms. Women were not admitted to Marlborough Street Training College until 1845.

Training was later more elaborate and better organised. Boys who wished to become teachers firstly worked as paid monitors in the National School and after three or four years of study and practical teaching, sat a public examination and if successful, were awarded a place in a Model School as a candidate teacher. This was followed by six months teaching and then by a further two years spent teaching in a National School and then final training in Marlborough Street.

Model Schools, due to their role in teacher training were superior to National Schools. Buildings and equipment were better and teacher's salaries were higher. They were expected to promote "united education" and because of this the Catholic Bishops opposed them. This resulted in most Model Schools being in Ulster where the Presbyterian populous warmly welcomed them.

While reading, writing and arithmetic formed the bedrock of the National School's curriculum, the National Commissioners set out plans in 1837 to give manual training in agriculture, considering that "it forms the only employment for a vast proportion of the labouring poor." Smallholdings were attached to some schools and practical instruction in agriculture was given.

At this point it is interesting to note that a residential agricultural school had been established in 1826, in Templemoyle, County Londonderry, one of the townlands owned by the Edwards family. It was known as the Templemoyle School or Templemoyle Agricultural Seminary and flourished for about forty years. It was an individual enterprise and was possibly encouraged by the Edwards family.

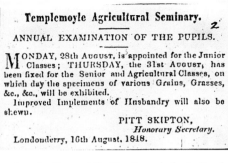

Templemoyle Agricultural Seminary.

ANNUAL EXAMINATION OF THE PUPILS.

MONDAY, 28th August, is appointed for the Junior Classes; THURSDAY, the 31st August, has been fixed for the Senior and Agricultural Classes, on which day the specimens of various Grains, Grasses, &c., &c., will be exhibited.
Improved Implements of Husbandry will also be shewn.

PITT SKIPTON,
Honorary Secretary.
Londonderry, 16th August, 1848.

An advertisement for Templemoyle Agricultural Seminary annual examination, from the News Letter, August 1848.

Some 2500 schools came into existence in Ulster between 1832 and 1870, but previous to 1835 school records of any kind, such as registers, class lists or inspector's reports, were at best haphazard and at worst non-existent. The first records kept after 1835 show that the Edwards Charity School came into connection with the National Board in July 1833. The schoolroom measured 22 and a half-foot by 14 foot and accommodated 47 males and 25 females. By any standards this was fairly overcrowded! It is also stated that Master Eglinton, who is defined by the letters "tr K.P."—presumably meaning that he was trained in Kildare Place, was "Inspected 23rd July 1835.... No class lists nor Registers." Inspections took place yearly and in 1836 the Inspector remarked, "The high rent paid for this house is injurious to this school," but the amount of the rent or the

exact whereabouts of the building or its type, are not stated. However, schoolhouses were known to be very basic, often with earthen floors and heating provided by a hearth fire, with fuel supplied by the parents in turn. The reports from the yearly inspections were very brief and the Inspection of 1837 stated, "Report rather favourable--- Teacher pays the rent of the School House."

The stamp of the Governors of the first school stating "The Governors of Hugh Edwards School, Castlesessiagh."

In 1839 it was noted, "A. Eglinton, aged 39; trained" and this was followed by a two pounds increment, which brought his half yearly salary up to six pounds.

Meanwhile the legal wheels were slowly but surely turning, as a large hand written parchment document dated the twenty sixth of March 1835 indicates an agreement drawn up between the Commissioners of Charitable Donations and

Bequests and Robert, Earl of Castlestewart, marking the conveyance of an acre of ground upon which to build a school and the payment of the arrears of two annuities which had accrued since the Earl of Castlestewart had taken possession of the estate. The ground surveyed was described as, "containing one late Irish Plantation measure, bounded on the West and North by the lands of Castlesessiagh and on the East by the road leading from Castlederg to Castlefin and on the South by the lands of Churchtown, the estate of Sir Robert Ferguson" and was to be free of rent whatsoever. The deeds were lodged in the Registers Office on the sixteenth of December 1835.

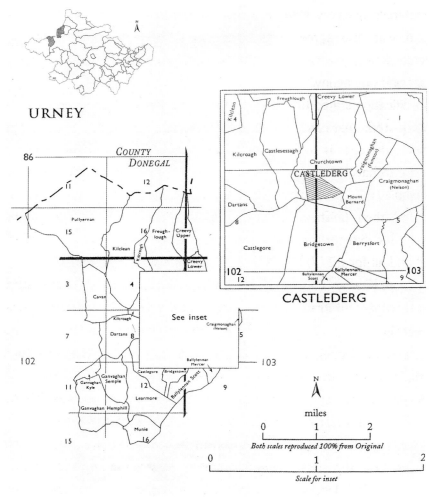

1901 Irish Census Index County Tyrone, map of Urney and Castlederg.

Finally in 1839 the wishes of Hugh Edwards appeared to come a step nearer to fruition when a contract for building the new school house was agreed between Mr John Kearney, Builder, and the Commissioners of Charitable Donations and Bequests.

Very detailed legal Articles of Agreement were drawn up proposing that Kearney would "in a good, perfect and workmanlike manner and subject to the inspection and approbation" of the Architect, finish the work of building the schoolhouse according to the specification and estimate contained in the document. Kearney was to "find carry and provide all manner of scaffolding, stones, bricks, timber, slates, iron, lead, sand, lime earth, holdfasts, cramps, pipes, gutters, paint, glass and materials of every kind" which were deemed necessary in completing the work. It was also agreed that after the work was completely finished and inspected, Kearney would be paid "two hundred and seventy seven pounds ten shillings and one penny."[1]

The specification stated that only the best materials were to be used—" the best quality of stone that can be procured, the timber to be of the best description of red pine...the roof is to be covered with strong Bangor slates...the entrance doors are to have very good draw back stock locks... the walls to be plastered----the whole to be done in the best manner.....the wood work to be three times paint and then finished oak colour grained......metal gutters of the best quality....the exterior is to be dashed with sized pebbles..." A very fine building indeed and all for £277/10/1!!!

Furthermore Kearney consented to a dispute clause, allowing the appointment of two independent arbitrators, should any disagreement arise between him and the architect inspecting the work. John McBeth and Moses Quentin, both of Ballindrate, Co. Donegal, agreed to act as sureties and the deal was completed with the seals of both parties.

The building work went ahead as planned and the new school was duly opened. In 1849 the Inspector reported "a change of school to these premises, in every respect suitable." It was also noted that the school was efficient and much good work was done. But strangely in the same statement the Inspector recorded the "dismissal by the Manager, of Eglinton, for having written an impertinent letter to Sir R. Ferguson, under an assumed name." Ferguson was the Landlord and why the letter was written or what its contents were, are sadly just a matter of speculation!

However, Norman Atkinson, in his book "Irish Education" suggests teachers were dismissed for all kinds of offences. He remarks: "Teachers were suspended or dismissed for such offences as "falsification of the accounts and loss of the free stock," "inattention and disregard of cleanliness," and "intemperate habits and being unfit for the office of schoolmistress."

Following Eglinton's dismissal, monitor Pat Connolly managed the school while James Lynch, John Crawford, G. Harper and James Wilson are also mentioned in connection with teaching in the school up to 1854, when on August 25th it was noted that the school was "in charge of paid monitor P. Connolly since the 30th June last. G Harper resigned on 17th June but left a lad named Jas Wilson in charge. On September 13th the Inspector stated that the Manager was "to appoint a competent teacher immediately."

Notes and references were frequently vague and it is difficult to tell who was appointed after that but an interesting series of notes in 1855 reveal that a Mr Thomas Orr had been "dismissed from the service of the Board when in charge of Croaghan N.S. Co. Donegal....owing to improper conduct" It then turned out on receipt of the quarterly returns on 5/12/1854 that Mr Wm Orr who had been appointed to Castlederg N.S. was identified as Thomas Orr, "formerly teacher of Crossan N.S. Co. Donegal and from which he was dismissed for bad conduct." While the spelling of the school differs, this appears to be the same man and following payment of salary due to him; he was to give up "instant possession of school which must at once be placed under a competent and suitable teacher."

Griffiths Valuation of 1860, a register of valuation for each Parish, shows the townlands and occupiers. In the case of the Parish of Urney and in the townland of Castlesessiagh the National School-house and land are shown exempt from rateable valuation. It is also interesting to note in that year a Robert Edwards was living in the townland of Castlesessiagh and the rateable valuation for his house, office and land amounted to £15. At the same time John Edwards, a member of the last Edwards family and another Robert Edwards are detailed in the valuation for Kilcroagh, their rateable valuations for houses, offices and land being

116

£46/15/0 and £17 respectively.

VALUATION OF TENEMENTS.

PARISH OF URNEY.

No. and Letters of Reference to Map.		Names.		Description of Tenement.	Area.	Rateable Annual Valuation.		Total Annual Valuation of Rateable Property.
		Townlands and Occupiers.	Immediate Lessors.			Land.	Buildings.	
		CASTLESESSAGH. (*Ord. S.* 16.)						
1		Samuel M'Cay, .	Earl of Castlestuart, .	Herd's ho., off., & land,	47 0 20	19 0 0	0 10 0	19 10 0
2	a	Robert Mitchell, .	Same, .	House, offices, and land,	29 3 15	18 5 0	1 10 0	19 15 0
—	b	Robert Sproule, .	Robert Mitchell.	House, . .	—	—	0 5 0	0 5 0
3		Matthew Knox, .	Earl of Castlestuart, .	House, offices, and land,	39 2 0	18 10 0	2 10 0	21 0 0
—	b	William Gilchrist, .	Matthew Knox, .	House, . .	—	—	0 5 0	0 5 0
—	c	Unity M'Nulty, .	Same, .	House, . .	—	—	0 5 0	0 5 0
—	d	John Carr, .	Free, . .	House, . .	—	—	0 10 0	0 10 0
—	e	Hugh Logue, .	Matthew Knox, .	House, . .	—	—	0 5 0	0 5 0
4		School-house, offices, and land, . .	(*See Exemptions.*)					
5	A	Robert Hemphill, .	Earl of Castlestuart, .	House, offices, & land, {	7 3 34	7 15 0	—	} 29 15 0
—	B				17 3 15	19 0 0	3 0 0	
6	A a				6 0 24	6 0 0	0 10 0	
—	B	Robert Edwards, .	Same, .	House, office, & land, {	5 3 7	7 10 0	—	} 15 0 0
—	C				1 1 0	1 0 0		
	A b	Matthew Browne, .	Robert Edwards, .	House, . .	—	—	0 10 0	0 10 0
7	a	Robert Kyle & Co., .	Earl of Castlestuart, .	Corn-mill, kilns, offices. miller's-house, yard, and garden, . .	4 1 21	2 0 0	20 0 0	22 0 0
—	b	Francis Gillespie, .	Free, . .	House, . .	—	—	0 10 0	0 10 0
—	c	John M'Devitt, . .	Free, . .	House and garden, .	0 0 25	0 5 0	0 15 0	1 0 0
—	d	National School-house and land, . .	(*See Exemptions.*)					
8		. . .	. .	Water, . .	1 3 8	—	—	—
				Total of Rateable Property, .	161 3 9	99 5 0	31 5 0	130 10 0
				EXEMPTIONS:				
4		Trustees of the Rossmore bequest, }	In fee, . .	School-ho., offs., and } land, . . }	1 1 30	1 0 0	4 0 0	5 0 0
7	d	. . .	Earl of Castlestuart, .	National School-house and land, .	1 3 8	0 10 0	1 10 0	2 0 0
				Total of Exemptions, .	3 0 38	1 10 0	5 10 0	7 0 0
				Total, including Exemptions,	165 0 7	100 15 0	36 15 0	137 10 0

Griffith's Valuation for the Parish of Urney, 1860.

In 1870 a Royal Commission, chaired by the Earl of Powis, reported on Primary Education and suggested some changes. Poor attendance was often a problem, but it was thought that compulsory attendance in a rural society was unworkable, due to the large numbers of children who were required to assist on the land at various times of the year, such as harvest. Instead, greater efficiency was to be encouraged by the "Results System" which had been operating in England since 1861. Fees were to be paid to teachers following inspections of children who had made a fixed number of attendances. However, in England the fees were paid to the school authorities but in Ireland, they were paid directly to the teacher.

An interesting letter dated March 19th 1885 appeared in the PRONI file relating to the school. It was from Rev. J. H. Gatchell, a trustee, and was addressed to the Secretary of Charitable Bequests for Ireland. It concerned the "school Mistress who has been teaching for the past forty years" and according to the rules of the National Board was disqualified on account of her age on January

1st '85. Names were not given, but Rev Gatchell had appointed another teacher and a problem had arisen when "The old woman now refuses to give up possession of the apartment to the new teacher." He wanted to know what steps were to be taken "to give the present teacher the apartments" and who was going to meet any financial costs involved.

Unfortunately what happened next is anyone's guess, as the correspondence has not been retained and there were no other references to the events!

A bill from James Robinson for extras done at Edwards School.

A tender from James Robinson for a school at Castlederg.

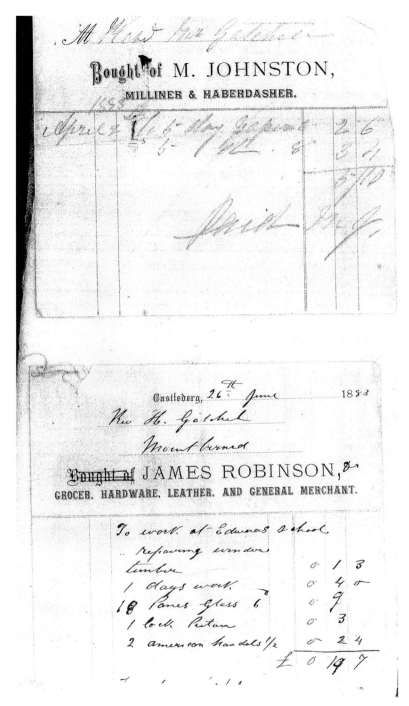

Invoices to the Rev. H. Gatchell for items purchased and work done for Edwards School. (1883 and 1893)

1. 1839 Contract for Building Edwards Charity School. PRONI: D/8/1

Edwards Boys And Girls Schools.

From Report of a Results Examination of *Castlederg Edwards*
National School, District _____6_____ Visited on 24th & 25th March, 1886
by *Mr. Nicholls,* District Inspector.

The School has, under present teacher, increased in numbers, improved in order, and made some progress in general efficiency. There are, however, some blots upon this general fair "character". Parsing of Seniors was bad, Explanation and notes in Reading Books not attended to, and above all the boys were confessedly never brought out into the School garden to receive practical instruction in Cottage Gardening. In Algebra, only one boy did well, and his name should not have appeared on the Examination Roll, as he has been attending an Intermediate School for the past five months.

    The room is clean and tidy.

    The children are well behaved and neat in appearance.

A school report from March 1886.

The first official register for "Castlederg (Edwards) National School" commenced in 1864 and contained boys' names only. It also included the following details: date of entrance, age, religious denomination, residence, occupation or means of living of parents and the last National School at which the pupil attended. Numbers of attendances were recorded as well as the subjects taught, which were reading, spelling, writing, arithmetic, grammar, geography and needlework. Extra branches often included agriculture, bookkeeping, algebra and geometry and the Inspectors' reports, while brief, covered all areas taught.

The exact date in which girls started to attend the school is not recorded, but Mrs Sarah Smyth, described as "First Grade Trained Kildare Street," was appointed on the 1st of April 1891 and from that date, female registers were kept. Boys and girls were taught in separate buildings and although the school went under the umbrella title of Castlederg Edward's National Public Elementary School, inspections were recorded in separate books. The "Inspection Observation Book: Boys School" began in 1875 while that for the Girls School began in 1893, the dates serving to underline the differing starting points.

While inspections were likely to have been serious at the time we now regard some of the remarks as quite amusing. For instance the report by Mr Cox in 1890.

In 1892 the same Inspector Cox, noted "the school, formerly a mixed one, has been recognised as a school for boys only, since April of last year." He suggested that the general proficiency was "by no means satisfactory and it will be necessary for the teacher to exert himself a great more vigorously if better work is to be obtained."

From Report of a Results Examination of *Castlederg Edwards* National School, District 6, Visited on 29th & 31st March 1890, by Mr. *Cox,* District Inspector.

Infants First and Second Classes are good on the whole; Third Class is good, except in Spelling and Grammar, which are only middling; Fourth is good except in Agriculture, which is decidedly bad; in the First Stage of Fifth Class Arithmetic Agriculture and Book-keeping are bad: in the Second Stage Book-keeping is bad: the Sixth Class is fair in Reading, Writing, Spelling and Geography; good in Grammar and unsatisfactory in Arithmetic, Agriculture, Book-keeping and extra subjects.

Discipline satisfactory.

An Inspector's report, March 1890.

The Endowment of Edwards School 1894.

Under the Educational Endowments (Ireland) Act of 1885, the final approval was given on the 13th of April 1894 for the Endowment of The Edwards School, Castlederg, which was to allow for the future government and management of the school by a Board of Governors, who were to be representatives of the local churches.[1]

The Scheme acknowledged the will and wishes of the late Hugh Edwards to provide **"a convenient country house for entertaining a master and six poor boys,"** along with a legacy of £24 sterling to pay a master and give the boys an apprentice fee of £2. By 1894 this amount had increased to £28, due to an accumulation of interest, and had been paid by The Commissioners of Charitable Donations and Bequests for Ireland to the Rector of Urney, the Presbyterian Minister of First Castlederg, and the Incumbent of Derg, towards the payment of a male and female teacher.

The Endowments in the Scheme included "all the lands, buildings, hereditaments, moneys, securities, chattels.... all rents, dividends and income thereof, and all other property, real or personal, held by any person or persons, in trust for or applicable to the purposes of the school."

Any endowments vested in the Commissioners of Charitable Donations and Bequests were transferred to the Governors who became responsible for their application to maintain the school buildings, defray the working expenses of the school and the scheme, employ and pay teachers and to supplement the salaries of any teachers or monitors and provide prizes for deserving pupils. Prizes were to be awarded in money or remission of school fees or in the manner thought best by the Governors to promote the progress of the pupils.

However, no movement of the school to another building or sale or letting or disposal of school property was to take place without at first being sanctioned by The Commissioners of Charitable Bequests and Donations who were to be satisfied that the move was for the benefit of the school.

The Governing Body was to consist of four "ex-officio" Governors, four Representative Governors and an additional Governor. The ex-officio Governors were to be the Incumbents of Urney and Derg and the Ministers of First and Second Castlederg Presbyterian Congregations, while the Representative Governors were to come from each the Select Vestries and the Sessions. If there were not less than ten Methodist children at the school, then the Minister of that denomination could become an additional Governor.

Along with Ministers, the first governors were Mr John Herdman, J.P., representing the Select Vestry of Urney, Mr William King Edwards, J.P., representing the Select Vestry of Derg, Mr William Gamble, representing the Session of First Castlederg and Mr Andrew Gailey representing the Session of Second Castlederg. They were to serve for one year.

If a Governor died in office or resigned or became bankrupt, or refused to act or was incapable of acting, his office would become vacant and the remaining Governors could co-opt another person from the same Congregation. It was notable too that any person employed by them could not hold office as a Governor.

Under the Scheme, the Governors were required to have quarterly meetings to examine the condition of the school and the efficiency of the education as well as having powers to exercise general supervision and control over the school in subjects taught, terms and vacations, provision for the maintenance of order and discipline and the hiring and firing of employees. They were also expected to manage the property and investments, pay expenses including salaries and audit their accounts. Minute books were to be kept and deeds and documents sealed with the common seal.

The School was to be maintained as a National School for the Elementary Education of children of both sexes and to follow the Rules and Regulations of the Commissioners of National Education.

Regarding the appointment of the Principal Male Teacher or Principal Female Teacher in the School, the Governors were to provide one from the Presbyterian Church and one from the Established Church.

The Governors were to permit children of poor parents belonging to the town of Castlederg to have free education and providing pupils attended on at least one hundred occasions they were entitled to free education but this privilege could be withdrawn if they failed to meet the stipulated number.

Religious Instruction was to be given in accordance with the Rules and Regulations of the Commissioners and no child was to be compelled to receive religious instruction to which his parents would object. Clergymen were to be given suitable opportunities to give religious instruction to pupils of their own denominations.

From time to time, as was considered necessary, the Governors could appoint a Committee or Committees to carry out any other orders, rules or business, such as a Committee of Ladies to assist in Domestic arrangements or in the supervision of female and infant pupils.

The Lord Lieutenant was to appoint an Inspector who was to inspect the school once yearly and report to the Governors, his remuneration to be defrayed by the Governors out of the Endowments. Inspectors appointed by the Commissioners of National Education, could be deemed to be the Inspector appointed by the Lord Lieutenant and in this case would not be entitled to receive any remuneration.

A sum of £248/17/5, representing the accumulations of the rent charge recovered in the Court of Chancery, (which enforced the will of Hugh Edwards), was invested in Government Stock and the produce of that amounted to about £28 per annum. This was then received by the Commissioners of Charitable Donations and Bequests and transmitted by them to the Managing Committee for the use of the school.

This Act then officially established Edwards as an Endowed School, a status that is still maintained, and to this day pupils derive benefits from the accrued investments.

1. This chapter is based on information contained in The Edwards School Endowments Scheme 1893-1943. PRONI: ED/27/83, a copy is held in the school.

The Burnside School.

According to the District Inspector in 1895, when he visited Edwards School he found "the general proficiency of the school is still low," but an improvement was beginning. Then, following the appointment of Mr Thomas James Burnside on May 1st 1898, the academic prowess of the school became legendary.

Master Burnside was classified in an Endowment Inspection as being "First of First Grade, First Class Honours Graduate, Royal University Certificated South Kensington, London." And when he began his career in Edwards in 1898, he had been teaching for twenty-five years previously. He was a Ruling Elder in Second Castlederg Presbyterian Church and was widely recognised as an excellent teacher.

In 1902 the teachers were Mr Burnside and Mrs Smyth and Inspector MacMahon reported excellent progress; proficiency in every subject was good or very good, while spelling, which had been weak a few years previously, was excellent! Excellency dominated the school in the Burnside era and to this day it is still referred to in respectful tones.

Mr Clements, Inspector, reporting in 1905 stated "A very good educational advance has been made during the annual period just completed. The teachers are doing and have done their best to foster the good and eradicate the bad habits of their pupils and the Principal teacher deserves great credit for the important reforms he has effected as regards the manners, politeness and general demeanour of his pupils."

In April of the same year a report in The Tyrone Constitution noted the appointment of Mr James Jack, "the genial assistant teacher in Edwards Boys School, Castlederg," as Headmaster in a school in Londonderry and expressed regret at his departure.

Subjects taught in the school were English, which was subdivided into Reading, Writing, Spelling, Grammar and Composition, Arithmetic, Kindergarten and Manual Instruction, Drawing, Elementary Science, Cookery and Laundry Work, Needlework, Singing, School Discipline and Physical Drill.

Since 1900 the "Revised Programme" had replaced the results system, English and Arithmetic were compulsory, as were other specified subjects where there were teachers qualified to teach them. Above the level of "Infants," classes were organised in six "standards" and the collective teaching of several standards in the same subject was encouraged. Manual instruction was confined to lower standards, while grants were made to encourage cookery, gardening and later domestic science. The Inspectors examined the progress and the proficiency of the pupils in each subject.

Following General Inspections, the teachers often received "an increment of continued Good Service salary" from the Office of National Education. Mr Burnside and Miss Susan Jackson, who had been appointed on July 1st 1919, frequently received these rewards. (See letters below)

County _Tyrone_

Roll Number _8438_

School _Castlederg Edwards B._

GENERAL REPORT OF _19th March_, 1919.

M _Thomas J Burnside_

is advised that _his_ Service since the previous General Inspection has

been of such a character as to qualify _him_ for the award of an increment of

continued Good Service salary.

W. J. DILWORTH,
A. N. BONAPARTE WYSE, } Secretaries.

To

M _Thomas J Burnside_

Principal Teacher,

Castlederg Edwards B. National School.

Entered _MH_

Checked _H_

OFFICE OF NATIONAL EDUCATION,

DUBLIN, _26th May_, 191 9.

N.B.—This advice is issued after each General Inspection to each principal and assistant teacher who is *not* in receipt of the maximum salary of his grade. It has reference solely to the efficiency of the teaching, and does not affect the teacher's eligibility for increment in respect of *training* and *average attendance*.

County ....

Roll Number ....

School ....

GENERAL REPORT OF ...., 191...

M... ....

is advised that ..... Service since the previous General Inspection has

been of such a character as to qualify ..... for the award of an increment of

continued Good Service salary.

W. J. DILWORTH,

A. N. BONAPARTE WYSE, } Secretaries.

To

M... ....

....

...........................National School.

Entered ....

Checked ....

OFFICE OF NATIONAL EDUCATION,

DUBLIN, ... 191...

N.B.— This advice is issued after the General Inspection to each principal and assistant teacher, who is *not* in receipt of the maximum salary of his or her grade, and to junior assistant mistresses who are not in receipt of the maximum salary of their scale. It has reference solely to the efficiency of the teaching, and, in the cases of principal and assistant teachers, the advice does not affect the teachers' eligibility for increment in respect of *training* and *average attendance.*

Letters from the Office of National Education, Dublin, giving notice of award of an increment of continued Good Service salary to Mr Thomas J. Burnside and Miss Susan Jackson.

In addition to his salary, Mr Burnside taught extra afternoon and evening classes, which supplemented his income. Pupils interested in entering further education travelled from far and near to avail of his expert tuition and indeed many went on to university and entered professional fields. (Some of these are listed in the recent publication "Castlederg and its Red River Valley" by Councillor Jim Emery and Rev. Canon H. Trimble.) In 1923 Mr Burnside's evening classes were in operation for twenty hours per week with an average attendance of 30. It is thought that his daughter Evelyn assisted him with the extra classes and the subjects were those of the King's Scholarship Examination and the Intermediate Programme.

The report of the Inspector in March 1920.

County Tyrone

Roll No. 8438

Post Town Castlederg

CONFIDENTIAL.

For the information of *Manager, Teacher, and Board's Officers, and to be preserved amongst the School Records.

Extracts from the General Report on the above-named National School, dated the 15th Feby., 19 20 by Mr. Coyne, Senior Inspector.

Office of National Education,   W. J. DILWORTH,

Dublin, March, 1920.   A. N. BONAPARTE WYSE, } *Secretaries.*

Inspector's minute of the result of the Inspection of the School.

This school is efficiently conducted. In the senior groups quite a respectable standard of proficiency is attained, while uniformly good progress is made by the pupils of the assistant's division

The reading of the first and second standard group – for which the master is responsible – is fluent, but should be more distinct and expressive; and an improvement in the style of the recitation of poetry by the pupils of the third and fourth standard group – in charge of the assistant – is desirable. In both divisions more frequent practice in interpreting the language of the reading texts is recommended.

Discipline and tone are very satisfactory.

The Report of the Inspector in March 1920.

Along with his assistant, Miss Susan Jackson, Mrs Sarah Smyth and her daughter Winifred, who had been appointed on December 1st 1919, Mr Burnside continued to develop a noteworthy school, receiving many complimentary reports.

As well as having the Inspectors from the National Board, the schools were yearly visited and examined by the Governors of the school, under the Endowment scheme. Full particulars were recorded in fourteen areas.

The interesting details of the Endowment Inspection of 1922 indicate that there were 83 boys and 69 girls on roll, with an average attendance of 128.9. Education was free. The buildings were regarded as suitable for the purposes of the School; they were in good order and sanitary arrangements, (2 dry privies for the boys and 1 for the girls) were described as adequate and efficient. It was noted that the "Principal Teacher and the Assistant in the Girls' School reside on the premises while Miss Jackson resides in the Main Street."

County...

School......Castlederg Edwards B.......................

Roll Number.....8438.....................

TABLE SHOWING THE EFFICIENCY OF THE TEACHING.

	Principal	ASSISTANTS.				
		1st Assistant	2nd Assistant	3rd Assistant	4th Assistant	5th Assistant
English—Oral	9 to VIII V.Good I & II Good	Good				
English—Written	V.Good	Good				
Arithmetic	V to VIII,V.Good I & II Good	Good				
History	V.Good	..				
Geography	Not tested	Good				
Object Lessons and Nature Study Elementary Science	Good	Not tested				
Cookery and Laundry Work	–	..				
Singing	Not taught by Principal	V.Good				
Drawing	V.Good	Good				
Needlework	–	–				
Training of Infants	–	Good				
Other Branches	–	Good (Manual Instruction)				

A table showing the subjects tested in the March 1920 inspection.

FORM No. 5.

ELEMENTARY SCHOOLS,

NOT UNDER N. BOARD

Sent out 28/12/22.

Letters, &c., should be addressed—
INSPECTION OF ENDOWED SCHOOLS,
THE UNDER-SECRETARY,
DUBLIN CASTLE.

Educational Endowments (Ireland) Act, 1885.

INSPECTION.

No. and Name of Scheme....170. EDWARD'S ENDOWMENT, CASTLEDERG.

No. and Name of School

Report of the above School for the year 1922 .

The Secretary, Manager, or other Officer, is requested to answer the following Queries
Nos. 1 to 14 inclusive, and to transmit this Form, before................24th January............1923.

to.......

N.B.—In answering Queries 1, 3, 4, 5, 6, 7, 8 and 9, it will be sufficient to note any changes which have taken place since last year.

A.—THE TEACHING STAFF. 1.—Enter the following particulars :—

Names of Master or Mistress and other Teachers.	Qualifications, Place of Training.	Length of Experience as Teacher.	Date of Appointment to present School.	Fixed Salary from Manager or Governing body.		
				£	s.	d.
Sarah Smyth	First Grade: Trained Kildare St.	55 years.	1-4-1891	5	15	0
Winifred M. Smyth	Trained Teacher C.I.T. Col. Kildare St. Dublin	7 years	1-12-1919	—		
J. Swain	First of F ... First Class Honor Trained High Royal University Trained Smith Marlboro London	25 yrs.	1-5-1893	5	15	.
A. Jackson		8 years	1-7-1919	—	—	—

B.—THE PUPILS. 2.—Enter the following particulars :—

Number of Pupils on Roll.				Number of Pupils in average attendance.			Scale of Fees for paying pupils.				
	Boys.	Girls.	Total.	Boys.	Girls.	Total.			£	s.	d.
Paying Pupils (if any) ...	—	—	—	—	—	—	Boys		—	—	—
Free Pupils	83	69	152	71.3	57.6	128.9	Girls		—	—	—
Total, ...	83	69	152	71.3	57.6	128.9					

2A.—Religious Denominations of the Pupils :—

—	Church of Ireland.	Presbyterian	Roman Catholic.	Methodist.	Others.	Total.
Boys	41	29	2	11	—	83
Girls	46	17	0	3	3	69

Wt. 4282—300. B.P.Ltd. 156/9/18

Referring to Religious Instruction the "Episcopalian boys go into Girls School and the Presbyterian girls come into the Boys' School." The course of Religious Instruction in the Boys School was "Reading the Holy Scriptures" while in the Girls' School it was "Reading and Explanation of Holy Scriptures and C. of I. Catechism."

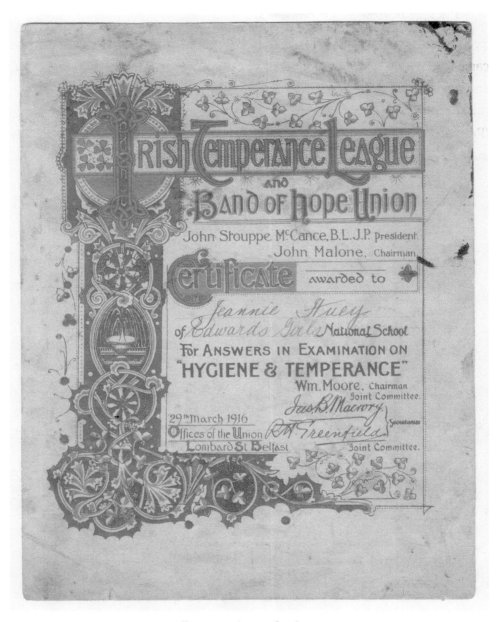

Temperance League Certificate

In the General Examination to assess educational proficiency, all pupils from Infants to eighth class in the boys and seventh class in the girls, were examined and everyone, except for one girl in fourth class, passed with merit. The final remarks were that in the Boys' School, "The instruction given is thorough and effective" while in the Girls' School, "The teachers work earnestly and effectively."

The accounts for the same year showed that £11/10/0 was spent on Salaries, Rent, Rates and Taxes amounted to £12/12/9, the Maintenance of the Premises came to £3/9/0, Insurance on scholars cost 4/3 and bank charges were £1/1/0, and a balance in favour of £17/3/2----- made the grand total for the running of the school for the year ---£46/0/2

(Present Principals and Governors struggling to manage their budgets will be most envious of the simple accounts!) See accounts sheet below.

A hand written account sheet for the same year (1922)

The school continued to flourish and in 1924 it was mentioned by the visiting Inspector that, "The Senior Division of this school is remarkable for a country town." Similarly, the Endowment Inspector, John Crockett remarked, "Good work is being done in both schools. The teaching staff are very diligent in their efforts." Rev. Macourt continued to act as Secretary for the Governing Body and the following document records the names of the Governors and the number of meetings they attended.

Form A124.

STATEMENT of the ACCOUNTS of the CHARITY called

Hugh Edwards

in the Parish of _Derg_

in the County of _Tyrone_

of which the following persons are the Trustees; viz.*

T.B. Morris, Rector, Church of Ireland.
A.W. McFarlane, Prest. Minister 1st Castlederg.
D.F. Henderson   Do   2nd   Do.
A. Deery, J.P. Farmer, Castlederg, Co. Tyrone.
James Colhoun   Do   Do.   Do.
D.F. Scott   Do.   Do.   Do.
C.P. Hamilton, Merchant   Do -   Do.
R. Scandrett, Rector, Church of Ireland, Urney, Do.
James Ritchie. Meth. Minister Castlederg   Do.

A list of Trustees in 1923

	Attendances	
	Ordinary.	Special
Rev. J. B. Morrin, The Rectory, Castlederg. resigned incumbency, 31.10.24	4	—
Rev. W. J. Macourt. The Rectory, Castlederg. appointed, 12.11.1924	0	—
Rev. W. F. Henderson. The Manse. Castlederg.	3	—
Rev. aw McFarland The Hotel. Castlederg.	1	—
Rev. James Ritchie. The Manse. Castlederg.	2	—
Rev. R. Scandrett. Sion Mills, Co. Tyrone.	0	—
Mr. W. J. Scott. Kilcroagh. Castlederg.	0	—
Mr. C. Hamilton Main Street, Castlederg.	0	—
Mr. a Deery. Goland. Castlederg.	0	—
Mr. J. Colhoun Castlegore. Castlederg.	1	—

A list of Governors and their attendances in 1925.

Unfortunately the Minutes Book of the Management Committee from 1898-1934 is missing and details of appointments and general day-to-day happenings are scarce for those years.

Governmental Changes.

In the wider field many changes were taking place in the political landscape, which also affected education. Under the terms of the Government of Ireland Act, in 1921, the Six Counties of Northern Ireland acquired a local executive and legislature of their own. A Ministry of Education was established in June 1921 and the educational administration for Northern Ireland was then transferred from Dublin to Belfast in February 1922. An Education Act was passed in 1923, which brought schools under the control of Local Education Authorities, appointed by borough and county councils.

The County Council of County Tyrone Education Authority was the umbrella body for the County while Strabane and Castlederg Regional Education Committee, whose offices were in 16, Main Street, Strabane, dealt with the local district educational matters.

Elementary education was simply defined as "both literary and moral, based upon instruction in the reading and writing of the English language and in arithmetic" and subsequent reports indicate that Edwards School followed that ethos.

To

Rev. T. B. Morrin M.A.,
The Rectory,
Castlederg.

Reverend Sir,

I am directed to inform you that Miss Elsie M. Porter has been recognised as substitute for Miss Jackson, Assistant Teacher, from 5th to 26th June 1924. I am to state that this recognition is exceptional and gives Miss Porter no claim to future recognition in this capacity. I am to request you to be good enough to advise Miss Porter accordingly.

I am, Reverend Sir,
Your obedient servant,

L. McQUIBBAN,
Secretary.

Ministry of Education for Northern Ireland,
Belfast, 15th July 1924.

1656. Wt.145/505. 4/24. 5,000. M'C.S.& O.Ltd.,Belfast. Gp.11.*

A letter from the Ministry of Education informing the Chairman of the Board of Governers of the recognition of Miss Elsie Porter as a substitute for Miss Jackson, who was off on sick leave in June 1924.

The Boys and Girls Schools Amalgamate.

By 1925 changes were also afoot for the two Edwards schools. The imminent retirement of the Principal of the Girls School, Mrs Sarah Smyth, forced the Board of Governors to examine the need for two principals. It was felt that "in order to secure greater efficiency and to effect economy" the two schools should be amalgamated under one principal and an assistant.

A letter was sent to the Ministry of Education informing them of their decision and the conditions involved. They requested that the "Ministry of Education give the Governors permission to let one of the existing teachers' residences, the rent therefrom to be devoted wholly to the upkeep of the amalgamated school," and secondly that "the Ministry shall take steps to have section 13 of the scheme altered," to allow the Governors, in the case of a vacancy in either the office of Principal or first Assistant teacher, to appoint as Principal, a member of the Presbyterian Church and as assistant, a member of the Church of Ireland.

This was a slight alteration to the previous clause, which had allowed the Governors to select one Principal from the Presbyterian Church and one from the Church of Ireland. Provided the candidate had the support of not less than six Governors, he or she could have been selected for either office, irrespective of denomination.

A letter was subsequently sent to the Ministry of Finance, (who in 1922, took over as statutory successors to the Commissioners of Charitable Donations and Bequests), from Mr A. N. Bonaparte Wyse, who was then Assistant Secretary in the Ministry of Education. (His rather grand sounding name came from his claim to descent from a brother of the Emperor Napoleon.) He pointed out that any amendment to the Endowment Scheme could only be made by the Ministry of Finance on receipt of an application by the Governors or by the Select Vestries of Derg and Urney and Sessions of First and Second Castlederg.

Mr Bonaparte Wyse also asked the Ministry of Finance to clarify if there was any condition in the lease that would be in conflict with the proposal to let the teacher's residence to someone who was not a "public elementary school teacher."

In considering the matter, the Ministry of Finance pointed out that of the Board of Works loans granted to assist in building the residences, £77 remained outstanding in the case of the Boys' School and £91 in respect of the Girls' School, and that the Bonds securing their repayment contained covenants that the premises should not be used for any other purpose than teachers' residences. However, it was felt that the Ministry could give the Governors permission to let to an outside tenant in spite of those covenants. The letter went on to say that, as the land on which the residences were erected was part of the original plot of ground on which the schoolhouses originally stood and which was vested in the Governors by the scheme, then there was nothing which would prevent them from agreeing to the condition and that they "might approve" if the Ministry of Education was satisfied that only one teacher's residence was essential for the amalgamated schools.

With regard to the amendment to Clause 13, it was felt that this would follow as a necessary consequence of the amalgamation.

A lot of correspondence passed between the Ministry of Education and the Ministry of Finance regarding the problems facing the Governors. Another problem was raised when the Ministry of Finance suggested that it might be held that if two residences were formerly provided for the two Principals, then the first assistant teacher in the amalgamated school would inherit the rights of the second principal, whose place he was taking, and that he might put forward a claim to occupy the residence. The Ministry of Education dismissed this, as under their rules no privilege of any kind was attached to the person recognised as first assistant or to any other assistant.

The final outcome was that the Governors amalgamated the two schools on June 1st 1925 and on the 20th of May 1926 they applied to the Ministry of Finance to have the Endowments Scheme altered to include the changes. Final approval was granted; the Governors were released from the Covenant of the Bond that provided that the residence should be used for a teacher only, and an amended scheme, dated June 1927, was drawn up.

Miss Georgina Elliott.

Meanwhile, another major change was effected on the 1st of November 1926, when Miss Georgina Elliott, from Letterbreen, Co. Fermanagh, who had been teaching in Convoy, Co. Donegal, joined the staff and became Vice Principal. Instead of living in one of the school residences, she stayed with Mrs Evans, who was the Organist in Derg Parish Church. She settled happily into life in Castlederg and immersed herself in the daily routine of the school. She was responsible for a lot of good work in the school, including the development of the Ulster Savings Scheme. She also played an active role in the local Parish Church. She is still remembered for her excellent teaching, firm discipline and striking fashion sense! The school continued to grow, causing Rev. W. T. Macourt, Secretary to the Board of Governors, (also sometimes called the Manager), to write to the Ministry of Finance in 1928, informing them that owing to increased attendance at the school, the disused teacher's residence had been handed over for extra school accommodation and he sought permission to remove internal walls on the first floor to make one large classroom.

This was granted as the sketch and plan of the school and Residence shows— see on following page.

In 1929 records show that 182 pupils attended the school and the teachers then were Mr T. J. Burnside, Miss G. Elliott, Miss S. A. Jackson, Miss P. C. Mitchell and Miss H. M. Morrison.

In what turned out to be Mr Burnside's final Inspection, which took place on the 20th and 21st of January 1930, the Inspector wrote, "There is an atmosphere of industry about this school, very marked in its upper end. The attention, application and demeanour of the pupils directly taught by the Principal speak eloquently of the value of the training they are receiving."

Miss Mitchell taught Infants and it was suggested that special instruction in Reading, Counting and Writing might be considered for pupils who were old for the class, but were late in commencing school life.

Standards 1 and 2, taught by Miss Morrison, indicated "quite good work" while in Miss Jackson's division, standards 3 and 4, the Inspector remarked, "If pupils are permitted to talk to one another time will be wasted, habits of inattention will grow, and progress will be impeded."

With regard to Miss Elliott's division----standards 5 and 6---"The weakest subject here is Oral English: it appears to give the teacher most trouble..... Study the treatment of Shakespeare---recitation from the play lacks expression and reality." One wonders what the pupils of "standards 5 and 6" today would make of the study of Shakespeare!

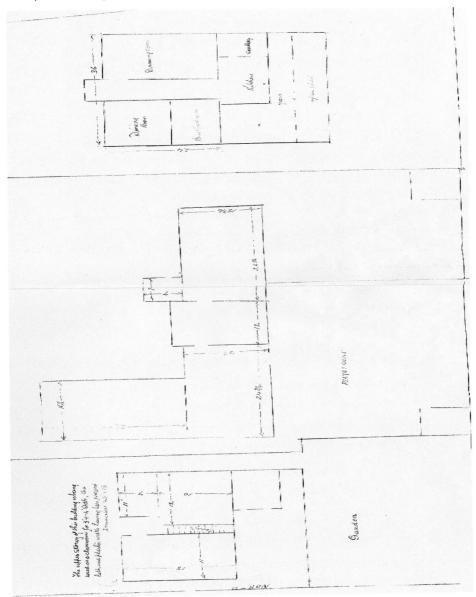

A sketch and plan of the school and residences showing that the upper storey of one residence was in use as a classroom.

Whereas the Edwards Male School Castlederg and the
Edwards Female School Castlederg in the County of Tyrone had
previously been carried on as separate schools AND WHEREAS
the Ministry of Education for Northern Ireland agreed that
said schools should be amalgamated and such amalgamation
has since been carried out. AND WHEREAS as a result of such
amalgamation the retention of the within named premises as a
teachers residence is no longer required AND WHEREAS the
within named Governors have applied to the Ministry of Finance
for Northern Ireland (hereinafter called the Ministry)in whom
the powers and functions of the within named Commissioners in
respect of Northern Ireland are now vested to release the
within named Governors from the condition in the within Bond
to use the within named dwelling house for a residence for the
teacher of the within named school and for no other purpose
whatsoever so that the Governors may let the dwelling house
and apply the rent therefrom to assist the funds of the
endowment AND WHEREAS said application has been approved of
by the Ministry Now this Indenture Witnesseth that in consideration of the premises the Ministry hereby releases the
Governors and the within named Sureties from the said condition
in restraint of using within dwelling house except for a
teachers residence to the intent that the within Bond shall
read as if said condition were deleted but all other conditions
shall remain in full force and effect.

In Witness whereof the Official Seal of the Ministry has
hereunto been affixed this 27th day of May, 1927.

The Official Seal of the Ministry   )
was hereunto affixed in presence   )
of -   )   (SEAL)
)
        G. C. DUGGAN.   )
    Assistant Secretary.   )

I Certify above to be a true copy of endorsement

A letter from the Ministry of Education releasing the Governors from the restraints of using the
schoolhouse as a dwelling, following the amalgamation of the boys and girls' schools.

The Burnside's Junior Class 1925/26.

Students of Dr Burnside's Afternoon Class 1926.
Front Row: Olive Bustard, ? , Ruby Robinson, Bessie Colhoun, Meta Speer, Ruby Sparks.
Second Row: Emma Stewart, ?, ?, ?,?, Doris Foy, ?
Third Row: Elsie Huey, Sadie Scott, ?, ?, Dorothy (Dosie) Robinson, Emma Fawcett, Mary Scott.

Miss Jackson and pupils pictured at Edwards School 1927-1928.

A copy of the accounts in 1928.

GOVERNMENT OF NORTHERN IRELAND.

T6 32/35

Telephone No. :- Belfast 4289.
Any reply should be addressed to -
The Comptroller and Auditor General,
Northern Ireland,
and the following number quoted :

EXCHEQUER AND AUDIT DEPARTMENT,

33, SCOTTISH PROVIDENT BUILDINGS,

BELFAST.

7th February, 1929.

The Secretary,
Ministry of Finance,
(Charities Branch).

I enclose a certified copy of the accounts of the Edwards School, Castlederg, for the year ended 31st December, 1928.

This account was formerly audited by a local auditor approved by the Ministry of Home Affairs. In view of the trivial nature of the work involved it is suggested that no fee be charged in respect of the audit carried out by this Department.

The item "Maintenance of premises etc." consists of

New desks............................£ 6. 5. 0.
" flooring........................£ 9.18. 4.
Setting range in teacher's residence..£ 2. 5. 0.
New range in teacher's residence......16.15. 0.
New stove for school..................12. 5. 0.
Setting stove in school............... 1.10. 0.
                                      £48.18. 5.

The item "Rent, Rates and Taxes" consists of

Instalments of loan charges on teacher's residences. £18.19. 0.
Cost of redeeming loan on teacher's residence.   £47. 8.11.
                                                    £66. 7.11.

Comptroller and Auditor-General.

no objections

Copy of Accounts in 1928.

The Development of the School Buildings.

Few photographs remain of the school buildings in the early days, but one that is most frequently referred to is an old postcard depicting four buildings, causing most people ask which is the school? The answer has to be that according to the plans and specifications drawn up by the builder, John Kearney, the building second on the left appears to be the original schoolhouse, constructed in the 1840's. The third building adjoins it and was also used as a schoolroom.

Following the building of the schoolhouse two Residences for the Principals of each of the schools were erected with the aid of a statutory loan of £250, granted on 29th October 1896 and another loan, also of £250, which was granted on 26th April 1898. These would appear to be the dwelling houses on the left and right of the photo. The residence for the Principal of the boy's school is on the right and following the amalgamation of the boys' and girls' schools in 1925, the upper floor of this house was converted to use as a classroom. It was later described as a "grossly over-crowded attic room."

The other residence, originally planned for the Principal of the Girls' School, was occupied firstly by Mr Burnside, then Mr Sloan and finally Mr Riddall, who vacated it in 1962 to move to a new house on the site of the 1938 school.

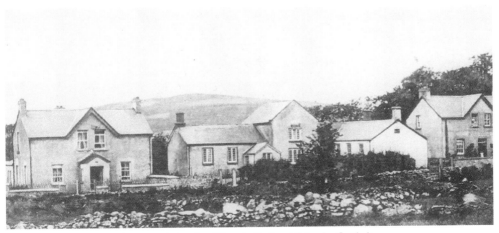

A postcard showing Edwards National Schools, Castlederg.

145

The Death of Mr Burnside.

The Burnside School on the Castlefin Road.

Unfortunately, Mr Burnside died suddenly on April 10th 1930, arousing widespread regret in the area. He had developed acute pneumonia, which had advanced rapidly and proved fatal.

A tribute in the Tyrone Constitution stated, "the outstanding successes attained by his pupils placed him in the forefront of educationalists in the North of Ireland." His funeral was large and representative of the esteem in which he was held. Upwards of two hundred pupils and most of the teachers attended and wreaths were sent by the staff and pupils of the school.

It is thought that his daughter left the area shortly after her father's death and went to live in Strabane, but the memories of their contribution to education in Castlederg still remain.

Few teachers can claim to have a building or houses named after them but the memory of Mr Thomas J. Burnside has been immortalised in the row of houses named Burnside Villas, which are situated near the present school,

Only a small number of people who were taught by Master Burnside are still alive today and those who remain have fading or confused memories, but according to the abiding accounts concerning his teaching, Master Burnside was regarded not only as a very stern disciplinarian but also as a very successful educator.

To read more about Mr Burnside please refer to the chapter featuring Headmasters Over The Years and also to the writings of the late Will Leitch in "Parliamentary Draughtsman Peculiar," and the memories of the late Mrs Jean Hamilton, who both recalled many anecdotes of their time spent in the Burnside School.

Mr J.G. Sloan Principal 1930-1955

Following the sudden death of Mr Burnside, the position of Headmaster of Edwards School was filled by Mr James Gilmore Sloan, who had been teaching in the local Garvetagh P.S. His was not an easy task, but one he met with a similar level of expertise and commitment, continuing to guide and advance scholars through Matriculation and Police Exams.

Mr Sloan also guided the school through turbulent times such as the poverty in the thirties as well as political and educational developments.

The following sections illustrate the depth of his involvement in the activities of the school and his contribution to the community in which he lived.

For more personal information on Mr Sloan, please refer to the Past Headmasters section.

Fair Days.

One of the features of life in the early decades of twentieth century Castlederg was essentially the Fair Day, recalled by many with great nostalgia. Country came to town in big way. The local farmers brought their produce; cattle, sheep, pigs, horses, fowl, potatoes, butter, oats, eggs, fish and fruit and the townsfolk assembled with eager anticipation to bargain and buy. By all accounts, these were great social occasions with all kinds of street entertainment and for many children they were the highlight of life in the quiet town. This observation is also reinforced by the Chief Inspector, who visited Edwards School on 31st of October 1930 and commented:

"Fair days are held in Castlederg on the last Friday of each month. Today (31st October, 1930), when I called at Castlederg Edwards School, only one pupil was present while in Castlederg school there were 139." (The school referred to was the Roman Catholic School.)

Subsequently, Mr Henry Garrett, Assistant Secretary in the Ministry of Education, sent a sharp letter to Rev. W. T. Macourt, informing him of the position and reminding him, "in 1908 the Commissioners of National Education gave permission to close Castlederg Edwards Schools on Fair Days."

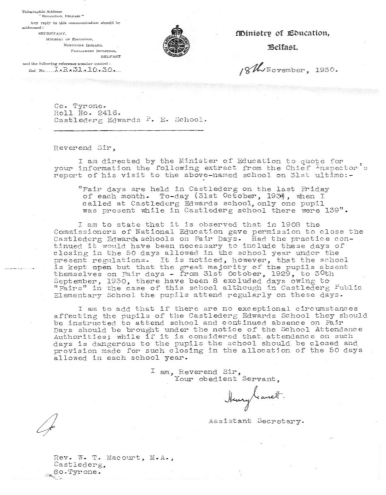

Telegraphic Address
" EDUCATION, BELFAST "

Any reply to this communication should be
addressed :
SECRETARY,
MINISTRY OF EDUCATION,
NORTHERN IRELAND,
PARLIAMENT BUILDINGS,
BELFAST

and the following reference number quoted :
Ref No......I.R.31.10.30...

Ministry of Education,
Belfast.

18th November, 1930.

Co. Tyrone.
Roll No. 2416.
Castlederg Edwards P. E. School.

Reverend Sir,

I am directed by the Minister of Education to quote for
your information the following extract from the Chief Inspector's
report of his visit to the above-named school on 31st ultimo:-

"Fair days are held in Castlederg on the last Friday
of each month. To-day (31st October, 1930), when I
called at Castlederg Edwards school, only one pupil
was present while in Castlederg school there were 139".

I am to state that it is observed that in 1908 the
Commissioners of National Education gave permission to close the
Castlederg Edwards schools on Fair Days. Had the practice continued it would have been necessary to include these days of
closing in the 50 days allowed in the school year under the
present regulations. It is noticed, however, that the school
is kept open but that the great majority of the pupils absent
themselves on Fair days - from 31st October, 1929, to 30th
September, 1930, there have been 8 excluded days owing to
"Fairs" in the case of this school although in Castlederg Public
Elementary School the pupils attend regularly on these days.

I am to add that if there are no exceptional circumstances
affecting the pupils of the Castlederg Edwards School they should
be instructed to attend school and continued absence on Fair
Days should be brought under the notice of the School Attendance
Authorities; while if it is considered that attendance on such
days is dangerous to the pupils the school should be closed and
provision made for such closing in the allocation of the 50 days
allowed in each school year.

I am, Reverend Sir,
Your obedient Servant,

Henry Garrett.

Assistant Secretary.

Rev. W. T. Macourt, M.A.,
Castlederg,
Co.Tyrone.

Had the school closed, these days would have had to be taken as holidays, from
the allowance of 50 days. However, it was kept open, although the children did
not attend. It was pointed out that the children should come to school, except in
exceptional circumstances, and that continued absence on Fair Days should be
brought to the attention of the School Attendance Authorities. If it was
considered too dangerous for the pupils to attend then there was no other option
than to close.

Obviously, the problem continued, as Rev Macourt again wrote to inform the
Ministry of Education of the small attendance in April 1931. Once more the
reply was as before, only this time it was underlined!

"They should be instructed to attend school and that continued absence on Fair Days should be brought under the notice of the School Attendance Authorities.

Telegraphic Address :
" EDUCATION BELFAST "
Any reply to this communication should be addressed
SECRETARY,
MINISTRY OF EDUCATION,
NORTHERN IRELAND,
PARLIAMENT BUILDINGS,
BELFAST.
and the following reference number quoted :
Ref No. E/2416/4

Ministry of Education,

Belfast.

18th May, 1931

County Tyrone: 2416: Castlederg Edwards
Public Elementary School.

Reverend Sir,

With reference to your letter of 20th ultimo in regard to the small attendance of pupils at the above-named school on Fair Days, I am directed by the Minister of Education to remind you of the suggestion contained in the concluding words of the official communication addressed to you on 18th November last to the effect that if there are no exceptional circumstances affecting the pupils of the Castlederg Edwards School they should be instructed to attend school and that continued absence on Fair Days should be brought under the notice of the School Attendance Authorities; while if it is considered that attendance on such days is dangerous to the pupils the school should be closed and provision made for such closing in the allocation of the 50 days allowed in each school year. In reply to your query as to whether days on which the attendance is under one-third of the average attendance for the month, *are allowed to be excluded,* I am to call your attention to the terms of Article 36(c) of Statutory Rules and Orders, 1929, No. 57.

I am, Reverend Sir,

Your obedient Servant,

Henry Garrett.

Assistant Secretary.

Reverend W. T. Macourt, M.A.,
Castlederg,
COUNTY TYRONE.

Attendance improved following the admonitions and no more warning letters were received.

However, the story is told of an Inspector visiting a Castlederg School (but not Edwards), on a Fair Day, and he reported that he "found the school empty and the Master full!!"

The School Is Transferred To The County Council.

In August 1930, the Governors of the school wrote to the Ministry of Finance offering for transfer to County Tyrone Education Authority, "the School Buildings, Teacher's Residence, Grounds and Endowments belonging to their trust." (See Proposal below)

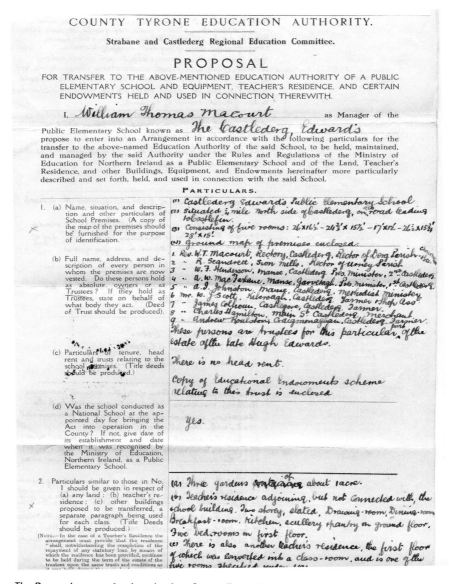

The Proposal to transfer the school to County Tyrone Education Authority in August 1930.

This had to be sanctioned by the Ministry of Education and Mr Thomas Elliott, Solicitor in Strabane, dealt with the many legal issues inherent in the transfer.

It was subsequently agreed that the Education Authority would accept the School and premises, including the Teacher's Residence, the equipment, the endowment, and debts, and these were transferred from the 1st of April 1831, subject to the following conditions:

(a)   A new school would be erected to replace the old one.

(b)   The rules pertaining to the Teacher's Residence would still apply.

(c)   The Trustees would have adequate representation on the School Management Committee.

(d)   The teaching staff would give Bible instruction.

(e)   The sum of £15 a year, from the income of the transferred endowment would be paid by the Education Authority to the School Management Committee for any purpose the Committee may think fit.

The Governors signed the agreement and the Ministry of Education applied its seal on July 15th 1932. The document was also sealed by the Ministry of Finance, who subsequently arranged the transfer of the funds in the Charities accounts, to the County Council of the County of Tyrone, the Education Authority responsible for the running of schools in the County. These funds amounted to a total of £180/1/1 in Ulster Loans and £640/0/5 in India Stock and were administered by a gentleman with the wonderful signature of **W. B. Spender**, Secretary, Minister of Finance!!

The Deed of Conveyance.

Following the arrangement for the transfer of the school to Tyrone County Council, a Deed of Conveyance was signed on the 27th of September 1932, between the Governors and Tyrone County Council, transferring the "one acre Irish Plantation measure with the school buildings and Teacher's Residence" to the control of the local authority."

The Conveyance was sealed and delivered by the Governors of The Edwards School Castlederg:

W. F. Henderson, Chairman,

W. T. Macourt

A. W. McFarlane

in the presence of W. J. Scott, Kilcroagh, Castlederg, Farmer,

Charles Hamilton, Castlederg, Merchant,

and C. R. Hill, Secretary of Tyrone County Council.

The document was then "Registered in the Registry of Deeds, Belfast at 31 minutes after 12 o'clock on the 18th day of October 1932."

With the legal documentation completed the next step in the development of Edwards Primary School was the progress towards a new building, but many complications were to arise before that was to happen.

Towards a New School.

Shortly after the school was transferred to the control of the County Council in 1932, the wheels were set in motion to meet the most urgent condition, which was the provision of a new school.

The old school buildings, which had been in use for over eighty years, were damp and deteriorating, in spite of attempts made to carry out repairs and general maintenance.

An application form for sanction to the erection of the new public elementary school was sent from Strabane and Castlederg Regional Education Committee to the Ministry of Education, in October 1932.

The application was for a new school to accommodate 220 pupils, "to supersede the existing one."

Three sites were listed as possibilities;

1. Kyle's site, 2a. 1r. 7p @ £160 per acre.

2. Greer's site, 4a. 0r. 26p @£200 per acre

3. Castlederg Board of Guardians site, 2a. 1r. 32p @£100 per acre.

The School Committee in 1932 comprised: Rev. W. T. Macourt, (Chairman), Rev. W. F. Henderson, and Messrs H. W. Ross, J. B. Wilson, Charles Hamilton, Robert

A. Lyons, Samuel Robinson, Robert Waugh and Mr J. G. Sloan (Principal).

At the October meeting, the Committee "passed that the erection of a new school be urged with all possible speed, with the recommendation that it be built on the present site of the Edwards School as the workhouse site was considered to be unfavourable."

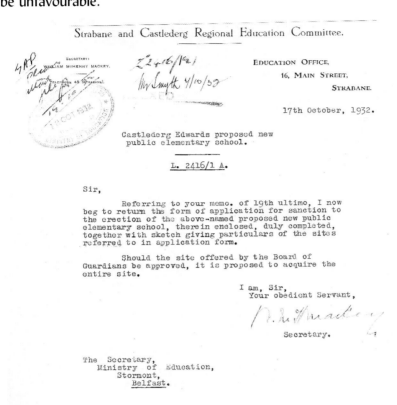

The letter seeking sanction for the erection of the new schoolhouse, October 1932.

This was contrary to any of the proposed sites recommended by the Regional Committee, who thought it was impossible to build on the present site as the layout there was unsatisfactory.

A lot of correspondence passed between the Regional Committee and the Ministry of Education and decision-making was slow. By January 1933 when the School Committee held its first meeting of the year, they agreed; "that this committee unanimously and most strongly recommend that the building of a new school be expedited as much as possible as the present conditions of dilapidation

153

and overcrowding make efficient work extremely difficult."

In February 1933 the School Committee met Mr Lawson, the Architect, and Mr Mackey, the Secretary of the Regional Committee, to view the proposed sites.

APPLICATION for sanction for the erection of a new Schoolhouse

at CASTLEDERG , Co. TYRONE

1. State area to be served by the proposed new school.

1. Same area as the existing Castlede Edwards P. E. School serves.

2. If proposed new school is to supersede an existing school, or schools, give particulars.

2. To supersede existing Castlederg Edwards P. E. School.

3. State number of pupils to be accommodated

3.   220.

4. Give particulars showing how this number has been determined.

4. There are 225 on rolls of existing school and practically all the summer months there were 200 in daily attendance.

5. Give particulars of sites available (area, dimensions, and situation in each case to be specified).

5. The following sites were offered b: Owners at the prices set opposite each site, and as delineated on sketch herewith attached:-
(1) Kyle's site, 2a. 1r. 7p. @ £16 per acre.
(2) Greer's site, 4a. 0r. 26p. @ £200 per acre.
(3) Castlederg Board of Guardians site, 2a. 1r. 32p. @ £100 per acre.

6. State which site is recommended by Local Education Authority, and why so recommended.

6. The sub-committee appointed to inspect the respective sites considered that the Guardians' si was the more suitable, being leve and having two approaches, and recommended its acquisition. This recommendation was adopted by the Regional Committee.

7. State the grounds on which the erection of the proposed new schoolhouse is considered necessary.

7. The existing schoolhouse is unsuited for modern requirements and it is one of the conditions of transfer that a new school would be built. It has been stated that the sites above mentioned would have the benefit of the town wate supply and sewerage system, while to build within the existing school grounds, this would not be possible, and the layout there would not it is stated be satisfactory.

8. Is the school intended to provide free elementary education for the pupils, or is it proposed to charge fees under Section 8 of the Act ?

8. Free elementary education.

9. (a) Will the school be under the direct control of the
   Education Committee,
   Regional Education Committee,
   or is it intended to place it under a school committee under Section 3 (1) of the Act ?

(b) If a school committee is to be in charge of the school, is it intended to delegate to it the functions specified at Section 3 (3) of the Act ?

(Signed) ....

Secretary to Local Education Authority
for County Tyrone

Date 17th October 1932

The application form seeking sanction for the erection of the new schoolhouse, October 1932.

The Workhouse Site.

At the following meeting in March, a letter was received from the Clerk of the Castlederg Union offering on behalf of the Board of Guardians, the Workhouse site for the new school. Acceptance by the School Committee was transmitted to the Ministry of Education in Stormont, who in turn wrote to the Senior Inspector of Schools in September 1933, asking him to investigate some objections to the Workhouse site.

These objections were mainly concerns for the safety of the roads for children during fairs. It was thought that many of the children would not be able to get to the school on fair days as so many animals created dangers. The Inspector was asked to visit the neighbourhood on a Fair Day and to furnish a report on the matter.

A former Chairman of the Board of Guardians raised further objections to the Workhouse site. His most serious objection was the site's proximity to the Reservoir. He had predicted that boys would bathe in the Reservoir and "boys would be drowned there every summer as long as the school was there." He reinforced his objection with a newspaper cutting – (see across).

funded debt of the Council at the 30th September, 1932, amounted to £26,817 11s 6d.

CONTAMINATED WATER.

Dr. J. L. Johnston, pathologist, Derry, submitted a report on a sample of the water taken at the Diamond, Castlederg, which stated that the water was quite fair as regards B.Coli, considering the hot, dry weather, but indicated dirty contamination somewhere

Dr. G. F. V. Leary reported that the water supply to the town was being contaminated and was dangerous to health. He recommended that the Council endeavour to completely control the water supply.

Capt. Williams said he was informed that children were bathing in the burn above the reservoir, and he believed this was the cause of the pollution. This was not a very pleasant thing as far as the water supply to the town was concerned and he thought the Council should take drastic steps to prevent this practice. The caretaker should attend to the matter and have notices erected at the place prohibiting bathing.

The Clerk said as far as Dr. Leary could ascertain, the contamination originated at a flax dam some distance above the reservoir.

Mr. Verner asked had the Council no power to prosecute these people found bathing at the place.

Mr. Henderson—Yes, but it lies in the hands of the caretaker to bring the prosecution.

Mr. Gamble said it was the caretaker's duty to look after this place. If he has not sufficient time himself he should en-

A newspaper cutting reporting the contamination of the water in Castlederg in 1933.

He also thought that the Creamery outside the Workhouse gate would provide another source of hazards—"boys would be tampering with the machinery.... surely would injure their hands, which would result in civil action by their parents."

Furthermore, he objected...."the graveyard in which the paupers are buried is outside the wall, a likely place to get a skull, with which to kick football."

He continued his objections with observations on Fair Days. He stated, "It would be absolutely impossible for children from Castlederg side to get to school on Fair Days as all the roads to and from the cattle market are completely blocked with cattle, then the horse market completely blocks the main road thereto, where horses ridden by, (in many cases) drunk men".

Castlederg. Workhouse site

13 SEP 1933 RECEIVED MINISTRY OF EDUCATION

71.3.087

11th Sept 1933

Dear Sir,

At a meeting of the Strabane & Castlederg Regional Committee held on 31st ult. Mr Gamble M.P. quoted me as the only member of the Council objecting to the above site for the school. I was the only one of my party at the meeting, and as Mr Gamble is head of his party the decision is not to be wondered at.

(1) My most serious objection to the workhouse site is its proximity to the Reservoir. My prediction of boys bathing in it has come true as can be seen from attached News paper cutting, I _said_ boys would be drowned there every Summer as long as the school was there.

(2) Another is the Creamery outside the workhouse gate. where the boys would be tampering with the machinery they surely would injure their hands, which would result in civil actions by their parents.

No Notices against Bathing in the Reservoir were issued, fearing I expect, that some person would send one to the Ministry, showing how they were attempting to deceive or defeat their foolish proposition (3) The graveyard in which the

A letter of objection to the Workhouse site for the new Edwards School

He scorned the recommendation that Mr Greer's field would be suitable as it was "for three months of the winter time.....a miniature lake."

In his opinion and he felt that of "many honest people, the most suitable and ideal site, is Mrs Devine's field, dry, elevated, open and healthy, within 400 yards of the town, away from all motor traffic and other dangers." He added that there would be no difficulty with sewerage as "the property goes to the River Derg." Spring wells were at either end of the field and town water was laid on to within 300 yards.

To prove his point he suggested a meeting with the Inspector at 9 a.m. at the Royal Hotel, on the 29th of September 1933, the Fair Day.

The Inspector's Report on Castlederg Fair.

The Inspector duly met with the former chairman on the agreed date and he reported, "the direct road to the workhouse for a distance of about 50 yards from the town square was occupied by sheep ranged along each side" and the roadway "was free from traffic." The back road, which passed by the fair green, "was blocked with cattle and was impassable," the only access being via an adjoining field. Horses were not exhibited for sale until the afternoon and there were only eight in total. These were in the square and were "quiescent and I saw no horses galloping up and down." Apparently the chief horse fairs took place in October and in the spring months.

Finally he noted that cattle and sheep fairs began at about nine or ten in the morning and horse fairs took place in the afternoon only.

His report was brief and to the point and it led the Ministry of Education to feel there were insufficient grounds to support the objections and they subsequently approved the Workhouse site.

1934-1938

The Regional Education Committee had many reasons for approving of the Workhouse site, not least of these being financial. The Board of Guardians were willing to sell the entire plot of five acres for £200, which was regarded by many as a sound investment.

It was also thought that although there were over 200 pupils on rolls, a new school would undoubtedly attract many more new pupils, therefore it was prudent to have a greater area.

Furthermore, it was agreed that if less ground was purchased, as the Ministry of Education proposed, then the site would be very crowded and playground space curtailed.

Not only that, but the Workhouse Authorities could sell their remaining land to a purchaser who could erect buildings or operate a business which would cause annoyance later on. The Regional Committee wished to avoid these problems by purchasing the entire site.

The Ministry also tried to suggest that heavy expense would be entailed in keeping the large grounds in good order, but the local Committee could see no problem with this.

Indeed, they suggested that if after the school was erected and occupied, the grounds were still found to be too large, they could then sell some, as land so near the town was in keen demand and they could provide safeguards in the conditions of sale to protect against aforementioned problems. Alternatively they could let what was not required.

In April 1934 the School Committee met and "noted with satisfaction that the site has been approved and urge the Regional Committee to hasten the erection of a new school as the present building is in a very unsatisfactory condition."

Another new year dawned and still there was no sign of the new building. Conditions were worsening in the old buildings on the Castlefin Road and at the January meeting the School Committee urged the necessity to begin building as they felt that "the unsatisfactory conditions are a contributory cause to the prevalence of epidemic disease that has had and is having on the attendance of pupils."

Miss G. Elliott and class 1930's

Pupils pictured Pre 1938. Anyone remember these faces?

MARY BELLA'S JOHNNY AT THE EDWARDS SCHOOL CONCERT.

Shure, last week they had a concert
  For the gran' oul' E.S.C.,
And A think a better evening
  Darg town'll hardly see.

Me an' my wife, Mary Bella,
  Thought we went an hour too soon;
Says the lad that tuk the tickets:
  "At the front there's stannin-room."

Well, we niver got sich crushin'
  All wur days, at any time.
But indeed, we'll not begrudge it
  For the programme, man, was prime!

There were cliver comic fellas,
  Match them elsewhere, if yez can!
An' a fine wee singing lady
  All the pride of fair Strabane.

There were three wee mice went happin'
  On the stage—till A declare
A cud see my own oul' wumman
  Felt like leppin' on her chair.

Shure, the like o' thon weans actin'
  A've not seen before nor since;
All the good oul' little people
  Dancin' roun' a fairy prince.

There were weans played ball wi'
    oranges,
  Niver drapped a single one;
When yon oranges' song was finished
  A just wushed it had begun.

Then there was a wheen a' Indians—
  Deed, their weemin's well kep' down
By their own account entirely!
  But A saw my wumman frown.

Though A'll say that Mary Bella
  Liked the rest as well as me,
But yon quare Red Indian notions
  Wudn't wi' her mind agree.

There was more than A cud tell yez,
  Songs an' sketches, everything!
But the rest clane left my memory
  When A heard thon gipsies sing!

For a lot o' lovely lassies
  Danced an' sang in gipsy dress,
Man, A lost my heart entirely
  If the truth A must confess.

There were "gipsies" from near Killeter,
  Darg, the Free State, fair Drumqueen,
Meaghy Hill and Magheracreggan,
  Sion Mills and Killen green.

Dear, shure even Mary Bella
  Says, jist till hersel' an' me,
"Ay, there's always bonnie lassies
  At the good oul' E.S.C."

Deed, A niver seen no better
  For a crowd of handsome girls!
Wan av them that tuk my fancy
  Had her hair in "kissing curls."

Ay, an' thon's a lively lassie,
  That wee Queen that danced an' sung;
When A saw her lead thon dancin'
  Man, A wished that A was young!

An' a gran' wee singing cutty
  Frae the town o' oul' Ardstra,
When she sang "The Gipsy Lassie"
  Ye cud hear a needle fa'!

The poem entitled *Mary Bella's Johnny at the Edwards School Concert* from *Tyrone Constitution* 1930.

Composition.
"Irish Mountain Scenery."

The Irish mountains as they loftily raise their towering, defiant peaks far above the cresty billows of the surrounding waters lure the ocean traveller to rugged awnings and peacefully secluded valleys over which paternally they sometimes frown or tearfully glisten when western winds have yielded to their granite peaks.

Legends and poems have in but modest attempt tried to paint for man a pen picture of the charms and unrivalled beauty of the Sainted Isle. They who have given of their verse but mildly touched upon her subtle charms. Words cannot describe the lavish beauty of the virgin, verdant heights.

To artists of delicacy nothing more irrestibly appeals than the purple-headed peaks capping the sturdy granite-sided and jagged elevations of Connaught's heights.

Nothing to compare with Kerry's bold and yet retiring pillars as they are reflected in the glassy smoothness of the nestling waters of Innisfree can be expected on this Hemisphere. To search for a successful rival must prove futile.

161

"Etd".

Sad must the misty eyes and heavy hearts of those who looking behind them from the departing vessel or emigrant ship ~~as they~~ gaze in some instance for the last time at the coasting mountains which in their fastness shelter the homes thus vacated and guard those whose tears are falling.

The beauty which enthralls the passionate lover of Nature in her primitive state can best be realized when man gazes on the sunkissed slopes of the Wiclow Hill or the Majestic slope of dark and sober Mourne.

Almost as if influenced by its rustic primary, the Highlands of Donegal cast a spell over the hearts of those who wander near the briged peaks of Errigal or those shadowed waters near Muckish blue.

Fair and without rival are those modest Malin slopes as timidly and with unostentious steps (~~like a blushing bride who leaning on her parental strength~~) they meet the lapping waters of the Atlantic.

Roy Evans. April. 19th 1934.

A composition written by Roy Evans in 1934.

Unfortunately the epidemic diseases worsened and in March the School Committee minutes recorded that "since June last the district from which the Edwards School children are drawn has been severely affected by epidemic diseases, Measles, German Measles, Scarlet Fever and Diptheria....thereby causing a serious decrease in the average attendance, both through direct illness and children being kept at home through fear of infection...... We are of the opinion that the unsanitary condition of the old building is a contributory cause of the epedemic."

The Ministry of Home Affairs had responsibility for health issues and the Medical Inspector, Dr. F. J. Deane, on his Inspection in May 1935, reported:

"The public elementary school situated adjacent to the town of Castlederg is overcrowded to a very marked degree, especially in the room used by the third and fourth standard pupils. The conditions here are deplorable as the room in use is the attic room of the teacher's old house and is grossly overcrowded and approached by a narrow twisting staircase. The sanitary conveniences are kept as clean as possible in the circumstances but are unsatisfactory; one being situated 12 ft from the open window of the classroom. The walls of the classroom are defective and damp and the floor in one of them is in a very bad state of repair. It is hoped that these insanitary and unhealthy conditions under which upwards of 200 children receive instruction will be remedied at an early date by the speedy provision of new premises."

Reasons for the long delay are not entirely clear but Mr Lawson, the Architect, indicated in August 1935, in a letter to the Regional Committee that he had been unable to prepare plans due to an accident to one of his staff. He went on to enclose drawings of the school building, playsheds and offices, block, water supply, details and site levels along with specifications for the school building and other works and for the Central Heating plant. Presumably it had taken some time to survey the area and draw up the necessary plans. He also pointed out that upon taking levels for the water supply, he found out that the "town reservoirs are much too low to be of service" and the only other recourse was to use that of the District Hospital behind the school. This supply was at a higher level than the town reservoirs but was still not sufficient to supply the school by gravity, so he had to arrange for a gravity supply to a sump tank at ground level behind the school from which the water would be raised to a Service reservoir by an automatic pump.

Meantime, the school management committee continued its quarterly meetings to deal with the general matters of running the school. Business was often brief and there were usually only one or two items on the agenda as the Strabane and Castlederg Regional Education Committee undertook the major administration of the schools in the area.

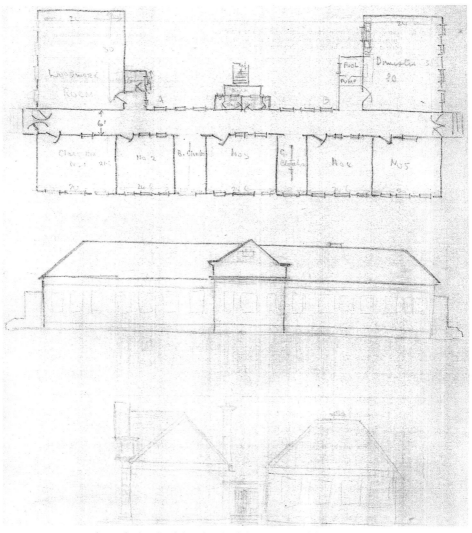

A rough sketch of the plans and the position of the new school

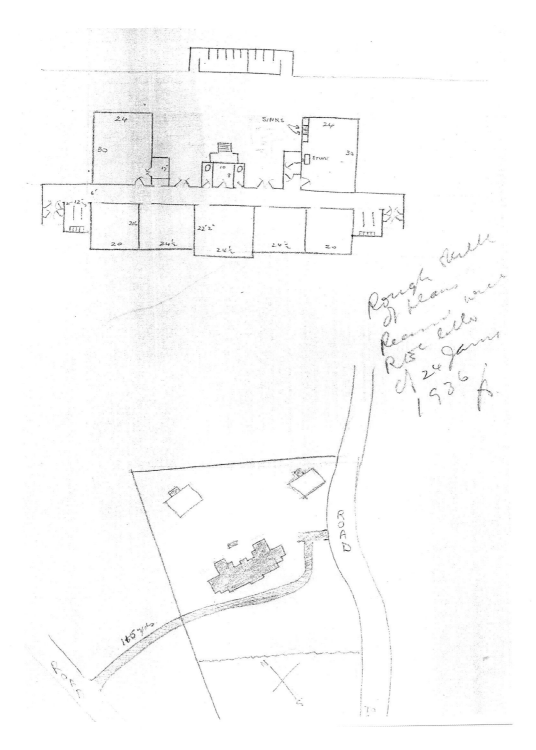

A rough sketch of the plans and the position of the new school

It was notable that in October 1934 the school committee had to remind the Regional Committee that one of the conditions of the transfer of Edwards School was to pay £15 annually to the school committee, out of the endowment fund. The Secretary recorded, "not one penny of this sum has been received although the school has been transferred for over three years."

The response could be described as tardy, as money in respect of payment only reached the school committee in July 1935, when arrangements were made to open an account with the Ulster Bank, in which to deposit the Endowment funds. At the same meeting, it was agreed to pay Mr Sloan £7/5/3, an amount paid by him for two years for supplying books to necessitous children. Occasionally, clothing and boots were also provided for "necessitous children."

It was also proposed that Mr Sloan "be authorised to establish a library with an initial expenditure limited to £5."

Unfortunately, the Regional Committee appeared to be unnecessarily slow in dealing with any business. It is hard to believe that two years after Mr Lawson had submitted his plans for the new school, the Edwards committee recorded that they "were of the opinion that they should have been shown a copy of the plans of the new school!"

The Regional Committee passed on the concerns of the School Management Committee to the Ministry of Education, regarding the delay in passing the plans and beginning the building.

Mr James Lawson, B. E., Civil Engineer, Architect and Surveyor, featured strongly in the discussions and recommendations in the three years prior to the commencement of building. He advised on such issues as the entrance roadway. The Ministry considered the main entrance to be the gate on the East boundary, while Mr Lawson, with his local knowledge, advised that the roadway to the West boundary of the site, had always been the "principal entrance to the ground" and he objected to the other one on the grounds that the tortuous road leading past the gate was a "narrow lane without footpaths, on which two vehicles would have difficulty in passing."

He also remarked on the provision of "Offices" or W.C. compartments, stating that in other new schools, too many had been provided and in some cases they were locked up and not used. These schools were in country areas where the pupils lived some distance away, but in the case of Edwards a large percentage of the pupils resided in Castlederg and could go home during the day!!

Mr Lawson commented on a range of other areas such as Cloakrooms, Flooring, the Cleaner's Store, Door Panels, Blackboards, Drains, Heating and Lighting and the Water Supply, the latter being the most major consideration. As stated earlier, the water supply was to come from the hospital and there was concern that in dry weather there would be an insufficient supply to meet the needs of both institutions.

The town supply at that time, (May 1936) was being cut off at night to conserve supplies and this also happened during the day in the summer months, therefore it was not going to be of much use, so a pump to bring water from the hospital reservoir and extra service tanks were recommended.

A letter sent from Mr Thomas Elliott, Solicitor in Strabane, to Mr Lawson, queried the whereabouts of the title deeds to the branch road from the water works' road to the school site and suggested that the original title deeds of Castlederg Union had had been lost in the Dublin troubles. This being the case they were in no doubt that the roadway had been dedicated to public use, at least since the erection of the workhouse.

The Cost Of The New School.

During 1936 the plans for the school were put out to tender and the costs of building and finishing the site were given serious consideration. Mr Lawson investigated the costs and negotiated reductions with the accepted Contractor, Mr J. J. Loughlin, of Castlederg.

In a letter to the Regional Committee, Mr Lawson pointed out that the site, excluding the recreation field, had an area of 3 acres, 1 rood and 23 perches. To leave it in a satisfactory state, a large amount of levelling, terracing and cleaning of the ground was required and that as there were more roadways and paths than in most other schools, these too would add to the cost.

The geographical position of Castlederg also caused enhanced freight charges. Mr Lawson remarked, "gravel, which has to be conveyed from Strabane, costs 4/0 per cub yd. over the price in Strabane and bricks cost an additional £1 per 1,000."

Increases had occurred in other areas too, including labour, which added twenty per cent more onto the original estimate.

With regard to the specifications of the school building itself, it was "to be faced with Buckley Junction Rustics and Reconstructed Stone, with the roof carried on steel principals and the floors constructed in hardwood."

Mr Lawson met with a sub-committee to try to reduce the costs and deleted all the items not considered absolutely essential and to substitute, in certain cases, cheaper materials. The result was a reduction of £1,156 and brought Mr Loughlin's original price down from £10,650 to £9,494. However Mr Lawson expressed some doubt as to the wisdom of doing this as he felt that "the exclusion of a considerable part of the external work from the scheme will detract from the appearance of the School grounds when the works are completed."

In reply, the Regional Committee indicated that while they approved of the effort to reduce costs, they hoped this would not be detrimental to the standard of the building as they looked upon "this school as being the most important in the Castlederg district."

Mr Lawson and Mr Gamble, representing the School Committee, met with the

Ministry to discuss their recommendations and then sent their findings to the Regional Committee.

The Ministry suggested sinking a well on the site, but Mr Lawson knew this would be rejected by the Regional Committee who would realise there was a risk of contamination from the old workhouse graveyard! In addition the costs involved were likely to be high due to the rocky ground.

They also found that an additional £290 for plumbing had already been included in the cost and should not have been added on to the cost of the water supply, a point that Mr Lawson discussed with the aptly named Mr Waters!

One of the most striking features of the new school was to be the central façade, which the Ministry wanted to remove. The Regional Committee was very much in favour of it, as they wanted the school to have a satisfactory appearance on its commanding site.

But the lengthy delays in starting the work incurred further costs. Mr Loughlin again wrote to Mr Lawson in April 1937, detailing increases in materials since he had submitted the original tender. (See letter) He was ready to begin the work and was awaiting the go-ahead. The changes were accepted and Mr Loughlin began work in June 1937.

Mr John J. Loughlin, Builder

Item	Cost as per Bill of Quantities			Increase	Amount		
	£	s.	d.		£	s.	d.
Asphalte	253	17	0	10%	25	7	0
Dampcourse (material only)	17	16	0	10%	1	15	0
Wood casing to Concrete	34	0	0	25%	8	12	0
Sarking Felt (material only)	36	0	0	10%	3	12	0
Timber (material only)	736	0	0	25%	184	2	0
Windows (material only)	265	0	0	20%	53	0	0
Coat Stands, etc. (material only)	41	0	0	15%	6	3	0
External Plumbing (material only)	87	2	0	100%	87	2	0
Sanitary Fittings (material only)	59	5	0	30%	17	18	6
Lead Wastes, etc. (materials only)	17	18	4	100%	17	18	4
Drain Pipes Gullies, etc. (materials only)	199	19	0	10%	19	19	0
Painter & Glazier (materials only)	109	0	0	15%	16	7	0
Offices and Playshed Timber	67	0	6	25%	16	15	0
Offices and Playshed Slates	69	0	0	15%	10	7	8
Steel Beams (material only)	10	0	0	10%	1	0	0
Main Building Slates, etc.	279	0	0	20%	59	16	0
Rainwater Goods, etc. (materials only)	78	5	3	20%	15	7	0
Mild Steel Bars Expanet, etc. (materials only)	109	0	0	20%	21	18	0
Water Main & fittings (materials only)	127	0	0	15%	15	17	6
Internal Plumbing (material only)	65	0	0	100%	65	0	0
					£646	17	0

Letter from John J. Loughlin, builder, indicating the increase in the bill of quantities.

J.J. LOUGHLIN,
General Steam Saw Mills and Joinery Works.
Castlederg, Co. Tyrone.

3rd April, 1937.

James S. Lawson, Esq., B.E.,
Strabane.

Dear Sir,

Following my interview with you on 23rd March re Edwards New P.E. School, I have gone into the various items that have increased in price since the date of my original tender, and find that it represents an additional 6% on the reduced contract price, which after deducting £1509 (for work omitted) from the original price of £10,650 leaves £9,141, plus 6% makes a total of £9,689, as the cost of the work.

If the Regional Committee is prepared to accept this price for the erection of the school I purpose to put the work in hand as soon as I receive notification, alternatively, if the Committee agree to pay the extra increase on the current invoice price, over the prices prevailing in July, it will be equally acceptable to me. I have given the above figures so that the approximate amount of increase can be known, and I enclose a schedule showing how the amounts have been arrived at from which it will be seen that the major items of the work are unaffected.

Brick Work, Concrete Work, and all labour skilled and unskilled remain unaltered, but the general tendency of prices is upward.

I remain,
Yours truly,

JOHN J. LOUGHLIN.

Letter

Monday 6th December 1937.

24°

Heavy frost during the night, all outside construction work suspended. stone breaking and fixing of lead pipe in school. dado bead being run & grounds for sundela board, being fixed

Tuesday 7th December 1937.

24°

Five asphalt workers arrived & at work on roofs. At noon Mc Lawson called, inspected, and discussed eves & flashing of flat roofs with foreman Asphalt worker,   weather frost & snow.

Wednesday 8th December 37.

20°

Work as above,   Hard frost,.

Thursday 9th December 37.

20°

Excavating for playshed, jointing of lead pipes for supply to offices, work at roofs continues,
                    Frost & Snow.

Friday 10th Dec. 37.

Owing to heavy snow, work on roofs, & nearly all work suspended,   Frost & snow.

Saturday 11th Dec. 37.

Frost and snow continues, work on roofs suspended, and work men left for Belfast, some labourers & plasterers at work, plumber & 2 joiners,
                    Frost & snow.

An insight into the building progress, materials used, workers involved, problems encountered and almost daily weather reports are to be found in a very detailed diary, fastidiously kept by Mr William Donnell, the Clerk of Works. He began his entries on 21st June 1937 and concluded them in July 1938, allowing us a fascinating glimpse of the developments as they unfolded.

As work progressed, Mr Lawson enquired about the use of the school for technical instruction and was instructed to advise the builder to equip two classrooms for Woodwork and Domestic Economy, "equipment being neither elaborate nor costly." This was carried out and by the end of the summer term of 1938 the school was nearing completion.

Despite poor weather in the early summer, teams of workers landscaped the grounds and put the finishing touches to the flowerbeds in preparation for the long-awaited opening.

However, the school committee did not discuss the opening plans or preparations until 20th May 1938, when it was recorded that the meeting was called for the purpose of making arrangements in connection with the opening of the school. Even then there are few details; the official opening date was given as Thursday 7th of July at 3 o'clock. Tea was to be provided for the children, their parents and visitors and the costs defrayed out of the funds of the School Management Committee.

The following meeting was held on 31st of May and tenders for catering were discussed. The same menu was chosen for parents and visitors, Mr Sparks being awarded the contract for catering for adults and Mrs McNutt to cater for the children.

A list of people from Castlederg who were to be invited, was drawn up (but not included in the minutes) and it was agreed that Rev. W. T. Macourt conduct the dedicatory service. This concluded all the business in connection with the opening, as at the next meeting the only business was to discuss a storehouse for the caretaker to hold his barrow, lawnmower and bags of sweeping compound!

Edwards School in the early thirties.

Mr Jim Sloan and Miss Susan Jackson pictured outside the okd Edwards P.S. on the Castlefin Road. (1930's)

The New Edwards Public Elementary School 1938

The 1938 Edwards Public Elementary School under construction.

Work on the new school had advanced quickly and less than a year after it had commenced, preparations were made for the grand opening on July 7th 1938. It was a greatly anticipated day and proved to be a most exciting and memorable occasion for everyone in Castlederg, particularly the children, who as adults still recall the move with great nostalgia.

Members of staff at that time were:

Principal; Mr J.G. Sloan (Classes 6, 7 and 8)

Miss G. Elliott (Classes 4 and 5)

Miss Jackson: (Classes 2 and 3)

Miss McArthur: (Class 1 and Senior Infants)

Miss Campbell: (Senior Infants)

The Tyrone Constitution of Friday July 8th carried banner headlines and almost two pages were dedicated to the wonderful event. The following paragraphs are extracts from the paper:

EDWARDS SCHOOL, CASTLEDERG, DECLARED OPEN.

School Accommodation Problem Solved.
BRIGHTER PROSPECTS FOR EDUCATION

Largest Rural School Erected Under Education Act.

Under particularly happy and pleasant conditions the new Edwards Public Elementary School, Castlederg, erected by Strabane and Castlederg Regional Education Committee, was declared open on Thursday afternoon, 7th inst., by Mrs Herdman, M.B.E., J.P., wife of Captain J.C. Herdman, D.L., Chairman of the Regional Committee.

The event aroused the utmost interest and enthusiasm in Castlederg district and there was a large attendance of the local people and a very representative company from all parts of the Regional area.

Provided at a cost of approximately £11000, the new school has the distinction of being the largest school of its class erected in any rural district in Northern Ireland under the Education Act, and not only solves the question of elementary school accommodation in the Castlederg district for a long period to come, but endows the district with accommodation for the development of technical or secondary education.

It can scarcely be stated however that the new building opens up a new era in education in Castlederg district for the records of the old Edwards School in past generations could not have been excelled and the only expectation for the future is that the splendid reputation that the school gained under the headmastership of the late Mr T. J. Burnside, B.A. and under the present headmaster, Mr J. G. Sloan, M.A., will be continued under more pleasant and modern conditions.

The school is a tribute to the operation of the Northern Ireland Education Act, but it is no less of a tribute to the foresight of the local public boards who availed of the opportunity of ridding themselves of the incumbrance of the old workhouse, with its forbidding aspects, and placing on its site a building of great service to the community and very pleasing architectural beauty.

DESCRIPTION OF THE NEW SCHOOL

The new school, which faces directly south, consists of five spacious rooms for elementary education, all leading off the same corridor, and two rooms for the teaching of special subjects.

It stands on its own grounds of five acres, with splendid playgrounds and ample accommodation for instruction in horticulture, and from its windows a charming view of the town and the Derg Valley.

The rooms are particularly well lighted and ventilated, and the system of central heating installed is of the very latest pattern, so that instruction will be imparted under conditions undreamt of a few years ago.

Surmounting the front of the school there is a very attractive façade, and the whole aspect from the charmingly laid out terraces is particularly beautiful. Throughout the entire scheme nothing has been omitted to equip the school on the most modern lines. The flagpole, from which the Union Jack was flown, is erected near to the Boys entrance.

In addition to the classroom accommodation there is a timber store (off the wood-work room), cleaner's store, male staff lavatory, teacher's room, female staff lavatory, fuel store and electric pump room. The corridor, which is 155 feet long from end to end, at each end of which is the boys' and girls' entrance door.

At each end of the classrooms there is spacious cloakroom accommodation, with wash hand basins for boys and girls, all approached from the corridor. In addition tot the two main entrances there are two back entrances leading to the heating chamber and to the boys' and girls' lavatories in the grounds on the north side of the building. The entire school building is centrally heated by a low pressure hot water system from a sectional boiler installed in the heating chamber , with radiators in the various classrooms, cloakrooms and corridor. A "Mrs Sam" cooking stove supplies the Domestic Science room with hot water, laid on to two fireclay sinks, to which a cold water supply is laid on.

The Regional Committee's architect, Mr J.S. Lawson B.E., was of course the designer of the building and the contractor was Mr J. J. Loughlin, Castlederg, who had already built Ballylaw and Killen P.E. Schools. The heating installation was carried out by Mr John Davison, Strabane, and the electrical work by Mr McLernon, Belfast. Great credit is due to the clerk of works, Mr William Donnell, Strabane, for his part in the erection of the building.

On the north end of the playground there is a fine playing shed erected, in front of which is a tarmac drill ground. The entire site is about five acres. This includes a field containing about two acres, which will be used a playing field, and which is separated by a hedge from the main school gardens.

The school has been built to accommodate 230 elementary school pupils, and the specialist rooms are designed to accommodate twenty pupils each under the Technical School Regulations."

The article went on to detail the illustrious history of the school from the will of Hugh Edwards in 1737 to the present Endowed state.

The red-letter day in the history of Castlederg, was described as an occasion when the whole populace turned out to witness the opening ceremony.

"The utmost enthusiasm prevailed and the grounds were very appropriately decorated with loyal colours, while the newly laid flower beds, ablaze with bloom, imparted singular beauty to the scene.

As Mrs Herdman entered the school grounds, Master John Gallagher and Miss Edwina Beattie, senior pupils, broke the Union Jack on the flagpole, and its folds, fanned by the breeze, floated forth, the symbol of loyalty and devotion to the British Crown. The Union Jack was kindly presented to the school by Captain J.C. Herdman."

The solemn dedicatory service was conducted by Rev. Canon Macourt, his first public ceremony since being elevated to Canon of Derry Cathedral. He said, "We dedicate this school to the honour and glory of God and to the education of the children and young people of the district. In the name of the Father and the Son and the Holy Ghost. Amen.

This was followed by an address by the Chairman, Mr James F. Gamble, M.P., who outlined the history of the school and thanked the architect, the builder, the clerk of works, the heating contractor and the electrician. He also paid tribute to the Regional Education Committee and their secretary, Mr W. McH. Mackey, and the parent body, Tyrone County Council.

He went on to thank the Council for their generosity in providing the capital needed, **"a sum that would have paralysed the original donor who laid the foundation for the first Edwards school, by the small endowment which he** bequeathed for that purpose, if he could have ever dreamt that this fine building today would have been the outcome after two hundred years.

I hope the harmony that has still prevailed among the Committee and the teaching staff, the parents and the pupils will continue and the new building will send forth even yet more famous scholars than have been educated in the old."

The opening ceremony was then performed by Mrs Herdman, using a gold key which the contractor, Mr Loughlin, presented to Mr Lawson. She turned the key and declared the school open, expressing the hope that it would be the means of equipping future generations for the battle of life.

Two junior pupils, Phyllis Carson and Gordon Faulkner, presented Mrs Herdman with a bouquet of flowers.

The Principal, Mr J. G. Sloan, then addressed the crowd, again expressing thanks to all who provided the new school. He said he remembered being a pupil in the old school and there was talk of a new school but it had never materialised. At last they were the proud possessors of such a worthy building—"a model of superior excellence!" He said they looked forward with pleasure to working in the new building, which was in marked contrast to the old one.

Captain Herdman, Chairman of the Regional Committee, acknowledged the vote of thanks and praised all who had been involved in building the new school. He agreed that it had taken a long time but was "better late than never." "I suppose, " he said, "that in, say, fifty years time, many of you children, as many as are left in Castlederg, will be able to point out this new school to your grandchildren and tell them how you were among the first band of pupils to enter its doors and do lessons within its walls. Probably by that time it will have lost its newness and perhaps be a trifle out-of -date, but at least it will have stood the ravages of time better than the old building just vacated."

He went on to talk about loyalty, to the school, to fellow pupils, to Northern Ireland, to the British Empire and the King.

Canon Macourt proposed a vote of thanks to Mrs Herdman and Rev. W.G.M. Thompson seconded this. Mr Samuel Robinson thanked Mr Gamble, seconded by

Mr J. J. Mitchell.

The ceremony was brought to a close with the singing of the National Anthem. The visitors then inspected the school and the School Management Committee provided a wonderful tea.

The following parts of the article paid tribute to all those who were involved in completing the school;

THE CONTRACTING FIRMS

CREDIT WHERE CREDIT IS DUE.

CENTRAL HEATING

Mr. John Davison, Main Street, Strabane, who is well known, not only in County Tyrone, but throughout the entire North-West, as one of the most highly skilled and experienced gentleman in the heating and plumbing trades, held the contract for installing the central heating system at the new Edwards School and carried out the work with the same efficiency which has always characterised his work.

Mr. Davison has ensured that the whole interior of the school will be maintained at a comfortable temperature, at minimum cost for fuel.

Mr. Davison has already carried out the heating of the Castlederg District Hospital and administrative buildings, and has gained a splendid reputation for really high-class workmanship. Anything entrusted to him in the installation of water services, plumbing, sanitary fittings and heating always receives his careful attention.

ELECTRICAL LIGHTING, HEAT AND POWER

Mr. B. McLernon, Main Street, Castlederg is already well known to the people of Castlederg and other towns in North Tyrone, which have been linked up by the Electricity Board's grid system, as a highly efficient electrician, and capable of giving the most valuable advice on the subject of electric lighting, heating and power.

Mr McLernon has already installed electricity in hundreds of dwelling houses, shops, factories and workshops with the utmost satisfaction to the owners, and with the development of electricity there is a steadily increasing demand upon his services.

We advise our readers to consult Mr.McLernon on all matters, whether for installing supplies from the Electrictiy Board, or private supplies in districts not yet linked up with the Electricity Board.

Mr McLernon carried out the contract and supplied all the fittings for the electric installation at the new Edwards School.

DUNGANNON BRICK CO., LTD.

The Dungannon Brick Co., Ltd, supplied all the 'Rustic' facing bricks and specials used by the contractor in the erection of the Edwards School – in fact this progressive concern are now manufacturing all classes of bricks of the very best quality, as well as beautiful fireplace designs in great variety.

The manufactures of the Dungannon Brick Co., Ltd are now used extensively in the erection of public and private buildings throughout County Tyrone and bear the hallmark of excellence.

The new Edwards P.E. School is a credit to the Strabane and Castlederg Regional Education Committee, but it is an even greater credit to their contractor, Mr. John J. Loughlin, Castlederg, who has carried out his contract in a very superior manner. The contract price was £9,699. Mr. Loughlin secured the contract in the face of the keenest competition, and we believe the building is the largest and most important public work with which he has been entrusted by any public board up to now.

He has already given the utmost satisfaction to the Strabane and Castlederg, and Omagh Regional Committees by the erection of new schools at Ballylaw, Killen and Gillygooley, but these were small buildings compared with the Edwards School.

There is some very beautiful workmanship in the school, and while Mr. Loughlin is deserving of hearty congratulation, we must express admiration for the skill and capability displayed by his employees, all local men.

It is exceedingly creditable to Castlederg that it has a contractor capable of undertaking such extensive work, and workmen so highly skilled in their trades. They have never failed to give satisfaction.

MODERN SCHOOL FURNITURE

Next in importance to good school construction comes the question of modern school furniture, and Messrs. James D. Bennet. Ltd. of 121, Avenue Street, Glasgow, have done much to solve this important problem for school committees by the great variety of very superior furniture they are manufacturing at very attractive prices.
The new Edwards School has been furnished by this enterprising firm, and Education Committees requiring school furniture should ask for catalogue and quotations. The firm also specialises in church and hall furniture.

BUILDING MATERIALS

The well-known firm of Messrs Robert Kirk Ltd, Builders Providers, Exchange Street, Belfast, supplied the materials used in the construction of the new Edwards School, Castlederg.
The firm stocks everything of the very highest quality in the building line and carries on an extensive business in County Tyrone.

Extensive advertisements and numerous photographs featuring the school, the Board of Governors and Teaching Staff and the Platform Party, accompanied the article; it's prominence matching its importance in the life of the small town of Castlederg.

With hindsight, it is rather amusing and somewhat ironic to study the events of the time and to see them echoed almost seventy years later!

1939-1978

The New School.

Mr Jim Sloan (circled) attending a teacher-training day in Horticulture in Portstewart in 1938

Following the opening of the school pupils and teachers settled happily into the new surroundings. Today, as adults, those pupils still reminisce about the bright, warm and airy classrooms and the contrast with the old buildings they had recently vacated.

The modern building and the spacious grounds led Inspector Benn in his report of June 1939, to comment, **"The excellent new premises provided for this school by the Regional Education Committee have now been in use for more than six months and are proving very satisfactory.**

Part of the grounds is being developed as a school garden in charge of the Principal, who has obtained the necessary provisional qualifications.

Special mention must be made of the high attendance percentage; whist the tone and discipline of the school are alike good. The standard of work improves steadily through the school, reaching a high level in the senior classes."

The Inspector, Miss L.R. Hogg in December 1951, noticed the importance of play and the attempt to use the wonderful facilities. (Incidentally, this was the first recorded visit of a lady inspector!) She remarked, *"The excellent playground gives opportunity to all teachers to develop the work on more modern lines. An attempt is being made in all classes to get away from mere formal exercise."*

The School Caretaker.

The Management committee continued to hold quarterly meetings and in July 1938, shortly after the opening, they met to discuss the salary of the caretaker, Mr Joe Speer.

At a previous meeting in 1932, the committee considered the remuneration of £16 per annum, fixed by the Regional Committee, to be insufficient payment for the extra work involved in the dilapidated premises and the fact that the rooms were not all under one roof.

Once again the committee felt that "he was not paid a salary commensurate with the amount of work he has to do in the new school and grounds." They pointed out that "in the old school he had five small rooms whereas in the new building there are seven large rooms, with a great many windows to be cleaned, a furnace to be lighted and tended and entire grounds to be kept in order and wash hand basins to be cleaned etc." It was then proposed that he should be paid at least 40/0 per week.

However the minutes of the next meeting in October confirm that he was still receiving 12/6 per week, "a totally inadequate wage," and they urged the Regional Committee to reconsider his salary. They also granted an "honorarium of £5" out of their own funds.

In November 1939 the committee once again convened, this time to consider applicants for the office of school caretaker. Tenders were received; one from Mr Joe Speer, the present caretaker, leading us to surmise that selection by tender was for a limited time. Mr Speer was agreeable to undertake the work for 25/0 weekly but the committee did not reach a decision and further tenders were discussed at the next meeting.

Finally it was agreed that Mr Speer would continue as caretaker.

The War Years

During the war years life in Castlederg, particularly in Edwards school, went on fairly normally. There were some changes, which usually injected a little excitement into the mundane daily lives of the children.

One of these was the arrival of evacuees from Belfast. The local children viewed their city lives and habits with curiosity and many still recall their different clothes and dialect. However, they were welcomed and integrated into the community and long-standing relationships were established in many cases.

The school Principal, Mr J.G. Sloan and members of his family were involved in Castlederg Air Training Corps.

Castlederg Air Training Corps.
Back Row L-R: Ruby Cather, W.J. Harron, Harry Barrett, Johnston Aiken, Joe Speer,
Tommy Sturdee, John Sloan, Maisie Nesbitt.
Second Row L-R: Mr Buss, Ella Semple, Cissy Robinson, Willie Charlie Hemphill,
Sam McNutt, Dr. Crockett, R.A. Scott, Mr Sloan, Elizabeth Scott.
Front Row L-R: Florrie Hamilton, Annie Crockett, Miss Park, Annie Cather, Charlotte Hamilton,
May Roulston, Mrs Crockett, Sadie Keatley, Maud Young, Kathleen McCracken, Ruby Irwin.

At a meeting of the school committee in March 1943, an application was considered from the Commanding Officer, Mr C. Boyd, requesting permission to use the Domestic Science room on three evenings a week for the purpose of giving instruction to the Corps. This was granted and the Corps met in the school.

The room next to the main entrance of the school was used as a Food Office and many past pupils also recall this and the issue of coupons and Ration Books.

In April 1943 a special meeting of the committee was convened to consider an application from the Divisional Food Officer, requesting the use of the wood store, which was the small room adjoining the Food Office, as they required more space. They also asked for permission to put four iron bars inside the window of the small room and steel sheeting on the inside panels of the door. The requests were granted.

The school building continued to be used by the Air Training Corps and in October 1943 they asked the Regional Committee for permission to erect a Nissan Hut in the school grounds. This was referred to the school committee who approved the erection of the hut for the duration of the war only and also under the condition that it was placed in a position that would not interfere with the amenities of the school.

The school Registers of the war years also reflected the national events. The occupation of Parents or Guardians was frequently listed as "Soldier" or "War Worker" and in some cases as "Widow."

Miss Jackson, who had been teaching in the school since her appointment in 1919, left in 1944, and the committee instructed the Secretary to write to her, expressing appreciation of her services and regret at her departure. Miss Isabel Millar, of Douglasbridge, replaced her.

In its early years the school was a useful focus for life in the community. It was regarded as a "Technical" and classes in Woodwork, Domestic Science and Agricultural Machinery were held. The School Attendance Committee also met once a month in the Domestic Science room while the A.T.C. continued its training in the building.

Edwards P.S. Pupils in 1944
(Kindly donated to school by Mrs Olive McKean (nee Hemphill)

The Post War Years.

Life continued in a humdrum manner after the war. The A.T.C. Nissan hut fell into disuse and the school committee sought approval from the Ministry to use it as a storeroom for fuel and gardening tools. In 1949 it was given a coat of "red oxide" paint and became home for the winter supply of coke.

Children were still bringing their "piece" to school for lunch, while some who lived near, walked home. With increasing numbers and a trend toward school meals the management approved the building of a school kitchen in the grounds.

The Food Office continued in use after the War and in September 1948 a letter was received from the Divisional Food Office in Belfast, complaining about the lack of heating in the building on Saturdays and in the holidays. The committee considered the matter and the unanimous response was that the cost of heating had increased considerably since the Food Office took over and disturbance and visitors caused upset in the normal working of the school. It was also felt that there was the danger of infection being carried into the school by "all types of people, including gypsies, who seem to be continual visitors." The final decision was that the room should revert to its former use, "viz Technical Evening Classes in Woodwork or if not equipped for woodwork, the room is ideal and is needed for Physical Training on cold wet winter days."

At the next meeting in October the decision was withdrawn as the committee was more fully informed of the requirements of the local branch of the Food Control Committee.

The boys continued to enjoy the large football field and in April 1949 it was decided to purchase a good football but at the same time the football field was let to Mr John Robinson for grazing at a rent of £5, until November 1949, with the proviso that the boys would have free access to the field for their games.

As numbers continued to increase in the primary school population, Miss Adelaide Blackstock and Miss Iris Blackstock were appointed in 1948. Miss Anna H. Scott (later Mrs McNutt) was appointed as fourth assistant and Mr William G. Starrett as fifth assistant in 1949 while Miss Mary E. Patrick (later Mrs Caldwell) joined the staff in the next year. The average number on roll in

1949 was 208.9 and this merited the appointment of Miss Elliott as Vice Principal.

Mrs J. Loughlin became Caretaker in 1949 and some members of the committee were concerned that there was a lot of work for one woman, however they were assured that her husband, an ex-service man, was willing to help her! She remained in the post until 1956. Her wages were increased by 2/6 per week in 1952, due to the fact that she had to carry the coke some distance.

In the early 1950's the school building began to show a few defects. There was some dampness and the plastering needed attention, windows needed fresh putty, internal decoration was necessary and the fuel store was too small.

The school residence, in which Mr Sloan still lived, had not been attended for years and required repairs and decoration. After numerous requests a bathroom had been provided sometime after 1938, but there was no electricity in the house, and the only means of cooking was on an old range, the oven of which was burnt out. A new modern cooker, a Rayburn, was quickly installed and was reported as "giving entire satisfaction."

One of the problems in the early stages of planning the school, concerned the water supply. These concerns proved genuine in 1952, as the committee reported that there had been no supply to the school lavatories or the school canteen, from the Derg Valley Hospital Well, and the health of over 200 children was a major consideration. They urged the County Education Committee to deal quickly with the matter.

Castlederg Rural District Council was contacted to see if the school could be connected to the town main water supply and the reply was that they expected the Lough Bradan water scheme to be operative in about nine months hence and they could then be connected, but the committee felt they were entitled to the town supply and as the supply was already at a house near the school, there should have been no difficulty in connecting it to the school storage tank. However, in mid 1953 there was still no sign of the Lough Bradan scheme and the local committee once again voiced concerns for the health of the children.

By 1954 Lough Bradan water had reached Castlederg but in March 1955 the committee was informed that the Rural District Council had refused to pipe the water to the entrance gate of the school. Air Commodore Churchman held an enquiry on Monday 27th September 1955 and at a later date the water supply was connected.

Another contentious issue was the roadway leading from the main road into the school. In 1954 it was in bad state of repair but as it was not a County Road the County Council could not spend money on its repair. In 1956 it was said to be in "a rutted condition" but by 1958 nothing had been done and the Management proposed that "when the repair of the school road was put out for tender, the removal of the old stone gate pillars would be included as one was about ready to fall and constituted a real menace to the children."

In 1961 Mr Thomas Kane acquired the land to the north side of the school road and as he was building a dwelling house he proposed to make a short footpath to the house. The committee agreed to negotiate the possibility of having it extended along the length of the roadway. This was met with a suggestion from the Architect's Department that it would be preferable to run a footpath over vacant ground along the back of the Breezemount Park houses, as there was an increasing danger to the children with the greater volume of traffic. The Rural District Council assumed responsibility for this work and in 1965 the school Committee expressed pleasure at the improvements effected on the school road. Over the years a lot of equipment was purchased for use in the school. The County Education Committee supplied many necessary and diverse items such as storage cupboards, notice boards, easels and drawing boards, tables and chairs, waste paper baskets, a duplicating machine, a rubber stamp, gardening tools— spades, forks, hoes, rakes and a lawn mower, a tumbling mat for P.E., a "Slate" globe, a rain gauge, a piano and piano stool, a sewing machine, a wireless set and the reception equipment, a film projector, maps, shelving in the staff room as well as replacing the boiler, floor coverings and curtains. These requisites, along with those purchased using the Endowment Fund money, meant that the school was very well resourced.

The Endowment Fund.

The subject of the Educational Endowment Scheme was frequently debated in correspondence between the school management committee, the Ministry of Education and the Ministry of Finance. The school management committee made decisions on spending the £15 per annum allowance out of the income of the transferred cash endowment. These ideas were forwarded to Strabane and Castlederg Regional Education Committee, who in turn passed them on to the Ministry of Education in Stormont, who gave final approval of any expenditure. Regular debates arose concerning the items chosen and on occasions the requests were turned down.

In 1953 the Ministry of Finance ascertained that the amount of capital in the fund was £189/4/11 of Conversion Stock together with £645/0/5 in Savings Bonds. The Education Committee had allowed its share of the income to build up to £64/12/11 with the intention of buying visual aid equipment for the school. In the previous year a lawn mower and schools meals equipment had been purchased and it was the intention to buy six dozen Bibles and another lawnmower for use in the horticulture plot. The Ministry of Finance was unsure that the money was being spent properly and they also questioned the auditing of the expenditure and who was responsible for that. The Ministry of Education suggested that it was the responsibility of the local Authority who had representatives on the school committee.

On another occasion the school committee, thinking they were acting in accordance with the terms of the Endowment Scheme to "make additions or improvements to furniture, appliances etc," decided to purchase cups, saucers and drinking glasses for the use of teachers, out of the Endowment income, but this request was refused and they were told that the sum had to be spent for "the benefit of the school and pupils."

Some items of expenditure that were authorised were £10 annually for the purchase of film strips, an electric plug in the staff room, a tape recorder and tapes, a mobile television set, visual aids, badges for sports day and prizes for deserving pupils, cricket and netball sets, books for the library, B.B.C. pamphlets, class pictures, Medici Prints, standardised and diagnostic tests and a record player and records,

Although the £15 allocation to the school committee was supposed to be paid yearly, the Minutes often indicate that it was not, and requests were often made to have it forwarded. Occasionally the larger accumulations were awarded in block and bigger items were purchased.

The fund still exists today and the Western Education and Library Board sanction the use of the money.

Changes in Education.

On the wider front in Britain, R.A. Butler's Education Act of 1944 raised the school leaving age to 15 and this was followed by a White Paper issued by the Northern Ireland Government in December 1944 announcing the intention to conform to the lines of the Butler Act.

Compulsory schooling was to begin at 5 years (maybe 5-6 years in rural areas) and continue to 15 years. There would be free secondary education for all, in three types of school, junior for basic subjects, senior for academically talented children and Technical for children aged 13+. The State would arrange an entrance test at age 11 with eighty per cent of places awarded this way and twenty per cent left to the schools to award as they wished.

The school day would begin with religious worship and religious instruction would be part of the curriculum. The right of access of the clergy would continue.

The plan also included expansion on a wider basis, including university scholarships, free medical and dental treatment in schools and free meals and milk in primary and junior schools.

The Education Act became law in Northern Ireland in 1947 and brought about some changes in schools. The Act recognised that all aspects of a child's development —physical, intellectual, imaginative, emotional, social and moral and spiritual are involved in the education process. The emphasis was moving from content-based teaching to considering the individual needs of the child.

A new primary education programme came into operation in 1952. Teachers were given guidance on various methods of teaching and the choice and presentation of material. They were encouraged to draw up their own schemes of instruction and aim for a balance of class, group and individual teaching.

III.—AMMUNITION BOXES.

Ammunition boxes (see photographs) can often be obtained from a " scrap " dealer. They are strong and when sealed down and painted, make a very useful piece of apparatus. They usually have handles at each end and can be moved about easily by quite small children. They are of special value for jumping, balancing and agility exercises, but also form useful starting points for trunk and abdominal exercises. They are suitable for free experimental work on the part of both child and teacher and add much to the interest and variety of the lesson. A unit of twenty-four such boxes allows for partner work on a class activity basis, and they can be used by individual children or piled up in various formations for group practices. When using them for some forms of jumping, e.g., Nos. 21, 33, 36, it is advisable to have a child sitting on, to make the base completely firm, leaving half of the top free for the jumper. The suggestions given below are only an indication of the type of work that can be done with these boxes, but free practice and experiment by the children should be encouraged while the teacher observes keenly and chooses worth-while activities for the whole class to try. The children are full of ideas which frequently need " tidying-up " by the teacher in order to give more valuable training.

(a)—JUMPING.

A teacher's guide to P.E. lessons using ammunition boxes, left over from the war.

Ammunition Boxes No. 38

Climbing Round Partner

Ammunition Boxes No. 30

Hand Stand in Two's

Ammunition Boxes No. 26

Diving through Partner's Legs

General View of Infants' Balancing Activities

Edwards in the Fifties

Edwards School Pupils in 1950

Back Row: Andy Robinson, Alan Wilson, --, Tommy Robb, Alex Robb, Willie Irvine, John Burke, David Henderson, Billy Mitchell, Noel Hemphill.

1st Row: Derek Louglin, Pearl Wilson, Audrey Boggs, Ann Boggs, Vena Rutledge, Laura Rutledge, ? Speer, -- , Hilda Wilson, Angela Turnbull, Noel Fallows, John Smith.

2nd Row: Sammy Semple, Maureen Blackstock, --, May Hemphill, Ann Hemphill, Heather Lyons, Ann Kane, Jean Walls, Gwen Kinnear, Ann Loughlin, Jean Kerrigan, Mary Bruce, Margaret Moore, Sheelagh Kinnear, Raymond Hemphill.

3rd Row: Doreen Robb, --, Ann Robb, Ann Monteith, Hazel Hemphill, Maureen Faulkner, Ann Ballantyne, Cherry Lyons, --, --, Frances McCrea, Barbara Cox, Uel Hemphill, -.

Front Row: Will Huey, Dave Henderson, Robin Wilson, Robin Lyons, Ronnie Watt, John Moore, Derek Wilson --.

The comprehensive range of subjects taught in Edwards in the early fifties included English, comprising grammar, reading, writing, spelling, poetry, creative writing or composition, maths and oral arithmetic, geography, history, music, games, such as football and netball, singing and gardening.

The teachers along with Mr Sloan in 1952 were Miss Elliott, Mrs McNutt, Mrs Caldwell, Mrs McFarland, Miss Millar and Mr Starrett.

Miss H. M. Neeson inspecting the junior classes in 1952 remarked; "The teachers are experienced, and the children seem secure and happy." This tone happily continued and the Chief Education Officer, Mr A. Gibson, wrote to Mr Sloan in 1954 to compliment him and the members of staff on the work being done in the school. He said, "My committee was particularly pleased to note that a pleasant tone pervaded the school as it feels such an atmosphere in a school has a marked effect on the work and character of the pupils."

Strict discipline was a feature of schools at that time. The cane was frequently used, even for very minor offences. Talking in class was not encouraged and a poor standard of work was often rewarded with "six of the best." Many children from Edwards remember the canes being bought in bundles from Sam Hemphill's shop. Mr Sloan kept his cane on top of the cupboard along with a globe and many times the children wished he would topple it as he rushed to bring down the offensive weapon!

The school was bitterly cold and former staff and pupils alike recall the freezing temperatures. There were major problems with the boiler and it was said that only for the tender nursing by the caretaker it would not have lasted as long. It was finally replaced in 1956 and the level of heating greatly improved.

The souvenir booklet presented to pupils to mark the Queen's Coronation in 1953

The Coronation of Queen Elizabeth in 1953 was a national event that was marked by the school. The children received souvenir medals and brochures and joined in a celebratory parade of the town.

Under the terms of the Education Act of 1944 all children received free milk in little third pint bottles, (albeit often frozen in the wintry temperatures in the school!). Dinner was also provided from the school's own kitchen, the cook being Mrs Martin from Omagh.

The school continued to suffer from the erratic water supply. It had been supposed that there would be sufficient to supply both the Derg Valley Hospital and the school from the Hospital source but there were difficulties in dry spells of weather. At times there was simply none and at other times it was turned off for lengthy periods to conserve supplies. Eventually the problem was solved when the town supply was laid on in 1955.

The Royal Family

Homage to the Queen

THE inevitable isolation of a Queen's office is assuaged by a happy family life. To her family the Queen can retire simply as Philip's wife and Charles' and Anne's mother. The greater cares of state become less in the personal cares and problems of bringing up a family; the joy of watching children develop their own character and inner drive. It is the highest office of the Queen's husband, the Duke of Edinburgh, that he provides our Queen with that family refuge from our cares and concerns. For this above all else we are grateful to him; his chivalry, as well as his energetic interest in public affairs, in science and technology, and in his profession as a naval officer, ensure him his unique place as reigns, the Royal Family is the ideal of British family solidarity everywhere. The family is the basis of all citizenship and self-forgetfulness.

To OUR QUEEN WE HAVE ALREADY PLEDGED OUR LOYALTY, FOR IT RISES naturally, with our love and respect for the woman, from full hearts. The office of kingship in the British family of nations to-day places an extraordinary burden upon the man or woman called to uphold it. The Queen must know all – all the uncertainties, all the dangers, that beset a hard-pressed country in a difficult time. Everything, wise or unwise, is done in her name. Yet she herself has no power beyond the gentle influence of a loving heart.

We all know that in times of stress action soothes the nerves, steadies the mind, mercifully restricts the imagination; a decision taken brings a sense of relief. No such relief is readily possible to a sovereign to-day. We require her to know all, to see all, to suffer all, reigning but not ruling, for she now is the symbol of the State and the community which shapes itself. We require her to be the visible link between a multitude of diverse peoples whose historic association is vital to peace and of immense material importance to us in Britain – yet only by personal friendship, charm and ceaseless social duty can she strengthen that bond. Hers is a lifelong vigil; an ever-renewed prayer that foresight, good sense and magnanimity will prevail in every crisis.

Do we realise what this must mean to human nerves, to an individual mind, however well schooled to take the strain, to a soul which knows that strain can never end save by death? It is to assure our Queen of our ever-renewed attempt to understand her burden that these words are written . . . in gratitude, in reverence.

4

The souvenir booklet presented to pupils to mark the Queen's Coronation in 1953

In 1955 Mr Sloan reported that valuable silver cups, which Captain Garnet Leary M.D., the local doctor, had presented to the school in February 1916, had somehow disappeared during the move to the new building in 1938 and "their whereabouts still remains a mystery." It was strange that this was the first and last mention of the disappearance.

Other problems encountered by the staff and pupils in the fifties included the condition of the roadway into the school and the playground that had deteriorated into a dangerous state. The latter was resurfaced in 1956 and was a great improvement while the road was not completed satisfactorily until 1965. However, over the years the condition of the road caused a lot of concern and seldom seemed to have been in a satisfactory state of repair.

Horticulture was regarded as an important facet of the curriculum. Mr Sloan was trained to teach the subject and the school garden became a regular feature in the lives of the senior boys who looked after its maintenance, grew all kinds of vegetables and sold them to the shops down town. It was considered a real treat to load the wheelbarrow and take the wares to the shops! Many boys remember sampling the tempting young vegetables as they carried out the various tasks!

Major Staff Changes.

Not only did the fifties bring major changes in the school curriculum, but Edwards school also witnessed a large turnover of staff.

Owing to an increase in the average number on rolls in 1953, the school was entitled to another assistant, so Mr Daniel McIlgorm of Coalisland was appointed to the position.

After only three years teaching in the school, he left to take up duty as Principal of Erganagh and the Management Committee expressed appreciation of his valuable work.

Mr W. H. Creighton of Dromara and Miss Mary F. Colvin of Warrenpoint were appointed as assistant teachers in 1956 while Mr H. Fox, a local man, was appointed as Caretaker.

In September 1957 Miss Millar retired after thirteen years service and Mr Norman Humes of Irvinestown filled her position. The committee wrote to Miss Millar conveying their thanks for her years of loyal service.

As the local population was increasing, this brought about an enrolment of 189 pupils in 1959, and the school required another assistant, so Mrs Margaret McCrea of Castlederg was appointed to the position.

Edwards School Staff 1962.
Mrs Caldwell, Mrs McCrea, Mrs McNutt, Mr Humes, Miss Elliott, Mr. Riddall (Principal)

The Retirement of Mr Sloan.

Mr J. G. Sloan retired from teaching in 1955, after twenty-five years as Principal. The committee recorded its appreciation of his excellent work and wished both him and Mrs Sloan health and happiness in the years to come. For a detailed report on Mr Sloan and his career please refer to the section on "Headmasters Over The Years".

The following article has been transcribed from a report in the Tyrone Constitution, of the quarterly meeting of Castlederg branch of the Ulster Teachers' Union, which was held in the Central Hotel on Wednesday 27th of July 1955:

"Mr. J. G. Sloan. M.A. (who has retired from the principalship of the Edwards School), relinquished his office of hon. secretary and treasurer of the branch, a position he has held since the death of his brother, in 1947. Mr. Sloan has been associated with the branch since its inception in 1933, when he was unanimously chosen as chairman, and since then he has taken an active interest in the work of the Union.

Mr. D. L. McIlgorm was appointed hon. secretary and treasurer, and a very enjoyable social evening followed.

The branch was happy to honour their general outgoing secretary and treasurer by making him the recipient of a very lovely automatic electric toaster as a token of their esteem and appreciation of his faithful attendances and discharge of his honorary duties.

Miss G. Elliott Chairman, in making the presentation, spoke of the cordial relationship for which the branch was specially noted, and wished Mr. and Mrs. Sloan very happy years of retirement and blessing in their new home. All the members present associated themselves with the chairman's remarks.

Mr. Sloan, who was deeply touched by the gift and tributary remarks of his fellow teachers, suitably replied.

Mr. Sloan, who, on Friday, 29th July, completed 45 years and one month in the teaching profession, 25 of which he had spent in the Edwards School (having acted as locum tenens during July) at a happy ceremony in the school, paid tribute to the loyalty and co-operation of his staff, past and present, and also to the friendly relationship which existed between teachers and pupils, many of whose parents has been taught by him when he succeeded the late Mr. T. J. Burnside B.A. He would always affectionately remember his pupils and with pride retain two letters received from gentlemen who visited the school with the late Mr. Wm. McHenry Mackey, secretary to the Educational Committee, commending him, as principal, on the very pleasant tone and genial atmosphere which prevailed throughout the Edwards School.

Miss G. Elliott, vice-principal, in wishing Mr. and Mrs. Sloan many happy years of blessing in their retirement, called on Miss May Hemphill, Listymore, a senior pupil, to present the pupils gift of a Standard Electric Lamp, to Mr. Sloan. This, May, very graciously and with well-chosen words did, amidst applause.

Miss Millar, on behalf of the present members of the staff, and with whom Mr. G. Starrett, a former assistant and now Principal of Letterbin P.S., wished to be associated, asked Mr. Sloan to accept the gift of a tea set. Mr. Sloan, having expressed his appreciation of their good wishes and gifts to himself and Mrs. Sloan, joined them in the words of "Auld Lang Syne" after which he said a personal good-bye to each one."

Mr T. F. Riddall   Principal 1955-1985.

When Mr Sloan intimated that he was to retire, the position was advertised and fifteen applications were received. Out of these Mr Thomas F. Riddall of Strabane, was chosen, and as he took up office in September of 1955 it was unlikely that he would have envisaged many of the changes he encountered during his time at the helm.

Like his predecessors, he too was a strict disciplinarian and expected high standards of work and behaviour throughout the school.

Mr Riddall believed in beginning the school day with Assembly and as there was no Hall, he utilised the long school corridor, lining classes along its length. He played the piano and many traditional hymns were sung. He maintained the tradition of encouraging hymn singing throughout his teaching career and many will recall two of his favourites--The Cowboy Carol and The Lord of the Dance. He also enjoyed the challenge of trying many new hymns, often having to persuade the staff to be as enthusiastic!

As a great lover of music he encouraged its development by purchasing recorders and percussion instruments and formed a school choir, to which many pupils were proud to belong.

He also ensured that the school had the latest audio equipment and every room was equipped with radio receivers so that BBC Schools' programmes were readily available.

Five years after he had assumed office, an Inspector stated, "the most pleasing feature of this six teacher school is the friendly open nature of the children, who are well mannered and hard working. All this is without doubt due to the careful planning and the general influence of a principal who is sincerely devoted to the interests of his pupils." Assistant teachers at that time were Miss G. Elliott, Mrs A. McNutt, Mrs M. Caldwell, Mrs M. McRea and Mr N. Humes.

The continuing success led to the presentation to the school in 1962, of the Carlisle and Blake Premium Prize, a much-coveted award for excellence. To mark the illustrious occasion each child received a pen.

From the mid sixties concerns were expressed about the increasingly poor state of repair of the school residence. "Ashburn," the home of the Riddall family, was one of the original dwelling houses erected on the Castlefin Road site in the early 1900's. It was suffering from damp and in poor decorative order. According to an evaluation it was worth about £1200. The County Committee was of the opinion that it was going to be too costly to repair it, so they proposed to dispose of it and supply two new residences, one for the Principal of Edwards and one for the Principal of the local Secondary school. It was placed in the hands of local auctioneers, "Robinson and Lecky" and the sum raised was used to assist in the building of the new residence.

By the mid sixties the new house, built in the grounds and adjacent to the school, was complete, and Mr and Mrs Riddall and their family moved in.

A sixties aerial photograph of the school and grounds with the hospital in the background.

Pupils in 1954

Edwards Sports Day 1959
Parents' Hoop Race
L-R: Mrs Kinloch, Mrs Connor, Mrs May Martin - now in her 90th year, unknown, Lady in behind unknown. Mrs Margaret Rowe, Unknown, Mrs Anna McNutt - teacher at the school, Mrs Moira Northridge (dec.) (Canon's Wife)

Parents and adults ball game at Edwards Primary School, Castlederg during their recent sports day.
2nd Cecil Patterson, 3rd Rev. Northridge, 5th Harry Trimble, 6th George Baskin, last Rev. Austin Hazard.

Messrs. Jack Buchanan and Roy Waugh, two of the organisers at Edwards School, Castlederg sports, pictured with a group of mothers and children during a break in the proceedings.

Miss Elliott's Retirement.

Miss Elliott's Retirement 1962
Junior Class with teacher Miss G. Elliott, David Young, Fred Kane, Thelma Roulston, Audrey Kerrigan,
Shirley Kerrigan, Keith Johnston, Oliver Marshall, Gordon McNutt, Ian Sturdee, Kay Marshall,
(not known), Maureen Sproule, James Caldwell, Robert Catterson, James Semple. Seated: Marie Catterson,
Thelma Fulton, Howard Irwin, Alan Wilson, Stephen Monteith, Joan Buchanan.

Teacher for 40 years

An insight into the emotions of Napoleon bidding farewell to his troops at Fontainebleau may have been gained yesterday by Miss Georgina Elliott, vice-principal of Edwards Primary School, Castlederg, Co. Tyrone.

She ended her 40 years' teaching career yesterday, and is shown in the smaller picture saying goodbye to the last generation of pupils she will teach.

However, while Napoleon was heading for exile at Elba and ultimately St. Helena, Miss Elliott is thinking of a

STORY BY T. G. M'Evoy
PICTURES: Cecil M'Causland

round trip—a world cruise, in fact—and will be returning to Castlederg at the end of it.

Trained at Kildare Place, Dublin, Miss Elliott first taught at Convoy, Co. Donegal, for four years. She went to Edwards School in 1926, and remained there for the rest of her teaching career.

> The school was founded by a bequest of Hugh Edwards, who owned Castlegrove Estate, Castlederg. Miss Elliott's present home, Dartan House, Castlederg, was formerly his residence.
>
> Teaching has not monopolised all Miss Elliott's energies. For 10 years she was chairman of Castlederg branch of the Ulster Teachers' Union; she was secretary of the Ulster Savings group in the school for 20 years, and has received the R.N.L.I. medal for her work as an area organiser. She is the only woman member of the select vestry of the parish church, and superintendent of the Sunday school.
>
> More than 400 former pupils and friends met yesterday to honour her.
>
> Her farewell words—"I'll miss the school very much,

In most organisations there are constant changes in staff and Edwards School was no exception. During Mr Riddall's reign there were many changes, one the most notable being the retirement of Miss Georgina Elliott in 1962. She had been teaching in the school from her appointment in 1926 and the Committee recognised the sterling service she had given over the thirty-six years spent in the school. A special presentation was held and glowing tributes were paid to her.

Although she retired from teaching she continued to take a lively interest in the school, acting as a member of the management committee for sixteen years. After leaving the area to live at Drumbo, near Lisburn, she paid frequent return visits and was always delighted to renew friendships.

In 1972 she presented a cup for the winner of an annual Story Telling Competition, beginning a tradition that continues to this day. (For more information on Miss Elliott see section on past members of staff.)

Sporting Chances.

10 GARNET TERRACE,

CASTLEDERG 23ʳᵈ Dec 19 55

The Principal
Edwards School Castlederg

ROBERT J. KING Dr.

Building Contractor

Dear Sir

As requested herewith Estimate amounting to £9-10-6 for supplying & erecting Goal Posts at Edwards School with Timber to sizes as specified & painted white

Robert J King

The estimate for the supply and erecting of new school goal posts.

Throughout his career Mr Riddall always endeavoured to make the school a better seat of learning. Not only was the academic side of life fully promoted, but also he aimed to provide as many opportunities as possible to enhance the all-round development of his pupils.

As a keen sportsman he encouraged cricket, football and netball, purchasing the necessary indoor and outdoor equipment, providing a pitch and transporting his young protégées to games in far-flung destinations such as Sion- Mills!

Large crowds came to watch the local sides play cricket and matches against past pupils and parents were keenly contested affairs. Many past pupils refer to the sport as the highlight of their elementary education and fondly recall those halcyon days. The cricket match reports from the "Con" manage to capture something of the flavour of those glorious occasions!

CRICKET

Edwards' Primary School v. Prior School (Lifford)

Above match, which was played at the Edwards' School ground, attracted much local interest. Prior batted first and put up the very respectable total of 57 runs. McCay, contributing 20. V. Porter, D. Baxter and D. Semple bowled well for the home side, the first two being particularly outstanding and John Forbes was a most confident wicket keeper. Edwards' opened their innings with Lindsay, N., and Baxter but a rot set in and four batsmen were dismissed for a small score. Lindsay continued to defy the bowlers and his total runs moved up to 25 when he retired and the wicket was now occupied by his brother. R. Lindsay, and B. Wilson, who knocked up 15 and 12 respectively. There were 15 extras, and with their total at 75 for 5 Edwards' declared. The batting of the brothers Lindsay was the subject of much comment, their fine stroke play contributing much to the evening's enjoyment by all present.

Mr Riddall regarded the importance of proper equipment as paramount and many boys still recall the excitement of having real goal posts for the first time. They proved much better than the thorn hedge! (See the estimate from R. J. King.) Good quality footballs were also purchased from time to time and the boys met after school to develop their skills.

But sporting occasions were not solely confined to games. Mr Riddall was responsible for introducing Sports Day as a major feature of the school year. Fading photographs record those wonderful family fun days and in 1957 the management committee congratulated the Principal and staff on their effort!

Mr Riddall began the tradition of marching down from the playground to the field in a long line, led by a bell ringer. Many adults still remember this and look back with amusement as they recollect the excitement and sense of anticipation as they made their way down, mostly in glorious sunshine! Such was the sense of occasion that the Union Flag was flown proudly from the flagpole!

The winners were presented with cups and badges, many of these being purchased out of the Endowment Fund. One of the first cups presented to the school for the Relay race was the Coyle Cup, donated by Mr Pat Coyle, who was asked by Mr Riddall to supply the treat of ice cream on Sports Day. That tradition continues to this day and is still eagerly anticipated by the children!

TYRONE COUNTY EDUCATION COMMITTEE

Nᵒ 890

1st June 19 57

Received from Mr J J Riddall

the sum of _____ four Pounds

_____ no Shillings and _____ no Pence

being for Sale of Scrap iron from Edwards P.S.

£ 4 : 0 : 0

Receipt for Scrap Iron

208

Sale of Old School.

The benefits of being an Endowed School were illustrated in a letter received by Mr Riddall in 1961. The County Education Committee informed him, "in or about the year 1939 the Strabane and Castlederg Regional Education Committee disposed of part of the property known as Edwards Old School and the proceeds of the sale amounted to £350 which was transferred to the County Council." The sum had been deposited and with interest it amounted to £580. This had been reinvested in Defence Bonds and interest of £29 per annum was to be added to the Endowment Scheme. The Principal was requested to suggest ways of spending the accumulated sum of £85/7/1 and a record player and records were duly purchased.

Staff Changes.

Following Miss Elliott's departure, Miss A. E. Hemphill (later Mrs Waugh) from Castlederg, joined the staff as an assistant teacher, while Mrs McNutt became Vice Principal, a position she relinquished in 1970. In 1965 Mr R. S. Stronge from Trillick was appointed and in 1966 Mrs I. Andrews was transferred from Gortnagross School, which was closing. Mrs McCrea was placed in charge of remedial education in 1967 and Mr Stronge moved to Omagh P.S. (although he was to return as Vice Principal in 1970). Mr D. McKittrick was appointed to replace him. Further changes took place in 1968 when Mrs M. E. F. Bleakley of Castlederg, was appointed and the next year saw the arrival of local girl, Miss M. E. Clarke, (later Mrs Watt) along with Miss Y. Hamill from Coleraine.

One of the most striking aspects of the appointments procedure was its apparent ease and simplicity. An application was received and considered by the school committee and a decision made. Interviews for positions began in 1969 for the first time. It is also worth noting that it was acceptable then to advertise for a "Male Assistant" and indeed if this criterion was not met, the post was often re-advertised until a suitable candidate was found.

School Uniform is Introduced.

In 1965 Mr Riddall again received an admirable inspection report. Mr D. M. Collie remarked, "The excellent administration of this school by the Principal, himself a very able teacher, the willing co-operation of his staff in implementing the liberally planned and comprehensive programme; and the ready response of the pupils, both orally and in writing, again call for very high commendation."

He took great pride in the school and expected his teachers and students to do so too. Canon A. H. Northridge, as Chairman of the Management Committee, remembers accompanying Mr Riddall to visit a descendant of the Edwards family in Sligo to ask permission to use the Edwards symbols of the chough and the fretted chevron in a school badge, with the ultimate intention of incorporating it into a school uniform.

The first Edwards woven badge features the blue bird on a yellow background.

The first badge was of cloth and featured a blue bird on a yellow background. The badge was sewn onto the school cap that was worn by many boys. To begin with, the uniform consisted of a Royal blue jumper with the badge sewn on it, a blue shirt and blue and yellow striped tie. The boys wore grey trousers and the girls had navy skirts. It was gradually introduced in the eighties, starting with the infant classes and building up to seniors. The Principal, staff and pupils, were indeed very proud of the new look and were complimented by many on their smart appearance.

The uniform has remained but has had some slight adaptations over the years. The badge was amended to include the name of the school, which was placed inside an outer circle. The symbols in the centre were altered to include the castle turrets at the top, the chevron, which many interpret as the bridge over the River Derg and the chough, the Edwards symbol. From being a sewn-on feature, the badge was later printed, in various sizes, on the jumper and P.E. shirts. Presently it is woven into the fabric and has been worn with pride by all Edwards' pupils since its introduction.

Royal blue jumpers were difficult to obtain so gradually navy jumpers replaced them. The trend today has been towards a more casual look and yellow t-shirts and navy sweatshirts are worn. On more formal occasions, such as when representing the school at any function, or when the choir is performing, white shirts and the blue and yellow ties are worn.

Enamelled brooches, incorporating the school crest were purchased in 1964 using the Endowment Fund. Some past pupils still have these mementos of their school days.

Edwards pupils in the early sixties.

Communications Improve!

While it is hard for us to envisage life without the many forms of communication that we take for granted today, the first television was obtained for the school in 1961 and a second purchased in 1971. It was the job of the Caretaker, Sammy Reid, to ensure that the set was taken to each room, as it was required. Initially Sammy carried the large, heavy set around but later a trolley was bought to help him transport it more easily.

The first colour television set was purchased from the Endowment Fund in 1978 and for many years it too was moved around the school on a trolley.

The first telephone was installed in the school in 1971 and an arrangement was made to have an extension to the Principal's residence.

Today we can't imagine how they ever existed without these items!

The Formation of the Special Unit.

Mr Riddall had a keen interest in all children under his care and he wished to provide equal opportunities for every one. Aware of gaps in the provision, he established an early "Special Unit" for children with learning difficulties. Mrs Gladys McKinley was appointed as Special Needs teacher in 1974 and although no classroom was available, she began work in a cordoned-off part of the corridor and since then the unique Unit has provided a valuable service in the school and has doubled in size over the years. A mobile classroom was provided in 1975 and the Unit became an integral part of the school building in 1978. Inspectors' reports have always been complimentary and many children owe their success to the assistance they received in the Special Unit.

The Troubles.

The seventies and eighties were turbulent years and few were untouched by the effects of bomb and bullet. The town of Castlederg was the target of bombers on a great number of occasions and sadly many members of the security forces were killed. These events brought trauma and grief into the schools too but staff endeavoured to keep the school open and to maintain a semblance of normality in the difficult times.

On one occasion in April 1990, following the detonation of a particularly large bomb at the local Police Station, the school suffered damage to six classrooms, to windows in the front of the school, and to the Assembly Hall roof. Consequently, it had to be closed for three days to allow staff to clear up broken glass and remove books and items that had been affected. The Principal thanked everyone involved in the clean up operation and expressed relief that there were no injuries to children as the bomb had exploded during the night.

Following the bomb there was concern about the safety of the children in the event of further attacks and there was even the suggestion of safety glass being installed in the Assembly Hall, although this never happened and the school remained unaffected.

The Computer Age.

Teachers in the eighties witnessed many changes in education but one of the most far reaching was the introduction of computers. Mr Riddall, who loved to be at the forefront of technology, was passionately enthused by the dreaded beasts! Members of staff found it hard to share his enthusiasm and tried to avoid them, muttering that they wouldn't be seen dead with one of them, but the Principal refused to give up. He endeavoured to help teachers come to terms with machines that had greater memories than themselves, mice which had no legs and didn't squeak, but could move rapidly and silently, cassettes which did more than play music and drives which weren't in the car. Teachers today would not recognise the ancient forms of prehistoric computers! Eventually he succeeded in his mission to convert teachers to modern communication technology and computers became the norm in every classroom.

School Trips.

Mr Riddall was a born organiser and for many years was responsible for the joint churches Sunday School Trips.

He realised the benefit of first hand experiences and encouraged children to go on educational visits. These might have only been to local factories and were certainly not far flung travels but they were new experiences for many children. The local Education Committee provided free transport, but this was withdrawn for primary schools in 1967, much to the dismay of the school committee. Children had enjoyed trips but the Principal did not wish to pass costs on to parents, so many of them ceased. A trip for senior pupils to the large exhibition

"Ulster '71" in Belfast was paid for using the Endowment Fund.

On one particular occasion a wonderful day trip to Girvan in Scotland was organised by Mr H. Faulkner. Senior pupils and staff set off at an early hour, travelled to Larne, took the ferry to Scotland, ventured up the coast to Girvan, spent a short time there and made the return journey, all within twenty four hours!! Some members of staff, who remained in a state of exhaustion for many days afterwards, thought that the epic journey should have been known as "The Longest Day!" Needless to say such excursions were not repeated.

Gifts.

Following the First World War, a Roll of Honour was presented to the school by a former pupil, George Nesbitt, Esq, M.P., N.S.W. Australia, naming all past "old boys" of Edwards who had been involved in the War.

George was a son of the late Mr J. S. Nesbitt, Master of the Workhouse, and he had emigrated to New South Wales in the 1880's. He became a commercial traveller and was recognised as a distinguished businessman, playing important roles in the society in which he lived.

Mr Nesbitt had made the presentation following a visit to the school, when he was so impressed by the splendid response of sixty-six "old boys" who had volunteered in the hour of their country's need.

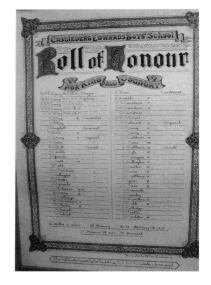

An article in the Tyrone Constitution in October 1919 stated, "Mr Nesbitt's kindness in presenting such an artistic and endurable record of these achievements is deeply appreciated, and it is most gratifying to all concerned that his name is to be permanently associated with the school by this memorial Roll of Honour."

It is a beautifully inscribed and decorative manuscript with copperplate handwriting and is highly regarded as part of the history of the school, when is referred to each November at the school's Remembrance Service.

Interestingly, in 1965 Mr Riddall received an unusual and greatly appreciated gift. Mr E. T. R. Herdman, son of the late Capt. J.C. Herdman D.L., presented the key that Mrs Herdman used to open the school in 1938. It was suggested that it should be displayed in a suitable glass case but this did not happen, although the key is still securely kept in the school.

Another gift, which is still seen and appreciated by many, is the Castlederg Market Bell, which was presented to the school in 1979 by Rev. Harry Trimble. The bell, which had been acquired by his grandfather, Mr Thomas Scott, who was the last full time clerk of the markets, had been rung to mark the start of trade. It was mounted on a plinth and placed adjacent to the door of the school and indeed tempted many children to give it a good ring as they passed by!
Rev. Trimble also presented the accompanying Market notice giving information about the times when trade commenced.
When the 1938 school was demolished, Mr Jack Sproule built a new plinth and the bell was moved to a prominent position on the paved entrance area of the 2005 building.
The school was also presented with the A.R.P. hand bell after the war and it is still in daily use, summoning children from the playground into dinner and for signalling the walk to the field on Sports Day.

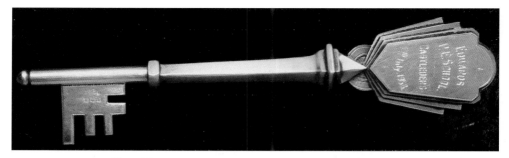

The gold key used by Mrs Herdman to open the 1938 building.

This 19th Century Market Yard Bell was presented by
Rev. Harry Trimble B.Th. to Edwards Primary School in 1979.
His Grandfather, Thomas Scott, was Clerk of the Markets
from 1900-1941

The A.R.P. Bell

Difficulties in the Sixties and Seventies.

The sixties saw a period of growth in the town population and this was reflected in the increasing attendance at Edwards. The average enrolment in 1969 was 260, and the school, which had been built for a maximum of 230 pupils, was bursting at the seams. Mobile classrooms provided in 1968 and 1971 helped to ease the accommodation problems but there were increasing problems with the aging building. The Committee requested the replacement of the iron window frames and the levelling of all wooden floors in 1966. They also welcomed the news that they had been promised a new extension.

Storage space was a continual problem and Mr Riddall provided additional shelving in rooms and on windowsills. Extra desks, chairs and equipment such as maths apparatus, sand and water trays, a balancing beam and mats, a Lego set and an art easel were also ordered.

Teachers and children frequently complained about the lack of heat in the school and in May 1962 Mr Riddall noted in the committee minutes, "Despite careful nursing by the Caretaker, the school heating system appears to be impaired by certain defects in the boiler" and it was hoped that the County Committee would consider converting the system to oil burning."

Unfortunately nothing was done and in 1968 a proposal suggested, "The Co. Education Committee should immediately investigate the present heating arrangements in the main building. The loose fitting iron-framed windows are considerably reducing the effectiveness of the rather old coke-fired boiler, when towards noon, this does succeed in sending any heat to the radiators." A year later the situation was no better and the management committee expressed the hope that it would be dealt with before the next autumn.

Perhaps one of the most constant recurring problems that was dealt with by the committee was the issue of the school road. In the fifties the County Council was reluctant to assume responsibility for its upkeep, as it was not regarded as a public road. Because no one else accepted responsibility for maintaining it, the road fell into a dangerous state and in November 1974 the committee noted with great concern that the potholes were two- three inches deep. An increasing number of vehicles were using it and by June 1975 the conditions were still worsening and debate rambled on over ownership. In April 1976 the Committee reported that there was still no progress but thankfully by October 1976 it was revealed that the Road Services would adopt and maintain the School road. In September 1977 it was noted in the committee minutes that the Road Services were asked to commence the repair of the road, which they said would be completed in time for the opening of the school extension in 1978!

Unfortunately the problems were only solved for a short time and in 1981 the committee recorded that the school road was once again deeply rutted and asked for "complete adoption by the Roads Service." It was not until 1984 that the road was finally brought up to standard—thirty years after first being an issue in the minutes!!

The old dry stone wall in the Sports Field was suffering from the ravages of time and the elements and was reported in 1978 to be in a dangerous condition. A request for urgent attention was made to the Western Education and Library Board and in March 1979 they agreed to replace the wall with a wire fence. Part of the wall along the western perimeter, which was considered to be secure and not causing problems, was untouched and the rest of the boundary was fenced. As far back as February 1959, the management committee had suggested converting the central meals kitchen into a dining room and central hall but progress was extremely slow. In 1961 Mr Riddall learnt that in response to his requests for additional accommodation, the Ministry had approved, in principle, to the provision of a 150 meals kitchen and the request for an assembly hall had been referred to an architect.

Almost ten years later the County Committee indicated that they had plans to begin an extension to the accommodation in the 1971-1972 school year. Mr Riddall continued to negotiate with officials in the Western Education and Library Board, (which had replaced the old County Committee), and finally in 1973 design plans for the new extension were forwarded to the Ministry of Education. They were approved in 1974 with some adjustments. A request for curtains in the Assembly Hall was rejected and instead blackout curtaining was suggested. It was also proposed that the play shed that had been used as a garage should revert to its former purpose.

By 1974 half of the school's pupils were being taught in temporary accommodation and the facilities for P.E. and assemblies were "totally inadequate." The committee was "not at all satisfied with progress of the building programme."

Over a year later the contract, which had been accepted by the builder, was still awaiting the final approval of the Department of Education. (Formerly the Ministry of Education) This frustrating situation dragged on and in March 1976 the Management Committee were said to be "extremely perturbed...in a building climate of rising costs."

At last, building work began in August 1976 and the Contracting firms were asked if they could finish the job in fifteen months. Unfortunately they were unable to meet the schedule and the work took 20 months to complete. The Principle Architect was Mr J. McFarland and the contractors were John A. Gamble and Co., Strabane, while the Supervising Architect was Mr Hubert Turner.

When the work was nearing completion the management committee then had to turn their thoughts to preparing for a Grand Opening. In January 1978 a sub-committee was set up to deal with the guest list, the plaque, hospitality and the printing of the invitations.

The Opening of the Extension in 1978.

WESTERN EDUCATION & LIBRARY BOARD

Edwards Controlled Primary School
CASTLEDERG

The Edwards School Management Committee
invites

Rev. Canon and Mrs A. H. Northridge

to be present at the Re-opening of the school after extension and renovation, on
Wednesday 31st May, 1978 at 2.00p.m.

(Management Committee)

R.S.V.P. before 15th May to the Principal   *Reception 1.45 p m.*

Invitation to the opening

The long awaited extension, costing £200,000, consisted of five new classrooms, a special unit for children with learning difficulties, an assembly hall and kitchen, offices, stores and a staff room and was ready for opening in May 1978. Renovations were also carried out on the existing classrooms; new windows and floors were installed and rooms were painted and decorated.

Many plans were laid in place for the official re-opening and Miss Elliott was invited to return to perform the opening ceremony. It was indeed a proud day for Mr Riddall and the staff.

The occasion took place on Wednesday 31st of May 1978, and was blessed by beautiful weather. Miss G. Elliott, who said she was honoured to play a part in the ceremony, unveiled a plaque and performed the grand opening. The Chairman of the management committee, Canon A. H. Northridge, thanked her and paid tribute to her long career in Edwards. He went on to briefly outline the history of the school and wished the Principal and staff every success in the future. Dr W. J. Patterson, vice-chairman of the Management Committee, thanked the Western Education and Library Board for the finance for the extension while Mr Riddall thanked the contractor and architects. Mr F. Horisk, replied on behalf of the Board and said that the building was unique, incorporating a special unit and saving children from having to journey to Omagh. He appealed for support and co-operation from parents and teachers in ensuring as good an education as possible for the children.

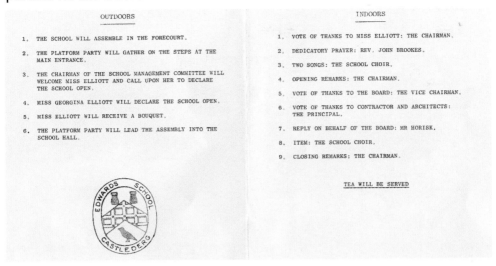

OUTDOORS

1. THE SCHOOL WILL ASSEMBLE IN THE FORECOURT.

2. THE PLATFORM PARTY WILL GATHER ON THE STEPS AT THE MAIN ENTRANCE.

3. THE CHAIRMAN OF THE SCHOOL MANAGEMENT COMMITTEE WILL WELCOME MISS ELLIOTT AND CALL UPON HER TO DECLARE THE SCHOOL OPEN.

4. MISS GEORGINA ELLIOTT WILL DECLARE THE SCHOOL OPEN.

5. MISS ELLIOTT WILL RECEIVE A BOUQUET.

6. THE PLATFORM PARTY WILL LEAD THE ASSEMBLY INTO THE SCHOOL HALL.

INDOORS

1. VOTE OF THANKS TO MISS ELLIOTT: THE CHAIRMAN.

2. DEDICATORY PRAYER: REV. JOHN BROOKES.

3. TWO SONGS: THE SCHOOL CHOIR.

4. OPENING REMARKS: THE CHAIRMAN.

5. VOTE OF THANKS TO THE BOARD: THE VICE CHAIRMAN.

6. VOTE OF THANKS TO CONTRACTOR AND ARCHITECTS: THE PRINCIPAL.

7. REPLY ON BEHALF OF THE BOARD: MR HORISK.

8. ITEM: THE SCHOOL CHOIR.

9. CLOSING REMARKS: THE CHAIRMAN.

TEA WILL BE SERVED

The programme for the opening of the extension in 1978

The school choir performed "I'd like to teach the world to sing" and "Killeter Fair" and Rev. J. Brookes, the Methodist Minister, said a dedicatory prayer. Bouquets of flowers were presented to Miss Elliott by Jacqueline Sproule and Desmond Thompson and to Miss Isobel Dick, (Schools Meals Supervisor), by Mrs McNutt. The ladies served tea and a special cake to mark the occasion.

Miss Georgina Elliott unveiling the opening plaque accompanied
by Canon A. Northridge and Mr T.F. Riddall.

Staff at the 1978 opening.
L - R: Group on left of Sign: Mrs A. McNutt, Miss Joan Wilson, Miss H. McNutt, Mr. T. F. Riddall, Mrs A. Waugh.
In Front of Sign: Mr H. Woods, Mr I. Gowdy.
To Right: Mrs G. McKinley, Mrs P. Bratton, Mrs H. Graham, Mrs M. Caldwell, Mrs M. Watt.

Mr Riddall, along with the staff and pupils, greatly appreciated and were justifiably proud of the spacious new facilities. The Principal at last had the luxury of a purpose built office, albeit a small one! He was also given an additional 15 hours of clerical or classroom assistance and Mrs Walls, the secretary, found herself in a dual role.

The ladies committee who were responsible for making and serving tea at the opening of the extension.

P.E. took on another dimension in the new hall, with its wide selection of large and small apparatus. The dual-purpose building was also used as a dinner hall and relieved the overcrowded rooms that had previously been used. The new kitchen provided Cook, Myrtle Lyttle and her team, with state of the art facilities while for the infant teachers the new classrooms were pleasant and bright and the Special Unit became a happy base for those with learning difficulties. Caretaker Sammy Reid was blessed with new equipment and a store in which to keep his cleaning materials and tools. New floors and fresh décor enhanced the other classrooms giving the school a new lease of life!

Miss Georgina Elliott receiving a bouquet of flowers from Jacqueline Sproule and Desmond Thompson, following the opening of the extension in 1978.

The onslaught of educational change was, and is, never-ending. In the early eighties the Government introduced "Primary Guidelines," far-reaching proposals for changes in every subject area. Mr Riddall held countless, long meetings, immersing the staff in all the details and preparing them to cope with the changes.

The expression "professional development" was virtualy unheard of, but the Headmaster who was ahead of his time, prompted members of staff to attend training days and to be fully aware of new ideas. Every detail of school life was planned with precision and teachers and pupils were left in no doubt about what was expected.

Parents were also kept informed of their child's progress, initially in the form of a simple report and later at "Parent Interviews," which were held twice yearly.

Panto Time!

In the seventies Mr Riddall was a member of the local amateur drama group, Omagh Players, and he went on to become a founder member of the Derg Players. His enthusiasm spilled over into school and he began to encourage teachers and pupils to promote the areas of speech and drama.

Photographs of some of the early pantomimes.

With the new hall at his disposal he launched into school performances with great gusto. A stage was erected in the corridor linking the hall with the other rooms meaning children had access from both sides. The improvised stage was made up of the old dinner tables covered with chipboard and carpet to inhibit noise. All children, from the smallest infant to the oldest seniors, were encouraged to become involved in drama.

Miss Heather McNutt helped to stage the initial productions, to which parents and friends were invited to come and witness their children's first attempts at

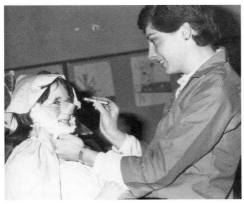

Miss Heather McNutt applying stage make up to a pupil.

treading the boards. This was to lead to shows being a regular feature of the school calendar for many years. They varied from short performances by each class to become two hourly pantomimes, held on two nights and planned meticulously by the Principal.

The author remembers writing many scripts and staging pantomimes with the willing help of all the other members of staff and pupils, who, uncomplainingly,

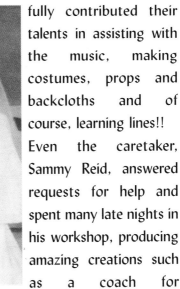

fully contributed their talents in assisting with the music, making costumes, props and backcloths and of course, learning lines!!

Even the caretaker, Sammy Reid, answered requests for help and spent many late nights in his workshop, producing amazing creations such as a coach for

Cinderella, trees for a forest, portable backcloths, wishing wells and fire places! The three corridor lights were the only stage lighting and that was considered totally inadequate for the "West End" of Castlederg! Once again, Sammy's expertise was called upon and in a very short time we had the first lighting bar made from large catering tins and 250-watt bulbs! Later on, at great expense, two spotlights were purchased, but Sammy's system was by far the best! (Lasting right up to the change to the new school in 2005)!!

Entire days were taken up with practising and the budding actors and actresses played to full houses! School life was less pressurised then and great enjoyment was derived from these productions. But no sooner was one performance over than the Principal was requesting the draft for the next show.........

Two narrators, Sharon Mortland (kneeling) and Irene Harpur who took part in the play "The Smiling Prince".

Over Three Decades of Appointments and Retirements.

The last three decades of the twentieth century witnessed huge changes in Edwards school, both in terms of the building and staff. This section attempts to record the changes in staff and because of their frequently occurring nature they have been grouped together.

The seventies began with the appointments of Mr H. J. Faulkner, Omagh, as P6 teacher, Miss E. E. H. Gardiner, Armagh and Mrs F. E. Marshall, Omagh, as assistants in 1971, the choice of Mr Sammy Reid as Caretaker in 1972, and the approval of Mr Faulkner as Vice- Principal in the same year. Mrs Marshall left in 1972 and was replaced by Miss G. M. Tate, (later Mrs Faulkner).

Mrs McCrea retired in 1972 after thirteen years in the school and Mrs McNutt who assumed responsibility for remedial teaching filled her position. Mr I. D. Gowdy and Miss Iris Barclay also joined the staff.

Also in 1972 Mr Sammy Reid was appointed to fill the important role of School Caretaker.

Edwards Staff in 1972
Back Row L - R: Mrs Margaret Watt, Mrs Georgina Faulkner, Mrs Ann Waugh, Mrs May Caldwell,
Mrs Iris Barclay, Mrs Yvette Brown.
Front Row L - R: Mr Henry Faulkner, Mrs Anna McNutt, Mr T.F. Riddall,
Miss Heather Gardiner, Mr I.D. Gowdy.

Edwards Staff 1973

Back Row L - R: Mr S. Reid (Caretaker), Mrs I. Allen, Mrs H. Graham, Mrs G. McKinley, Miss J. Wilson, Mrs M. Watt, Miss J. Acheson, Mr I. Gowdy.

Front Row L-R: Mrs G. Faulkner, Mr H. Faulkner, Mrs A. McNutt, Mr T.F. Riddall, Mrs M. Caldwell.

The year 1973 brought the appointment of Mrs F.V. Hall who succeeded Mrs Y. Brown.

The management committee continued to be busy in 1974 when Miss E. E. Roulston, Miss C. J. Acheson, Miss H. Wilson (later Mrs Graham) and Mrs G. McKinley were all appointed to the staff. A new management committee met on August 1st 1974, with Canon A. Northridge in the Chair and Rev. Dr W. Patterson as Vice Chairman.

Miss H. McNutt, daughter of Mrs A. McNutt, qualified to teach in 1975, and joined her mother on the staff. The committee advertised several times, unsuccessfully, for an infant teacher to replace Miss Acheson.

1976 saw the arrival of Mr T. S. Bratton, as Vice-Principal, and Mrs P. E. Bratton as assistant teacher for P1. Mrs E. C. Walls was appointed as school secretary as administration was ever- increasing.

Mr Bratton left in 1977 to become Headmaster in Ardstraw and Mr H. J. Woods was appointed as his successor. Mrs Jean Bogle was also appointed as a part time cleaner in the same year while Dr. M. Brown became a new face on the committee.

Miss Joan Wilson, who had been teaching temporarily, left to return to Australia in 1978 and Miss H. Bleakley (later Mrs McCay) filled her position.

The new Special Unit attracted more children and in 1978, out of seventeen applications, Mrs V. McKibbin was appointed as the first Classroom Assistant for the Special Unit and Infants while an additional fifteen hours of clerical or classroom assistance time was granted to help manage the increase in work levels.

Due to the growing numbers of children walking to the school, the committee felt it was necessary to provide supervision to assist crossing the Strabane Road, so the Western Education and Library Board appointed a School Crossing Patrol man at "The Points." It was also agreed that the Hospital Road Gate should be restricted to children and parents on foot.

Staff Photograph 1979/80
Back Row L - R: Mrs Helen Graham, Miss Myrtle Lyttle, Mr Sammy Reid,
Mrs Darragh, Mrs Hazel McCay,
Middle Row: Mrs Elizabeth Walls, Miss Patricia Fergie, Mrs R. Irwin,
Mrs May Henderson, Mrs Irvine, Miss Hazel Beacom, Mrs Patricia Jones.
Front Row L - R: Mrs Pamela Bratton, Mr Ivan Gowdy, Mrs Margaret Watt,
Mr Thomas Riddall (Headmaster). Mrs Anna McNutt, Mr Harry Woods (V.P), Mrs Gladys McKinley.

Miss H. McNutt left in 1980 and was replaced by Miss E. M. Beacom, who was selected from twenty-two applicants.

After serving thirty-one years on the school management committee, most of them in the role of Chairman, Canon Northridge resigned in 1982. He was retiring from his incumbency in Derg Parish Church and was leaving the area. His expertise and sound advice had been greatly valued by the Principal and staff, who extended their good wishes.

Staff Photograph 1980
Back Row L - R: Mrs H. Graham, Mrs V. McKibbin, Miss M. Keys, Mrs E. Walls,
Miss E. Beacom, Mrs G. McKinley, Mrs H. McCay, Mrs P. Bratton.
Front Row L - R: Mrs M. Watt, Mr I. Gowdy, Mrs M. Caldwell, Mr T.F. Riddall,
Mrs A. McNutt, Mr H. Woods, Mrs A. Waugh

Rev. Dr. W.T. Patterson, who had been Vice Chairman since 1974, succeeded him as Chairman, with Rev. W. Quill in place as Vice-Chairman, but this situation was short lived as Dr Patterson moved to Killinchy Presbyterian Church in 1983. Rev. Quill took over the position of Chairman and Mr Ernest Young became Vice Chairman.

Sadly Mr Young passed away in 1984, having served on the committee for ten years.

Miss Beacom, who had been an asset to the school as its "resident pianist" and had willingly assisted at many school productions, resigned her position and moved to Castledawson in 1985. Miss Lorna Harron from Castlederg, replaced her.

The year 1985 was remarkable for the number of major staffing changes; Mrs

Caldwell retired after "34.5 years," as the Minutes precisely state, Mr Riddall retired in August 1985, after thirty years, and Mr A. S. Orr was appointed to succeed him. However, Mr Orr was not released from his present position to commence in September, as he had hoped, and was only able to begin in Edwards in December.

Following the Education Act of 1984, when it was recommended in the Aston Report that every school should have a separate Board of Governors, Edwards P.S. adopted the recommendations of the WELB and Mr Orr attended the first Board of Governors meeting on December 10th 1985. Just before Christmas they made their first appointment of Mrs I. Crockett as an additional Classroom Assistant.

Teachers with musical ability are always welcome in Primary Schools and in May 1986 Miss Judith Anderson from Belfast, was appointed to the staff to take Year 3 with special responsibility for music. She too was an asset to the school as she helped out at many functions in her capacity as pianist and choir mistress.

Mrs McNutt retired in 1986 after thirty-seven years and Mrs Waugh took her remedial post.

In March 1988 Mrs S. Sproule was appointed as a Classroom Assistant in the Special Unit, a position that she still holds, and Mrs V. Anderson became a supervisory assistant, helping out with duties in the dinner hall and playground After three years in Edwards Miss Harron left Year 5 in June 1988 and was replaced by Mrs H. M. Robinson, while Mrs Watt moved to the Special Unit to take the Infants. Miss M. W. Condy from Castlederg, (later Mrs West), who was appointed in October 1988, took her position in the Year 3 class.

The extension of the Special Unit in 1988 meant that a classroom had to be converted to suit that purpose, so Room 9, in which Year 3 had been taught, became the home for the Seniors with Mrs G. McKinley and Miss J. Anderson moved with Year 3 up the corridor to Room 2. Room 10 was renovated to suit Mrs M. Watt and the Infants. New windows were fitted and the room was carpeted and furnished. Additional storage space, a washroom and changing facilities were also provided.

In December 1988 Miss C. J. Cummings, (later Mrs Hawkes), was appointed to the staff to teach Year 3 when Miss J. Anderson left. She also became responsible for taking the choir and had responsibility for music throughout the school.

The first appointment in January 1989 was Mrs S. M. Quigley, who became the second Classroom Assistant in the Special Unit. In March Mrs O. E. Reid became a supervisory assistant,

Also in 1989, Rev. W. Quill, Chairman of the Board of Governors, became a Canon of Derry Cathedral and was congratulated by Mr Orr, the Governors and staff.

In 1990 the Board planned to establish an Outreach scheme in the Castlederg area using a peripatetic teacher to help poor achievers in reading. Following negotiations it was agreed to base a teacher in Edwards, allowing them to travel to surrounding schools within a ten mile radius to provide help to a number of children with reading difficulties. Mrs H. Robinson moved to the Outreach position in 1991 and Mrs H. McCay moved up to Year 5. Mrs C. Hawkes then moved down to Room 8 to teach Year 2.

Staff Photograph 1988/89
Back Row L - R: Mrs H. Robinson, Miss M. Condy, Mrs G. McKinley,
Mrs P. Quigley, Miss C. Cummings, Mrs S. Sproule, Mrs E. Walls.
Front Row L - R: Mr. I. Gowdy, Mrs H. McCay, Mrs P. Bratton, Mr A.S. Orr,
Mrs M. Watt, Mrs H. Graham, Mrs A. Waugh, Mr H. Woods.

Mrs Waugh took early retirement in 1991 following a drop in the school's enrolment figures and in order to continue the valuable work with children who needed Remedial help, Mrs P. L. Stewart was appointed in June 1991.

Mrs Waugh's departure meant that there was a vacancy for the Teachers' Representative on the Board of Governors, so Mrs G. McKinley took her place. In the same year Mrs A. E. Sproule was appointed as a Supervisor to deal with lunchtime duties.

Miss J. Douglas from Tandragee joined the staff in June 1992 to replace Mrs West who moved to Dungannon. Up until 1998 Miss Douglas taught Year 2 but when Mrs Bratton took over reading recovery she moved to take Year 1.

Temporary caretakers, including Mr Bobby Sproule and Mr Joe Wauchop, have cared for the school over the years and following Sammy Reid's retirement the position was advertised in 1994 and Mr Billy Gilchrist was appointed.

When Mrs I. Crockett left her position as Classroom Assistant in 1995, Miss M. J.Young took up the post with Year 1. In the same year Miss N. Moore from Londonderry took up a temporary teaching position in Key Stage 1, and was appointed as a permanent member of staff in April 1996.

Mrs P. Stewart accepted a position in Castlederg High School in October 1998 and Miss K. Johnston assumed her post in a temporary capacity. Miss L. Morrow also joined the staff in 1998 as a temporary teacher for Years 2 and 3. Her position was made permanent in 1999. Also in the same year another Classroom Assistant post was created and Miss E. McKane was appointed.

When agreement was reached to provide a Nursery in the school Mrs Bratton was selected in April 2000 to take charge. Miss M. Young was given the post of her assistant in June 2000 and Miss Morrow assumed responsibility for Reading Recovery.

As the number of children with special needs increased, extra help was required. This led to the appointments of Mrs I. Forbes and Miss K. Waugh (later Mrs Cowan) in November 2000.

Mr H. Woods who had been teaching in the school since 1977, and was Vice-Principal, retired in 2000 and Mr I. Gowdy was awarded the V.P. position and he also moved up to teach Year 7. Miss C. Roke from Banbridge took over in Year 6 in June 2001.

The General Teaching Council of Northern Ireland was formed in 2002 and Mr Orr was appointed to serve on the new committee.

To bring the series of staff appointments to a conclusion before the opening of the new school, Miss Z. Johnston was appointed in January 2004 as a Special Needs Assistant.

A large number of temporary vacancies, including Maternity cover and Sick Leave, have been filled over the years by many competent and willing people. The Principal and staff are indebted to all those who have assisted in bridging gaps, and although too numerous to mention individually, each one is valued for their useful contributions to the life of the school.

The Retirement of Four Senior Members of Staff.

The eighties and early nineties signalled the end of an epic era in the life of Edwards School with the retirements of four eminent and highly respected, senior members of staff. First to retire was Mrs Caldwell, who relinquished her post in January 1985, after almost thirty-five years of exemplary service. Staff and pupils alike will long remember her kindly nature and willing disposition. A retirement function was held in the school and Mr Riddall and members of the committee paid tribute to her commendable teaching career before presenting her with a luggage set, a gift cheque and a bouquet of flowers and wishing that she would enjoy many years of travel.

Later in the year it was the turn of Mr Riddall to hand in his chalk! After thirty years in office it was the end of an era for everyone! His retirement in June was marked with a concert and presentation of a video recorder and a gift cheque. Staff and past and present members of the Board of Governors, including Miss Elliott, attended it. Wonderful tributes were paid to his fine example and exceptional leadership during his time at the helm, which had been punctuated by the introduction of many new initiatives. A bouquet of flowers was presented to Mrs Riddall and everyone extended their good wishes to both of them for a long and happy retirement.

After a marathon teaching career spanning thirty-seven years, Mrs McNutt retired in 1986. Members of staff, who had been so benevolently looked after in their fledgling years by this mother figure, were sorry to see her go. A special ceremony, attended by her husband and family, was held to mark her retirement. She was accorded the best wishes of everyone and was presented with Tyrone Crystal, a dinner service and flowers.

Falling numbers of children in the school's catchment area meant that Edwards' Board of Governors had to deal with a redundancy in 1991. Mrs Waugh, who had been teaching in the school since 1962, decided to take early retirement and a reshuffle of the staff took place.

To recognise the sterling work that Mrs Waugh had done, a ceremony to mark her retirement was held in the school. Her mother, husband, children and members of the Board of Governors attended it. Tributes were paid to her excellent service and she was presented with a Tyrone Crystal Lamp, a gift cheque and a bouquet of flowers.

For more information about these members of staff please refer to the sections on Past Headmasters and Past Members of Staff.

Mrs Caldwell's Retirement 1985
Mrs A. McNutt, Mrs M. Caldwell, Mrs. A Waugh, Mr. T.F. Riddall.

Mrs Caldwell's Retirement 1985
Jill Irwin, Linda Baird, Mrs M Caldwell, Roy Forbes.

Mr Tom Riddall (centre, front row), who was presented with a video recorder to mark his retirement after 30 years as principal of Edwards Primary School, Castlederg. Also in the photograph are his wife, members of the school management committee and staff.

Mr Orr, Canon W. Quill and pupils, Christopher Monteith and Rhonda Lecky presenting Mrs McNutt with her retirement gifts.

Alison Irwin presenting Mrs Waugh with flowers to mark her retirement

239

Ballad of a Schoolboy.

A long time ago, or so it seems today,
My mummy sent me on my way,
"To school," she said, "you must go,"
So I walked along with steps so slow.

I had been there before, but for part of a day,
No problem for me, sure they only play.
I thought it was great as I approached the gate,
When a jangling bell told me I was late.

I ran this way and that, for I'm not too bright,
And I couldn't find a door that was right,
When all of a sudden a nice lady in glasses,
Said, "Come with me, I look after new classes."

The tears were tripping down my face,
As I looked at this angel, saving me from disgrace,
In a tone both gentle and kind she said,
"Don't worry now dear," and patted my head.

The tears dried up and wasn't I glad,
For the lady looked down saying, "I know you, little lad,
I recognise your face, you can't be bad,
Sure, it was only yesterday I taught your dad.

So, she's a teacher, I suddenly thought,
I was beginning to like her such a lot,
Then to a cloakroom she brought me, hung up my coat,
And into a book my name she wrote.

She brought me to a room full of girls and boys,
Some crying, some playing with toys,
"Don't leave me now," I started to cry,
She said, " I'll be back in the twinkle of an eye"

Another lady came offering comfort to me,
I looked at her pleadingly, "Please who is she?"
"Oh, " she replied, "Mrs McNutt is her name,
She's been here for so long, she's a lady of fame.

"Mrs McNutt", sure I'd heard it before,
My dad often said she had taught him more.
A wonderful teacher, and so kind to all,
A knowledgeable expert was what he'd recall.

Well, ever since then she has been a great friend,
Offering help and advice right up to the end.
Her pleasant manner and ready smile,
We'll surely remember for a long while.

Just recently she said, " I'm retiring, the time has now come,
To enjoy my hobbies, of which I have some.
I'll have more time to spend at my leisure,
The thought of which brings me very mush pleasure

Her expertise and example will be hard to replace,
We will certainly miss her pleasant face,
But good health and good wishes to a dear friend,
As today brings an era to an end.

By H. McCay   June 1986.
Edwards P.S.

The Present Era.

Mr A. S. Orr Principal 1985

Mr A.S Orr, who had been Principal in Kesh P.S, filled the vacancy following Mr Riddall's departure.

This was a period of great change with the Education Act of 1984 and the 1989 statutory Education Reform Order. The Aston Report "recommended that every school should have a separate Board of Governors" and this was accepted by the WELB, so from December 1985 Boards of Governors replaced the School Management Committees, although essentially they performed the same role.

At this time members of the Board of Governors for Edwards School were:
Chairman: Canon W. Quill,
Vice-Chairman: Dr M. Brown,
Transferor's Representatives: Canon W. Quill, S. Crawford,
R. Montgomery, Dr. M. Brown,
Parents' Representatives: Mrs P. Quigley, N. Donnell,
Board Representatives: E. Turner, I. Clarke,
Teachers' Representative: A. Waugh.
Secretary: Mr A.S. Orr (Headmaster).

The statutory reforms proposed by the Government were debated by the Board of Governors in May 1988 and although the changes were welcomed there were some reservations about testing at seven or eight years and the unfair pressure that would be put on teachers of classes being tested. Despite the varied responses the proposals went ahead and became law in 1989.

For the first time schools were bound by statutory requirements to deliver a defined curriculum and to make arrangements for testing. Changes in teachers' terms and conditions of employment were introduced and Boards of Governors were responsible for the delivery of the curriculum as well as shouldering the financial administration of the school.

The curriculum was completely revamped with changes in every subject. English, Maths and Science were regarded as the core elements and along with Geography, History, Art and Religious Instruction the areas to be studied became highly structured. New subjects, reflecting the age, such as Technology and Design and Information and Communication Technology became compulsory, as did the introduction of cross-curricular themes such as cultural heritage, economic awareness, education for mutual understanding and health education. The far-reaching changes brought about:

- The new Common Curriculum.
- End of Key Stage Assessments
- Publication of school performance results against those for N.I.
- Pupil Profiles
- School Development Planning
- Special Needs Provision
- Annual Reports
- More Inspections
- Publication of Inspectors' Reports

All of these reforms put an incredible onus on the Principal and the staff to adapt to the sweeping changes but with determination they managed to get to grips with the new Northern Ireland Primary Curriculum and gradually everyone became familiar with Programmes of Study, which were the contents of the curriculum, Key Stages 1 and 2, which previously were Infants and Seniors, Attainment Targets and Assessment.

Because of the myriad of changes, many courses to train teachers were provided by the Western Education and Library Board. Mr Orr encouraged staff to use these. Coordinators in each subject-area were appointed to help disseminate the vast amount of information received. Awesome changes were made but the teachers managed to cope and began the painstaking process of writing new schemes of work for each subject. This represented a huge volume of work on top of the daily teaching tasks.

Teachers were also expected to show adequate planning, so monthly or six-weekly planners replaced weekly notes, which had been the norm in Mr Riddall's day. At first these were hand written but now they are completely produced on computer.

Computers, which had been introduced in the early eighties, were spiralling to dizzy heights and Mr Orr was particularly interested in keeping abreast of the modern technology. Many new computers and printers were purchased, each one far in advance of the previous one, and staff had to learn of the extra benefits each time a new computer was introduced. The W.E.L.B. supplied new computer equipment to the Special Unit and the School Governors recorded their appreciation.

The new technology also included such interesting items as video cameras and Mr Orr was frequently seen with a large piece of apparatus on his shoulder, filming a group of pupils on an educational outing or performing within school. This brought a host of new opportunities for the children and provided parents and friends with chances to see their children in action. Videos of pantomimes and Nativity Plays became the norm and were eagerly anticipated after a performance.

After years of performing on an improvised platform, Mr Orr decided to purchase a purpose built, portable, foldaway stage. This was a great boon and has witnessed many performances and events. New stage curtains on a pulley system replaced the motley combination of cast off curtains that had been used for many years, and these proved to be useful additions in the hall.

Mr Orr, who was very keen on travel and its educational benefits, encouraged trips to a host of local educational venues and events, which broadened the curriculum, such as the History Park at Gortin and the Ulster American Folk Park near Omagh, Gortin Glen, Barrontop Open Farm, Castle Archdale, Enniskillen Museum, the Millennium Forum in Londonderry, Eglinton Airport, train trips to Castlerock, the Ardhowen theatre in Enniskillen, the Grand Opera House in Belfast, the Butterfly Farm at Seaforde, the Zoo in Belfast, Bessy Bell Wind Farm, the Ulster Museum, Big Houses such as Castlecoole, Florencecourt, the Argory and Springhill, the Marble Arch Caves as well as local farms and industries, to name but some!

Initially he introduced trips to Scotland and England as part of the school curriculum. For many pupils these presented the first opportunities for them to venture further than the shores of Northern Ireland. Even the bus and ferry trips were exciting!

Pupils and staff from Gillygooley P.S. joined Edwards' pupils in 1995 to visit Edinburgh. They experienced many of the delights of the Capital, including the Castle, the Honours of Scotland, a ghost tour and the Zoo.

Those who visited London will always remember the famous sights such as Madame Tussauds, The Tower of London, Buckingham Palace, The Thames, Tower Bridge, Big Ben and the Houses of Parliament as well as the delights of a West End musical.

To enhance a greater awareness of European affairs, Mr Orr involved the school in the Comenius project, which developed links between Edwards and schools in France, Spain and Switzerland. Exchange teachers have visited the school and pupils have benefited from these new experiences as well as enjoying exciting trips to Disneyland Paris and other areas of France. Pupils delighted in the sights of Paris--- the Eiffel Tower, the Sacre Coeur, Notre Dame Cathedral and a boat trip on the Seine, they visited a French farm, stayed at a chateau and relished their first experiences of French cuisine, even venturing to try snails!

During a difficult time in community relations in the eighties Mr Orr worked closely with Mr Sean McCarron, Principal of St Patrick's P.S. and together with the staff from both schools, endeavoured to promote harmony through educational links. The Western Education and Library Board, through their Education for Mutual Understanding venture, provided funds and encouraged joint partnerships with local schools. Edwards' pupils frequently met with the children from St Patrick's P.S. to enjoy educational trips, talks, drama and musical events.

A lot of success in this field must be attributed to well-respected bodies such as The Speedwell Trust, which was established to encourage children to form harmonious relationships when they came together for educational purposes in a neutral venue. These ventures have continued up to recent times but due to a reduction in funding by the W.E.L.B., schools and organisations such as The Speedwell Trust are now forced to meet the costs out of their own budgets. Consequently fewer events are possible although established friendships and good relationships between both schools still continue.

The Special Unit continued to thrive and was increased in size. In 1988 it extended to two classes and Mrs M. Watt joined Mrs G. McKinley. A changing room and washing facilities were provided and the needs of more children were accommodated.

Children in the Special Unit were, and still are, encouraged to integrate into school life in as many ways as possible. These involve participation in art, music, dance, swimming and Riding for the Disabled, with many notable successes in each area.

Creative expression has always been encouraged throughout the school and for a number of years the children from the Unit were involved in the Pushkin Prizes, which encouraged their creative writing skills. They enjoyed visits from the Duchess of Abercorn in her capacity as Patron of the Pushkin Trust and in 1995 were delighted to be invited to Baronscourt, home of the Duke and Duchess of Abercorn, to receive a prize for their work.

1995
Pictured at Baronscourt to receive a Pushkin prize, children from Edwards Special Unit.
William Galbraith, Jonathan Hyndman, Robert Walsh, Mrs G. McKinley, Anne Roulston.

The L.M.S. Budget.

The L.M.S. budget made an unwelcome intrusion into schools in 1991, forcing Head teachers and Boards of Governors to become familiar with accounting and balancing the finances needed for running a school. The "Local Management of Schools," a Government initiative, handed over the running of schools to the Head teachers and Governors. It was not an easy option and Headmasters, like Mr Orr, had to "learn the tricks of the trade" and become experts in accounting and management.

The Department of Education allocates a yearly sum of money to each school and from it, everything from staff salaries to the maintenance of the building, has to be paid. Many factors govern the sum allocated including the geographical position of the school and the socio-economic status of the pupils.

In the year it was introduced the Governors expressed dissatisfaction with the funding provided and yearly since then there has been a lot of discussion surrounding the budget and how it is allocated.

In the present difficult economic climate it has not been easy to balance the books and all schools struggle to meet the financial strictures, particularly if extra money is required in any particular area.

The Formation of the Parent Teacher Association.

The growing trend in involving parents in the education of their children led Mr Orr to help set up a Parent Teacher Association, which initially was formed in the late eighties. Its original purpose was to provide social opportunities for parents, staff and pupils and to raise funds that could be used to provide extra resources. The P.T.A. in Edwards has always been a most supportive body; always ready to assist staff in events and raising many thousands of pounds over the years. Numerous functions have been held, ranging from auctions, concerts, discos, bazaars, beetle drives, a Brides of Yesteryear event, an Antiques evening, fashion shows, table quizzes, cookery demonstrations, craft fairs and draws, to name but a few.

As a result the extra funds generated have been utilised to provide such things as additional computers and printers, video equipment, new reading schemes and subsidise trips.

The work of the P.T.A. is of great benefit to the school and is much appreciated by staff and pupils alike.

Edwards P.T.A Auction Great Success

As our photographs show there was a very large crowd at the Auction last saturday which held in the Enterprise Centre.

A very wide ranging number of items were sold from childrens toys right up through to almost every household item and even a piano which was delightfully and tunefully demonstrated by Miss Cummings before its sale.

The auctioneer's ham-
mer was in the capable and very experienced hands of William Smith. Auctioneer and Estate Agent Castlderg.

Every single item was sold and this was the first auction ever carried out by Edwards P.T.A Castleder. They would like thank the Enterprise Centre and a special word of thanks to all who donated items to the auction, and of course a deep felt gratitude to the large
crowd who supported it and to William Smith whose experience was very much valued.

Please Note that Furniture Auctions are carried out at this centre every three months by William Smith. If you have unwanted furniture for sale contact William Smith, Castlederg 71279. Next Auction is at the end of April.

Photographs kindly submitted by Mr. Tommy Maguire

247

Thanks to :

Castlederg High School

Diane and Violet of Silhouette.

Steven and Hazel Allen of Erganagh Ayrshires.

Mrs Pollock (Flowers).

Alan Armstrong and staff.

Thanks to all those who donated raffle prizes and to everyone who supported the event.

Edwards Primary School
PTA
Brides of Yesteryear

Castlederg High School
Wednesday 1st April, 1998 at 8pm

P.T.A. Fashion Show
Photographs of one of the first P.T.A. events, a fashion show

EDWARDS PS PTA
PRESENTS

YARNS AND SONGS

An opportunity to hear two of Irelands greatest Storytellers.
Edwards P S Castlederg
Tuesday 25th March 7.30 pm
Admission including supper £5
Tickets available from PTA or Edwards Primary School

Members of the P.T.A. and staff at the launch of the Millennium Calendar in 1999.
Mrs. A. Waugh, Mr. M. Robb, Mrs D. Stevenson, Mrs D. Baskin, Mrs S. Kane, Mrs M. Caldwell,
Mr A.S. Orr, Mr T.F. Riddall, Mrs A. McNutt

The Globe Project.

Children at the Earth Day Celebrations of the Globe Organisation in Dubllin.

*Photogtaphs of the Kennedy family on display in the Phoenix Park home of Mrs Jean Kennedy Smith,
American Ambassador in Ireland.*

For many years Mr Orr encouraged the senior pupils to become involved in the Globe Project, which is an organisation that promotes environmental awareness and encourages pupils to look after the earth. It began in America and has expanded to the U.K. Each year some pupils were invited to visit the Phoenix Park home of the American Ambassador in Dublin (who at that time was Mrs Jean Kennedy - Smith, sister of the late President J. F. Kennedy), and present a special project based on environmental conservation.

A fascinating glimpse of the sphere of Presidents and world leaders was gained from a study of the array of photographs on display in the Mansion. The groups also enjoyed lunch, met famous people such as astronaut John McBride, who had been on the Space Shuttle Challenger, and local Members of the Irish Parliament, saw the displays and presentations of children from all over Ireland and were taken on visits to such places of interest as the R.T.E. Weather Forecast Centre and the Smurfitt paper-recycling factory, as well as receiving "goody bags" to take home.

Unfortunately for Edwards' pupils the Globe project trips to Dublin stopped when Globe became based in the U.K. and we were required to subscribe to the English base, however we greatly benefited and enjoyed the welcome and hospitality received from our counterparts in Dublin.

Charities.

Like all organisations, schools are frequently asked to contribute to appeals for help in natural disasters and tragedies or with general fundraising. Mr Orr and staff have always encouraged pupils to consider those who are less well off and endeavour to assist a number of charities each year. Annual draws and collections in many forms take place and the proceeds are donated to those in need.

Large and small donations have been presented to such groups as the Royal National Institute for the Blind, The National Society for the Protection of Cruelty to Children, Doctor Barnardo's Homes, Earthquake and Famine Appeals in Honduras, Nicaragua and Africa, Orphanages in Romania, The Ulster Wildlife Trust, The Woodland Trust, The Samaritan's Purse, Guide Dogs for the Blind, Lepra and Cancer Charities such as the Malcolm Sargent Appeal, Diabetic Research and help for many Missionaries, to name but a few.

The organisers of
Readathon wish to thank
the children of

EDWARDS PRIMARY SCHOOL

for participating in this
event and for raising

£528.60

which has been donated to

The Malcolm Sargent Cancer
Fund for Children
and
The Roald Dahl Foundation

READATHON
READING FOR LIFE
ORGANISED BY BOOKS FOR STUDENTS
BIRD ROAD, HEATHCOTE, WARWICK CV34 6TB
TEL: 01926 314366 • FAX: 01926 450178

Miss J. Douglas and Mr A.S. Orr handing over a cheque to Mr and Mrs E. McAnirn and Karen following an earthquake in Mrs McAnirn's homeland of Honduras.

Big Charity Effort by Edwards PS. - Romanian Orphanage Appeal

RNIB Presentation £1530 Autumn '96

R.N.IB £1530 Autumn '96

Assessment.

Assessment has become a regular feature during the school year with two statutory Key Stage tests.

Key Stage One children, (those up to and including Year 4) follow set Programmes of Study, as prescribed by the Northern Ireland Curriculum Order, and at the end of their fourth year are formally assessed and the results collated to form Northern Ireland statistics. Key Stage 2 children (those up to and including Year 7) do likewise and have a formal assessment at the end of their last year in primary school.

More informal or class tests are usually carried out in January and June for Key Stage 2 pupils, while Key Stage 1 usually have tests at the end of the year. Written reports are sent to parents at the end of the summer term.

Throughout the year teachers constantly monitor the progress of pupils and any child with difficulties may be assessed by an outside agency, such as the Educational Psychologist from the local Board, to determine future help.

Over the years the school ethos has been to look after the needs of all children and in order to do this, remedial help has been provided. Today this takes the form of Reading Recovery, a one to one intensive reading programme, which was introduced in 1997 with the help of financial assistance from the E.U. support programme for Peace and Reconciliation. It has proved very beneficial and has encouraged many children to be comfortable, confident readers.

The "qualifying" or 11+ examination was introduced by the Government following the 1944 Education Act, in order to decide the direction of a child's post primary education. This controversial examination has been the subject of much debate and many changes, yet nothing suitable has been found to replace the system of selection.

Pupils begin to prepare for the two-part examination, which tests their knowledge in the core subjects---English, Maths and Science, in Year 6. They sit the exams in the autumn term of their last year at Primary School. The results are released in the spring term and the child is offered a place in a Secondary level school, at present either a Grammar or High School. From either of these they may then go on to third level or University education.

The Fiftieth Anniversary in 1988.

Mr Orr was at the helm as the school approached the fiftieth anniversary of its opening. To mark the event the Management Committee decided to launch a competition to produce an Anniversary Tea Towel while Mr Riddall generously donated the prize money. The pupils were asked to enter a design incorporating the Edwards symbols and the dates 1938-1988. There were many excellent entries and two of the best, submitted by Claire Sproule (now Mrs Ferry) and Christopher Monteith, were chosen. A tea towel was produced and sold and many people have retained theirs as a memento of the occasion. Here is what Claire had to say about her memories of the competition.

"I was in P7 at Edwards Primary School in 1988. As part of the 50th anniversary celebrations we had to design a tea towel. I decided to re-create a design that incorporated both the view from the front of the school on the top half and the uniform, showing the tie, shirt and jumper on the bottom. In the middle was the school crest. The colour scheme was the traditional blue and gold of course. I can still remember it very distinctly—eighteen years on!!

I was joint winner with another boy from my class. His design was used as it had less detail and was easier to print. The tea towels were then printed and sold, raising money for school funds. I was delighted and proud that I won the competition, as art and design were always favourite subjects of mine. This was one of the fondest memories of my time at Edwards."

A special Open Night was held in the school on May 31st 1988, when parents, friends, past pupils and the community enjoyed many exhibits and displays reflecting the past years. Every classroom was open and visitors enjoyed reminiscing and the staff served tea and an anniversary cake. (See photographs)

Tea Towel produced for the 50th Anniversary.

"Founders Day" 50th Anniversary, 31st May 1988
Back Row: Harry Woods, V.P. Pamela Bratton, Lorna Harron, Helen Graham, Margaret Watt, Ivan Gowdy.
Front Row: Gladys McKinley, Judith Anderson, Alastair Orr, Ann Waugh,
Hazel McCay, Rhonda Armstrong (Sub).

ORDER OF SERVICE EDWARDS P.S. 1938-88.

Derg Parish Church
Wednesday, 1st June, 1988

Introduction	Mr. Orr
1st Hymn No. 232	Thank you Lord for this fine day
Introductory Prayers	Rev. W. Quill
2nd Hymn No. 134	Jesus' hands were kind hands
Old Testament Reading	Rev. S. Jones
Anthem - School Choir	Make Way/Seek ye first
New Testament Reading	Rev. D. Anderson
3rd Hymn No. 169	My God is so big
Prayers	Children
4th Hymn No. 188	One more step
Final Prayer	Rev. W. Quill

Hymns announced by:	David Sproule, Robert Hogg, Johanne Muldoon, Lisa Montgomery, Celia Rankin.
Prayers led by:	Samantha Galbraith, Olivia Clarke, Tracy McNamee, Johanne Loughlin.

The Order of Service marking the Fiftieth Anniversary of the School.

Mr Sammy Reid and the late Mr Jack Verner admire a display at the 50th Anniversary of the School Opening.

258

The following poem was composed by the Primary Three children and Mrs M. Watt to mark the Jubilee:

Fifty Years Ago.

Fifty years ago,
When granny was a girl,
This Edwards School was opened,
For those children, what a thrill!

They didn't have a uniform,
 Like us--- we're all so smart.
Our sweatshirts with the Edwards crest,
Make us look quite apart.

They had no school buses then,
To travel here each day,
Those children got up early,
Many walked all the way.

Very shortly afterwards,
In 1939,
The Second World War started,
What a dreadful time.

Some children came to Castlederg,
For Belfast was in danger,
They left their homes and families,
To stay here with a stranger.

While here they came to Edwards School,
And learned to read and write,
Evacuees they were called,
This school was their delight.

There used to be a garden here,
The children worked quite hard,
When busy digging up the soil,
No one was ever bad!

Master Sloan was in charge,
Many vegetables here were grown,
In '46 a cup was won,
For that garden was well known.

Things are very different now,
We have dinners, books and toys,
Television and computer discs,
All for modern girls and boys.

I wonder, all those years ago
Was Edwards School a dream?
Like this school was it bright and shining?
Was there a "Sammy" to keep it clean?

We are proud of Edwards School,
As we surely now should be,
When we think of all that's past,
On this our Golden Jubilee.

Mrs M. Watt and P 3.   June 1988.

1988 Tree Planting at Mitchell Park with Strabane District Council Chairman James O'Kane. Also included at P7 Teacher Mr H. Woods and Principal Mr A.S. Orr.

Edwards Staff in 1993/94.

A cartoon drawn by Tyrone Forsythe to mark the retirement of Mr Sammy Reid, the caretaker.

Caretaking with Honours.

It was no secret that Edwards P.S. was the envy of all the local schools when Mr Sammy Reid was appointed as Caretaker in 1972, and his wife was assigned as his assistant cleaner along with Mrs Jean Bogle.

The standard of their caretaking was, and still is legendary; on many occasions the Management Committee, Inspectors, staff and visitors admired the gleaming rooms and shining floors. But Sammy was not just a caretaker and custodian of a building. He was a kindly father figure, always ready to help a child or member of staff in distress! He was the ultimate odd job man, the painter and decorator, the carpenter, the plumber, the inventor, the gardener, the first aider, the football referee, the comforter and above all, a friend to everyone. He took pride in his work and at all times gave his very best.

Unfortunately Sammy became ill in 1992 and was forced to take time off work. It was no surprise however, that news of his supreme talents had reached the Queen and in 1993 he was honoured by being included in the New Years' Honours List. Sammy was modestly pleased and felt "very honoured." Mr Orr, the school Principal, and staff were bursting with pride. It was not every day or every school that could boast of a Caretaker with an M.B.E.! Later on in the year Sammy and Meta travelled to London and enjoyed not only a rare visit to Sammy's late brother, but the unique reception and award at Buckingham Palace. Despite wanting to return to work Sammy's health did not improve and on the advice of his doctor he reluctantly decided to retire in 1994. It was one of the saddest decisions the Headmaster had to accept and a function was held in the school to mark the retirement of both Sammy and Meta.

Members of the Board of Governors, Parent Teacher Association, staff, Western Education and Library Board, parents, friends and pupils gathered for a Presentation on the 20th of May 1994. Sammy, Meta and members of their family attended. Tributes were paid to the exceptional qualities of Sammy and Meta and gifts were presented followed by entertainment and tea.

Pictured at the presentation to Mr. and Mrs. Sammy Reid who retired as employees
of Edwards Primary School, Castlederg.
Front Row, left, Canon W. P. Quill, Chairman of the Board of Governers, Mr and Mrs Reid, Mr. Alistair
Orr, Principal. Back Row, Mr. Jack Walls, Mr. Tom Riddall, former Principal,
Mr. William Montgomery and Mr. Sandy McKinley.

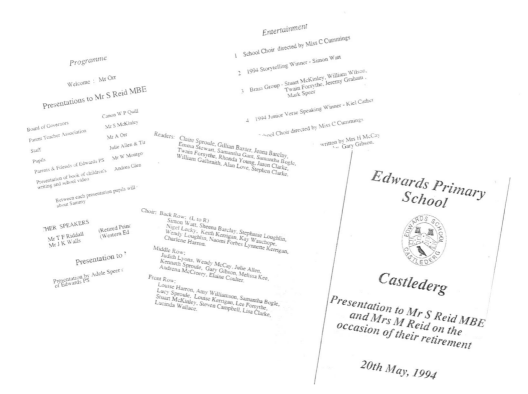

Ruth Griffin chirismas 1984
Sammy

sammy is or care taker
and he is a very busy man
and he dekarokesed the
chirsmas tree too. sammy
holds the rain deers for father
chirrismas. I like sammy
becaue he plays games with
Tanza Lesley Davina and me.

Davina Henderson Christmas 1984.
Sammy

Sammy is the teartaker of Edwards
primriy School he does lots and lots of
work, he puts up the Christmas tree at School
for Christmas, and mops the floor, and
cleans the wall and also the windows too
and at Christmas when Santa Comes with
is raindeers Sammy looks after his raindeers
until every person has got a present.
I think he disevares a very very good
present.

MBE for a 'terrific' school caretaker

School caretaker, Mr. Samuel Reid (61), of Learmore Road, Castlederg, got the shock of his life when he heard he had been nominated for the MBE.

"I thought it was a joke at first, but now I feel very honoured. All I was doing was my duty in the best way I could," he said.

Mr. Reid and his wife, Margaret, have two sons.

He has been caretaker at Edwards Primary School in Castlederg since March 1972, but has been off work since April of last year with heart trouble.

However, he went in over the festive period to erect the Christmas tree and help with props for the school's pantomime. He hopes to be able to return to work full-time soon.

Mr. Reid thanked to the chairman and members of the school's board of governors who, he says, nominated him for the award.

As a pastime, Mr. Reid enjoys gardening.

The school principal, Mr. Alistair Orr, described Mr. Reid as a terrific caretaker who kept the whole place shining.

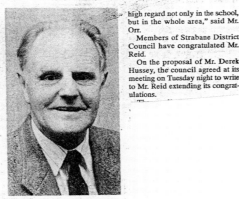

MBE recipient: Mr. Samuel Reid.

And Mr. Orr went on to say that Mr. Reid was devoted to the whole school.

"He has a great love for the pupils and they have an unbelievable rapport with him," said Mr. Orr. "If he saw a child in any kind of distress he would immediately go to their assistance."

Mr. Orr also praised Mr. Reid for his help with props and lighting for the school's pantomimes each year.

"It is everyone's hope at the

high regard not only in the school, but in the whole area," said Mr. Orr.

Members of Strabane District Council have congratulated Mr. Reid.

On the proposal of Mr. Derek Hussey, the council agreed at its meeting on Tuesday night to write to Mr. Reid extending its congratulations.

The following poem was written to mark the retirement:

No Trouble At All.

This is a story, which began twenty years ago,

When someone we all love and know,

Came to this school to look for a job.

He wasn't a Jimmy or a Willy or a Bob.

But at interview when asked his name,

He said loud and clear,

"I'm Sammy and working's my game."

The Head said. "Great, you're just what we need,

Get started now and clean the school with speed!"

So without hesitation came the reply,

"No trouble at all sir, I'll give it a try!"

And that is the story of Sammy's life,

Backed so well with Meta as his wife.

From early morning to late at night,

He kept the school shining and bright,

No job too big, no job too small,

Sammy willingly did them all.

You only had to say, "I think I need...."

When it arrived with the utmost speed.

And without hesitation would come the reply,

"No trouble at all, I gave it a try."

From runny noses, little mistakes and cut knees,
Sammy tended them all with kindly ease,
His patience, his love, every child will recall,
But birthdays were always the best of all,
For when Sammy learnt of that special day,
He'd say, "That's just great, come this way,"
And then he'd give the "bumps and the shakes!"
What a memory that special treat makes!
For without hesitation had come the reply,
"No trouble at all, I'll give it a try!"

Children and staff have come and gone,
But for all one memory lingers on,
And that is love for Sammy, one of the best,
Whose shining example has stood the test.
Few visitors ever came through the door,
Who didn't mention the shining floor,
Or the wonderful way the school was kept painted and clean,
Sure, even the Queen knows what we mean!
For she too has heard the reply,
"No trouble at all, I'll give it a try!"

Sammy, we were so proud of you,

When you went to the Palace for that "do,"

We were all with you in spirit that day,

When at eleven o'clock we heard the Queen say,

"Sammy Reid, what a Caretaker you've been!

Unfortunately your work I've never seen,

But it's said it is fit for a Queen.

I award you the M.B.E. with the greatest of pleasure,

But now I hope you'll enjoy deserved leisure.

And without hesitation came the reply,

"No trouble at all, Ma'am, I'll give it a try!"

Now Sammy, as we pay tribute to you,

We say sincere thanks for all you do.

It was much appreciated we'd like you to know,

We'll miss you, but we wish you well as you go.

You can reflect you've done your best,

Now look forward and enjoy a rest,

But come back to see us now and then,

For you never know the day and hour when

We'll need your help and you'll reply,

"No trouble at all, I'll give it a try!"

H.McC. 1994.

For further information on Sammy see the section on past members of staff.

Storytelling

Edwards Celebrate 25 Years of Storytelling

Edwards Primary School in Castlederg has been complimented by well-known storyteller, Billy Teare, speaking at a recent celebration of 25 years of storytelling at the school. He commented that the school was years ahead of the national revival in storytelling and he congratulated the 41 children who took part as he awarded their certificates.

Twenty-two children had taken part in the final adjudication where the judges were Mrs. M. Creighton, Mr. T. Riddall and Mr. D. Baxter. All finalists received a special commemorative medal and a certificate. The winner was Jeremy Graham with "Me Turf Spade." In second place was Melissa Kee with "What a lot of nonsense!" and in third was Gillian Baxter with "Sports Day". Fourth place went to Kathryn Bratton with "Wolf and Goat" followed by Emma Stewart with "The Curly Freckle Gang." A cup which had been presented to the school 25 years ago by the late Miss Georgina Elliot was awarded to this years winner.

A short humorous history of the competition was given by Mr. T. Riddall, who was Headmaster at the inauguration of the competition. Many previous winners, judges and friends were among the audience who enjoyed the stories related by Billy Teare and the top five of this years finalists.

The evening concluded with supper provided by the members of the Parent Teacher Association and Staff.

" Me Turf Spade "

The whistle blew. Murphy has won. Begorra, I don't believe it! That cunning, scheming, wee man has beat me again. 'Tis cheating, he was cheating, I tell ye, Up to his old tricks again! I thought I'd sorted him out once and for all. Murphy I'll murderlize ye!

Do you know anything about wee people? Now I just don't mean vertically challenged- I'm talking really badly vertically challenged leprechaun-style. Patrick Shaun Murphy style. He's the pain of my life He's me worst nightmare. Always up to no good. Well yesterday was the last straw.

I woke up in the morning. Looked out the window. Nice day for cuttin' turf. So I got up and went out to me shed, opened me shed door and there was me new turf spade sitting where I left it.......GONE! "Murphy! says I, Murphy, come here, show yourself man."

"Ah,ah,Patrick S. Murphy at your service. Tap o' the morning to ye. How may I help ye?"

" You know very well, where's me spade?"

" Your spade. Ah well de ye see sir, its like this sir. Ah good luck tay ye sir. Good luck tay ye sir."

" Murphy, come back here, me spade please."

" Well I didn't exactly take yer spade. I just sort of borrowed it. Ye see, I was this close, this close to finding the biggest pat o' gold you've ever seen and I figured I needed a really good spade to dig it out. So I borrowed yers, but to tell you the truth it was no good. Sure me own wee spade is a thousand times better."

" No good! What do ye mean? That's the best spade in all Scraghy. Ah Sure you canny use it right. There's neither a man can dig better than me! Well patrick Murphy you've got a nerve, I'll challenge you to a diggin' competition to prove me turf spade is better than yours any day."

" Diddly, Diddly, Dee, yer on. We'll mark out the course in the morning and I'll show ye whose spade's the best."

And so here we are. I don't believe it, Murphy's finished! Well blow me! Here's me sweating me guts out and there's him dancing a jig with his spade at the far end of the garden.

" Murphy" says I, " How did you do that?"

" Begorra now, 'tis a fine job you made o' me garden. I'll be able to plant me spuds in the morning. 'Tis a fine turf spade ye have after all."

" What! You've tricked me into digging yer garden! But how did you finish so quickly? "

" Ah meet the family. Come out me boyos, put the poor man out of his misery."

And now I've seen it all. There's MURPHY, and Murphy and Murphy and Murphy and Murphy all over the garden, laughing and shouting at me.....Such excitement...... and such a fool I am, and all because of me aul turf spade!!!

Jeremy Graham

Since its inception in 1971 the Storytelling Competition has been keenly contested each year. Miss G. Elliott presented the Storytelling cup and independent judges adjudicate the children's stories. Although the original cup was replaced following the twenty-fifth year of the competition, the new cup is a coveted award and pupils are proud to have their names engraved on it.

The following is a list of winners since the beginning of the competition:

1971—1972	Neil Hazard
1972—1973	Neil Hazard
1973—1974	Margaret Burke
1974—1975	Jane Marshall
1975—1976	Susan Scott and Alan Porter
1976—1977	Alan Porter
1977—1978	Sharon Crawford
1978—1979	Karen Jack
1979—1980	Karen Quigley
1980—1981	Karen Jack
1981—1982	Elaine Quigley
1982—1983	Danyl Quigley
1983—1984	Ian Quigley
1984—1985	Ian Quigley
1985—1986	Wendy Clarke
1986—1987	Danyl Quigley
1987—1988	Laura Griffin
1988—1989	Laura Griffin
1989—1990	Keith Kerrigan
1990—1991	Laura Griffin and Trudy Robb
1991—1992	Simon Watt
1992—1993	Simon Watt
1993—1994	Simon Watt
1994—1995	Wendy McCay
1995—1996	Jeremy Graham
1996—1997	EmmaStewart
1997—1998	EmmaStewart

1998—1999	Jonathan Kane		
1999—2000	Leeza Sproule	Year 4:	Andrea Bustard
2000—2001	AdamLecky	Year 4:	Rachel Gowdy
2001—2002	Nathan Robb	Year 4:	Sophie Harpur
2002—2003	Joanna Baskin	Year 4:	Kirsty Gillespie
2003—2004	Joanna Baskin	Year 4 :	Abigail Clarke
2004—2005	Candice Gathers	Year 4 :	Scott Gordon and Shirley Harpur

Edwards Primary School Story Telling Finalist '96 Jeremy Graham with Billy Teare.

Back Row Claire Hunter, Gillian Baxter, Judith Loughlin, Jennifer Mooney, Janine McMullan, Tina Sproule, Melissa Kee, Samantha Bogle, Louise Kerrigan, Nicola Hunter, Emma Stewart.
Front Row: Catherine Doherty, Claire Kerrigan, Christopher Speer, Adele Speer, Jeremy Graham (winner), Samantha Gant, Ashleigh McSorley, Mark Lecky, Kathryn Brratton, Shirley McCay.

The Millennium.

Despite all the threats of major computer crashes, Millennium bugs and impending disasters, the pupils and staff of Edwards approached the year 2000 with ease.

To mark the new Millennium each child and member of staff in the school planted a native tree in the corner of the football field with the intention of creating a wood for future generations of children to enjoy. This was a most enjoyable event and it was pleasing to see the development of the young saplings. However, no one had foreseen the advent of a new school to be situated in the field, removing the chances of the anticipated wood ever reaching fruition.

When the site was cleared many of the little trees were uprooted and planted in other areas of the grounds and at present they are being used to develop wooded areas in the new environment.

The P.T.A. was also very active in preparation for the Millennium. They composed a commemorative calendar featuring photographs from the past along with the classes from Reception to Year 7, the Special Units, the teaching and ancillary staff.

Tree planting Dec. '99

The New Nursery.

As the trend for pre-school provision became more pressing, Mr Orr recognised the growing need for a nursery attached to Edwards P.S. The Management Committee had firstly discussed it in June 1979, when it was proposed, "a Nursery Classroom should be built, staffed and equipped as soon as possible." But the rusty wheels of progress grind so slowly and although a sub-committee was set up to visit a Nursery School in 1991, nothing concrete was done until the late nineties, twenty years after it was first mooted. The 1991 Inspection had also drawn attention to the number of underage pupils in the school and emphasised the need for Nursery provision.

In October 1996 the Board of Governors applied to the Childhood Fund for a grant to provide a Nursery and further proposals were submitted to the Department of Education. Hopes were high for a favourable outcome but these were dashed in 1997 when it was revealed that Edwards was not one of the five schools to have received approval. St. Patrick's P. S. Castlederg had been given the green light and this encouraged Mr Orr to engage in further discussions with the Western Education and Library Board and the Department of Education, putting forward an urgent case for nursery education at Edwards. Numbers of children in the area were increasing and in 1997, 31 pupils applied for entry to Year 1.

Finally the case was considered positively and after inspecting the facilities in the school it was decided to start a Nursery class in one of the vacant classrooms. Furnishings and equipment were provided and in September 2000 Mrs P. Bratton moved to assume charge of the Nursery with Miss M. Young as her assistant and Mrs I. Forbes providing Special Needs help.

They opened the doors to receive the first Edwards Nursery pupils sporting their uniforms of Royal Blue jumpers, featuring a logo of two small children and the name of the Nursery. The staff and children were very happy in Room 6 but it was slightly cramped and did not quite meet all the required provisions for nursery children, such as their own toilets and an outdoor soft play area.

Eventually permission was granted to provide a purpose-built nursery in the school grounds on the site of the old schoolhouse.

It was a most interesting development for the staff and children to watch. The site was prepared and the sectional building was delivered on two large lorries and lifted off by a huge crane. Very quickly it took shape and the interior was prepared. It comprised of an entrance foyer, an office, a main classroom, a quiet room, a kitchen with a washing machine, and toilets and wash hand basins especially sized for little folk. Bright, new, colourful furnishings were provided and Mrs P. Bratton along with her assistants Miss M. Young and Mrs I. Forbes, eagerly unpacked all the new items and prepared to receive the first pupils in their special home.

Outside there was a paved entrance, a soft play area and a garden. It was fully fenced and was an ideal safe site in which the pre school children prepared for the rigours of a full school day.

The school opened at Easter and Mrs Bratton, Miss Young and Mrs Forbes helped twenty-six pre school children to settle into a happy and structured learning environment, paving the way for them to adapt easily to mainstream school.

After settling in, Mrs Bratton and her staff prepared for the grand occasion when the building was officially opened by the Duke of Abercorn K.G. on Friday 25th of May 2001. Taking part in the proceedings were Mr Joe Martin, Chief Executive of the Western Education and Library Board, Mr Pat O'Kane, the Chairman, Canon W. Quill, Chairman of the Board of Governors and Mrs Sheila McCaul, Senior Education Officer, WELB. Following the opening ceremony tea was served in the school assembly hall.

The staff and pupils settled happily into the lovely surroundings and it was delightful to watch the fledglings playing outside on their tricycles and happily using both the indoor facilities and all the larger outdoor playthings. They walked over to the main school building for P.E. in the hall and also to watch performances such as the Nativity Play. Dinner was served from the school kitchen, having been delivered by a school bus to the Nursery door.

These experiences helped the children to feel comfortable when they came into the larger building and proved invaluable in helping them settle into school when their turn came.

The Nursery remained their home until the facilities attached to the new school were completed in November 2004, when again the staff and pupils had to make another move.

"Watch the Birdie" - the height of the VIP's posed no problems for 4 year old pupil Leah Lowry as she stood on a table to photograph the guests - Joseph Martin, Chief Executive of the Western Education and Library Board, Pat O'Kane, Chairman of WELB, The Duke of Abercorn who unveiled the plaque, Shelia McCaul, Senior Education Officer, WELB, and Canon Quill Chairman of the Board of Governers. The budding photographer lined up her subjects during the opening of Edwards PS New Nursery Unit in Castlederg.

Pictured at the opening of the New Edwards Nursery Unit on Friday 25th May 2001. L - R: Mrs P. Bratton, Mrs I. Forbes, Miss M. Young. Hannah Hawkes, Olivia Keatley, Kyle Duncan, Jason Kilpatrick, Leah Lowry, Scott Gordon.

The Rector writes

My dear Parishioners

Friday 25 May was a red-letter day for Edwards Primary School. His Grace The Duke of Abercorn KG officially opened the Nursery Unit which is situated within the school grounds. Edwards Primary School was built in 1938 and extended in 1978 with the addition of a Special Needs Unit. The provision of a state-of-the-art Nursery Unit, complete with professionally trained staff, will be of tremendous benefit to the children of Castlederg and district.

Among the VIPs present were Mr Pat O'Kane, Chairman of the Western Education and Library Board, Mr Joe Martin, Chief Executive WELB and Canon Aubrey Northridge.

We were all delighted to hear the Chief Executive state his hope for Edwards to be given a new school in the not too distant future. Mr Martin emphasised that although he couldn't give a date, he was fairly optimistic that a new building would be provided before too long. His announcement was greeted with much applause.

The future for schools in the Castlederg area looks healthy for some years to come judging by the fact that the NurseryUnit and the local play groups are all full. This does not surprise me when I consider the number of children in the Junior Sunday school. Incidentally, it's sometimes said that 'the children of today are the church of tomorrow'. Recently at the General Synod in Dublin, a member reminded us that 'the children of today are the church of today'. That's good theology. Baptism admits a person, whether child or adult, to membership of the Church of Jesus Christ. Maybe if more adults accepted that fact, children's participation in worship would be encouraged and not simply tolerated.

Following the official opening, framed paintings were presented to those who had taken part in the event. Each painting (four in total) was the work of one of the children in the Nursery. The Duke of Abercorn said he was going to put his in his library at Barons Court. My wife has put mine(a painting by 'Olivia') in the family room of our house in Coleraine. I shall treasure it along with a pair of socks that a Castlederg lady knit for me when she was 101 years of age! There can't be many people who have been presented with a framed painting by a 3-year old and a pair of socks knitted by a 101-year old!

I hope all of you have a good holiday, but please, don't take one from church!

Your sincere friend and Rector

Walter P. Quill

NEWS BULLETIN

DERG AND KILLETER

JUNE/JULY/AUGUST 2001

CANON WALTER P QUILL

TEL/FAX: 81671362

History Repeats Itself.

The maintenance of property always features high on a school's agenda and it became a regular feature of the Edwards Board of Governors' business in the last three decades of the twentieth century.

After almost fifty years in use, the school building was showing the effects of "wear and tear," so in February 1987 the Governors inspected the building and asked the Maintenance Officer from the Western Education and Library Board to meet with them to discuss their concerns. There was praise for the excellent standard of caretaking and interim repairs were carried out to the building.

Only eleven years after the opening of the 1978 extension there were serious defects in the felt roof and from September to December 1989 there were five leaks in the roof and the windows needed replacing. In March 1990 new windows were installed, with single glazing only, as Primary Schools did not get double-glazing! The roof was to be repaired and the playground required resurfacing. However, the Caretaker was forced to continue catching the rain in buckets as the Governors reported that by the end of the year the roof was still leaking and the ceilings were not repaired!

By 1990 Mr Woods had left the school residence in which he had lived since his appointment and discussions were held on its future. The WELB wanted to sell it but the Governors disagreed and various suggestions were put forward such as using the building for extra storage space, using it as a base for practical subjects or to provide accommodation for therapists who visited the school. All these suggestions were rejected by the Board who felt security of resources was an issue. The debate continued and the Governors still insisted that it would be shortsighted to sell the property and suggested that the building could be converted to a Nursery. A meeting with Mr P. Mallon, a Senior Board Officer, was arranged, and he considered the latter request. However the WELB reply was that there was no money for Nursery Education and finally in 1992 the Governors, who were witnessing the deterioration of the property, offered to remove the house at no expense to the Board.

In the eighties and nineties there were many problems concerning lack of room for storage of resources, for caretaking equipment and for the Speech and Occupational Therapists who paid regular weekly visits to the school to assist pupils. The Medical Inspection Room was being used on too many occasions and often when required for its original purpose it was unavailable. Mr Mallon, the Board Officer, suggested that a new resource/library area could be made at the Year 7 cloakrooms and part of the play shed converted to make a store for the Caretaker.

The wet Castlederg climate proved unkind to the brickwork in the 1938 building, causing it to decay and become absorbent, so in 1991 the WELB suggested plastering over the brick. However that was rejected as it was felt that the character of the building would be lost. Rendering was also considered and rejected so finally the bricks were sprayed with silicone, which arrested the problem for a short time.

The cellar, which originally held coke for the old boiler, became a store for extra tables, chairs, pantomime props and excess equipment of all kinds. It was damp, dark and dingy but worsened on one occasion in the nineties when it flooded and most of the contents had to be dumped. Pumps had to be employed to drain the water and the cellar was not fit for use again.

From the outside, the school did not appear to have had many changes over the years but the interior underwent constant developments to suit the changing requirements of a busy school. The mobiles were removed when the extension was completed in 1978 and the old kitchen became Room 6 and accommodated Year 3 for a number of years until falling numbers meant it was no longer needed as a classroom. It then became a Nursery for a short time in 1999 and following that it became a Resource centre as well as being used for a multitude of purposes such as displays, the Book Fair, music lessons, choir practices, medical examinations, tests and special help.

The classroom situated directly under the façade at the front of the school was that used by Mr Gowdy and Year 6. In latter years it suffered greatly from damp and leaks, particularly around the windows. Various remedies were tried and at one stage the removal of the façade was suggested but this was never carried out, as it could not be guaranteed that the removal would solve the problem and it would have been detrimental to the appearance of the building. However, towards the end of the nineties the damp was severe and large pieces of plaster constantly fell off the walls.

Rooms 7, 8 and 9 in the 1978 extension were originally meant for infants but when the Special Unit expanded in 1988, the Infants from Room 9 moved up the corridor to Room 2, vacated by Mrs Caldwell. Room 9 was adapted for the Senior Unit pupils while in 1995 Room 10 was structurally altered, enlarging it and including toilets, a new changing room and wash facilities.

Room 2 also became vacant in the late eighties as numbers continued to fall and was changed to become a library, with some space provided for the Outreach teacher. The new library was praised in the Inspection in 1991 and was widely used and enjoyed by the pupils.

Room 1 became the new Medical Inspection room, while its store and the adjacent cloakroom were combined to provide a small room for remedial teaching. After a few years, the room, which had always been very cold and had significant damp problems, had to undergo serious renovations. The walls were completely re-plastered; new windows and new radiators were installed, the interior suitably decorated and furnishings provided. Mrs P. Stewart then occupied it for remedial teaching, following her appointment in 1991.

Mr Orr and the Governors always tried to act prudently within the budget to maintain the classrooms and corridor areas in good decorative order. Rooms were decorated on a rota basis and the high standard of caretaking and cleaning ensured that the school was well presented. Indeed the school inspection in 1991 praised not only the good behaviour of the children and the hard working teachers, but also mentioned the cleanliness of the school. However, the roof continued to leak and the outside was criticised in the Inspection as being "dirty and drab," so arrangements were made to have the external walls painted and the deteriorating playground tarred in the summer of 1993.

In early 1993 work started on the extension to the Special Unit. The existing classroom wall was extended, windows moved to new positions, toilets, changing and washroom facilities were added and storage facilities provided. The room was decorated and a new carpet provided, giving the infants in the Special Unit much needed comforts.

Disabled access to the school was also given consideration, with ramps at the front and side doors being provided for wheelchair users.

Finally the old school house, which had been rapidly deteriorating since Mr Woods had left it, was demolished in early 1993 and the site cleared, leaving a greater area of grass on which the children played.

Health and Safety measures introduced by the Government in the nineties forced schools to consider relevant issues. Chairs, which were used at dinnertime, were stacked in a line along a wall in the assembly hall and this was not regarded as safe practice, so provision had to be made to allow safer storage. The existing equipment store was already full to capacity, so was of little use. The very small office in which the secretary worked was considered suitable, so she had to move out and was given the slightly larger office of the Headmaster, while he moved up the corridor and into the former Medical Room/Library. The existing door to the corridor was closed up, a new door was created, opening into the assembly hall, and from then on the little office became a chair store. A glass service hatch was created in the secretary's new office, new furniture and fittings were provided along with up to date office equipment, including a photocopier and computer.

In March 1996 a serious incident took place in a Primary School in Dunblane, Perthshire, Scotland, when a deranged gunman entered the school and shot dead many children and teachers. Security in schools and the safety of children and staff became urgent issues. In Edwards new procedures for visitors entering the school were drawn up and the children became aware of the enhanced safety measures.

Concerns were also expressed about the number of unauthorised people who were using the school grounds. On occasions cars sped along the road through the school grounds and caused hazards to the children. Football matches were being played in the field and people were exercising dogs in the grounds without permission. Although notices were erected they were taken down. Both school gates were locked in the evening and this helped in a small way to combat the problems.

Strangely enough for a school of its size, there were only two staff toilets, one male and one female. In the nineties this led to storms of protest from the ever-increasing numbers of females on the staff. (In true Ronnie Barker fashion they said they had nothing to go on!!) Eventually, their requests were met with the provision of an extra staff toilet in the former store of Room 6, providing much relief for teachers in the upper corridor!

In the year 2000 Mrs Graham and Year 4 moved out to a mobile classroom situated near the back gate and Room 5 which was also suffering from damp and was continually cold, was renovated, the interior door to the store removed and the walls plastered and redecorated. The store was then accessed by a door opening into the corridor and became a storage room for the cleaning staff. Year 4 remained in the mobile and Room 5 became a new library with carpet and fittings supplied by the WELB.

From then on Mr Orr and the Governors concentrated their efforts in securing a deal for a new school and no further decoration or changes were made.

There is almost a sense of deja-vue when one looks at the minute books kept by the Board of Governors in the nineties and compares them to the minutes kept by the Management Committee in the thirties. The same problems occurred and were discussed each time; the deficiencies of the boiler and the heating system resulting in cold conditions, and the deteriorating fabric of the building resulting in damp, leaks, decaying walls and floors. Each time efforts to remedy the situation have been painstakingly slow and conditions in the school have worsened.

Although the 1938 building had been very well maintained, both inside and outside, and it appeared to be robust, there were serious underlying problems. In the main building there were many damp areas and the ravages of time and the effects of bombs rendered the flat roof of the 1978 extension to a sieve-like state, causing numerous leaks which in turn decayed the woodwork, creating constant demands on the budget as interim repairs were carried out.

The Board of Governors was very concerned and continual approaches were made to the Western Education and Library Board and the Department of Education, with regard to replacing the school. Following much debate and many meetings it was agreed that the costs of repairs were outweighing the effects and eventually Mr Orr and the Board of Governors gained a foothold on the ladder of progress towards a new building.

Finally, in March 2002 the Department of Education made the monumental announcement of a £2 million funding package to build a new school to replace the 1938 building. Mr Orr, the Governors, staff and pupils were absolutely delighted and excitedly awaited to ascend the next steps on the ladder. The football field was chosen as the site as this meant that there would be the minimum disruption to school life as the work progressed.

Edwards PS principal 'absolutely delighted'

"ABSOLUTE DELIGHT" was the reaction of Mr Alastair Orr, principal, of Edwards Primary School, Castlederg, to the announcement of a £2 million funding package to build a new school.

Edwards PS has more than 200 pupils. It was built in 1938, and extended in 1978. Staff say the building is now "showing its age".

The new school will be built on the sportsground beside the present building. No timetable for the work has been fixed, but staff hope the new school can be up and running within three years.

Edwards has a busy school community, providing facilities not only for pupils in P1 to P7, but having a unit for pupils designated as having Moderate Learning Difficulty (MLD) and a nursery unit.

Mr Orr explained the new building would have 10 classrooms, seven for the main school and other facilities for the MLD and nursery pupils. The building would have a new kitchen and dual-purpose sports/dining hall.

He added: "Staff, parents and governors began campaigning for a new school about four or five years ago and it has come along comparatively quickly."

It is perhaps ironic that the original part of the school has a good slate roof and poor walls, while the newer extension has a poor roof and good walls.

Commented Mr Orr: "We are all absolutely delighted. This is good news for the school, and good news for Castlederg".

Mr Orr travelled to Belfast for the announcement last week, accompanied by three pupils and the chairman of the Board of Governors, Dr. Morris Brown.

Pictured on the playing fields that will form the site of the new building for Edwards Primary School.

At last when the Department of Education gave the green light, the Principal and staff, along with the Board of Governors discussed the new site, drew up plans, sought tenders, appointed a contractor and waited with anticipation for the new building to evolve.

However, it was with great sadness that staff learnt that the old school building would be demolished following the completion of the new building, so with this in mind it was decided to have an Open Evening in June 2004 to allow past pupils, staff and members of the public to come and reminisce. Staff and pupils set about collecting memorabilia from the past and assembling displays. Past pupils and staff, from near and far, attended the evening and enjoyed meeting old friends and reminiscing.

EDWARDS P.S.
1938—2004

OPEN EVENING
Wednesday 23rd June 2004

We bid you a very warm welcome to our Open Evening and we hope you enjoy meeting old friends, reminiscing, browsing through the displays and chatting over a cup of tea, provided by our Parent and Teacher Association

AU REVOIR

Thank you for coming to our Open Evening. We also wish to thank all those who contributed items for display. We sincerely hope that you have enjoyed the time spent with us and that it has renewed many happy memories for you.

NEW SCHOOL

We look forward to welcoming you again to our new school. If anyone wishes to be associated with the new school through sponsorship of any items or for example in planting a tree in the grounds, please leave your name and contact number on the sheet in the foyer.
Thank you and our good wishes to you from everyone in Edwards Primary School.

EDWARDS PRIMARY SCHOOL,
26, HOSPITAL ROAD,
CASTLEDERG,
CO.TYRONE.
N.I.
BT 81 7HY
Tel : 028 816 71642
Fax : 028 816 71995
Email : aorr@edwards.castlederg.ni.sch.uk

PRESENT STAFF IN EDWARDS P.S.

Principal : Mr AS Orr Cert Ed B.Ed. (Hons)
Vice Principal : Mr I. Gowdy Cert Ed. B.Ed (Hons)

Teachers :

Mrs P. Bratton Cert Ed. B.A.

Miss J. Douglas B.Ed.

Mrs H. Graham Cert Ed.

Mrs C. Hawkes B. Sc.

Mrs H. McCay B. Ed

Mrs G. McKinley Cert Ed.

Miss L. Morrow B.Sc. (Hons) P.G.C.E.

Miss N. Moore B. Ed.

Mrs H. Robinson B.Ed

Miss C. Roke B.Ed

Mrs M. Watt Cert Ed.

CLASSROOM ASSISTANTS

Mrs I. Forbes   Miss K. Waugh

Miss Z. Johnston   Miss M. Young B.A.

Miss E. McKane

Mrs P. Quigley

Mrs S. Sproule

SECRETARY Mrs E. Walls
CARETAKER Mr W Gilchrist
CLEANERS Mrs J. Bogle, Mrs G. Glass
COOKS Mrs M. Burke, Mrs H. Keatley

A New Beginning

The following photographs and newspaper cuttings record the building progress from Monday 17th November 2003, when the first digger moved onto the site. The children and teachers watched the progress every day and many classes completed diaries of the events, using the excavation and building processes as learning experiences. Pupils whose parents worked on the site were particularly interested and pleased to see the building take shape.

Unfortunately some of the pleasant aspects of the school grounds gradually disappeared; the hedge was the first to go, followed by the row of large trees, then the two cherry trees in front of the school and rapidly the football field became unrecognisable. The trees that had been planted to mark the Millennium were moved to temporary sites and now many have been replanted. A large swathe of ground was cleared from in front of the school and as digging progressed a section of the old workhouse wall was uncovered but it was not considered viable to retain it. Work went on through the winter of 2003-2004, even continuing in the snow. Cranes arrived to assist with the heavy steel girders and roofs and the children were enthralled as they watched the workmen carry out skilful manoeuvres. The building began to take shape and pupils tried to work out the position of their new classrooms. For the teachers there were many decisions to be made concerning new furnishings and fittings and there was an air of excited anticipation.

Finally, just a year after work had begun, the new Nursery was ready and the pupils and staff moved in. Shortly afterwards the rest of the new school was ready and staff began the process of packing and moving. Large containers were supplied by the WELB and a team of helpers arrived to move the contents into the new building. A lot of work was carried out before Christmas as the pupils were given extra holidays, while the staff worked overtime to prepare for the opening in January 2005.

*The first digger enters the football field on Monday 17th November 2003
to begin work on the new school.*

The site is cleared and foundations are being laid.

January 2004, building above ground level.

A large crane helps to erect the steel work.

Steel work continues with roof trusses in position on the Hall and Nursery.

Large lorries come and go using the Hospital Road entrance.

Building continues despite the snow.

Rooms begin to take shape as brickwork increases. Windows are put in.

Scaffolding enables the builders to work on the roof.

Work continues on the Hall roof and the glaziers begin to put in the glass.

Parishes of Derg and Termonamongan

Rector: The Revd Canon Walter P Quill
The Rectory
13 Strabane Road
Castlederg
Co Tyrone   Tel/Fax: 028 81671362 (Mobile: 07801921697)
BT81 7HZ   Email: walter.quill@talk21.com

I wish to pay tribute to Mr Alistair Orr, Principal, and to the Board of Governors, under the chairmanship of Dr Morris Brown, for their untiring efforts in bringing about the building of this excellent new school.

As a former chairman of the Board of Governors, I can appreciate the satisfaction they must feel at having achieved such a successful outcome after much discussion and debate.

The old school building, while holding many happy memories for all those associated with it, had long past its sell-by-date. It was a constant source of concern regarding matters of health and safety.

A new chapter has begun in the life Edwards with the provision of this very impressive new building. However, it needs to be remembered that it is the people at the school – not the building itself - who contribute to its history, its story.

My prayer is that God will richly bless governors, staff and pupils in the years that lie ahead. May Edwards continue to attract, educate and nurture children from the Castlederg area. May those same children reach their potential and grow up to be an influence for good wherever they travel.

293

Derg pupils settle into their new surrounds

by Olga Bradshaw

PUPILS at Edwards Primary School, Castlederg, have been settling into their new, £1.7 million state-of-the-art primary school this week.

The new facility boasts a total of seven classrooms, which are fully equipped with all 'mod cons' to ensure a quality education experience for the children

In addition, there are what are known as two 'moderate learning difficulties' units, which are specifically geared to helping children overcome any difficulties they may have, as they take their formative steps on the academic ladder.

At present there is an enrolment of 201 at the school, and the classroom provision is fitted out with a full range of cloakroom and toilet facilties, specifically designed so that 'little people' have no difficulty learning to be independent, where health and hygiene is concerned!

The architects for the new build were W D R and R T Taggart, Belfast, while the building contract was awarded to McCann Bros (Ireland), of Seskinore.

Support accommodation at the school includes an assembly hall, four offices, a group teaching room facility, as well as three 'resource' areas.

While for most the start of January signalled the end of the festive fun and games, the return to school for pupils in Castlederg meant a completely new environment to explore.

The old school building closed, the principal, Mr A S Orr, and his staff then had to work faster than Santa's elves to ensure that all the books and resource materials were packed away for the journey to the new building, and then taken out of their protective packaging and housed in their new 'home'.

The new building includes a nursery unit, and children enrolled there moved into their new accommodation just before Christmas.

For everyone associated with the school, January 6th 2005 was a real red-letter day. After all the excitement of parties, Santa and Christmas, the new term was about to begin within the walls of the hitherto forbidden building—the new Edwards Primary School!

The staff of the school had carried out a lot of behind-the-scenes work to enable the children to begin the New Year in the most exciting way possible. Anticipation and nervousness hung heavily in the air as pupils were brought into the wonderful state-of-the-art building. Mr A. Orr conducted a welcome service in the cavernous hall and children were brought to their new classrooms, where they delighted in bright, spacious rooms with carpeted floors, beautiful new furniture, interactive whiteboards, resource areas, cloakrooms and toilets adjoining classrooms and a large playground. During the day classes were taken on tour of the interesting new facilities and everyone was impressed as they drank in all the new sights and sounds.

Dinnertime brought another set of rules and ideas into play as both kitchen staff and pupils adjusted to working and eating in the different surroundings. However, everything went smoothly, although a little slowly, but this improved as the days passed.

At home time pupils had to become accustomed to the new rules and find the correct exit doors. Then they had to find their parents or the buses. Each one had a story to tell, but everyone agreed that they had learned a lot on that first momentous day in their new school! What a day it had been!!

To mark the occasion, each family received a souvenir colour newsletter recording the events of January 2005 and featuring comments and photos, and it is hoped that each will value this little piece of history. In time, it too could become a collector's item. Who knows what will happen in another seventy years time?

Year one pupils, Jayne Young, Scott Monaghan, Scott Montgomery, Emma Reid, Jamie Reid and Hannah Thompson, leave the old school behind and enter their new school with their teacher, Miss Jill Douglas and Mr Alistair Orr, principal.

Primary 7 pupils, Sophie Harpur and Denver Lecky, ring the bell on their first day in the new Edwards Primary School, Castlederg. The bell, formerly the Old Market bell sited in Castlederg town centre, was presented to the school by Canon Harry Trimble.

Testing the computers in the new Edwards Primary School, Castlederg, are Year 2 and 3 children, Chloe Gannon, Mark Hamilton and Mark Keatley, under the supervision of Year 3 teacher, Miss Nicola Moore.

Year 6 and 7 children, Leanne Lindsay, Caroline Irwin, Julie-Ann Sproule, Heather Sproule, Travis Gordon, Dean Irvine and Adam Patterson, excercising in the Assembly Hall in their new school.

Children from the special unit at work in their new surroundings with teachers,
Mrs Margaret Watt and Mrs Gladys McKinley.

Year 4 and 5 pupils queue for their dinner in the new Edwards Primary School, Brett Wallace,
Abigail Clarke, Charlene Hemphill, Chloe Hall, Emily Maxwell and Alan Boyd,
served by kitchen staff, including supervisor, Mrs Maria Burke.

EDWARDS SPECIAL EDITION NEWSLETTER JANUARY 2005.

NEW SCHOOL OPENS ITS DOORS.

Thursday 6th of January 2005 was a momentous day in the history of Edwards Primary School when the doors of the newly constructed school were opened to the pupils for the first time.

Little ones were apprehensive, some felt tummy twinges, some felt really excited. Older children quietly entered the new portals in wonderment and awe at finally being in the building which they had watched being constructed from the moment the first digger entered the football pitch on November 3rd

2003. It's amazing the difference a year makes!!

The day began with pupils being taken to their rooms and shown their new cloakrooms, toilets and exit doors.

Mr Orr addressed the pupils at their first Assembly in the Hall, welcoming everyone and wishing staff and pupils continued success and happiness in the new school.

During the day classes settled happily into their shining new rooms, trying hard to find all their belongings and acquainting themselves

with the lay-out of the new building.

Dinner in the Assembly hall was exciting as was the first lunch-time spent in the spacious playground. Before the end of the day many classes took a walk around and enjoyed the interesting features, everyone agreeing that the school was "lovely".

Mr Gowdy practises using his new white board.

Special points of interest:

☺ Read what pupils think about their new school.

☺ Enjoy browsing through the photographs.

☺ Barney the Barn Owl is the first visitor.

☺ Scottish Country Dancing begins.

☺ Forthcoming events.

MEMORABILIA
A small quantity of items will be available for a short time. If you wish to buy, please place your order as soon as possible.

WISE OLD BIRD MAKES HIS MARK IN NEW SCHOOL HALL!!

For most schools the first visitors are usually well known people, but the first officially invited visitor to our new school was in fact a very attractive bird, of the feathered variety of course.

Barney the Barn Owl accompanied by his minder, Seamus Burns of the Ulster Wildlife Trust, met the children of Key Stage 2, on Tuesday 11th of January — see inside for further details.

The 1938 Building is Demolished.

For those who worked in or attended the 1938 Edwards Primary School, the necessary demolition of the property was a sad sight to behold. The staff that had worked there for decades and indeed even those who had only been there a short time, watched poignantly as many years of happy memories and a splendid part of history disappeared under the harsh, cruel and unrelenting force of a digger bucket.

Even the children felt sad and some were afraid as they witnessed the awesome sight of the majestic building tumbling down.

Within a short time, the roof had been stripped, timbers removed, walls crushed, rubble removed and the site levelled as if the building had never existed.

The new playing field was then prepared and it is hoped that it will witness as many happy sporting occasions as the old football field, now the scene of the new Edwards!

WESTERN EDUCATION & LIBRARY BOARD

The Chairman and Board of Governors of
Edwards Primary School
request the pleasure of the company of

---

at the Official Opening of
Edwards Primary School
on Thursday, 29 September 2005 at 11 am

R.S.V.P. (Regrets only) before 22 September 2005 to:
Mr A S Orr, Edwards Primary School, 26 Hospital Road,
Castlederg, Co Tyrone, BT81 7HY
Telephone: 028 8167 1642

*Buffet Lunch will
be provided*

**WESTERN EDUCATION
& LIBRARY BOARD**

OFFICIAL OPENING

of

Edwards Primary School

on

Thursday, 29 September 2005

by

Her Grace, The Duchess of Abercorn

303

OFFICIAL CEREMONY

INTRODUCTORY REMARKS

Dr J M Brown
Chairman of Board of Governors
Edwards Primary School

WELCOME

Mr Alistair Orr
Principal
Edwards Primary School

OPENING REMARKS

Mr Barry Mulholland
Chief Executive
Western Education & Library Board

OFFICIAL OPENING

Her Grace, The Duchess of Abercorn

CLOSING REMARKS

Mr Dominic McElholm
Chairman
Western Education and Library Board

Vote of Thanks and Presentations

Guest of Honour

The Duchess of Abercorn

Sacha Abercorn was born in Tucson, Arizona and brought up in Leicestershire. She is married to James, the Duke of Abercorn and they have three children. They reside on the Baronscourt Estate near Newtownstewart.

Increasingly concerned with the unrest in the Province, she decided she wanted to work with children and teachers. This led her to evaluate a method to bring children together and so The Pushkin Trust was founded in 1987. This would involve Protestant and Catholic schools from both Northern Ireland and Republic of Ireland coming together for environmental and creative arts workshops.

Sacha has made an immense contribution to the education of children and teachers on this island for the past 18 years. She has focused her energy on developing opportunities for people of different communities on both sides of the border to develop their creativity and find their own voice.

DESIGN AND CONSTRUCTION TEAM

Architects: WDR & RT Taggart, Belfast

WELB Design Consultant: Mr H Turner, Property Services Division, WELB

M&E Engineer: Delap & Waller, Londonderry

Structural Engineer: Doran Consulting, Belfast

Quantity Surveyors: FCM Partnership, Belfast

Main Contractor: McCann Brothers Ireland Ltd, Seskinore, Omagh

Mechanical Sub-Contractor: Thomas Hanna & Co, Brookeborough

Electrical Sub-Contractor: Campbell & Slevin, Omagh

Landscaper: Cloon Nursery, Castlederg

Clerk of Works: Mr Jack Sproule, Castlederg

Board of Governors and guests.
Back row: Mr Robert Montgomery, Mr Thomas Kerrigan, Mrs Anne Hunter, Mr Ivan Clarke,
Mrs Gladys McKinley, Mr Desie Williamson, Mr Jack Walls.
Front row: Mr Barry Mullholland, (Chief Executive of the W.E.L.B.), Dr Morris Brown,
(Chairman of the Board of Governors), The Duchess of Abercorn, Mr Alistair Orr, (Principal)
Mr Dominic McElholm, (Chairman W.E.L.B.)

(News Letter) Duchess Planting a tree

The choir performing at the Opening.

The unveiling of the plaque.

Guests and children.

Mr Orr, Canon Trimble at Market Bell.

The Official Opening Of The New School
Thursday 29th September 2005.

The official opening of the school took place nine months after the doors had first opened to receive the pupils. The day was in sharp contrast to the opening in 1938, when just about everyone in Castlederg attended. This time, under the direction of the W.E.L.B., most pupils were given the day off, while those taking part in the programme came to school, but remained in a classroom until they were required.

The Western Education and Library Board played a major role in planning the occasion, liasing with the Principal in finalising details. This meant that the month of September was even busier than usual. Teachers and pupils had only just begun to settle into the new term when they were thrown into the chaos of organising the event. A guest list was collated, invitations extended, a menu for the buffet lunch selected, a programme compiled, entertainment planned and practised, last minute jobs completed, the grounds finished and wall displays erected.

These were duly accomplished and the W.E.L.B. was proud to show off its latest masterpiece. The guest of honour was Her Grace, the Duchess of Abercorn and senior representatives of the Western Education and Library Board, the school Governors, past members of staff, local clergy, some parents and Principals of local schools attended.

The Duchess performed the Opening Ceremony, remarking on the sadness of closing the old school and the end of an era. She commented upon the "new school, with excellent facilities, a school fit for the 21st century," with the common aim being "the best possible education for all of our children."

The Chairman of the Board of Governors, Dr Morris Brown, thanked the Duchess for performing the opening and praised the work of the staff. He acknowledged the efforts of the W.E.L.B. and the Department of Education in bringing the school to fruition and observed that it was a momentous and special occasion for everyone.

Principal, Mr Orr, also paid tribute to the dedication and professionalism of the staff, and thanked the Western Board for funding, remarking, "we are delighted to be able to teach in such a bright and spacious environment."

The chief executive of the Western Board, Mr Barry Mulholland, commented that they were "acutely focused on providing a suitable environment" to promote teaching and learning. "Edwards P.S. and Nursery Unit provide modern state-of-the-art facilities in which to implement the Northern Ireland Curriculum," he stated.

Western Board chairman, Mr Dominic McElholm, commended the innovative design and the construction teams. "You need more than just good buildings to provide quality learning experiences. You also need quality teaching. I am delighted that Edwards P.S. now has both firmly in place," he said.

The Duchess of Abercorn unveiled the plaque to officially open the school and following a short entertainment program, she planted an oak tree. The visitors then toured the new facilities and enjoyed a buffet lunch in the Hall. This was provided by the W.E.L.B. catering services.

In the evening an open invitation was extended to parents and the community to visit the school and view the facilities. The members of the P.T.A. provided supper and visitors enjoyed a leisurely stroll around the building and an informal chat with staff.

Murals and Paintings presented to the New School

Presented by
Castlederg Junior
Gateway Club
September 2005.

Presented to
the School by
former pupil
Samantha
Bogle.

Presented by the P.T.A. to mark
the opening of the New School
29th September 2005

A School Year.

Reflecting on the many changes since Hugh Edwards' dream of a "convenient country house" became reality, leads one to realise that although buildings may have altered beyond recognition, the greatest transformation has unfolded in the school curriculum and the events in a school year.

The following details outline some of the happenings over a typical year in Edwards School and indicate the changes that have evolved up to the present day. From the days of chalk and talk to the more child centred approach with hands on activities, life in school has been marked by continual modifications. As well as the curricular changes, many events and competitions have been incorporated and the school year is increasingly busy.

The present school year for pupils is 190 days long with an allowance of 71 days for holidays while teachers work 200 days. Some holidays are "fixed" and must be taken as prescribed, while others are taken at the discretion of each school.

"Baker Days"—named after the Government Minister, who introduced them in the early nineties, enable teachers to undertake preparation and training and give the pupils extra holidays! Teachers have found their holidays shortened as they fit in the extra days. At least three days in August are now taken up with preparations for the impending year while the other days are taken, as needed, for in-service training.

The busy term begins in early September and staff and pupils settle in. From the age of three children are welcomed into the nursery by Mrs Bratton and Miss Young and they enjoy a wide range of experiences that prepare them for their future school life. For those beginning mainstream school, the day is short— (9.30 a.m. to 12.30 p.m. for a number of weeks) while those starting Primary 4 have to become accustomed to a longer day (9.30 a.m. to 3.15 p.m.) Classes and teachers adapt to the busy routine and they look forward eagerly to the mid term break at Hallowe'en when they have a few days off, and Christmas is only around the corner!

The present system of grammar school selection at eleven years of age means that pupils have to sit the Transfer Tests in November. For them this incurs extra preparation classes, additional homework and a series of preparatory tests. Hard work for everyone involved!

Key Stage 1 teachers, Miss Douglas, Mrs Hawkes, Miss Moore and Miss Morrow meet parents regularly. This ensures that the Infants settle well into school and acquaint parents with the areas being taught, as well as giving help and advice to parents of those with special needs.

Miss Morrow is also responsible for teaching Reading Recovery, an intense one-to-one teaching system that helps children improve reading skills and strategies. She is also responsible for special educational needs throughout the school.

The story of Christmas is told in the form of Nativity Plays performed each year by the infants or Key Stage One children, while the older pupils contribute choir items. This sounds simple but involves a lot of extra work and practice. In latter years the trend has been to have the Key Stage 2 pupils performing class productions and again a lot of extra work is required to reach a satisfactory level. Parents and families have always supported and enjoyed these occasions.

Following the Christmas break, school begins in early January, usually with tests for Key Stage 2, in preparation for Parent Interviews, (which were started by Mr Riddall), and these happen early in February. For Key Stage 2 pupils this brings revision and extra homework! For teachers its means mountains of marking!

The old emphasis on Handwork for boys and Needlework for girls has shifted to a much more integrated approach and the time allocated to those subjects is now taken up by "Clubs," which offer all pupils from Year 4 to Year 7 opportunities to try various sports and creative and expressive activities.

Over the course of the year a number of special weeks are held, focussing attention on a particular area of the curriculum. In Music Week, co-ordinated by Mrs C. Hawkes, Music Advisors from the Western Education and Library Board visit the school and encourage children to join in a range of musical activities. Children are invited to write songs and hymns and to try different musical instruments. Various musicians and bands also visit and contribute at different times of the year. Mrs Hawkes is also responsible for auditioning, selecting and training members of the choir, who perform at various functions throughout the year.

In Year 4 a member of the Western Board Music staff assesses pupils to ascertain musical aptitude and some children are given the chance to learn a brass instrument.

During Safety Week, coordinated by Miss N. Moore, different aspects are studied, ranging from road safety, personal safety and bullying issues and home safety to farm and electrical safety. Various speakers are enlisted and talks and displays have always been beneficial. At the end of the week the Key Stage 2 pupils take part in a Quiz and the winner receives a Cup and prize, while the representatives from each class also win a book or book token.

The Cycling Proficiency Scheme aims to help young cyclists to improve their skills, develop good road sense and promote safe cycling. Miss Moore has taken this scheme since 1999 and has been assisted by Miss Douglas.

The Story Telling Competition, which began in 1972 after Miss Elliott had awarded the Cup, has always been keenly contested. Mr Orr encouraged the continuance of the competition, which is organised by Mrs McCay, and various ideas have been tried. Pupils originally took a story or fable, interpreted and told it before a panel of judges. Later they tried creating their own stories and telling them to their peers and independent judges. Many stories have been written down and kept and make interesting reading!

Mrs P. Stewart started a verse speaking competition in 1994. Pupils were asked to learn and recite a poem and this tradition still continues as a yearly competition for both Key Stage 1 and 2 pupils.

Various tutors from the Verbal Arts Centre in Londonderry have visited the school to work with classes for a term and pupils have been encouraged to improve their creative writing talents. This has been most enjoyable for pupils and teachers and some have even seen their efforts published.

Religious Education is now taught less formally but teachers still promote Biblical knowledge and an awareness of other religions, while Ministers from the local churches take Assembly once a month. Missionaries are also welcomed and pupils have gained valuable insights into far off Mission fields and the difficulties experienced by the staff in spreading the gospel and coping with different climates and cultures. Mr Gowdy and Miss Douglas also organise the Scripture Union group, which meets for Bible Study, talks, quizzes and games and there is a weekend Youth Club for past pupils.

Under the auspices of the Speedwell Trust and as part of the E.M.U. programme many classes have visited places such as The Folk Park, The History Park, Baronscourt and Beltrim Castle to study History, Science and Nature topics. This has allowed children to visit interesting venues to gain practical experiences and to form friendships with pupils from their partner school, St Patrick's P.S. Castlederg.

Mrs Graham is responsible for the promotion of Art and Craft throughout the school. With the children she has produced many memorable displays, one of the most noteworthy being the mural of the past three schools, created by Year 4, and with the assistance of Miss Jill McFarland. It now hangs proudly in the new school foyer and has also been used as the cover for this book.

There are many visitors to the school over the course of a year. Representatives from various charities make appeals for funds, entertainers, such as Story Tellers Billy Teare and John Campbell, musicians like Len Graham, Willie Drennan and Different Drums of Ireland, Horace the Magician, and actors from travelling theatre companies such as The West Midland Theatre Company, all enhance the curriculum, while other visitors such as Ian Patterson with his Birds of Prey, staff from the Zoo and the Ulster Wildlife Trust provide opportunities to see and handle live birds and animals.

Teachers from France and Switzerland have also contributed to the children's learning, when they were hosted as part of the school's involvement in the Comenius programme, which fosters greater links with Europe.

Children are encouraged to have an environmental responsibility and have taken part in various Recycling schemes promoted by the local Council such as collecting old telephone directories and Christmas Cards and have been successful in many Council competitions.

Healthy eating is also promoted and for many years the school has received Smart Snacks Awards. Children can purchase milk at a subsidised rate, daily fruit tuck shops operate and the cafeteria-style kitchen encourages pupils to make healthy choices.

The Police Service for Northern Ireland visit the school over a period of six weeks and involve Year 5 children in their CASE programme—- Citizenship and Safety Education. Acting Sergeant Alan McGonagle, from the local station, helps children to become responsible members of society and provides a valuable insight into the role of the PSNI.

Handwriting has always had an important place in the curriculum and Mrs McNutt presented a Handwriting Cup on her retirement. Each year pupils submit their efforts and the Cup is awarded to the best entry.

Sport has continued to feature as an important aspect of the school curriculum. Extra curricular activities have included football, taken by Mr Gowdy, hockey taken by Mrs McKinley and Mrs Graham, netball taken by Mrs McCay and latterly tag rugby taken by Miss Roke. The Youth Foyle Sport Scheme in conjunction with Castlederg High School has also provided coaching in a number of sports.

The children of the Special Unit 2 and the Year 7 class also enjoy swimming lessons. They travel to Strabane High School Pool for a period of four months, during which time they learn basic swimming strokes and are awarded Certificates marking their attainments.

Easter holidays provide a welcome break in the school year and according to when Easter occurs; the summer term is often brief. Many trips and outings take place during this term as well as outdoor activities. Pupils enjoy preparing for Sports Day and the field is in regular use.

Sports Day has long been the highlight of the year and is awaited with great expectation. Pupils prepare for their races and when the big day comes around they are in peak condition! Parents gather on one side of the track to watch the budding athletes while pupils and staff assemble on the other side. The ARP bell is still rung to signal the start of the parade to the field and classes in turn follow the bell-ringer. Mr Gowdy and the senior pupils organise the equipment and the events and many keenly contested races take place. Badges marking first, second and third place are presented and following their races the exhausted competitors enjoy ice creams. Cups, which have been presented to the school by local families, are awarded to the winners of the Infant and Senior Sprints, Relay and Long Distance races.

June brings end of term tests and reports, a very busy finish to the year for both pupils and staff. The school year concludes with a special service and presentation of awards followed by the welcome break for the July and August holidays, when both staff and pupils recharge their batteries in preparation for another challenging year.

Reflecting on all these activities and including day-to-day planning for teaching, preparation and marking, in-service training, curriculum meetings, testing, record keeping, staff meetings, extra-curricular activities and PTA events, it is easy to see that this very hectic programme of events over the course of the school year is in marked contrast to the more leisurely school years of the past. With frequent changes to the curriculum, ever increasing paper work and record keeping, planning, teaching and marking, teachers are now placed under pressure of overload, which is increasingly leading to stress, disillusionment, loss of confidence in one's ability to cope and exhaustion.

Maybe a step back in time would be the answer!

Bibliography.

Irish Life in the Seventeenth Century.   Edward MacLysaght, M.A. D.Litt. M.R.I.A.

The Siege of Derry—A History. Carlo Gebler.

Ardstraw—Historical Survey of a Parish 1600—1900. John H. Gebbie.

A History of Irish Education. P.J. Dowling.

Irish Education. Norman Atkinson.

Tyrone- History and Society. Charles Dillon and Henry A. Jeffries.

The Plantation in Ulster 1608—1620. Rev. George Hill.

A Guide To Irish Country Houses. Mark Bence Jones.

A Genealogical and Historical Sketch of the Stuarts of the House of Castlestuart in Ireland. Rev. Andrew Godfrey Stuart M.A.

A View of Society and Manners in the North of Ireland. J. Gamble Esq.

Ordnance Survey Memoirs of Ireland, Parishes of County Londonderry VII, 1834-35, Volume 25. J. Rodrigo Ward 1835

Ordnance Survey Memoirs of Ireland, Parish of Skirts of Urney and Ardstraw, County Tyrone. J. Rodrigo Ward 1836

A History of the Family of Cairnes or Cairns. H.C. Lawlor.

Burke' Peerage and Patronage.

Castlederg and Its Red River Valley. Councillor James A. Emery and Canon H. Trimble.

An Old Ulster House—Springhill. Mina Lenox-Conyngham.

Irish Education---A Historical Survey. James Johnston Auchmuty. M.A. Ph.D.

Valuation of Tenements—(Griffith 1860) Parish of Urney

Topographical Dictionary of Ireland 1837. Samuel Lewis.

Hayes Manuscript Sources for the History of Irish Civilisation.

Memoirs of the Archdales. Henry Blackwood Archdale.

Tombstones of the Omey. William J. McGrew

A History of the Parish of Tullanisken 1793-1933. Eileen Elizabeth Donnelly M.Sc. B.A. Dip Ed.

Ulster Journal of Archaeology. Extra Volume 1903. (Old Castles of County Tyrone)

Clogher Cathedral Graveyard Burial Records—Cairns/Cairnes Nos 257-264. P30.

THE

PEOPLE

OF

EDWARDS.

Headmasters Over the Years

- Mr Alexander Eglinton 1833 - 1849

- Mr Thomas J. Burnside B.A. - 1898 - 1927.

- Mr James G. Sloan M.A. - 1930 - 1955

- Mr T.F. Riddall 1955 - 1985

- Mr A.S. Orr B.Ed. 1985 -

From 1849 until 1898 school records are scarce but it would appear that a series of paid monitors contucted the teaching.

Mr Alexander Eglinton 1833-1849

Early educational records are very scarce; hence little is known about Alexander Eglinton or Eglintoun, as it is sometimes spelt. He is first mentioned in the National School records of 1835, where his pay was noted as £4 quarterly. J. Rodrigo Ward's Ordnance Survey Memoirs for the Parish of the Skirts of Urney and Ardstraw in 1836 also describe him as the Protestant master of the National School. There are no records of his education but he is referred to in the school records of 1833 as "tr K Pl"-presumably meaning trained in Kildare Place in Dublin. Later he is mentioned in April 1839 as "aged 39, trained" and in 1840 received an increase in salary of £2 per quarter. Numerous letters exist which indicate that he had been brought to teach in Lord Castlestewart's school but had not received any remuneration. The Trustees of the Hugh Edwards Charity pleaded on his behalf and stated that he "has a large family and is miserably poor." This correspondence is described in detail in "Schools in Ireland in the 19th Century" but it is not known if the master actually received any support.

In 1849 a new school building opened on the Castlefin Road and Alexander Eglinton was the Master. However, in the same year he was dismissed from the post for having written an "impertinent letter to Sir Robert Ferguson, (the Landlord) under an assumed name."

This brought his career in Castlederg to an abrupt halt and following that the school was managed for many years by paid monitors.

MR THOMAS J. BURNSIDE. B.A. 1898-1927

and MISS EVELYN BURNSIDE M.A. LLB.

Mr Thomas James Burnside B.A. became Principal of the old Edwards School on the Castlefin Road in 1900. He was a local man and for many years was a Ruling Elder in Second Castlederg Presbyterian Church. He was widely recognised as an erudite educationalist and the seat of learning, often referred to as "The Burnsides' School," was highly regarded in the area. He taught Classics, (the study of Latin and Greek and the literature of ancient Rome and Greece), among other subjects such as Irish, French, English, Geography, History and Arithmetic. Inspectors' Reports of the early 1900's describe the proficiency of the pupils as "excellent" or "very good." In 1905 Mr W. Clements, the Inspector, said " the Principal teacher deserves great credit for the important reforms he has effected as regards the manner, politeness and general demeanour of his pupils."

He taught Junior and Senior classes as well as an evening class for secondary level pupils and his daughter, Evelyn, assisted him in this. She obtained the degrees of M.A. and LLB in Trinity College, Dublin, and also was highly regarded as an educationalist. The school was fee paying and pupils came from miles around to attend it. Many pupils sat Matriculation examinations that enabled them to enter University.

In 1915, Mr Coyne, the Senior Inspector reported that "the Principal is a highly efficient teacher, and the educational proficiency of his classes is very satisfactory on the whole." Indeed his service was considered to be of "such a character that he was awarded an increment of continued Good Service salary." A letter from the Office of National Education in Dublin in 1921 records his annual salary as £430 and that of his assistant teacher, Miss Susan Jackson, as £205.

Mr Burnside died in 1927 after a brief illness and his wife also died within a very short time. (See obituary notice following this article.) His daughter, Evelyn, moved to Strabane, where she continued to give private lessons. Mrs Ivy Lambert, of Ballygawley, sent the following information regarding Miss Burnside.

She wrote,

"I was brought up on a farm at Ballymullerty, Douglas Bridge. As there was no secondary or grammar school in Strabane then, in common with lots of Protestants I went to the Convent. Because I had got fifth place in the Old Strabane and Castlederg Regional Exam I was put into Form 2, but I missed out on the beginnings of Geometry and Algebra. Consequently I got behind and did badly in first year exams. I was sent to Dr. Burnside, as she was known, for extra lessons in these subjects. She had a lot of pupils for the same reason. She also did a lot of "cramming" for junior and senior exams.

She had a flat in a three-storey house in Upper Main Street above the Town Hall. It was very musty and we went upstairs to it. She was very plain looking but very erudite. I don't know how she became friendly with my mother but she used to come up to our house for tea and to spend the evening with us. She came in the bus. She was not in any way domesticated and liked home made bread, scones, tarts and cakes, which my mother made. I have lovely memories of her but don't know when she died."

(A copy of the tribute in Tyrone Constitution, April 1930)

Death of Mr Thomas J. Burnside. B.A.

LOSS OF DISTINGUISHED EDUCATIONALIST.

No death in the Castlederg district for many years has aroused more sorrow and sympathy on the part of the people than that of Mr Thomas J. Burnside, B.A., the esteemed principal of Edwards Public Elementary School, who passed away after a brief illness, on Thursday night, the 10th inst and the regret at his sudden call to the Grand Beyond is shared by all classes over a very wide area of North Tyrone. The leading part which the deceased took in educational affairs in the Castlederg district, and the outstanding successes attained by his pupils placed him in the forefront of educationalists in the North of Ireland. He devoted his life with the utmost self- sacrifice to the interests of his profession, and had the distinction of numbering amongst his pupils many of the most successful men in the learned professions and in important commercial positions. He manifested a kind and personal interest in his pupils by whom he was greatly beloved and was particularly pleased to learn of their progress and success in after life, whether at home or abroad. His loss to the district of Castlederg, where he laboured so zealously and acceptably, is irreparable, for it can scarcely be hoped that his place in the Edwards school will be filled by a teacher with the same enthusiasm and talent.

Mr Burnside's final illness developed with great rapidity and his condition on Thursday afternoon 10th inst became so critical that little hope was entertained for his recovery. Stricken with an acute attack of pneumonia, he never rallied and passed away at 9.30 pm. the same night. His work in Castlederg district will stand as a perpetual memorial of a devoted life.

A prominent member of the Presbyterian Church, he was a ruling elder in Second Castlederg, and manifested a very keen interest in the affairs of the congregation.

With Miss E.M.G.E. Burnside, M.A. LL.D.,---his daughter---herself a distinguished educationalist, and a member of the local Castlederg boards and the Strabane and Castlederg Regional Education Committee---there is the utmost sympathy in the severe bereavement into which she has been plunged.

In Derg Parish Church on Sunday, Rev. W. T. Macourt made sympathetic reference to the deceased and expressed sympathy with the Presbyterian Church in the loss of such a useful member

The funeral on Monday afternoon was one of the largest that has been seen in the neighbourhood of Castlederg for many years, and bore striking testimony to the esteem in which the deceased was held. Many travelled long distances to pay their respects. Immediately behind the hearse came the relatives, followed by the Governors of Edwards School. Then came upwards of two hundred pupils of the elementary and secondary schools, with most of the teachers. Prior to the funeral a service was conducted in the Infant's School in the presence of a large number of people, by Rev W. T. Macourt, Rev W. F. Henderson who with Rev.McFarlane, officiated at the graveside.

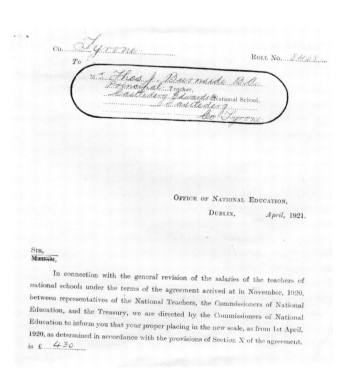

Co. Tyrone.   ROLL No. 8468

To

Mr Thos J. Burnside B.A.
Principal Teacher,
Castlederg Edwards National School.
Castlederg
Co Tyrone

OFFICE OF NATIONAL EDUCATION,

DUBLIN,   April, 1921.

SIR,
~~MADAM,~~

   In connection with the general revision of the salaries of the teachers of national schools under the terms of the agreement arrived at in November, 1920, between representatives of the National Teachers, the Commissioners of National Education, and the Treasury, we are directed by the Commissioners of National Education to inform you that your proper placing in the new scale, as from 1st April, 1920, as determined in accordance with the provisions of Section X of the agreement, is £ 430

Wreaths were sent from the following: Widow and Daughter, Staff of the School, Pupils of Elementary School; Pupils of the Secondary School; Session and Committee of the Presbyterian Church; Governors of the School; S and C. M. Gailey and family; Elsie Huey and A. Friend."

Mr James Gilmore Sloan M.A. (T.C.D.)

Mr Jim Sloan

Mr James Gilmore Sloan was one of three brothers whose names were synonymous with education in the Castlederg area from the thirties to the fifties. Mr George Sloan was Principal in Erganagh P E. S. while Mr Tom Sloan was in charge of Garvetagh P E.S.

Mr James Sloan, or Jim as he was more commonly known, was born on 22nd of May 1890, at Knockbrack, and after a successful school career he trained as a teacher in Kildare Street in Dublin and for some years taught in Garvetagh P.E.S. During his time there he sat an external examination to gain the degree of M.A. from Trinity College, Dublin, which was quite unusual in those days.   He was appointed Principal of Edwards Public Elementary School in 1930, a position he held until his retirement in 1955, when Mr T. F. Riddall succeeded him.

Following the excellent reputation that had been built up by the Burnsides, Mr Sloan also coached students for Matriculation and Police Exams. His broad ranging curriculum provided resources for those wanting to study shorthand, typing and book- keeping while students going to higher level education were given tuition in Latin and French.

During his time in office Mr Sloan facilitated the change over from the old premises on the Castlefin Road to the new building on the Workhouse site. Records indicate that this was not an easy move. There were many problems relating to the purchase of the site, access, water supply, cost of building and issues relative to the technical subjects, which were to be taught in the school as extra evening classes. Finally, after much correspondence between those involved, and of course many meetings held to resolve the difficulties, Mr J.M.Benn, the Inspector, reported in June 1938 that, "this school will shortly be transferred to a new building in which the ideal conditions should have a beneficial effect not only on the standard of the work done but also on the general health and well-being of the children." Of course the school was officially opened on July 7th 1938, a red-letter day indeed for Mr Sloan, the staff and the pupils as well as the wider community.

During the next year the same Inspector re-visited the school and remarked, " the excellent new premises provided for this school have now been in use for more than six months and are proving very satisfactory. Part of the extensive grounds is being developed as a school garden in charge of the Principal, who has obtained the necessary provisional qualifications. Special mention must be made of the high attendance percentage, whilst the tone and discipline of the school are alike good. The standard of work improves steadily through the school, reaching a high level in the senior classes."

By 1940 Mr Sloan had put his gardening skills into operation and the subject had become well established in the curriculum, causing the Inspector to comment "special mention must be made of the excellent start made in teaching of Horticulture, especially on the practical side."

The school continued to go from strength to strength under Mr Sloan's leadership and he was complimented by Mr A. Gibson, the Chief Education Officer of Tyrone County Education Committee, following a 1954 Report from the Senior Inspector. In a letter he stated, " My Committee was particularly pleased to note that a pleasant tone pervades the school as it feels that such an atmosphere in a school has marked effect on the work and character of the pupils."

After serving the educational needs of the area to such a high standard for twenty-five years, Mr Sloan retired in 1955 and went to live near his daughter Ann in Finaghy. Following her emigration to Canada he stayed on his own until the early seventies when he moved to live with his other daughter Elaine and her family. When his health deteriorated he went into Greenisland Hospital, where he remained until his demise on October 16th 1975.

In addition to his teaching duties Mr Sloan played a very active role in the community. He was Congregational Secretary and Clerk of Session in First Castlederg Presbyterian Church. He was Secretary of the local Masonic Lodge and during the Second World War was Chief Air Raid Warden for the town.

In September 1924 he married Miss Annie McCaffrey, from Omagh, who had taught in Erganagh P.E.S. with his brother George. They lived in the School House on the Castlefin Road and had three children, Elaine, John and Ann. Sadly John passed away in 1978 after developing leukaemia, Ann lives in Canada and Elaine, who is married to Rev Victor Ryan, lives in Ballynure, Co. Antrim. Their daughter Alison is married to Rev. Harold Agnew, who is at present the Methodist Minister in Omagh.

Erganagh P.S. circa 1920, showing Mr George Sloan and Miss Annie McCaffrey, who married Mr Jim Sloan in 1924.

Mr T. F. Riddall – Principal 1955—1985.

Mr. T.F. Riddall

Thomas Frederick Riddall was born and raised in Strabane where he attended the local primary school. He proved to be a bright student and following his success in the 11+ examination he went to Foyle College in Londonderry. After his education there and aged just eighteen, he enlisted into the R.A.F. He was subsequently sent to the Shetlands where he was unfortunate to develop double pneumonia and pleurisy, which meant he had to be invalided out in 1943. He spent some time recovering in a sanatorium and decided that if the R.A.F. was not for him, then teaching would be his chosen career.

He entered Stranmillis Training College in 1943 and in 1945 began teaching, first in Glenwood and then in Lisnasharragh in Belfast, for ten years. His first schools provided him with a wealth of experiences and he was appointed as Principal of Edwards in 1955, a position he held until his retirement in 1986. He moved from Belfast to Castlederg with his wife, Joyce, and they settled down to a way of life in the little town that was to be their home for the rest of their days. This was the beginning of an illustrious career as a headmaster and Mr Riddall will long be remembered as a great innovator, a man ready to accept a challenge and someone who was ahead of his time.

Teachers and pupils alike recall his passion for music and his promotion of it throughout the school, with the introduction of singing and the playing of musical instruments. Mrs McNutt, who taught with Mr Riddall for thirty years, remembers the first Assemblies with children filling up the long corridor in the absence of a proper Hall and teachers encouraging reluctant pupils to join in the hymn singing as Mr Riddall accompanied them on the first school piano. Prospective teachers long remember the sinking dread of being asked to do an impromptu performance of "All on an April Evening" to prove their musical competence! Also remembered with some amusement, (but no disrespect) was the hymn "St Patrick's Breastplate" which everyone was required to sing around the middle of March every year! It was a difficult tune with equally difficult words and much to Mr Riddall's disappointment, the renditions could only be described as very poor musical efforts and are best forgotten!

Inspectors visited schools every two years and Inspector's Reports were always complimentary of Mr Riddall. A report of 1961 remarked on the "friendly, open nature of the hard working and well-mannered children". This was attributed in no small measure to the "general influence of a principal who is sincerely devoted to the interests of his pupils."

In recognition of this excellence, the school was awarded the prestigious Carlisle and Blake Premium Prize for 1962, and each child received a special pen.

A 1965 Inspector's Report described Mr Riddall as a " very able teacher" who carried out "excellent administration" of the school. Indeed many teachers who worked with him recall his fastidious attention to planning and lesson notes, which had to be handed in on time, and were subsequently examined and marked! Spelling errors or any omissions were duly indicated and commented upon!

Under his direction the school continued to develop and by the early seventies enrolment had reached a peak of just over 300. The school, which had opened in 1938 with a compliment of five teachers, had spiralled to a teaching staff of twelve and by 1974 half of the pupils were being taught in mobile classrooms.

Conditions in the school were definitely cramped, as would be confirmed by anyone who ever entered Mr Riddall's office. Mrs Joyce Riddall amusingly relates the story of sending her young grandson, Stevie, over to the school with a message to his grandfather. On his return she asked him if he had found his grandpa, to be met with the reply, "I found him in the tubbard (cupboard) with another woman!" Of course he had simply been at work in his office with the secretary, Mrs Elizabeth Walls!

Lots of people recall their school days as being the foundation of a life-long love for a particular subject or area and for many who attended Edwards when Mr Riddall was Headmaster, the love of sport must rate highly. Football and cricket became regular features of the curriculum and Mr Riddall, who was himself an Ulster schoolboy representative in cricket, coached a team, described by the Tyrone Constitition in 1957 as a "force to be reckoned with." Matches were held against past pupils and parents and were wonderful social occasions, when large crowds gathered on good evenings for some lively entertainment. Football too, was given much encouragement and it was considered an honour to represent the school in matches. Goal posts were bought by Mr Riddall and were considered by the boys to be a vast improvement on the thorn hedges of the field. Many boys will remember the team transport being Mr Riddall's old blue Capri with the lads tightly packed in! No mention of Health and Safety rules spoiling the fun!

A lively interest in drama led him to acting in Omagh Players and establishing the local Derg Players drama group. Naturally, his enthusiasm bubbled over into school-life and it was not long before he was promoting drama as part of the school curriculum. He began Pantomimes in the late seventies, with Miss Heather McNutt assuming the role of Producer. The older pupils were involved and I am sure many will recall their antics, both on and off the stage, back-stage disasters and first night nerves! Scenery and props were made by the versatile caretaker, Sammy Reid, who was known to turn up anything from a wishing well to a coach for Cinderella. Mr Riddall took great delight and pride in these two–night productions that continued for many years and were regarded by parents and pupils alike as the highlight of the year. Indeed, no sooner was one Pantomime over than he was planning the next!

The welfare of children with special needs was another area that was also dear to Mr Riddall's heart. He was aware of the acute lack of provision for these pupils and with this in mind he approached the local Education Board with the idea of establishing a Special Unit within the school. Mrs Gladys McKinley was appointed to the position of Special Needs teacher in 1974, and as no classroom was available, she began her teaching career in Edwards, tutoring eight pupils in a cordoned-off area of the corridor. The following year a mobile classroom was made available and many children were given the help they required. An Inspector's Report of 1976 records that "the Unit operates throughout the whole school day and this has been of considerable benefit to the pupils as it gives them a base of their own and of belonging to a full time group." It was recognised that "much of real value is being achieved" and the Unit flourished to become a two-teacher facility and is unique in the Western Board area, thanks in no short measure to the initiative of Mr Riddall.

A proud day for Mr Riddall, the staff and the members of the School Management Committee, was the opening of the long-awaited extension, on 31st of May 1978. At a cost of over £200,000, five new classrooms, a Special Unit, an Assembly Hall and kitchen, a staff-room, toilets, cloakrooms and stores were added to the existing accommodation. Miss Georgina Elliott, a former vice-principal and member of staff for thirty-six years, declared the new extension open.

The advent of computers in schools occurred in the early eighties and of course Mr Riddall was at the forefront again. Now anyone who remembers the first BBC B computers, will not have forgotten the unwieldy beasts that they were, having to be operated with cassette drives and booted with special instructions. If Mr Riddall was far from being an expert, the members of staff were even further off the mark and most were reluctant learners!! However the intrepid Headmaster was undaunted and before long everyone was hooked and all classes were encouraged to brave the difficulties and keep up with the latest technology. Technical hitches were common but the "Jim will fix it" of Edwards did his best to keep everyone on track!

The idea of school trips was largely unheard of until Mr Riddall introduced them into the curriculum. While they may not appeal to the pupils of today, many of whom are used to foreign travel, they were regarded as brilliant occasions and were eagerly anticipated.

As well as being concerned with the welfare of the pupils in his care, Mr Riddall took an active interest in the pastoral care of teachers, through his membership of the Ulster Teachers' Union. He acted as Chairman of the local branch and for many years attended the yearly conferences. On retirement he continued to work for the good of all through his involvement in the Retired Teachers' Association. After a long and illustrious career of thirty years as Headmaster, Mr Riddall retired in August 1985. Members of the staff and the school management committee marked his retirement with a concert and the presentation of a gift cheque and a video recorder. Glowing tributes were paid to Mr Riddall's excellence and to the many initiatives that had marked his career.

While school obviously occupied a lot of his time, Mr Riddall still found time to play a very active role in the local community. For many years he was a member of Castlederg Silver Band, playing a cornet and appearing at many events.

He was also a committed member of Second Castlederg Presbyterian Church, where he served on the Church Committee. He was Treasurer for many years, and kept a watchful eye on the Church finances. As a choir member he helped enrich the Sunday worship and as a dependable organiser he was responsible for the combined Sunday School excursions to Portrush each summer, happy events that linger in many memories.

His love of sport never deserted him and he was a keen bowler in the church club until declining health prevented his involvement. Playing golf was a favourite past time of both Mr and Mrs Riddall and he played regularly up to a year before his death.

For many years he was also a member of the local branch of the Royal British Legion and was prominent at the Remembrance Services. He always made the children in school aware of the events of history and the sacrifices paid by the Armed Forces.

Sadly, in his eighty -fifth year Mr Riddall suffered a stroke and was admitted to a local Nursing Home, where he passed away on the 8th of March 2002. His death caused widespread regret and many past pupils and members of staff along with a large representation of local people, attended the funeral service in Second Castlederg Presbyterian Church on March 11th, to pay tribute to a most influential and innovative gentleman. Following the service interment took place in Strabane.

For those who were privileged to work in any capacity with Mr Riddall, he will long be remembered as a distinguished gentleman, who could best be summed up in the words of Sir Walter Scott as "one who had the will to do and the soul to dare."

Castlederg Silver Band featuring two teachers from Edwards P.S. - Mr T.F. Riddall and Mr D. McIlgorm.
Back Row L - R: J. Verner, S. Huey, S. Walls, T. Henderson, S. Semple, R. McKinley,
D. McIlgorm, D. McCay, D. Cairns, J. Gordon, E. Rowe.
Front Row L - R: T. Riddall, R. Leitch, C. Monteith, F. Wilson, W. Kyle, H. Fox, H. Cooper,
C. Gamble, J. Forbes.

Mr A.S. Orr B.Ed 1985 -

Mr A.S. Orr as President Ulster Teachers Union 1995

The present Principal is Mr Alistair Orr who was appointed in 1985. He is one of only three principals who taught in the 1938 school, the others being Mr Jim Sloan and Mr Tom Riddall.

Mr Orr was born in Londonderry and attended Christ Church Primary School and Foyle College. After studying Chemistry, Physics and Biology at A level he went to Stranmillis Teacher Training College studying Mathematics, Science and Art. He would be the first to admit that Art was not his subject but a broad range of subjects was demanded at that time so Art was the college decision. Very few of his paintings, sculptures or other art works remain from this period! However he met his future wife Anne at Stranmillis and she still remains at his side.

In 1971 he was appointed to a P5 class in the recently opened Tullycarnet PS in East Belfast, where he taught a class of 36 which changed regularly as the troubles meant a constant flow of disturbed children moving out of the Short Strand, Woodstock Road area to the new housing estate at Tullycarnet.

The next year he and his wife Anne were both appointed to the new Artigarvan Primary School where he totally embarrassed her by asking the principal at the first staff meeting the dates of the summer holidays.

In 1976 he became Principal of Drumlegagh PS, a two-teacher school and persuaded his wife to apply for the assistant teacher post. The school was very different from the then state of the art Artigarvan PS – no water, no telephone, no school dinners and chemical toilets. However, it did have a pet deer called Bambi who visited the school at break and lunchtime. They thoroughly enjoyed their time there and claim to be one of the first schools in Northern Ireland to have had a computer, a Sinclair Spectrum. All three of their children were born whilst he was principal there. While there they had a visit from the then Education Minister Lord Melchett who noting the apparent remoteness of the school, asked did they ever had the opportunity to meet another teacher!!

It was from there that he took the first school trip to London and to France – a day trip to Calais.

Seven years later he was appointed to Kesh Primary School and two years later in December 1985 to his present post in Edwards PS where he has remained ever since.

There have been dramatic changes in Education since 1971 and especially in the past twenty years whilst he has been principal. The education reform order of 1987 introduced new challenges for schools. The introduction of LMS and schools having their own budgets meant a total rethink for all staff and Mr Orr endeavoured to bring the staff along with him towards the new philosophy. New ideas had to be embraced as the school looked to develop not only within the building but to a wider world.

There were many innovations including the appointment of subject co ordinators for the new curriculum with all staff working together at subjects instead of in isolation in the own classrooms. Many polices were devised and the introduction of new strategies such as the Reading Recovery programme added momentum to the new ever increasing pattern of 'change' in education.

In 1994 Mr Orr obtained a B Ed Hons degree in Educational Management at the University of Ulster, which proved to be very useful in the business administration of the school.

At this time schools began to work more together and this saw the beginning of EMU work with St Patrick's PS Castlederg and Mr Sean McCarron, the then

Principal. This continued even through the most difficult days of the troubles and still continues today. Educational school visits in line with the new curriculum increased dramatically and spread to include visits to Scotland, London and to France. Links were formed with schools in France and Spain and visits were made to these schools, as were visits to Edwards by teachers from France and Switzerland. These were challenging situations, which were thoroughly enjoyed by the pupils and teachers.

The PTA committee was formed in 1989 and continues to be a very active and valued part of school life.

Throughout this time Mr Orr was a dedicated member of the Ulster Teachers' Union and in 1995 was elected as the Union's President. This was a great honour for him and for the school and during his year as President he attended many conferences at home and abroad, including the week long Education International Conference in Washington which was attended by 2000 delegates from all over the world and was addressed by then US President Bill Clinton. He has served on many committees in the Education sector in Northern Ireland and in 1999 was asked to be part of a Department of Education Committee setting up the General Teaching Council for Northern Ireland. In 2001 he was appointed to the first GTCNI Council. Also in 2001 he was invited to a reception in Buckingham Palace for teachers from all over the United Kingdom. In 2005 he was appointed as a member of the Western Education and Library Board for a three-year term.

In spite of his heavy commitment to school and to education Mr Orr has many interests outside school, including his family of two boys and a girl, travel, reading, technology, photography and gardening.

The last few years saw tremendous problems with the old school building and Mr Orr, the WELB and the Board of Governors worked very hard to convince the Department of Education that a new school was necessary.

The decision to provide funding was announced in March 2002 and since then he and the staff have worked hard to obtain a building and facilities suitable for twenty first century teaching and learning.

The opening of the new school was the realisation of a dream and he is very proud that he was principal when the new school finally opened in 2005.

Some Past Members of Staff.

The following chapter details the lives of some past teachers and other staff and the dates they worked in Edwards P.S.:

- Miss Georgina Elliott 1926—1962

- Miss May McArthur (Mrs McFarland) 1931—1949

- Miss Isabel Millar 1944-1957

- Miss Anna Scott (Mrs McNutt) 1949-1986

- Miss Mary Patrick (Mrs Caldwell) 1950—1985

- Miss Ann Hemphill (Mrs Waugh) 1963-1991

- Miss Margaret Clarke (Mrs Watt) 1969—2005

- Mr Tom Bratton (1976-1977)

- Miss Elizabeth Beacom (Mrs Kissick) (1980-1985)

- Miss Myrtle Condy (Mrs West) 1988-1992

- Mrs Pearl Stewart 1991-1998

Other Members of Staff

- Mrs Elizabeth Walls, Secretary, 1976----

- Mrs Sadie Emery, School Meals, 1978—2000

- Mr Sammy Reid, Caretaker, 1972—1994.

Miss Georgina Elliott.

Miss Daisy Kelly a niece
of Miss G. Elliott

Miss Georgina Elliott

Mr Bertie Lyons

Georgina Elliott was born on the 29th of August 1899 at Drumderg, Letterbreen, Co. Fermanagh, the youngest of a family of nine children, three boys and six girls. She began her early education at Corryglass National School where Mrs Thornton was the Headmistress. She went on to Kildare Place, Dublin and when she completed her training she returned to Corryglass under Mrs Thornton's care and taught there for a year. She proceeded to a school in Convoy, Co. Donegal, where she taught for four years.

In 1926 she began her legendary teaching career in Edwards P.S. Castlederg where she was to happily remain until her retirement in 1962. Initially she stayed with Mrs Evans who was the organist in Derg Parish Church and who became a life long friend. Many pupils still recall her excellent teaching, her strict discipline and her meticulous fashion consciousness. Within the school, she has been long remembered for the presentation of a Cup for Story Telling, a competition that is still running annually. Many pupils also refer to the oak tree in the school grounds as one that was grown from an acorn by Miss Elliott and then planted out in the grounds as a young sapling.

For ten years she was the Chairman of the Castlederg Branch of the Ulster

Teachers Union and for twenty years she was secretary of the Ulster Savings Group in the school. She also was a keen supporter of the R.N.L.I. and received a medal in recognition of her work. When women held a low profile in Church affairs, she was the only lady serving on the Select Vestry of the local Parish church and was Superintendent of the Sunday School for many years.

For some years her home was on the Castlefin Road where she was joined by her niece Miss Daisy Kelly, who later married Mr Bertie Lyons and they moved to live at Dartans House. Eventually the family moved to live at Drumbo, Lisburn. She remained in that area until she passed away on the 29th of January 1991, aged 92 years, leaving behind many memories of a wonderful teacher and friend.

Mrs May McFarland (nee McArthur)

Miss May McArthur (later Mrs McFarland) at the 1938 opening.

Miss May McArthur was born on the 10th of March 1909 at Listymore, Castlederg, the eldest child of James and Elizabeth McArthur. She was one of a family of three girls and two boys and she attended Erganagh P.S. when Mr George Sloan was Principal.

She was a bright pupil and when her potential as a teacher was recognised she was sent to Omagh Model School as a monitor. During this time, when travelling was not so easy, she stayed with an uncle and aunt at Rosnamuck, between Omagh and Gortin. Her uncle, Mr John Hutchinson, was Principal of Dunmullan, and her aunt, his sister, was the assistant teacher. Both took a keen interest in May's welfare and education, encouraging her to progress to Stranmillis Teacher Training College, Belfast, in 1928.

After three years in Belfast her training was complete and although posts were scarce, she was fortunate to be appointed as an assistant in Edwards P.S Castlederg. She often mentioned that many students who trained with her were not so fortunate in securing jobs in teaching and often ended up working in places such as Woolworth's.

Mr Jim Sloan was Principal and Miss McArthur taught in both the infant and senior school. She has long been remembered for her strict but fair teaching.

She married Mr Arthur McFarland in the late thirties and moved to live at Mountjoy East, but probably due to the scarcity of posts, she continued to travel daily to Castlederg. During the war years she had to obtain petrol coupons, enabling her to make one journey each way. While teaching in Edwards she raised a family of twin boys, John and Herbert, and a daughter Jill.

She drove an Austin 7 and on one occasion John and Herbert mischievously filled the petrol tank with pebbles from the driveway and obviously the car wouldn't start! Their furious father had to be restrained from severely punishing the boys and the car had to be turned upside down to remove the offending stones!

The family moved to live at 74, Dublin Road, Omagh in 1948 and Mrs McFarland still taught in Edwards, bringing the twins with her until 1949, when she was appointed as Principal in Altdoghal P.S. a small two teacher school near Newtownstewart, which closed in 1978 and was demolished in 1993.

Mrs McFarland retired from Altdoghal in 1972 and sadly passed away on 31st December 1984, aged 75, leaving her daughter Jill who now lives in Leeds and is also a teacher, John, who resides in Canada and Herbert who lives at Cultra.

Miss Isabel Millar

Miss Isabel Millar

Many past pupils have paid tribute to Miss Isabel Millar who taught in Edwards P.S. from her appointment in 1944 until her retirement in 1957.

She was born on 24th of September 1895, a daughter of Thomas and Margaret Millar of Douglas. She attended the local National School and from there she went to Marlborough Street Training College in Dublin as a King's Scholar. She completed two years training (see certificate) and began her first teaching post in Bailieborough in Co. Cavan. Some time later she returned nearer home and taught in Letterkenny National School but before the border was formed in 1920 she obtained a post in Sion Mills.

In 1944, Isa, as she was popularly known, was appointed to the staff of Edwards P.S. on the retirement of Miss Susan Jackson, who had been teaching there since 1919.

She continued to live at her home in Douglas and travelled daily to school in her Morris 8 car, bringing with her William G. Starrett, a teacher in the school, her nephew Wesley and some other children. Past pupils, who recall her gentle but firm nature and her fairness and compassion to everyone, remember her very fondly.

She retired from Edwards in 1957 and the Management Committee expressed their appreciation of her service to the school.

Following her retirement from teaching and giving up her job as Sunday School Superintendent in her local chuch, she resided for some time in Belfast with her younger sister and then moved to Bangor, Co. Down where she remained until her death. She passed away on 2nd of July 1976, in her 81st year, and is buried in Douglas Presbyterian Church Graveyard, opposite the home of her birth.

NATIONAL EDUCATION, IRELAND.

MARLBOROUGH STREET TRAINING COLLEGE

THIS DIPLOMA

IS GRANTED TO

Isabel Millar

WHO WAS A KING'S SCHOLAR IN

THE MARLBOROUGH STREET TRAINING COLLEGE

FOR A COURSE OF *Two* YEARS' ENDED *July 1917*

AND WHO HAS FULFILLED THE PRESCRIBED CONDITIONS OF

TRAINING, INCLUDING THAT OF SATISFACTORY PROBATION AS

TEACHER IN A PUBLIC ELEMENTARY SCHOOL.

By Order of the Commissioners of National Education, Ireland.

A. N. Bonaparte Wyse } Secretaries

Dated *4th* day of *May* *1920.*

ALEX. THOM & CO. LD. DUBLIN.

347

Mrs Anna McNutt

Mrs McNutt's Retirement June 1986.

Pupils who attended Edwards P.S. from the fifties until the eighties will fondly recollect Mrs A. H. McNutt's sound teaching and her gracious manner. With her customary charm she provided this information about her personal history.

Anna Scott was born in 1926 and raised on the family farm at Bridgetown, close to the town of Castlederg. She recalls her school days with great affection and wonderful clarity. Although living near the town, her parents chose to send their offspring to Garvetagh Public Elementary School as they thought it was safer to walk to Garvetagh than into town. They also considered the fact that Edwards School on the Chapel Road in Castlederg often closed on Fridays, which were the Fair Days, and this was regarded as disruptive. She fondly recalls walking to school in all kinds of weather and that on occasions when there were thunderstorms the children were met by their parents. With a twinkle in her eye she remembers getting a new bicycle and proudly she was able to ride it to school, much to the envy of many of the other pupils.

It is interesting to note that the Headmaster in Garvetagh then was Mr Tom Sloan, his brother Jim was Headmaster in Edwards and another brother, George, was Headmaster in Erganagh School.

At the age of fourteen she sat the Elementary Certificate Examination in Edwards School. This examination consisted of English Grammar, Dictation and Maths, including Algebra. She even recalls that one of the words in the Dictation was "coconut!" What an excellent memory!

Following that exam Anna was then sent to a private school that was upstairs above Eric Robinson's shop in the Main Street. The teacher was a Miss Devlin, who travelled daily on the bus from Omagh. Anna's parents paid for her tuition and she studied Maths, English, French, History and Geography.

At around the age of sixteen she sat the Junior Certificate and having excelled in that, went to Omagh Academy for the next two years. She has happy memories of her two friends, Mary Patrick (Mrs Walter Caldwell, deceased) and Beatrice de Zeuw (Mrs Jim Cather, deceased) who travelled on the bus with her to the Academy. The Headmaster of the Academy at that time was Mr Arthur Simpson and under his direction Anna sat the Senior Certificate.

Her ambition was to become a teacher and on leaving Omagh Academy she became a Junior Assistant Mistress in Magheracreggan School where she taught infants for one and three quarter years. She recalls school inspectors staying in the town and taking taxis out to the various schools. There was quite a number of Junior Mistresses and they were also inspected. Anna obviously made a favourable impression on her inspector who recommended that she should go to Stranmillis Teacher Training College, which she did in 1945. This was a great adventure for the young student, as she had to go to Victoria Bridge or Omagh to catch the train to Belfast. At Stranmillis she stayed in the bungalow accommodation and had her meals provided. The areas she studied included Methods, Principles of Education, Speech Training and of course Teaching Practice. She still remembers Nettlefield and Brown Square Schools in Belfast, where her Teaching Practices were spent.

In spite of all the worldly difficulties at this time, life in the post-war years continued with a degree of normality and Anna finished her two years at Stranmillis only to find that no jobs were available locally. She found employment in Sion Mills where she taught for two years and was then delighted to be appointed, in 1949, as fourth assistant to the staff of Edwards in Castlederg, where she remained until her retirement.

Mr Jim Sloan, a firm, fair and kind man, was the Headmaster and Anna taught along with Miss G. Elliottt, Miss I. Millar, Mrs M. McFarland and Mr W.G. Starrett. The school consisted of seven rooms and the Caretaker was Mr Joseph Speers. Over 200 children attended and for many years Anna taught infants. The school was in need of repair and she remembers members of staff complaining about the bitter cold. School dinners were the highlight of the day and were enjoyed by pupils and teachers alike. The kitchen was conveniently situated opposite Anna's room and the cook was Mrs Martin from Omagh.

In 1950 Anna's good friend, Mary Patrick, was also appointed to the teaching staff and both of them witnessed many changes over the years. Anna became Mrs Lesley McNutt in 1952 and they had a family of twin boys, Gordon and Alan, and two daughters, Heather and Elaine. Heather, the only one to follow in her mother's footsteps, became a teacher and actually taught in Edwards for a few years, leaving in 1980 to take up a post in Bangor, Co. Down.

Most of us in a lifetime experience some huge- impact moments. For the young Robert Northridge, son of Canon A. Northridge, the time when Mrs McNutt informed the infant class that King George VI had died, was one of those never-to- be-forgotten instances, as he recently informed her at the school's Open Night in June 2004. Many children also recall the events that followed the King's demise; the accession of Princess Elizabeth and the Coronation in June 1953. Anna remembers the children being given souvenir medals and brochures and after assembling at the school, parading around the town. Many still have those souvenirs to this day.

During the fifties the erratic water supply to the school came from the Derg Valley Hospital and eventually mains water from Lough Bradan reached Castlederg in 1954. A new boiler was installed in 1956, improving the level of heating throughout the school.

Mr J. Sloan retired in 1955 and was replaced by Mr T.F. Riddall who was responsible for many innovative changes, including a great emphasis on music, singing and playing instruments, the introduction of school uniform and the scary days of the first computers in schools. Anna recalls Mr Riddall conducting Assemblies in the long corridors in the absence of an Assembly Hall.

Many teachers came and went but perhaps the most memorable retirement for Anna was the departure of Miss G. Elliott, in 1962, after thirty-six years spent in the school. This marked the end of an era and she was replaced by another local girl, Miss Anne Hemphill (Mrs Roy Waugh) who also taught infants.

High winds and storms have always been with us and Anna recalls a very bad storm in the sixties when two temporary buildings in the school grounds were very badly damaged and lots of books and literature were found in the school hedges.

By the mid sixties the school enrolment was reaching two hundred and fifty pupils and plans were drawn up for an extension, but meanwhile the staff had to endure the temporary classrooms and walking outdoors in all kinds of weather. When the plans were completed in 1974 half of the pupils were being taught in mobile classrooms.

Anna enjoyed her work and was seldom ill, despite the somewhat difficult working conditions. She remembers on one occasion having 'flu and the ever - attentive caretaker, Sammy Reid, checking in on her to see how she was!

June 1978 brought about the fulfilment of the extension plans and the school now expanded to include more suitable infant accommodation, a kitchen and dining hall, offices and a staff room. By this time Anna had taken over responsibility for the provision of remedial education and it is in this capacity that many pupils recall the help that they were given.

Mr Riddall continued to play a major role in the development of the school and the professionalism of the staff right up to his retirement in 1985 when Mr A.S. Orr occupied the position of Headmaster. So within her years in Edwards Anna worked happily with three Headmasters. After teaching thirty-seven years she decided to call it a day in 1986 and a special ceremony was held to mark her retirement. She was presented with a Tyrone Crystal candleholder, a dinner service and flowers and all her family attended the special occasion. Many tributes were paid to her wonderful dedication and commitment to teaching and she received a book featuring the thoughts and good wishes of the children. What better way to end this profile than in the words of some of those pupils?

"Everybody is sad that you are leaving." Marcella Robinson.

"You helped me very much when I went in to you."   David Humphrey

I have enjoyed my classes with you as you have been a very kind teacher." Clive Reid

"We hope you will be very happy but we will be very sad." Adele Sproule

Mrs May Caldwell

Mrs May Caldwell

Mary Elizabeth Patrick (May), was born at Bridgetown, Castlderg and attended Garvetagh Public Elementary School where she was taught by the Junior teacher, Miss Henderson, (Mrs Scott), who taught all subjects, including knitting sewing, making garments and cooking. On reaching third standard. May moved into the senior room where the teacher was Mr Tom Sloan. Around the age of twelve May sat the annual Scholarship exam and having passed, went to Omagh Academy, travelling daily by bus. While attending the Academy she passed Junior and Senior Certificates and chose teaching as her career. She went on to Stranmillis Training College, where she gained the Teacher's Certificate with Honours. She first put her newly acquired skills into action in Killen Primary School, where she attained great success. In 1950 she was appointed to the teaching staff of Edwards Public Elementary School and she taught there under the direction of Mr Jim Sloan and Mr Tom Riddall until her retirement in 1985 having given almost thirty-five years of dedicated service. However, school life did not take up all of her time and she had many outside interests. She was especially interested in Girl Guides and often took girls away to Camp and G.G. Jamborees. She also loved to travel and went to America many times. One of the highlights of her travels was a trip to the Holy Land, which she thoroughly enjoyed and which she loved to relate to people. She also undertook many bus trips to England, Scotland and Wales, enjoying the scenery and meeting people along the way. She married Mr Walter Caldwell of Knocknagrieve, Killen, where they farmed for many years. They were blessed with a family of two sons, James and John who remain on the farm, and a daughter, Mary (Mrs Montgomery). May was always devoted to her Church and as a Methodist after her marriage, she was totally committed and was exemplary in living out her Christian beliefs. In school she was highly respected and was a very generous, patient and kindly teacher Many students will recall her utmost respect for those who gave their lives in the Wars and how she always asked the class to stand for an Act of Remembrance on each Armistice Day. She is also remembered for her Needlework skills and many girls loved her lessons and are indebted to her for their proficiency. Sadly Mrs Caldwell passed away on November 7th 2001 but is still very fondly remembered by pupils and colleagues alike.

Making a Retirement Presentation to Mrs May Caldwell are L - R:
Mr Ivan Clarke, Mr Sammy Crawford, Mrs May Caldwell, Mrs Pearl Quigley, Canon Walter Quill,
Chairman of the Board of Governeors and Dr. Morris Brown.

Mrs Ann Waugh.

Mrs Ann Waugh

Ann Hemphill was born and raised at Listymore and began her early schooling in Erganagh P.S. but after a short time transferred to Edwards P.S. Her first teacher was "Miss Millar, from Douglas Bridge, a lovely lady."

She has vivid memories of the large class discussion pictures in subjects such as geography, history and nature study, particularly recalling the picture of the Wooden Horse of Troy and learning the appropriate poems connected to the pictures.

She travelled to and from school by public transport, meaning that she had to get out early to catch the bus in John Street.

She was very happy at school and had many good friends. She sat the qualifying, which was a much larger exam than the present transfer test, and went to Omagh Academy in 1951. She took Junior Certificate in 1955 and Senior Certificate in 1957. After successively passing her exams she went on to Stranmillis Training College, fulfilling her ambition to become a teacher.

She specialised in teaching in the infant and upper schools and her first post was in Sandville P.S. (between Strabane and Londonderry), where she taught P4 and 5, beginning on 22nd August 1960. She taught in the church hall of Donagheady Presbyterian Church and each Friday was required to completely clean the room in preparation for Sunday School and any other church functions that were held during the week.

A vacancy arose in Edwards P.S. in 1962, following the retirement of Miss Elliott, and was advertised several times in the hope of securing a male teacher. In those days the preferred sex could be stated, but as no male teacher was forthcoming, Miss Hemphill was appointed to fill the position.

She began teaching in Edwards on 25th of March 1963 with 38 P5 and P6 children in Room 1a. It was a small room and sitting was the order of the day. On the last day of term in June 1963 she delightedly remembers having afternoon tea with the rest of the staff in the new residence built in the school grounds. On that special occasion she was presented with a wedding present prior to her marriage to Roy Waugh in July.

Following in the footsteps of Miss Elliott she carried on the Ulster Savings scheme and was presented with a 10-year service medal, although she actually continued for longer.

During her busy teaching career she and Roy also managed to raise four children; Janet, who is now a Consultant in Muckamore Abbey in Antrim, Diane, who works in the Western Education and Library Board in Omagh, Alison, who is a Cook in Bready, and Robert, who helps to run the family business.

In 1965 Mrs Waugh moved to the Infant school to teach P2 in Room 5, as Ronnie Strong had been appointed and was better suited to the upper school. Mr Riddall was still a teaching Principal and the school was growing steadily. Due to this expansion she then moved in 1967 with the P2 class, to a mobile in the grounds.

In 1980, due to changes in the Primary Curriculum, she became responsible for the organisation and supervision of Infant Maths.

She was also renowned for teaching needlework skills and during her career assisted in many changes and developments in education. She also acted as teacher tutor to probationary teachers, helping new recruits to settle in.

Following Mrs McNutt's retirement in 1986, Mrs Waugh then moved to the Special Class, working with children who required remedial help.

She continued this work up until her early retirement in 1991, having had a very successful teaching career spanning over thirty years. A special presentation was held in the school and Mrs Waugh was presented with a Waterford Crystal Lamp and a gift cheque. Tributes were paid to her professionalism and her contribution to the school, particularly her work with those who needed extra help.

Since then Mrs Waugh has greatly enjoyed her busy retirement, helping Roy in the business, moving into a new home, gardening and travelling, as well as delighting in her grandchildren and caring for her mother and brother.

Mrs Margaret Watt.

Mrs Anna Patterson, Mrs Joyce Adams, Mr Herbie Watt,
Mr William Watt, Mrs Margaret Watt.

Miss Margaret E. Clarke, from Lislaird, Castlederg, was a pupil of Lisnacloon and Gortnagross Primary Schools until she was successful in the 11+ examination and went to Strabane Grammar School in 1960. Her ambition was to become a teacher and she went to Stranmillis Training College in 1966.

Having completed three years and gaining her teaching certificate she began her career in Edwards in 1969, at the same time as her youngest brother, aged four, started P1 with Mrs McNutt.

She began teaching in Miss Elliott's mobile classroom and inherited an acorn that her predecessor had grown in a pot and then planted outside the classroom. As the sapling grew larger it was too near the classroom, so with the help of Mr Sammy Reid, the Caretaker, it was transplanted to its present position in the school grounds. It has always been known as Miss Elliott's oak tree and it has borne many acorns over the years.

During her long career Margaret witnessed many changes. In 1969 she recalled eight members of teaching staff; Mr T. F. Riddall, Mrs A. McNutt, Mrs M. McCrea, Mrs M. Caldwell, Mrs A. Waugh, Miss Y. Hamill, Mr McKittrick, herself, a part time Caretaker and no secretary.

In 1970 she married local businessman Herbie Watt and together they have two boys, Andrew, who is teaching in Lytham-St-Anne's, Lancashire, and William, who has recently graduated in Business Studies from the University of Ulster.

Margaret continued to teach P3 in the mobile classroom until the new extension was completed in 1978 and for the first time in her career she had a classroom in the main building.

The Special Unit in the school also extended over the years to require two teachers. In 1988 she joined Mrs McKinley and cared for the education of the younger children. She enjoyed her work with those pupils and was proud of their developments.

With all the new developments in education during the eighties Margaret was given responsibility for Infant Reading and led the staff in their attempts to get to grips with the changes.

As well as teaching, Margaret found time in her busy life to indulge her favourite passion; playing golf at her local Club in Newtownstewart. She enjoyed many successes and was Lady Captain in 2002.

For many years she organized an annual competition at the Golf Club to raise funds for the Special Unit. It was very well supported and the money raised was used to provide extras for the children such as horse riding lessons, special musical activities, P. E. equipment and various outings and trips to Pantomimes in Belfast and Londonderry.

In June 2005 Margaret took early retirement and after six months in the new school building she said goodbye to her pupils, her classroom assistant, Sally Sproule, and the staff of Edwards, where she had taught for all of her career. She had seen it develop from an eight-teacher school to one with 12 teaching and 10 non-teaching staff.

At a presentation in the school, attended by her husband and family members, Principal, Mr Orr, and Dr. M. Brown, Chairman of the Board of Governors, paid tribute to her career and wished her a long and happy retirement. She was presented with a Tyrone Crystal bowl, a golf bag, a bouquet of flowers and a gift cheque. In reply Margaret read the following poem:

On Leaving Edwards

I'm sorry to say
That the time has come
For me to move on,
My work here is done.

Edwards P.S.
Is a wonderful place
Where children are nurtured
And given their space.

It was in September '69
That 2 Clarkes came to class.
Brother Mervyn joined P1;
In charge of P3, I was still only a lass.

For the last 36 years
Edwards has been much of my life.
In fact I've been here longer
Than I've been Herbie's wife.

College was marvellous,
Work and play some of each:
But it was here in Edwards School
That I really learned to teach.

Mr T.F. Riddall
I shall never forget.
To his vision of teaching
I am always in debt.

A lady with proper speech
Was Mrs McNutt.
With her dedication and gentleness,
Above all others she was a cut.

I learned about phonics
From Mrs McCrea.
Her "icks" as in fox
Always with me will stay.

As for dear Mrs Caldwell,
She learned not to fuss.
Another new idea, she said,
Would come along like a bus.

After many years with us
Mr Riddall retired.
Mr Orr took his place
And another era was fired.

Then another stalwart
Had to leave Edwards' fold.
Sammy, with Meta beside him,
Was worth more than gold.

Mrs Waugh was the senior
During many events here.
Her knowledge and expertise
Were relied upon year after year.

As for dear Mr Woods:
He kept a close watch
On all comings and goings:
For him there was no match.

Then it was Sadie's turn,
And the kitchen she left.
How the children all loved her!
Everyone felt quite bereft.

Now many more new faces
To Edwards have come.
Their contribution is immeasurable:
And with this a great sense of fun.

Mr Orr has done us proud,
Our new school is a dream.
With this latest technology
He has sorted out his team.

Edwards P.S.
Is a King among schools,
With a band of professionals
Who are certainly no fools!

Out in the Nursery,
There's a wonderful start
Given by Pamela and Michelle,
With children at the heart.

Into the main school,
Where Jill operates in Year 1.
Helped by Kyra and Andrena,
She makes computers such fun.

Caroline, our musician,
Has a marvellous choir.
Claire helps her with Year 2,
But reading books are Caroline's desire!

Our maths expert, Nicola,
In Year 3 is to be found.
With Irene and Zara to help,
Many bright ideas do abound.

In Year 4 we find Helen
Whose displays are pure joy.
Joan tries keeping things tidy....
But art is just Helen's toy!

Hazel is so busy
Writing this Edwards book.
Her talents she uses
While working in her little nook.

Pretty Julie Ann
Is our newest recruit.
She learned a few skills
As Year 5 she undertook.

Claire's the sporty lass
Who's at home with Year 6.
Jill and she have a second job.....
But teaching and PTA do not mix.

Ivan, our unassuming V.P.,
Does everything he can -
Teaching, administration
And Christine really does stand by her man.

Now Lillian, this year,
Of Special Needs took care.
With Gladys beside her
They're a formidable pair!

Next door is Heather
Who travels around.
No-one ever knows
In what school she can be found!

In S U 2
Gladys reigns supreme.
With Nurse Quigley beside her
They make a great team.

Ethne's our Honorary
Member of Staff.
In many emergencies
She's been our life raft.

Mrs Walls in the office
Really does her best,
But keeping track of everything
Means she doesn't get much rest.

Don't forget our Board of Governors,
Sometimes working late at night,
Who give of their time and knowledge
To keep everything at Edwards just right.

Maria, Heather and their team
Keep us all well fed.
With Dorothy and Tracy in charge,
Dinnertime is well led.

Billy is always in demand,
A busy member of our team.
With Geraldine and Jean to help
Our new school is kept clean.

Our Community Nurse,
Known as "Patsy" by all,
Sorted out all our problems
When on her I did call.

Now what about my own class,
SU1 is a special place
Where Sally keeps us organized
And Elaine can keep the pace.

I'll miss the birthday parties,
Horse riding and trips far and near.
We were a good team together,
So please excuse a tear.

Sadly my time in Edwards
Has come to a full stop.
In future I promise I'll visit,
But that won't be a lot.

I'll go down to the golf course
When the weather is good,
And maybe I'll go travelling
To Australia, if I get Herbie in the mood.

To all my friends and colleagues,
I bid you fond farewell
May Edwards School continue
To always do things well.

Margaret E. Watt June '05

A Special Year - a very special time. By Tom Bratton

My very first visit to Edwards Primary School was to meet Mr Tom Riddall. His office which was probably the smallest I have ever been in. Mr Riddall went through the door first and sat behind a small table, the door was closed and a small folding chair, which was located just behind the door, was pulled out for a visitor to sit on. While I had not come looking for a job, he encouraged me to complete an application form for the vacant post of Vice-principal. I applied and was successful and I had the privilege of working with, and learning from, a dedicated professional, who was highly respected locally and across N. Ireland. How Mr Riddall managed this school from that tiny box office amazed me.

Mr Riddall was a commanding figure — a man well ahead of his time in education. He had high expectations for himself, high expectations for his staff and high expectations for the children. Everything had to be done "by the book" and there was little room for innovative thinking or practice. Good discipline was expected and maintained rigorously and only the best behaviour tolerated in Edwards School.

I remember suggesting that the children might go on an educational visit to Scotland, but Mr Riddall quietly declined, as it might place additional financial burdens on parents. On another occasion, he agreed that I organise a Christmas Book Exhibition for parents and children, with the books supplied for purchase by a leading bookshop in Enniskillen- the night was a great success and new ground was broken. I remember leaving the school keys over to the school residence, where Mrs Riddall, sitting on a pure, white sheepskin rug, was carefully plucking a pheasant which had been given as an early Christmas present.

Another innovation was the school Sports Day, which had always been organised along very traditional lines to determine the best at running, long jump, and high jump. The strong focus which now is on enjoyable events for all of the children, has remained a feature of current Sports Days.

A gifted singer, Mr Riddall ensured that "All in the April Evening" was a part of every Easter celebration. He was often seen adorned in his body-warmer waistcoat, overseeing the school and leading by example. His moral teaching at assemblies encouraged the children to develop Christian living, respect themselves and respect others. The microphone attached to the speaker of the reel-to-reel tape recorder provided the children with opportunities to perform in front of the whole school and to develop confidence and communication skills.

Mr Riddall provided wise counsel for the staff on their own professional development. He promoted health and safety, always stressing the importance of healthy eating, chewing food for the appropriate number of times before swallowing, not lifting heavy objects such as the cylinders of gas for the classroom heaters and certainly not pushing a car unless there was plenty of help. Tom Riddall had a "presence" as he strode along the corridors and as he interacted with the children and with their parents.

Mr Riddall kept very tight purse strings; I remember a teacher who regularly ordered plastic storage boxes for the children's work and resources, but each year he struck them off the order, suggesting instead that empty shoe boxes, which he felt would serve the same purpose and could be obtained free of charge from Watt's! When the first extension to the school was completed, the Board officers had a time persuading Mr Riddall that the brand new furniture supplied by WELB should be used, rather than the old furniture which would look totally out of place.

The staff were a group of individuals who cared passionately for the children's development, their education and their growth as individuals. Kindly and caring teachers such as Mrs McNutt and Mrs Caldwell always searched for, and found, the best in children and encouraged success in little things. Everything was "wonderful" and praise was used to encourage better effort and amending any wayward behaviour.

A memorable event was the football match between the school football team and the staff. While the expert training of the boys by Mr Gowdy ensured that the staff would never win, the teachers really tried hard. The towering figure of Joan Wilson, a teacher from New Zealand, must have sent shock waves through the boys. While we did our best, players like Adrian Leckey, Alan Irwin, Colin Lowry and John Scott made it quite clear that this was a battle that the boys would always win.

Sammy Reid, the caretaker, was a man in a million, a dependable and caring friend to all, a father figure to the children, and someone who went out of his way on very many occasions to help the teachers. He could bring comfort to the tearful child in the playground. A true craftsman, he regularly used his skills to keep the building looking its best and in good repair and Sammy even made and repaired toys and equipment for classroom use. A particular achievement, which illustrated his many skills, was the working coach which he created for the pantomime Cinderella.

Many children and many staff have had the privilege of spending time in Edwards Primary School. It has been, and is a very special place which has formed and developed very positive attitudes to life and to the community. Over many years, the impact of the principals, the teachers and the friends who learned and grew together, has been tremendous. There is rightly much gratitude to Edwards Primary School and all that it stood for in the past and all that it continues to do, in the new school, within the community of Castlederg and beyond. Everyone wishes Edwards Primary School continues success in the wonderful new building which includes many technical resources which Mr Orr has personally insisted on, resources rarely found in schools across N. Ireland and which will support the teaching and enhance the children's learning and education.

I only taught in the school for one year but it was a really special year for me.

Tom Bratton

Elizabeth Beacom

I was delighted to get my first teaching post in Edwards P.S in June 1980. Mr Riddall was the Principal and I was in charge of the P5 class. Ivan Gowdy taught the P6 class on one side and Helen Graham was in charge of the P4's on the other. I have very fond memories of my time there.

What thoughts immediately spring to mind when I think of Edwards? I recall:
My enthusiasm and the enthusiasm of my first pupils......
Mr Riddall and the memos he used to send around the teachers ..
Sammy the caretaker, having hot milk ready for the teachers' coffee every break time....
Mrs Graham preparing Art displays in the main hallway in the afternoons......
The kindness and friendliness shown to me by all the staff and the parents of my pupils.

The children at Edwards had many wonderful opportunities to perform on stage. Weekly assemblies helped prepare them for the bigger school productions. The Infants took part in the Nativity Play and in the Spring term a wonderful pantomime was produced by the upper school under the direction of Mrs McCay. I can picture in my mind's eye Mrs McKinley, Mrs Watt and Mrs Bratton working away on the costumes while Mrs Graham and Mr Gowdy helped with the scenery. The Story Telling Competition was another highlight. Every year the standard seemed to get higher.

In the Summer Term there was Sports Day. Mr Riddall made sure Sammy raised the flag if the weather was fine enough for it to take place. Following the customary bell ringing, long processions of children made their way to the school field. The 1st, 2nd and 3rd placed competitors walked back up the track to the applause of the onlookers.

After school activities became very popular among the children, Mr Gowdy took groups of pupils for football and a thriving Scripture Union was established in Mr Wood's room with quizzes, choruses and games.

One of the things I most enjoyed teaching was needlework. On Monday and Thursday afternoons the pupils were divided into groups of boys and girls for needlework and handwork. I recall the girls making beautifully embroidered aprons and gloves, the P7 girls knitting jumpers and sewing dresses! Somehow everything seemed so relaxed and ordered back then.

Elizabeth Kissick (Beacom).

Mrs Myrtle West (Miss Condy) 1988-1992

Some of my most memorable times were spent at Edwards Primary. I only taught for 4 years in the school but this was my first teaching position. I took over from Mrs Watt who moved to the special unit in the building. I was employed to take 27 P3 children in Room 6, with Mrs Quigley as my classroom assistant. During my time there I participated in many different school events and I have condensed these memories into terms as a guide.

*Myrtle West pictured with
Samantha Gant and
David Thompson*

Term 1

This was always a settling in period for pupils and teachers. Once this had been accomplished there were parental interviews and 11 + exams. At this time in the year my class were also involved in the Sponsored Readathon where children read books over a couple of weeks to raise money for charity. The school exams also took place before Christmas. The school Nativity was always a busy time with performances by the infants for the school and parents. The last day always saw Santa arriving for a visit and a school Carol Service.

1988

1st November - Off school early due to school being very cold. 30th November- received Reading 360 books as new reading scheme.

1990

22nd November - we got new tropical fish for school. 28th November - planted trees with Mrs McNutt, a former teacher.

1991

2nd December - general inspection started for several days in school.

Term 2

Mr Redmond came to my class for music and enthusiastically took us on a singing journey with his guitar. Miss Coulter was another asset to the classroom and she led the children in their Bible studies. The storytelling competition was another event which played a great part in school life with children retelling stories.

The older children had their pantomime performances in this term and all the teachers were busy with the production, costumes and make up.

1988
23rd February - school closed at dinner time due to heavy snow.
25th February - three children from our school were on Roland Rat Race on TV.
17th April - pupils were out planting trees.
26th April - school trip to London.

1990
26th - 28th March - school closed due to bomb in town which put out front windows in school. We spent our days tidying and making the rooms safe for the pupils returning.

Term 3

Road safety week was a great way to make children more aware of how to keep safe on the roads with the help of Tufty and his friends. This was a busy term also with the Book Fair coming to sell books and exams to be completed for the reports to be written. The children particularly enjoyed the school trips at this time and my classes over the years went to the Tayto factory and to Enniskillen. This concludes my visit to the past and it has brought back fond memories. The staff throughout the school and the children I taught were tremendous and they gave me a fantastic start to my career in teaching. I wish the new school continued success and all the staff many happy years, like mine, in Edwards. My final memory comes from an answer I received in a child's homework at the school. My pet's name is Maxa 1000.000. Did you guess it? Maxamillion!!

Ah, memories!

In 1991, I arrived at Edwards Primary School full time to fill a Year's post as Special Needs teacher. I stayed for 7!

Having done Heather Robinson's first maternity leave the year before and various other days, it was like a reunion of old friends and I slipped into the staffroom as if I had never been away. (Much more fun that side of the door than as a dutiful mummy propping up the radiator in the foyer at 2.15 every day!)

I took up residence in what was to become the library and within weeks had set up a Special Needs Register and was t-t-t-ing and b-b-b- ing like a good'un! The mad, spikey haired characters in the Fuzzbuzz books became my night-time reading and sometimes even provided inspiration at the hairdressers! (Note present hair creation. Obviously even 14 years later the influence is still there!) Therapy is helping, though.

Of course, one can only hope that the influence is still there for those you have taught. I have been in the privileged position for the past 7 years of seeing some of those I helped teach to read as they progress, blossom and flourish through KS3, GCSE and even A level. It is a very humbling yet rewarding experience to follow the lives of those you may not even have realized you have touched.

But I digress. Age probably!

Edwards was always a fun place to be. Mr Orr was frequently non-plussed. Especially when he returned from lunch duty to find a roomful of hysterical ladies (Mr Gowdy and Mr Woods Included!) Eventually he learned it was safer not to ask!

Pantotime was always "fun" as was the obligatory Nativity. Few will forget the "Look at the big......... (Silence) "Look at the big........" (Blank, confused look from child). Audible prompt from stage right. "Star?"!

I will never forget my time in Edwards. My wee room at the end of the corridor (which was almost as far away from the loo as Helen Graham's but, in compensation, had its own blow heater.) Hazel McCay's relentless teasing of Mr Gowdy and her presentation of the badge "So many women so little time!" (Pre Christine, of course!) The place where it was always "wile warm", everything was always "all right my end" (of the school, presumably?), some were "not stappin" when asked to visit the remedial department but there was always the double puddings to look forward to from Maria and co in the canteen!

Nor will I forget the pupils. During my time as a Reading Recovery tutor, I had to take a pupil to Londonderry for a "show" lesson. She was the only one _ever_ to notice the camera in the corner, remark on the gold filling at the back of my mouth rather than read her book and hear the laughter of the other tutors on the other side of the two-sided mirror! The look of absolute relief as you got someone's friend to speak to them again. The wee chubby hand in yours after a fall in the playground on the way to Mrs Quigley. The wee lad who just found it all a bit much. "That word's wile hard, miss. Sure you'd need a hammer to break it down!"

The memories will remain with me not just because of the many laughs but because they helped mould me into the teacher I hope I am today. Having seen where pupils begin it is so much easier to help them achieve their full potential when you meet again. Why make life difficult when there's an infinitely better way and someone has already read the map?

When I hit retirement I know I will have given it my best shot. Thank you Edwards for giving me the opportunity of teaching the whole caboodle from 4 to 18. For many, many reasons I will never forget you.

I wish you many more successful and "fun filled" years on your never ending journey of educating the nation!

Pearl Stewart, 1991 - 1998

Elizabeth C. Walls

I was appointed as part-time secretary at Edwards Primary School in 1976, one of the first appointments of this type in a new initiative in primary schools. When I met Mr. Riddall, the Principal, to discuss the terms and conditions of the job he also explained the pro-rata system of remuneration, which, when worked out meant that I would be working for the princely sum of 98p per hour, 7 hours per week to be worked on three mornings, no holidays to be taken during term time and no retainer fee during school holidays. I tendered my resignation right away but was prevailed upon by Mr. Riddall to 'stick it' for a week. Many changes and 29 years later I am still in the post. To begin with there was no office either for the Principal or secretary and a small store outside Room 4 was shared by both. Now it hardly accommodated one chair, let alone two, so that when the person who sat furtherest from the door wanted either in or out, the person at the door had to go out into the corridor. When a visitor came to see the Principal I had to take some work with me and sit in a cloakroom until the office was free again. The desk was a broad shelf, filing was stacked up on the shelves around the store. I requested a typewriter but Mr. Riddall insisted that a new one was out of the question and so a "re-conditioned" one was requisitioned and eventually a battered old specimen was received. It dropped every e. This, with a very old spirit duplicator (the Banda) which invariably flooded, made up all the office equipment. I was given a razor blade, albeit one with a guard on one side, as a pencil sharpener and it remains in the office wrapped and labelled as I received it. In the absence of a Staffroom, breaktime for the teaching staff and myself was held in Room 6. A saucepan of milk was boiled each morning, more often than not boiling over before anyone reached it. All this was to change when a new extension was completed in 1978 at the school, and as well as incorporating several new classrooms, a Staffroom, Medical Inspection Room, Kitchen and Assembly Hall, the Principal and Secretary had separate offices. On my office door was the sign 'Clerk' and to my amusement one parent thought this was my name and used to address me as 'Mrs Clerk'. I never corrected her. New equipment was at last available and a new typewriter, new spirit duplicator and an ink duplicator (Gestetner) were provided as was a typist's chair, filing cabinets and a cupboard. One further move of the office accommodation was at the behest of the Inspectorate who deemed that a chair store was essential for safety purposes. My office was earmarked for this purpose, I moved into the Principal's former office and the Principal moved to the former Medical Inspection Room. The workload of the post gradually developed as time went on - the 7 1/2 hours became 15 and finally 30 per week as schools took responsibility for their own budgets, computers replaced typewriters and photocopiers became indispensable. Eventually came the news that a new school building was planned and in what seemed a very short time another move was on the way and in January 2005 I found myself in an office of which I could only have dreamed about in 1976. What would Mr. Riddall have made of it all??!!!

Elizabeth Walls

My views of Edwards School Through "The Hatch"

On a cold January day in 1978 I began work in Edwards School Kitchen, after having been a year in the County Secondary Kitchen. At first I just worked ten hours per week, but very soon a permanent member of staff (Mrs Duncan) retired and I got her Post to work along side of Rosemary Irwin. She and I worked well together and formed a great friendship, which we still share to this day. Over the dishwashing many things were talked over, and we regularly put the world to rights and reared our families. At that time Myrtle Lyttle was the Supervisor. She went on to marry Andy Bogle. She stayed on for some time, and when she left Maria Burke took over, and is still Supervisor. I had some great times with the children. I enjoyed them so much, listening to their little stories as they took their plates from the hatch. If, and when, I had free time from the "Sink", I would go out through the dining hall and have some fun with them as they ate their dinner. There was one group of children I was very attached to. They were in the Special Care Unit. Their smiling faces and good humour was always a tonic. Jason was and still is very special to me. It was also amazing to see the progress they made through the years in the school. Over the years in the school I saw some changes in the Kitchen Staff and the Teaching Staff. The teachers all treated me very nicely. In September 2000 I retired from the kitchen. I felt I was there long enough and as well the school meals were changing over to cafeteria, which I thought at my time of day would take some getting used to. I got a great send off from the teachers and pupils, which I appreciated very much. I really enjoyed my 22 years at the school, regardless of what side of the "Hatch" I was on, and I still hold Edwards School very close to my heart.

Sadie Emery

Caretaker in a Million.

Sammy Reid (Caretaker) showing Mr Orr the Christmas tableau that he made for the school foyer.

In the course of collecting materials from past pupils and teachers one of the most constant fond references has been to a much loved member of staff who will long be remembered for his contribution to the life of the school for over twenty years. I refer of course to Mr Sammy Reid. Sammy was the school caretaker from 1972 until his retirement in 1994 and in his usual unassuming and modest manner he told his story.

Sammy is a native of Castlederg and has always lived in the same house, his father being the first tenant in 1910. He went to school in Killen and remembers Masters Brown, Black and Kelly and Mrs Verner. While at school Sammy never enjoyed academic work but loved the gardening, which was a very important part of the school curriculum then. Indeed one of the masters told him that he wished he was as good at lessons as he was at gardening! He also said, "You'll never be able to count your money, that is, if you could ever get a job!" How wrong Sammy proved this forecast!

At the age of fourteen he left school and started with Alex. Ballantyne, as a helper on a milk lorry, collecting creamery cans, and earning the princely sum of £1.00 per week! He then went on to work for John Alexander, also collecting milk for Killen Creamery, this time for the enhanced wage of £2.10.

After his "apprenticeship" Sammy was employed for eighteen and a half years in Nestle's in Victoria Bridge, emptying milk tankers and washing them out. Every day he rode his bicycle in all kinds of weather, to Victoria Bridge, doing shift work and often starting work at six o'clock in the morning.

Following the closure of the Nestle factory, Sammy went to work with Jim Hemphill doing contract work, building houses and carrying out school maintenance. He often found himself up at Edwards P.S. mending broken windows, filling in cracks, fixing guttering and doing a myriad of other general maintenance jobs. Pay was £12.00 a week and Sammy enjoyed the work.

Then in 1972 he noticed an advertisement in the paper looking for a Caretaker in Edwards school and he decided to apply. He clearly remembers the interview and feeling very nervous in front of the Committee, chaired by Canon A. Northridge. When asked why he was interested in the job, Sammy honestly replied that the pay was good, in fact, at £18.50 a week it was fifty per cent more than what he was currently earning! Sammy was duly appointed and began in September 1972, beginning with a probationary period. He started work at 7.30 a.m. and finished at 5.30 p.m. His duties included dusting, cleaning and sweeping out the classrooms, washing the wooden floors, cleaning toilets and windows, as well as keeping the grounds clean and tidy. The most onerous task was the care of the solid fuel furnace. Ashes had to be cleaned out on a daily basis and it needed refilling two or three times a day. Every evening it was stoked up so that it stayed lit overnight and was ready to go at full throttle when refuelled next morning. Every Sunday night Sammy came into school to light the furnace in preparation for the new week ahead. As Sammy was the sole caretaker/cleaner and furnace care took such a lot of his time, it was decided to appoint a fellow cleaner and who better to fill the post than Meta, Sammy's wife? This was a partnership that was to prove very successful and beneficial to the school. While Sammy had more time to work on the furnace, Meta dealt ably with the cleaning tasks, a job which she retained up until her retirement in February 1994.

Life in school threw up all sorts of tasks for Sammy and each one was always met with great generosity of spirit and ready willingness to do what was asked. In fact, teachers were almost afraid to say that they needed something, knowing from experience that no matter what it cost in terms of time, money or materials Sammy would ensure that they would have it. I'm certain there wasn't another school in N.I. that could boast that their caretaker made backdrops for plays, castles, fireplaces, dressers, wishing wells, carts, trees, numerous small but important items such as bows and arrows, axes and tools. Perhaps one of the most memorable props he made was the moving coach to carry Cinderella to the Ball.

Well before Christmas the largest tree from the forest was chosen to adorn the school hall and Sammy and his willing sons, Jimmy and David, spent long hours decorating it and adorning it with lights, much to the delight of everyone who entered the school on the following Monday morning. Some time ago he made a beautiful crib scene, which for many years graced the entrance hall and intrigued the children in the run up to Christmas.

In the days before professional stage lighting Edwards School was the proud owner of a very useful homemade lighting system built out of a number of large catering tins cut in half to provide reflectors and placed at regular intervals along a lighting board, which was put up and taken down with great a great deal of care and pride.

Screens were made for the side of the stage to allow a degree of privacy for the stagehands and carpet was laid on the stage to help sound proof it. Props were provided and painted with the minimum of fuss and the maximum of attention to detail. On the nights when plays were performed, Sammy was always there, parking cars, carrying on props and helping children on and off the stage. Nothing was too much trouble and he will long be remembered for his valued contributions.

When Sammy started work in Edwards technology was not quite as advanced as it is today. There was only one television in the school and it had to be carried from room to room according to the viewing timetable. It was Sammy's job to move it around and to ensure that teachers had it on time to watch their choice of programme. So often and so efficiently did he do his job that the T.V. repairman commented on the coloured sides of the T.V. being worn away from constant carrying!

When asked about their memories of the school so many pupils reply without hesitation that they remember Sammy and the way in which he looked after them with such care and kindness. He was a much loved and trusted father figure, always ready to comfort any child in distress and to join in happily to celebrate birthdays or successes. He knew every child by name and attended to each one equally. Cut knees were lovingly washed and soothed, clothes were changed without fuss and dirty arms and legs were secretly washed so that many mums would not despair! Dinner duty was seen by Sammy as yet another chance to help and reassure the children in his care. For small children meat was cut up and reluctant eaters were encouraged to try the food provided. Then outside, an ever-watchful eye was kept to ensure the well-being and safety of the children as they enjoyed all kinds of weather in the playground. Sammy recalled one occasion when a ball became stuck up in a tree and some boys had thrown up a stone to dislodge it but it too had become stuck. Sammy then brought along a pole to move the ball and as he did so the stone fell and struck him on the forehead, causing a cut and the blood to run profusely down his face. Of course the boys were scared but Sammy remained undaunted and treated the incident as part of the day's work!

Visitors to the school frequently commented on the obvious high standard of cleanliness and maintenance of the building. Indeed, those who worked in it knew that if it hadn't been for Sammy's selfless efforts and pride in his work, it would not have looked so well! Paintwork that was showing signs of wear was touched up, plaster was replaced in damp areas and every room was washed out in rotation in the early morning, long before teachers or pupils arrived. Desks and chairs were faithfully scrubbed and the floors were burnished and shone like mirrors.

So, it was with great pride that the Headmaster, Staff and pupils learnt that the Queen in the New Year's Honours List of 1994 had honoured Sammy with a well-deserved M.B.E. He described how he had been informed of his nomination and of his total surprise, but after recovering from the shock and talking it over with Canon W. Quill, he decided to accept the honour. Preparations were made for the journey to London, new outfits becoming the royal occasion were purchased and Sammy and Meta duly flew to London for the ceremony. They stayed with Sammy's late brother in Luton and travelled to Buckingham Palace to receive the award. Sammy was very nervous, as anyone would expect to be on such a major occasion, but the Palace staff were very helpful and made sure that everyone knew what to do. He lined up with the other recipients and when a footman called out his name he went forward to the Queen, who congratulated him, pinned the award on his lapel and spoke briefly to him. After shaking hands, Sammy described how he took five steps back, bowed and went back into another room, the whole ceremony completed in a few brief minutes.

Unfortunately Sammy was troubled by ill health and sadly for the whole community he was forced to take early retirement in April 1993. A special evening was held in the school to mark his retirement and presentations were made from the Staff, from pupils, from the P.T.A., from the Board of Governors and from parents and friends. Glowing tributes were paid to Sammy in appreciation of his work and dedication as a Caretaker and for his contribution to the community. Tributes were also paid to Meta, Sammy's wife, who retired at the same time and whose sterling work in the school deserved rich recognition. Since his retirement Sammy tried to overcome the problems of poor health and continued to take an interest in his home and beautiful garden. He enjoyed the close proximity of his son, David, his wife Joycelyn, and grandchildren, Kelso, Kylie and Kasey and he takes a keen interest in their well-being. His son Jimmy still lives with him but sadly Meta passed away in January 2005 after a long battle with cancer and the community shared in the great loss.

Sammy still looks back on his days in Edwards with enormous affection and pride. He enjoyed everything he did in the school and he feels especially privileged to have worked for and with so many lovely children and staff. In turn, so many children and staff echo the reflection that they were honoured and privileged to have had such a wonderful caretaker who is indelibly etched in their fond memories.

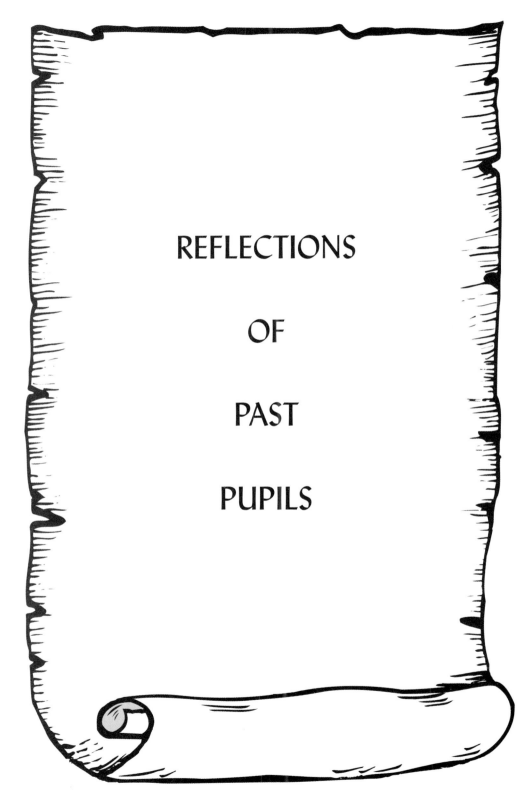

REFLECTIONS

OF

PAST

PUPILS

Remembering

Come take a look at days gone by,
Linger here and let memories fly,
Back to days of care-free fun,
When days were longer and there was always sun!
Stop and read with Janet and John,
Browse over reports of people long gone.
Study 'roll books' for familiar friends,
Note the uniform and its different trends.
Look at maps and distant places,
Remember friends and teachers' faces!
Sit at the desk and ponder a while,
Could there be a wistful smile
As you remember when you were a child?

Remember the reading, the writing, the sums to be done
The tables recited by everyone,
Three times three is nine,
Stand very still and toe in line.
Open 'reading' books and begin to read,
Get your copy book and work with speed.
Watch those letters do them well,
But you'll be in 'til after the bell.
Life was slower then and much less complicated,
When you were told sit, you silently waited,
Until 'teacher' had time to look at you,
And show you what you had to do.
But times were good and there was laughter,
No thought then of what comes after.
It's only now we wonder a while,
That we remember 'This Edward's Child.'

Author Unknown

Oldest Surviving pupil of Burnside School reflects

Born in 1912, Doris Wilson holds the record for the oldest surviving pupil of the Burnside school to contribute to this book.

A native of Moyrafferty, County Armagh, she was the eldest child of a family of four. Her father, Alex Foye, played football for Cliftonville and was also an Irish International player. He was Headmaster in Urney, but Doris, her sister Mona, brothers Bob and Harry, and a friend, "Loney" (John) Anderson, cycled to the Burnside school in Castlederg. On very wet days they were excused the long trek and Doris recalls occasions when they stopped for a rest at a big hill near Urney. With an admirable memory for her years, Doris described Mr Burnside as a severe, very well dressed man, who stood no nonsense and "loved to write on the board." His favourite topics were Geography and Nature Study and she remembers boys being taught on Saturdays as they were prepared for Matriculation and entry to university. Children rote learned facts and figures and to this day Doris is able to recite the counties of Ireland, names of County towns, rivers and mountains as well as large chunks of Shakespeare!

Doctor Evelyn Burnside taught French, Latin and Music and although she was not as severe as her father, she was an "odd" person. Fees were paid for the tuition and Doris remembers being given an "envelope" for the teacher, although she was unaware of the contents.

Doris also recalls the enjoyable Christmas Concerts to which parents and friends were invited. On one occasion she remembers being dressed in a purple bandana and a gypsy dress, as she and her best friend, Elsie Huey, assisted with the production. Boys wrote sketches and Doris played the piano. For her this was the beginning of a life long passion for music. She thinks she was sent to Londonderry for lessons and studied for an Entrance Examination and was accepted to London School of Music but didn't go as her brother Bob was accepted to study Chemistry in Belfast.

The family moved to live at Ardstraw when her father became the Master in the local school. She then taught piano lessons and trained choirs, often playing the organ in the Church. She also taught music in the school and she used the "tonic solfa" method. Her love of singing encouraged her to join choirs in Castlederg and Newtownstewart.

In 1937 she married Fred Wilson and they lived in Killeen, Fyfin, where they raised a family of five children. Doris insisted that they attended Edwards School although other schools were nearer. Her only daughter, Helen, continued the close link with Edwards when she returned as a teacher in 1974 and is presently teaching in the Special Unit.

Music has always been a part of Doris' life and although she is now a resident in Bell Gray Nursing Home in Newtownstewart, she still enjoys visiting choirs and likes nothing better than joining in with the singing, contributing her familiar alto role.

Despite being widowed for many years she has maintained a courageous and lively spirit, always interested in the world around her and enjoying visits from her family and friends. Finally, she attributes the fact that so much of her early education has remained with her during her long and healthy life, to the excellent instruction she received in Edwards National School, or as it was better known then--- the Burnside School!!

Mrs Doris Wilson

Memories of the late Mrs Jean Hamilton.

Perhaps one of the oldest people to contribute to our book was Mrs Jean Hamilton, (nee Watt), and we were delighted when she was able to share her memories with us through past member of staff, Mrs Margaret Watt. Unfortunately Mrs Hamilton passed away on 31st May 2005, before her recollections went to print, but we are indebted to her family for permission to include her valuable contribution.

Mrs Hamilton was a member of the well-known and highly respected local Watt family, her brothers being Samuel, Albert and Jack and a sister Margaret, all of whom sadly are also deceased.

In the early 1900's, before electricity, television, fridges and even cars, Jean Watt and her siblings, Margaret, Samuel, Albert and Jack, attended Edwards School on the Castlefin Road, Castlederg. Jean began school at about the age of six and wore a little petticoat and a chemise. Many children came to school in their bare feet but Jean wore shoes costing 4/6. She laughed as she recalled that it was a novelty to copy those who were barefoot but it wasn't funny when you stubbed a toe, so the shoes went back on again! She carried a little leather schoolbag, which had been made in the workshop belonging to the family business. Some children carried their books in a simple strap. Everyone had a pencil and they sometimes used slate and chalk but she doesn't have any recollection of ink being employed. They sat in a long row of about seven or eight children to a desk.

The boys' and girls' schools sat comfortably side by side, and although the pupils were mainly educated in a segregated fashion, the girls and smaller boys came together each morning for Religious Instruction in the Boys' School. Miss Fry or Miss Jackson took this lesson and Mr Burnside took the older boys separately.

The Headmaster was Mr J.G. Burnside, who ruled inside and outside with a rod of iron. He was known to go down town every afternoon and the children were terrified of him. Jean remarked that he was very strict but obtained great results. Teaching in the Girls' School was Mrs Smith and an assistant, Miss Young. Mrs

Smith was also remembered, as "cross, she didn't spare the rod," but was "a very good teacher." She was a great old lady who almost always wore black clothes and a beautiful gold chain. She had three daughters and a son. One daughter, Winnie, taught in the school and wore lipstick and rouge; she had hair coloured like straw and often referred to Jean and her sister Margaret as " the Miss Watts" and treated them like ladies! The other two daughters worked in government positions in England and homecomings were treated with "such embracing." Sadly her son died at around fifteen due to a weak heart.

An open hearth fire graced one end of the school room and a circle was drawn on the floor around the fireplace and pupils had to stand with their feet touching it—hence the saying "toe the line." The pupils paid 5/0 annually for the fuel but as the fire was kept slacked up, it emitted little heat and they were often very cold. Lamps and a Primus Stove were used and there was great excitement when electricity arrived in Castlederg. Jean thinks she may have been around eight or nine years old.

The whole class did sums from the board and pupils stood back to back to do mental arithmetic. Jean hated school and particularly "sums," but she loved singing and playing the piano. It was the tradition in the school that whenever the children were changing classes, for example for cookery, they marched along from room to room to the sound of the piano being played. Jean often had to perform this task and children took it in turns to play. She had piano lessons with Miss Daly, a Belfast lady, who taught singing and piano and stayed in rented accommodation in Gas Lane. She was a Methodist Minister's daughter and was very poor. Mrs Watt dreaded the bills as Miss Daly sent the bill and added on postage as an extra expense, but the family felt sorry for her and Margaret used to make her apple tarts to help supplement her means.

General maintenance of the school and grounds was considered to be everyone's responsibility, so every Monday morning the windows were cleaned with newspaper and occasionally the playground was given a thorough weeding.

Lunchtime was half an hour long and Jean and her siblings ran down from school to have their dinner at home. If they took lunch to school it usually comprised of home made bread with jam, which by lunch time had soaked horribly into the bread, accompanied by a bottle of milk.

Cookery and sewing were given prominence in the curriculum and Jean mirthfully recalled one occasion when they had made rice puddings on the tiny stove. They were placed on a board and left to one side to cool. Rev. Moran just happened to drop in to the class that day, when in childish spirits Dosy Robinson jumped on another child's back and sent the board of puddings flying.........What happened next is probably best left to the imagination!!

Jean loved sewing and her mother sent her red thread to use but the teacher said to use blue thread, as it didn't show up bad stitching! She bemoans the sad demise of needlework over the years and it's lack of importance in the current curriculum. Her father encouraged her love of sewing and when she moved to Belfast he bought her a hand sewing machine, costing £4/10. It was frequently used to make clothes and household furnishings and it was later converted to electricity and is still going today! Not bad value for £4/10!

Children were expected to work hard in and out of school but Jean remarked that she was a bit lazy. On one occasion she borrowed an exercise from Lily Porter, whose family worked on the trams, and as she copied it at home her mother spilt porridge on it!!

In school pupils were often given responsible jobs and Jean recalled being "housekeeper" when an exam was taking place. She made just one mistake that she has never forgotten—she replaced a sweeping brush or besom, the wrong way up, and this was regarded as serious! The Inspector just happened to be Miss Jackson who was later to drown in the sinking of the Princess Victoria.

Painting lessons were rare, still life drawing was much more common, but the pupils often struggled to draw a bowl or jug with symmetrical sides!

Water was not readily available in those days and had to be carried in buckets from the nearby well. Hence it was used sparingly. Cooking utensils were cleaned with sand and then rinsed off in fresh water.

The Watt family members were not beyond high jinks and Jean remembered the day when Albert got into trouble for throwing a paper bag of something resembling red cement over the boys! She also says that many of the children hated school and would have tried to get out early. Jean's sister Margaret tried this ploy on more one occasion when she wrote notes to the teacher asking to be released at 2.30 p.m.

Mrs McSorley was the teacher in the Catholic School and she grew roses behind the wall. Jean remembers at the age of nine or ten, on the way to school, being caught trying to pinch some of them. When Mrs McSorley put up the window and asked Jean her name, she ran away and never tried to take any more after that scare.

During the First World War many men from Castlederg answered their country's call and Jean recollects the eerie sound of a whistle being blown for five minutes by a soldier returning to battle after being home on leave. As a young child she wondered if he would ever come back. She also recalled hearing an aeroplane for the first time as they were swimming in the river. They were terrified and ran home, forgetting youngest brother Jack's new sandals. The aeroplane was dropping notes asking people to join the army.

Sweets were rationed and the allowance was a quarter pound weekly.

The Fair Day was held on the last Friday of each month and many children stayed at home as it was not regarded as safe for them to walk to school, hence the school was closed. Cattle were weighed in the centre of the town and sold in the area behind the barracks, horses were traded on the "Horse Hill" and produce was sold in the centre of the town. She can still see the cups and saucers spread out on straw and herring for sale—thirteen for the price of twelve!!

The bags of corn were full of rats and killing the vermin was a favourite pastime of the boys. They used to climb onto the roofs and poured water on the slates. When the rats came out for a drink the boys stabbed them with nail-covered sticks!!

Play stations and electronic games were not even the stuff of dreams and the children had to use their imaginations and develop their own amusement. The boys fished in the river with sticks holding a pin and a worm as the bait.

Although the town of Castlederg was much smaller then, it boasted Gailey's Hotel, where teachers, assistants and Inspectors, who lived a distance away, stayed. She clearly visualised many buildings and their occupants—Leary's, McCaskie's, McCay's, Parkes' Drapery and Wool shop and Dr Mowbray and his son Curzon. Beside the Watt family home was the butcher's, owned by the kindly Mrs Gallagher, who kept a few hens running around her yard. Then there was Barber Kane's and McGlinchey's who made exquisite traps for horses. Next came

Scott's who sold boots and kept cross dogs. Jean liked to walk her little dog Togo, but he was scared of the awesome opponents in Scott's and refused to go in their direction.

Parke's shop was very tiny and was situated on the other side of the street. One particularly warm twelfth of July, Freddie Parke ate a large breakfast of bacon and eggs and to cool off went for a swim in the notorious Castle Hole and unfortunately drowned. Following this sad incident the bands did not play in the town centre at the Twelfth parade.

Smith's of Magheralough delivered milk in pewter jugs around the town. People weren't so fussy and standards were not quite as stringent as today, but Mrs Watt used to warn the children not to drink "the dregs as they were all gritty!"

Jimmy Keenan was the Baker at the bottom of the town and it was a great treat when their mother sent down for a dozen of his jam puffs. With Cantrell and Cochrane's lemonade to wash them down, the children enjoyed a proverbial feast! There was a hotel at the top of the town, owned by Mr Buss, and he too made excellent pastry. So from time to time and to add a little variety to their diet, Mrs Watt would have sent Jean to purchase a dozen of his specialities. Jean was the family message girl and every Saturday night her mother sent her round to all her customers with an order.

Many residents in the town were very poor and Jean remembers her father sending paper to very poor folk to cover their clay floors. Her mother also provided jugs of broth or stew to help augment the frugal diets.

The Diamond or The Square as Jean referred to it, was vacant, with no buildings and she remembers playing ball against the Courthouse wall and hopscotch and rounders in the street, along with many of the other local children.

The Methodist Church still stands in the same position and Jean has vivid memories of the big fire in W.J. Kyle's on Christmas Eve 1938. It began in the bottom of the yard in a paint and turpentine store at around ten o'clock at night and Jean smelled the smoke. Fire Brigades were called from Strabane and Londonderry, in the absence of a local service. River water was used to fight the fierce flames and as they spread, the Methodist Church acted as a buffer in between the buildings and saved the rest of the street from destruction.

Jean sadly recalled the tragic sinking of the Princess Victoria, on a cold blustery day in 1953, as she sailed to Larne from Scotland. One of the people who tragically lost her life was a Miss Jackson, a School Inspector who was known locally.

Mr Burnside, although noted for his strict discipline, was highly regarded as a very erudite man and a sound educator. Subjects taught included Irish, Latin, French, Greek, English, Arithmetic, Geography and History. Clever students were able to sit exams that enabled them to enter university. The successful teaching of Mr Burnside was reflected in the number of students who went on to professional positions and Jean mentioned many fondly-- Roy Hamilton who went to Queen's University, Belfast, to study Medicine, Bill Hamilton who also went to Q.U.B. and studied Pharmacy, Norman Whitcroft who went to T.C.D. and graduated as a Chemist and his brother Fred who went on to become a Canon in the Church of Ireland, among of course many others who became lawyers, vets, businessmen and teachers.

Jean also recalls Mr Burnside's daughter, ...who was so clever that she was eccentric and is remembered for her peculiarities. Unfortunately Mr and Mrs Burnside died around the same time and Jean reflected on the sad funerals, which were widely reported in the papers. Their daughter was left a lot of money, but being of a flippant nature, she frittered it away on silly frivolities, such as unnecessary reams of lace and ribbon.

Many students left school from the age of twelve and Jean, aged seventeen, went to Shaftsbury Square in Belfast to do a typing and shorthand course. She stayed in a hostel for £1.00 a week until she completed the course. Subsequently she went to work in Ulster Tin Canister Company, a firm that made everything out of tin. (There was even a tin factory beside the river in Castlederg that made tin dishes and mugs.) She didn't like the job and only stayed a short time until she went to work in the Bank Buildings in Belfast, (which now house Primark.)

Her childhood sweetheart was Bill Hamilton, who for many years had lived opposite her in Castlederg. At the age of fourteen their relationship was serious and Bill gave her a half-pound box of chocolates as a Christmas Box! He also made a will in a book and bequeathed all he owned to the girl he loved—Jean Watt!! He served his time in McCay's Chemist Shop. Everyone paid for their medicines, which were dispensed in glass bottles, and it was Bill's job to wash the bottles outside in a big tub of freezing cold water!! On leaving, his generous employer gave him a parting gift of 10/0. Jean maintained a close friendship with him and when Bill went to work in Canada, Jean joined him in Toronto in November 1931. They were married and lived there until September 1933. She came home to give birth to her daughter, Eileen, and remembers that night with total clarity.

Nurse Muldoon and Dr. Huey were in attendance and as usual the Saturday night gospel preachers were spreading the word in The Diamond. The nurse, only concerned with the serious task in hand, "wished they would be quiet!"

For some time her husband Bill had temporary work in Banbridge and Jean and the baby remained in Castlederg. But then he obtained a permanent post in Tandragee and Jean and the baby joined him there. During the war he bought the business on the Crumlin Road with money he borrowed from Jean's father, Thomas, and which they diligently paid off on a monthly basis. They lived in a house in Wheatfield Crescent but when the bombing of Belfast took place Bill, Jean and their two children, Eileen and Brian, moved back to the Glebe Hills in Tandragee, while Bill travelled daily to work in the city. They moved back when it was felt safe enough to do so and purchased their house from a customer who gave him first offer and they continued in the business until they retired. It is still carried on today by their grandson.

Sadly Bill passed away in May 1979 but Jean remained in the family home, successfully managing to take care of herself until she passed away in her ninety-ninth year.

Recollections of Mrs Elaine Ryan.

School days for all children create many memories but when your father was Principal and you lived in the schoolhouse, a totally different perspective was achieved. This was the case for Mrs Elaine Ryan, nee Sloan, who vividly remembers her school days and dwelling in the adjacent schoolhouse on the Castlefin Road. She sketched out a plan of the house with its ground floor, consisting of an entrance hall, a drawing room to the front left, a dining room to the right, a pantry/ scullery and kitchen with a breakfast room to the back and five rooms upstairs. She described it as a great place for children to grow up. There was a large backyard with a garden complete with a burn running along side. Her father created a badminton court and she and her brother John and sister Ann, spent many happy hours playing outdoors. Their housekeeper was Mrs Jennie Scott and while her mother was a teacher, she did not teach when they were growing up.

Thinking of the old school she recalled the open fires in the classrooms in winter, ink wells in the desks for the nibbed pens, which were topped up by the senior boys using a vessel like a mini watering can. Teachers she remembers were Miss Mitchell (Mrs Davidson), Miss McArthur (Mrs McFarland), Miss Jackson and Miss Elliott and of course her father, Mr Jim Sloan. School was a centre of great discipline and caning took place regularly. Canes were purchased in Sam Hemphill's in half dozen bundles!

During the war she remembered the evacuees coming from Belfast. They were brought up to school and allocated homes. The front room of the school was used as a "food office," where ration coupons were issued but apart from that school carried on as normal during the war years.

As well as being a strict disciplinarian in school, Mr Sloan was also firm at home. Mrs Ryan has clear memories of being made to sit a scholarship examination to go on to Secondary level education and although she passed it, she was not granted a scholarship as it was means tested and with her father's position she didn't have a chance. She says he would have been fully aware of the situation but she was not excused.

So much for the myth that teacher's children have it easy!

Parliamentary Draughtsman Peculiar.

William Andrew Leitch CB LLM

The following excerpt is transcribed exactly from the unpublished memoirs of the late Will Leitch, formerly of Fyfin, a pupil of the Burnside School, who went on to become a lawyer and for many years was a Parliamentary Draughtsman. I am deeply indebted to his son David and daughter in law, Anne, who visited the school and granted permission to use his writing.

"The alleged skill in getting out of trouble was not an inherited trait. On the contrary, it was common to all who, like myself, suffered, at Castlederg Edwards Public Elementary School, the various slings and arrows of the headmastership of "Parry" Burnside. There, even for schools of the kind and time, discipline was of the strictest kind, detection of even the mildest misdemeanour was nearly almost certain and punishment invariably of barbaric severity. It behoved you to get off the hook if you could and heaven help you if the attempt failed. To this day, despite medical evidence to the contrary, I attribute my deafness to the frequent beatings he used to give me about the head with his favourite weapon, a hazel rod. Others who were less afraid of him fared even worse. Once, Willie Kyle, later a respectable merchant and pillar of society, was driven to desperation by Parry's vicious thumping, seized by the stem one of the potted geranium plants on the nearest window-sill and swung it at the old boy's head. Fortunately, centrifugal force threw the terra pot off line but the clay and roots landed fairly and squarely on the bald pate it was aimed for, much to the delight of the observing ranks of Tuscany, who, nonetheless were too cowed to cheer. If we could get away with it we would put hard-to-see nicks in the hazel rod currently in use with a cutthroat razor, temporarily borrowed from the bathroom at home. This was of little avail because if the rod broke, there was always another in reserve to hit with harder than before.

We learnt many things at Castlederg Edwards EPS but the pressing need to get out of, and stay out of, trouble, was first among them.

On the more positive side, we acquired at an early age, a healthy disrespect for some of the idiocies of bureaucracy. One of the major political controversies of the time related to religious instruction in the primary schools. All the clergy wanted it but the majority of teachers rightly thought it was a waste of time and detested it. The difficulty might well have disappeared but for the fact that it had unfortunate sectarian undertones. A compromise was reached which provided for a half hour's religious instruction every day. During this time a large notice, about two feet by eight inches, with the words "RELIGIOUS INSTRUCTION" had to be posted in the classroom. At other times the back of the notice which solemnly carried the words "SECULAR INSTRUCTION" had to be exhibited. But the only time "RELIGIOUS INSTRUCTION" ever faced us was when the Inspector of Schools made his appearance at Gailey's comfortable hotel, an event of which Parry always managed to receive early warning and immediately ordered us to bring copies of the New Testament to school. The "instruction consisted of making each pupil in turn read a verse of the gospel of which no explanation was ever forthcoming. Even this practice was abandoned on the Inspector's departure from the district and "SECULAR INSRUCTION" returned to its pride of place. The effect of the government regulation which lay behind this performance was to encourage small boys to treat the whole thing with contempt, which was hardly what the administrators had in mind. Shorn of Victorian hypocrisy, the system of education which Northern Ireland inherited, with its concentration on the "3R's" was primarily intended to provide cheap labour for the business man, whereas the aim ought to have been to make us more civilised. At one time we had a payments system under which the teacher's remuneration was made to depend in part upon the number of attendances of his pupils. Parry, who was exceptionally tight-fisted, then made a rule that (1) if every member of his class was present throughout the entire week, the class was excused homework for the week-end but (11) if even one boy was absent, even for a mere half day, the whole class had ten hours' homework and woe betide you if every bit of it wasn't done. My class had the Monteith twins, sons of a farm labourer, who were frequently absent, mainly to assist their father's employer and to supplement a meagre family budget. In consequence we were rarely excused homework and, not unnaturally, retaliated one day by throwing the Monteith brothers, fully clothed, into the nearest stream. Here, the result of an administrative effort designed to secure better school attendance had the direct result of making a group of young savages more savage than ever.

However, I am running ahead: Parry had his good qualities too. If he took care of his own money (he died leaving more than a modest fortune) he took even greater care of what was entrusted to him. The school was originally founded mainly by the local Protestant churches and his boast was that he had never cost the governors a penny. The government, of course, paid the teachers' salaries. Two boys from each classroom had to stay behind on Fridays to sweep out the floors after liberally sprinkling the rough and crudely repaired boards with a thin mixture of Jeyes Fluid and water. This was done on a rota basis but the other task for which the governors paid nothing was the occasional clearing out of the two-hole dry earth privies. This was usually reserved for larger boys who had stepped out of line and the contents were also spread by them over the master's garden on which, after the German fashion, he grew excellent potatoes and other vegetables. He and his daughter Evelyn, who had graduated with a Ph.D from T.C.D., taught Classics, modern languages, higher mathematics and much else that was outside the official curriculum. Indeed they even learnt sufficient Sanskrit and Hebrew to be able to coach former pupils who, as theological students at Trinity or Magee College Londonderry, were having difficulty with these subjects. Recently, looking through the Intermediate Examination Board's results for the late 1920's, I was amazed to see just how many successes they had. Their fees were modest, and but for them, many young people (incidentally more R.C's than Prods), would never have been able to carve out successful careers as bankers, teachers, ministers or priests, chemists or doctors (one of the latter obtained the gold medal in his M.D. at Q.U.B.) In those days one did not have to attend a secondary or grammar school in order to matriculate or pass the state examinations.

In 1927 I was definitely not looking forward to completing my schooldays under the Burnsides. Of my three best friends, Freddy Kyle was going to Wesley College in Dublin and the two McCay brothers, whose mother was the only parent courageous enough to protest about the ugly red welts left on our wrists by the hazel stick, were to go to Portora Royal School.

My chances of escape seemed slim when, quite unexpectedly, there came the offer of the "William Campbell" free tuition scholarship at Methodist College Belfast. This, apparently, was the result of my having entered, considerably under age, for the Elementary School Leaving Certificate. The offer surprised my father as much as it did me, but, very fairly, he left the choice to me, adding that he was perfectly prepared to pay for my boarding if I wanted to go. I was to show the letter to Burnside before I decided to go either way.

For a boy of thirteen it was not an easy decision. Though losing some friends I still had others: Andy Kane, already at fourteen an accomplished angler; Sammy Gailey not yet departed to South Africa on account of his asthma; the Robinson brothers, sons of the local blacksmith whom, in terms of service to the community no finer family ever existed; the Hendersons headed by the brilliant Sam, the Whitcrofts, the Toorishes and the Muldoons. In fact we were a close-knit bunch who had played together in exciting times in a school barely a mile from the border and on a road frequently used by black and tans in Crossley tenders and "A" special constables in their Model "T" Fords. Out of Old Parry's reach and sight our days were carefree and happy. But most of all I would miss Castlederg itself since nowhere on this earth---outside perhaps of the Parliamentary Counsel in London, have I encountered more colourful characters to the square inch than in this tiny County Tyrone village. There was "Wing" Sproule who had lost an arm on the Somme, Robert James "time enough" Walker, the Sir Gasser, the Black Doctor who was neither black nor a doctor and "the Cubit" so called because it was alleged there was no bottom to his stomach. Once my mother decided to put that theory to the test and instructed the current housemaid Winnie, a cheerful refugee from the Convent in Ballinasloe, to give him all he wanted. For the next two and a half hours his jaws moved with the monotonous regularity of a football manager chewing gum on television and he was still prepared for more when a halt was wisely called: with the Cubit enough was never enough. And the friendly Tom Galloway was always ready to invite you to join him on the footplate of the Castlederg and Victoria Tramway to show you how it all worked.

At school, next day, Burnside really made the decision for me. On going (with permission) to the privy I noticed, overriding its other odours, the unmistakable aroma of Wild Woodbine and the air was thick with its blue smoke. As I emerged from it, he was lying in wait and accused me of smoking and demanded to see my hands. They were entirely nicotine free when I produced them and denied the charge. I had not been smoking but he would not believe me, giving me two hard whacks on each hand for smoking and a further two for lying. I said nothing and did not produce the MCB letter until shortly before school ended for the day. He asked me what I was going to do. I told him I would accept the offer because he had wrongly punished me that morning. He was very angry about it but beyond saying---which in all fairness was true enough----that I would not have had the scholarship but for him, there was little he could do. The summer term ended in another three days and I told my father I did not want to go back as I was fearful of what might happen to me. To my surprise he agreed------guessing I would "mitch" anyway---- and that was the last I saw of Castlederg Edwards, at least from the inside!"

Those Were The Days.

Mr Tommy Sturdee with the A.R.P. Bell

Tommy Sturdee was born in 1928, one of a family of nine children of Alex and Harriet Sturdee, and he was brought up in William Street. His father was a railway man and Tommy grew up with a passion for trains and the railway.

He remembers a very happy childhood, playing on the streets with his friends and watching the few cars trundling along. Mischievous boys who liked to play pranks, like tying a string on a doorknocker and hiding some distance away, then pulling it, enjoyed the innocent fun as they watched the puzzled faces of the occupants when they opened the door and found no one there.

He recalled the fascination with the big engines as they travelled along the line, through where Jimmy Lyon's garage is now, and into the station.

It was a carefree time filled with many exciting developments. The streets were roughly stoned and he recalls one great day when he watched William Street being tarred. A big steam engine pulled a roller wagon with screenings and it was a boy's dream to watch the huge roller moving slowly back and forward, pressing the stones into the tar and creating a smooth surface.

Kindly neighbours were fondly recalled as Tommy reeled off many familiar names--- Master Quinn, Headmaster of the Catholic school, who lived next door, Old Tom Watt in his shoe shop, W. J. Kyle, Harry McAnea, and Cassie Loughrey in her shop, who sold about everything!

Friday Market Days were the highlight of young Tommy's life. He can clearly envisage the horses running up and down the Horse Hill and the weighbridge and the cattle pens in front of Kyle's shop. He frequently schemed school to go to the market and often collected sixpence for helping to herd cattle. A man by the name of Beattie had a huge Clydesdale stallion, and though very small in stature, Tommy lacked nothing in boldness and enjoyed being given the job of leading the magnificent horse down to Walls' yard for his owner.

At one time Tommy's grandmother took over the family home and opened a shop selling sweets, tobacco and snuff. The sweets were sold out of open boxes and cigarettes were sold singly. The sweets were obtained from Malseeds of Derry, whose traveller was a man named Joe Speer. Occasionally Tommy had to go on the bus to Strabane to collect sweets. These were procured from Tom McDevitte, father of the recently deceased Tom McDevitte, otherwise known as Barney McCool.

In addition to caring for her large family, Tommy's mother also ran a sweet shop in the middle of the town. Tommy remembers the sugary confections such as Dolly Mixtures and Liquorice Allsorts.

He recalls his schooldays with a twinkle in his eye and sprinkles his memories with many humorous anecdotes. He referred to the school as "The Burnside School," although Mr Burnside had already passed away when Tommy started, aged about 4. His first teacher was Miss McArthur and he sat at a long desk. It was a cold room, heated by an open fire at one end, nearest the teacher, of course. Lunch was his "piece," brought in his pocket and often eaten by ten o'clock. Bigger boys brought in a daily bucket of water from the well in the "moors," a patch of open ground behind the school. An enamel mug sat beside the bucket and was used by anyone wanting a drink. Everyone had books and pencils and there were no toys. He went on to Miss Elliott's class and she was very, very strict. Miss Jackson was his next teacher, followed finally by Master Sloan.

Again he recalls the long desks and the inkwells, which were often thrown at the Master by the more foolhardy boys. Tommy didn't like school lessons but his favourite time was spent in the garden, learning the rudiments of Horticulture, under the watchful eye of the Master, who occasionally checked the progress of the vegetable patch.

Inspector's visits to the school were always awaited with trepidation. In his last year Tommy recalled that rumours were circulating that the Inspector was doing his rounds. Tommy was given the very responsible task of keeping an eye out for his arrival and had to let the Master know immediately. However, Tommy missed the crucial moment and was duly slapped for his inattention.

The school buildings were nearing one hundred years old when Tommy was in his final years. There was great excitement on the grand occasion when the new school opened in 1938. In his mind he could clearly see the line of children marching over from the old school, along the Priest's Lane and up to the splendid new building. This represented a vast improvement in conditions for the staff and pupils; well lit rooms, heating, cloakrooms and flush toilets, large playgrounds and new equipment.

However nice the school was, Tommy was glad to leave and he proudly stated that he left school one day and began employment the next. He "served his time" with Joe Lindsay, a general blacksmith and he spent his days learning how to make carts and barrows. The working day began at eight o'clock and finished at six in the evening. Saturday was a shorter day, ending at three o'clock. His first wages were two shillings and six pence for the week and his employer remarked, "You should have been paying me," meaning that he should have been paying for his training! For three years he continued to work hard until he decided to move to Motherwell in Scotland, where he worked as a builder. He thoroughly enjoyed this work, which he was to continue until his retirement in 1968.

He returned to Northern Ireland and worked for the Housing Executive for around fifteen years followed by seventeen years in the employment of Robert Harpur. Many pupils of Edwards School will remember Tommy's friendly smile as he carried out frequent repairs for Billy Harpur, who was in charge of the maintenance of the building.

Tommy recalls the formation of the Air Raid Patrol in Castlederg during the War years. Master Sloan was the Air Raid Warden and he and John Sloan were the message boys. (See photograph on page 185) Of course there were no phones, mobile or otherwise; the only mobile messages were those transmitted by the message boys on their old bicycles, dimly lit by a light on the front that had a cover, which reflected the light downwards and prevented them from being detected.

In 1956 Tommy married Miss Elizabeth Patterson and they lived at 14,

Breezemount. They had three children, Ian, Hilary and David, who all went to Edwards School. At present Hilary is married and lives in Omagh, Ian lives in Enniskillen and sadly David passed away at the age of twenty nine, following a heart attack. Unfortunately, Elizabeth also died a few years ago but Tommy still remains in the family home and enjoys visits to and from his family. He has also had bouts of ill health but thankfully at present he is very well.

Although there were nine in Tommy's family, he was the only one who was to remain in Ireland; all the other siblings immigrated to Australia. They spread around to different parts and Tommy went out to visit them for the first time after thirty-three years. He scarcely recognised them but greatly enjoyed renewing the family ties. One brother, Ronnie, who had always had a great love of horses and spent a lot of time in the yard of Roland Walls, became a professional jockey and was Queensland Champion. It was a tough life, with very early morning starts but he made a lot of money and is now retired.

Tommy is also enjoying his retirement and is shortly to undertake a fourth trip out to see his family and renew old friendships—not bad for a man who is nearing eighty years of age! I thank him for sharing his memories and our best wishes go with him for a wonderful trip.

Boys Will be Boys!!

Teachers, and indeed parents, know that when you put two boys together they will often tell stories about each other and that is exactly what happened when I spoke to the Waugh brothers, Willie and Roy, about their schooldays!

Both attended the old Edwards P.S. on the Castlefin Road and while Willie had moved on, Roy clearly remembers moving into the new building, which opened in 1938. Looking at the photograph of the three old school buildings transported them back to the days in which they walked to school with their little "piece" for lunch, usually bread and jam, in their bags or pockets. Depending on the level of hunger pangs, the lunch was often eaten by the time they made it to school and then they had to fast all day! While they always wore shoes many children came to school in bare feet. They wore short trousers and knitted jumpers and some boys even sported shirts and ties.

In common with many children from farming families the boys enjoyed the seasonal tasks such as gathering potatoes or harvesting the corn and Willie vividly remembers Roy crying and not wanting to go to school because the thresher was coming to thresh corn at their house.

Children have always loved doing jobs for the teacher and the Waugh boys regarded these requests as great excuses to get out of schoolwork. Water had to be carried from the well behind the master's house, and of course the slowest and longest route brought it in. Hence, water was used very sparingly and hand washing was rare. A small pan for providing drinks was kept beside the enamel bucket of water that was kept at the back of the room.

The absence of running water meant dry toilets that were situated in a small building at the back. There were two toilets and a large effluent storage tank secured with two sheets of tin! One day an unfortunate pupil testing the security of the tin sheets fell in and had to be rescued from his malodorous dip!

Willie also recalled the times when five or six tonnes of coal were dumped beside the road. The boys were not afraid of hard work and gleefully wheeled barrows of the fuel through one of the houses and stored it around the back of the buildings.

Next door to the school was Matthew Knox's orchard and it was always a great attraction in the autumn. Mathew was renowned for his generosity and often gave the boys apples when they asked for them, but he did not take kindly to attempts to steal them. Some boys chose to hang their coats in Matt's stable and Roy recalled occasions when Matt tied the coat sleeves in knots and filled them with apples. One day Roy found his coat heavy with what he expected to be apples, only to find that Matt had played a joke on him and his sleeves were full of potatoes!!

Football was a popular past time among both the boys and girls and was played on the field behind the school buildings. They both remembered the day in which one of the girls suffered a broken leg as she played a game and had to be carried out to the road by the boys.

The change over to the new school, built on the workhouse site, took place in 1938 and was remembered as a grand occasion. The children marched over in classes from the Castlefin Road, up the Priest's Lane and across to the new school. There they had tea and Paris buns, which they considered a luxurious treat.

Gardening, which has been recalled fondly by many past pupils, was also a favourite pastime of the Waugh boys. Roy can still picture the occasion when he was sent out to garden and was enjoying a secret feast of tender cabbage hearts. Mr Sloan appeared to carry out an inspection of the work and suspecting something was amiss, flicked his hair back and shouted, "Open your mouth boy!" to find Roy's mouth full and as green as grass.......so that was the end of gardening for him!!

Mr Sloan, they recollected was a firm, fair man, who tolerated no nonsense and the cane was frequently used, as much for poor work as for bad behaviour. He kept the cane on top of a cupboard along with a globe and in some of his sterner moments would grab the cane and rock the globe but in spite of the boys' prayers the globe never fell!

Roy and Willie recalled the family names of Bell and Kirk, evacuees from Belfast, who attended the school during and after the War. Mr Sloan was delighted to welcome the families but when one girl arrived attired in trousers, "the master went mad and the child had to be sent home." Apart from having blackout blinds, school life proceeded as normal during the War years and Willie said there were collections in school for the war effort. The generous donation of £100 by one of the teachers was the first time in which the pupils had seen a note of such a denomination.

Recalling lessons, the brothers remember standing around the room to do reading, mental maths, tables and spellings. Reading, writing and arithmetic books were the same for the whole class and a slap per error was commonplace. Bad language was not tolerated and offenders were sent to the back of the room to the washbasin to wash the offending tongue with soap!

Inspectors visited all the schools in a locality each year and news of their arrival was quickly passed around. In Edwards some children were posted as lookouts and warned the teacher of the arrival. Some children, perhaps those who wouldn't give the best impressions, were asked to stay at home at this time. The name of one Inspector remains with the Waughs and that was the inaptly named Mr Tulip.

Some teachers were remembered for their rather wicked sense of humour. A local teacher, (not from Edwards), went off to Bundoran on his bike and terrorised many teachers in lots of schools as he visited in his capacity as an "Inspector!"

Both Willie and Roy completed their education at Edwards and what an education that was! The days are fondly recalled but neither would wish to repeat them!

Reflections of Jack Walls.

Jack Walls, a member of a very well known local family, attended Edwards P.S. during the years 1942 until 1948. Although it is often said that schooldays are the happiest days of one's life, he acknowledges that while his time at Edwards may not have been the happiest time of his life, he did enjoy being there and has many treasured memories, some of which he shared with us.

Like many past pupils, Jack's love of sport brings memories of happy days spent on and off the sports field. He recalls the first leather football being bought for the school, and it cost each pupil two shillings.... a small price to pay for so much pleasure!! The first match to be played with it was against old rivals, Killen, and of course Edwards won, with the score standing at 3-0!!

There is no doubt that times were hard during the war years and he remembers many children coming to school in bare feet—winter and summer—and there wasn't the luxury of a school bus. Many walked over two miles to get there and indeed he remembers those who were late, being caned; the long walk was not considered to be a good enough excuse. Jack also is reminded of the time when he was sent out by the teacher to cut a sally cane from the hedge surrounding the school, hardly the start of the next nature lesson!

During the War years British and American soldiers often carried out military manoeuvres in the locality. Naturally these were great attractions for young boys, so much so that Jack recalls two boys being injured by shrapnel when finding an unexploded shell on the ground close to the school! Imagine the full-scale alert if that was to happen today!

School dinners were unheard of in Jack's time at Edwards and the country pupils brought their "piece;" usually bread, butter and jam, in their pocket or in their schoolbag. Some even ate it as they walked to school and then had nothing left for the remainder of the day. Town children were somewhat more fortunate in that they walked home for lunch. The school minutes of 1948 include the recommendation that a kitchen should be erected in the school grounds and after that school meals were provided.

Sad times are often evoked in past memories, and it is with regret that Jack recalls the death and funeral of a young pupil and friend of his during his time at the primary school.

Even to this day there still remains, (perhaps more in secondary level education,) the custom of challenging new boys to prove themselves by performing a particular feat. When Jack attended Edwards the old custom was alive and well and boys were required to wrestle and fight to prove themselves.

Nicknames were in vogue in those days too and he mirthfully remembers some delightful ones! Now he says his own is amongst these but he leaves it to our imaginations to choose the one to match! Here is the selection: Snozzle, Pug, Perky, Porky, Baggats, Tinkpins, Sonny, Snipe, Hoaky, Banty, Rusty, Slogger, Bunyan, Bonzo and Lefty. What a fine collection! I wonder where they all are today?

Following his years at Edwards, Jack proceeded to Omagh Academy and from there entered Stranmillis College. He undertook a four-year course, specialising in Physical Education. On graduating he returned to Castlederg to teach in the County Secondary School from 1958 until 1966.

Youth organizations were very much to the fore in the mid sixties; consequently Tyrone County Education Committee appointed him as County Youth Officer, a position he held until 1973, when he then became a Youth Advisor to the Western Education and Library Board and became Senior Advisor prior to retiring in 2000.

Jack was a keen sportsman and captained Omagh Academicals 1st XV, the North-West Tyrone and Fermanagh XV and represented Junior Ulster on a number of occasions. As a student at Stranmillis he continued to play football and rugby and was vice captain of the prestigious college team, King's Scholars, in his final year. When he returned to Castlederg to take up his teaching post he played soccer with Crewe, Spamount and Derg Villa.

Jack is now enjoying retirement and is often seen browsing through books in the library or pottering in the garden. He also maintains close links with Edwards as a member of the Board of Governors and his wife Elizabeth is the present school secretary and has been for many years.

Some Memories of Edwards in the Forties and Fifties.

Wesley Millar

I attended Edwards Public Elementary School, as it was then called, in the late forties and early fifties, after the Second World War. I travelled to school with my Aunt, Miss Millar, who taught in the school. She drove a Morris 8 car and I remember the rattle of her bunch of keys on the dashboard as we travelled on the bumpy road from Victoria Bridge to Castlederg. Everything must have been kept locked!

We picked up another teacher, Master Starritt, at Victoria Bridge, and he was wearing his R.A.F. great coat as he had served in the Air Force during the war. He later left Edwards to take up the principalship of Letterbin, which is now The Hunting Lodge.

I was always at school early and we played outside until the bell rang. There was an old army Nissan hut locked up at the back of the school and outside it was part of an engine from an aeroplane. The boys spent a lot of time working at it trying to get bits off it. I remember John Hyde from Spamount having a great interest in it. I wonder did he become a mechanic? One boy got a magnet off it and it might as well have been a fortune, such was the excitement. He was lifting pins and sticking it to metal all round the school to the entertainment of the other envious children. I remember a deal that was done in the playground when Bert Huey bought a second- hand bicycle from another boy and paid him with savings certificates! I don't know the cost!

The school garden was fenced in at the front of the school and was used for growing vegetables. The boys were taken out by Master Sloan on selected days for Horticulture. We grew peas, beans, lettuce etc. The girls went to Needlework at this time.

One room in the school at that time seemed to have been used by the Government to provide cod liver oil and orange juice to the pupils and I feel that people from outside school may also have come with ration books for supplies of food, But I'm not sure about that. I do know that the room wasn't used for school at that time but was later used for school meals.

Miss Elliott, the teacher of infants, came to school on a bicycle with a basket of books etc on the handlebars. She was accompanied by the Lyons family from Dartans—Robin, Heather and Cherry, also on bicycles.

The principal, Mr Sloan, also rode a bicycle with high handlebars and a basket and he wore a hat. It must have been a tight fit! Other members of staff were Mrs McFarland, Miss Scott, (Mrs McNutt) and Miss Speer, whose father may have been the caretaker and who may have been on teaching practice.

I particularly remember Mrs McFarland, as I seemed to spend most time with her. Music lessons stick out in my mind. She used the tuning fork to start the singing. We learnt to sing The Keel Row, John Peel, The Minstrel Boy to the War Has Gone and All Through The Night. I remember how active she was on her feet as she moved around the classroom with her skirt swinging. Her hair was tied back in a bun. When she slapped with the cane your fingers would tingle for ages and you had time to think that you would avoid a repeat performance. She drove an Austin 7, I think, and had twin sons, John and Herbert. She later became Principal in Altdoghill.

We sat at double desks with the seats attached. There was a hole for an inkwell as we used little wooden pens with detachable nibs and constantly dipped into the inkwell to write. Writing was an art, as too much ink made a blot or too much pressure on the nib caused it to bend and spray ink in all directions. We used blotting paper as the ink took time to dry and would mark the opposite page if turned over without blotting. We used copybooks to learn to write when we copied a line of writing onto a lined space below. The blackboard was against the wall and could be pulled down or up. I thought it was a great idea as I had always seen it on an easel.

Generally I didn't like school and longed for the day when I would be free from it but I have pleasant enough memories of my time at Edwards.

Wesley Millar.

Memories by Eric Faulkner.

Edwards P.E. School, 1950.

Back Row: Dai Lindsay, Bertie Stewart, Jim Porter, Jackie Hemphill, Albert Porter, Freddie McMullan, John Hyde, David Patrick. Joe Rutledge, Jim Patrick. John Burke, Eric Faulkner, Raymond Kane, Thomas Loughlin.

Second Row: Milton Porter, Eileen Sproule, Etta Quigley, Madge Hetherington, Marion Gilchrist. - -, Jean Speer, Joan Williamson, Shirley Burke, - -, Florence Semple, Helen Loughlin, Beryl Loughlin, Phyllis Turner, Jim Scott, Percy Robb, George Gilchrist.

Third Row: Bert Kinnear (D), Martha McCreery, Winnie Lewis, Betty Ballantyne, Lily Matthews,

Olive Hemphill, Dorothy Cox, Barbara Cox, Isobel Speer, Ann Hemphill, Beck Kane, Dawn Henderson, Ann Faulkner, Joan Clements, Florence Bruce, Ann Forbes, Margaret Loughlin, Betty McMullen,

Violet Bruce, Billy Matthews, Dave Henderson.

Front Row: Sandy Caldwell, Ian Millar, Wesley Millar, Geordie Semple, David Young, Bertie McCutcheon, Norman Cooper, Wesley Maginnis, Tommy Robb, Jimmy Hamilton, Bill Trimble, Derek McCutcheon.

Alex Sproule, Bertie Lindsay, Bertie Hemphill, Bobby Tomlinson, Ronnie Watt.

410

I attended Edwards from I was five until I was fourteen. I could write a book on my time there. Mr Sloan was the Headmaster and he was strict but fair. I remember the garden where we grew vegetables and sold them down town. Geordie Semple was my mate and we worked two to a plot. There were no lawnmowers then and we had to pull the grass by hand.

I remember once when there was snow and we were out playing in it. Some of us decided to throw snowballs at the 'o' in the word boys above the boys' entrance. We were having great fun until I felt we were being watched. When I looked up Mr Sloan was standing at the window, beckoning us in. We each got six good slaps and that ended the snowballing!

I also remember Miss Elliott very well. She was very cross but a great teacher. I remember not being able to do subtraction and she took me to the side and showed me how to do it and from then on I had no bother.

Miss Millar was also a great teacher, a very gentle person. She always seemed to be so smartly dressed in a red skirt and navy blazer and was very kind to all the pupils. She had special pictures, I recall the Royal Family, and we used these for discussion and for composition.

Cricket was always great in Edwards, we used to be frightened of Freddie McMullan, he used to hit the cricket ball so hard and he was never afraid of being hurt, he was more worried about being put out!

There were no dinners until later on; when I was at school, we used to bring a 'piece' and later on soup was made in school and you had to bring your own bowl. I remember the boys fighting over bowls, we only got soup, and there was nothing else with it. I remember the dinners starting and some people thought them too dear, they were 2/1.

I will always remember my schooldays in Edwards and it's sad to look at the photos and see so many faces that are gone now.

Eric Faulkner.

Happy Days.

I went to Edwards Public Elementary School in 1948 and I clearly recall those early years. In my mind's eye I can see the long corridor with the six rooms off it. One room was used as a cookery room and one was a food office, used for issuing ration coupons, as this was just after the War. It was later used as a woodwork room for evening classes and in the absence of a staff room was a real meeting place for the teachers who were Miss Millar, Miss Elliott, Mrs McFarland and Master Sloan. All of them were cross but very fair. Mr Sloan, the Headmaster, was strict but kind. Pupils did not wear uniform and they carried leather school bags, which lasted all their school days. They travelled to school by service bus or by walking—school transport was unheard of. On the last Friday of the month the start of school was delayed due to the Fair and I can remember walking past horses that had been brought into town for sale and were tied along "Horse Hill," which is now known as High Street.

There were outside toilets and a playground with steps leading from it up to the hospital. The furnace that was used to heat the building was located in a cellar with the steps down to it being enclosed behind railings, which were often used as a base or "den" for games such as tig or catchers. A supply of coke was kept in the yard and the children, mostly boys, used to slide down it! There was a vegetable garden near the front gate on the right hand side and I remember the older boys going down town and selling their produce. In summer we too were allowed down town to get ice cream, while occasionally older pupils were sent out with a note to the shops.

School was very regimental- when visitors knocked at the door we jumped up out of our seats and stood to attention, without a sound! I can't imagine that happening nowadays! When we were spoken to we replied politely and only sat down again when we were asked to do so. We sat at heavy dual desks with a slot for the pen and little inkwells that were filled daily by the boys from Mr Sloan's room.

The curriculum was not as wide and varied as today but we were well versed in the basics. In reading, everyone was given the same book and we had to stand around the room to read. Pupils who did not know their reading were caned. Spellings were underlined in the readers and had to be learned thoroughly. The punishment for mistakes was two slaps for each wrong spelling. In Arithmetic we had to do a lot of rote learning and in written work we used to add, subtract, multiply and divide big long sums that children nowadays would never see! Handwriting was very important and we wrote in a looped style on red and blue lines. We did transcription or copying neatly from the board or from our readers and sometimes we had to do dictations, which I thought were so difficult. We paid for writing books and pencils, which were bought by the teacher from my uncle, S.L. Hemphill.

Art for us was a real treat and only happened very occasionally; we did still-life drawings with a pencil—no painting. We sang songs once a week and enjoyed that. P.E. was unheard of and there was no Hall or equipment, but sometimes we did exercises outside in the playground. We had no such thing as Sports Day as the school field was let out to a local farmer and he grazed cows on it!

Needlework for the girls and Handwork for the boys were highly regarded. The girls made useful items, such as aprons, jumpers, skirts and underwear; materials were bought and were not wasted! The boys did raffia work and things like bookbinding.

As an occasional treat we did Nature Study, which sometimes involved a Nature Walk to look at seasonal changes, but we never went any further than the school grounds.

The 11+ was in vogue in those days too and it involved two Verbal Reasoning Tests, Arithmetic, a Grammar Test, Story Writing and Comprehension. The Verbal Reasoning was held on two Friday mornings and the other subjects on an all-day Friday. That day everyone taking the exam received a cooked meal, which was a real treat for those who did not yet have school meals. The school closed on the days of the tests and children came from as far away as Drumquin to do the exams in Edwards.

School dinners were introduced during my time at the school. We used to bring a lunch, often jam sandwiches, and we had a small bottle of milk to drink. In summer it was warm and I hated that, but in winter it was often frozen and I used to bring a spoon to consume the "iced" milk! Dinners were cooked on a big range and they were delicious! We had a main course, such as Irish Stew, and a pudding, usually custard and sponge. They cost 2/1 a week and some families thought this was very expensive. The teaching staff dined in the room and of course table manners were paramount.

We didn't have any special awards or certificates, we were always expected to produce the best work that we could, and otherwise there was the threat of the cane!

Visitors to the school included the Inspector, the Attendance Officer, the dentist, school nurse and doctor. The local Minister came every Thursday and we were tested on our Bible Knowledge. We did Bible work every day and had a hymn and a prayer.

The Caretaker was a Mr Joe Speers and children helped by dusting the tables. We liked doing those tasks!

School was very different then and there have been many changes. It was very disciplined but we respected the teachers and the cane never did us any harm!

I don't know if today's children would like it very much but I certainly look back on my schooldays in Edwards with great affection.

Ann Waugh. (Nee Hemphill)

Betty Waibel

*Betty Waibel (left)
and her school friend Florrie Irwin*

Memories. When I was three years old in 1934 I started school. I walked up the Chapel Rd. to the old Burnside school every day with my friend Florrie Irwin (nee Bogle). We are still friends to this day and she visits me regularly in America. At school I sat on a long bench with the other babies. There were also infants and high infants and 2 or 3 other grades in the room. I played with small wooden bricks which I fitted into a tin box. My main concerns at that time were the holes in the floor, where, if anything dropped through, we were warned not to put our hands down. For lunch we got scalding hot oxo which I disliked and still do. Worst was the outside toilet -a three holer- an older girl always accompanied us babies in case we fell through. Miss McArthur was my teacher and I loved her dearly. Every day before school got out she went behind the blackboard and easel and combed her waist long hair and put it up in a big bun, while we all watched. Then the exciting day came when we moved to the new school. The dignitaries, the flag the flowers. Light and air and sunshine poured in the big windows. A new era had begun we had a beautiful new school, we were going to learn great things and we did. Miss McArthur was still my teacher, and her patience and good common sense helped me overcome many difficulties like long division. I often think of her and the lessons I learned which I still find useful. She got married and became Mrs. McFarland and had twin boys. The next excitement was the arrival of the evacuees. They came from the big city of Belfast. They brought their own teacher and when we were all sorted she became my teacher too. Miss Wilson was glamorous although I didn't know the word then. She was so interested in country life she perked our interest also. We had great discussions and even the shyest guy in the class talked about cattle and crops. From her we learned there was a world outside Castlederg and some day we would venture there. Miss Wilson boarded in town with the Misses Parkes who had a small drapery store in the centre of town. Every Friday at 12 noon it was my job to run down to the store and pick up a basket of lunch, as Miss Wilson went home to Belfast every weekend. When I returned the basket Miss Parkes gave me a special treat. Looking back on those days with the evacuees, some were happy and adjusted, while others were unhappy and got into trouble. Eventually they all went home and life settled down again. I am very proud of the fact that every child who attended school in those years could read and write and do maths when they graduated., but we also learned about making friends, being kind, how to play fair, loyalty and being able to laugh at ourselves. These lessons are equally important in the world we live in. I know the pupils nowadays are so much smarter than we were and so it is these other skills that I pass with the baton to the students at the NEW NEW SCHOOL.

Betty Waibel (nee Simpson) (class of '45)

Happy Musings.

Looking back over the years (almost seventy) to my days in Edwards School Castlederg, what a lot of fun we had, before degrees were the "be all and end all" of everyone's life. I remember vividly the day the school opened, so much excitement, having flush toilets and hand basins, water fountains and lots of pegs to hang our coats on! I can still see the beautiful green crepe dress Aunt Jane had made for me by Minnie Dolan. There was pink smocking on the yoke—I felt like a princess!!

What a big change all this was after the old Edwards School where we had dry toilets, a muddy playground and a fireplace at the end of each classroom; there was always a scramble for the desks nearest it!! No such thing as school dinners in those days, lots of us ran home for lunch and others brought "pieces." There was a nice cookery room where Miss Elliott taught us how to make potato bread, stew and lots of other things—to this day I remember her words when I'm baking "wee buns"; "Now always remember if the mixture curdles, add a little more flour." Strange how some sayings stick in one's mind! I always thought she was an amazing woman, she taught us sewing, cookery and singing plus all the other subjects! Sewing was my favourite subject and that was the start of my love for dressmaking and my career for the next sixty years.

Our families never worried about us if we were an hour late getting home from school, we would play ball, often using three or four balls at once. Wish I'd been as clever at my sums and spellings! Wintertime, we'd spend ages sliding on the puddles in the Cow Market!

The boys loved the new school too as they had a proper football field with real goal posts, the nice big play shed was a Godsend on wet days, (and often used in our teenage years to go courting in!) I was eleven when the school opened in 1938, then the war came and great excitement when the evacuees came from Belfast when the bombing started, so many city children amongst us!

Miss Jackson was a delightful teacher and all the children loved her; she was so gentle and caring. I was always a bit scared of Master Sloan, perhaps it was because I wasn't a very clever pupil and I couldn't wait to leave, to get started on my sewing career.

As I sit here looking at the picture in the "Con" of all those boys and girls—I wonder where they all are now? Many have gone all over the world and some to their Heavenly home, others to the war never to return.

Several years after leaving Edwards I married and lived a hundred yards from the school gate. My daughter Florence went there when she was four years old and was taught by Miss Elliott! We left Castlederg a few years later but I still talk of going "home" and after fifty years when I visit I still drive past my old home in Breezemount Park and have a look at the school of which I have many happy memories.

I'm looking forward to visiting again for the "Big Opening," hoping I will meet lots of old friends and recall our happy childhood days. I know my dear friend Betty Waibel (Simpson) will be there—she's coming from U.S.A. for the event. I took her to Edwards on her first day to school—a good way of reminding me that I'm four years older than her!!

I wish all the teachers and pupils much happiness in their new surroundings and may they enjoy their time in Edwards!

Florrie Irwin (Bogle)

Vera Hamilton MacDougall
EDWARDS PRIMARY SCHOOL 1940-1948

My first memory is of being with my mother, who was pushing a pram, at an open air event on a pleasant day. I have worked this out to be the opening of Edwards Primary School and I was 2 and the baby in the pram was my brother Mervyn, aged 6 months. I hope you noticed that I didn't say that I was 2 years old or that Mervyn was 6 months old because Master Sloan taught us that we must not say "I am 8 years old" because "when you are 8 you are not old". We had to say "I am 8 years of age". I no longer need to worry, I am now 69 years old! Master Sloan had a cup of coffee brought to him in the classroom in the morning, obviously a skin had formed by the time he got it. I remember his long, bony fingers removing the skin and placing it on the side of the saucer. We had the option of a small bottle of milk - yuck! I remember Mrs MacFarland, her twin boys and her maroon Austin Seven. I expect it was in the younger classes, but when the teacher wanted to leave the room, we had to fold our arms, place them on the desk and put our head on our arms. We had to keep quiet and still until the teacher returned. Miss Elliot also taught us cookery and all I remember about that was how she showed us to break an egg and make sure the shell was properly cleaned out so that none of the egg was wasted. Miss Stevenson from Strabane also taught us cookery for a time and I met up with her again in Glasgow when I discovered she was one of my lecturers at College. On my first day at school, aged 4,1 sat beside Gladys Mitchell. We weren't greatly taken with each other but we became good friends and I am glad to say that 64 years later we are still good friends and see each other regularly. These are just a few scattered memories - but what do you expect after all this time? I look forward to reading other peoples' memories and hope that their memories fill some of my gaps.

I Remember...... I Remember by Mr Jim Emery.

Mr Jim Emery

One of the best known local faces must be that of Mr Jim Emery, a Castlederg resident, historian, author, prominent Unionist, Councillor and immediate past Chairman of Strabane District Council, Clerk of Session in First Castlederg Presbyterian Church, an officer in the Boys Brigade for many years and most importantly, an old boy of Edwards Primary School! Jim was born at Aghakinmart, Castlederg, from where he walked two miles to attend Clare school, for three to four years until his family moved into the town of Castlederg in 1952, when he transferred to Edwards Primary School. His formative years were spent there and he has many memories of work and play under the direction of the Principal, Mr Jim G. Sloan, who was later succeeded by Mr T. F. Riddall. Other teachers he recalls were Miss Millar, Mr McIlgorm, Mrs Caldwell and Mrs McNutt.

The usual school subjects were taught: English; Poetry, which Jim especially enjoyed, Spellings, Grammar, Maths, Geography, History, Music, Gardening, and best of all, a variety of sports, particularly cricket and football! Jim sat at a heavy double desk with his friend Stanley Baxter, who now resides at Erganagh. Good discipline was always expected and the cane was sometimes used as punishment for the minor offence of talking.

The school garden was situated just inside the main gate, on the right hand side, and the boys loved planting, weeding and harvesting their crops of lettuce, beans, peas and potatoes. The lawns between the plots were well-tended and Jim smiled as he recollected the unsuccessful attempts to grow carrots in the hard ground! Produce was brought down into town by the older boys and sold by the local grocers, Mr Dick McCay and Mr Jack Fulton. As well as having a good knowledge of horticulture the boys gained valuable insights into running a business. This surely must have been the forerunner of the subject now known as

Business Studies!

The radio was introduced to the school during Jim's time there and "Singing Together" was a great personal favourite. I am sure many people can recall the songs they were taught through this medium and Jim is no exception. Many of the melodies were of far-off places and Jim loved the songs "Westering Home" and "Shenandoah." Only recently the latter song came flooding back to his memory when he visited America and the city of Atlanta with some of the production team of "On Eagle's Wing," an ambitious musical based on the story of the Scots Irish settlement in America.

Sport played an important part in the life of the young schoolboy and Jim fondly remembers staying after school on two evenings a week, for football in the winter and cricket in the summer. Initially, the thorn bushes were the goal posts until Mr Riddall brought in proper football goal posts, much to the delight of the boys. Being an avid sportsman himself, Mr Riddall was keen to see his pupils develop the best possible skills and to this end he encouraged them in every way. He introduced cricket and brought teams in his car to Sion Mills, the cricketing capital of the west. He also encouraged parents to play too and the teams of boys often played their fathers, making for wonderful social events in which the whole community became involved--- see the match reports below.

CRICKET

Edwards Primary Schoolboy's cricket team have reason to be proud of their latest achievement, and are now a force to be reckoned with in local cricket circles. Last Friday evening, at the Edwards School grounds, they decisively defeated a Past Pupils team by 87 runs. Details :—

Edwards (who batted first) :— N. Lindsay, run out, 5; O. Lewis, bowled Baxter, 0; R. Lindsay, bowled McCay, 3; D. Semple, bowled Baxter, 27; V. Porter, bowled McCay, 3; K. Robb, bowled Baxter, 6; J. Emery, l.b.w. bowled McCay, 5; H. Baxter, c Henderson, bowled Forbes, 29; R. Hanna, c Gilchrist, bowled Huey, 0; V. Simms, n.o. 1; K. Hanna, c Baxter, bowled Huey, 1; Extras—31; Total—111.

Past Pupils :— A. Robb bowled Porter, 1; N. Fallows c Lindsay, bowled Porter, 2; D. Baxter bowled Porter, 6; J. Forbes n.o. 3; G. Huey bowled Semple, 2; D. McCay bowled Semple. 0; D. Baxter run out, 0; A. E. Watt run out, 3; D. Gilchrist bowled Porter, 0; J. Kinnear bowled Porter 0; D. Henderson run out 1; Extras—6; Total—24.

For the Schoolboys, Victor Porter returned the remarkable bowling figures of 5 wickets for 6 runs.

It is on the cards that a match is being arranged between the boys and the Derg Senior Cricket team, and what an attraction it would be.

CRICKET

The pupils of the Edwards Primary School were in a joyful mood on Tuesday evening last, when they defeated their elders in a match labelled " Edwards v Parents XI." Batting first on a good wicket, the youngsters amassed the splendid total of 70 for 7. The Lindsay brothers, by consistent and steady batting, contributed 32 and 19 respectively. It was a worthy performance. The parents' bowling was only moderate.

With the exception of J. Young, who contributed 18, the batting of the elders was very feeble indeed, but, on the other hand, they had to face keen fielding and a deadly attack mustered by Victor Porter and Derek Semple, who bowled unchanged throughout, gave the excellent analysis of 6 for 12 and 4 for 10, and the side were all out for 32.

The game, which attracted much local interest, was watched by a big crowd.

Sports Day was another highlight of the school year and again in his usual innovative capacity, Mr Riddall introduced badges for the winners: red for first, blue for second and yellow for third. A local man, Mr Pat Coyle, who was married to an Italian lady, was very well known for his ice cream and Mr Riddall invited him to supply ice cream to the children on Sports Day and so began the tradition of this treat. In return, Mr Coyle presented the school with a silver cup that was annually awarded on Sports Day for the Relay race. The cup remains in school until this day.

Uniform was another facet of school life that was introduced by Mr Riddall. Jim remembers the school tie, which had broad blue and yellow diagonal stripes, the school blazer and cap complete with badge, featuring the castle and the bird (a chough), which was the emblem of the Edwards family.

A sense of responsibility was fostered in the older children when they were made prefects and Jim was a prefect at both Edwards and the Secondary School.

At the age of fourteen Jim left the firm foundation of Edwards School and went on to the local Secondary School at Castlegore, where he stayed for two years. This was followed by employment in McManus' Shoe Shop in Omagh where he worked for four years and then went on to become a Sales Representative for the company until 1994.

Edwards School Prefects - 1957
Back Row (left to right): Norman Gilchrist, Jim Emery, Derek Semple, Ken Robb, Norman Lindsay.
Front Row (left to right): Violet McCreery, Florence Muldoon, Jean Burke, Ruby Sproule, Cynthia Forbes.

He became involved in local government and was elected to Strabane Council in 1989, a position that he still holds and was indeed the Chairman in the year 2003—2004. His grandfather was a staunch Unionist and this influenced Jim's political affiliation, as he is still an active party member, being the Secretary of the local Association.

Presently he is Chairman of the Board of Governors in Bridgehill Primary School and also serves as a governor in the local High School. In all, Jim contributes much of his learning to the days spent in Edwards and feels he has every reason to say they were the happiest days of his life!

1954
Back row: Scott McFarland (Training Teacher), George Hemphill, Harold Hamilton, John Kinnear, Bert Wilson, Uel Hemphill.
2nd Row: Joan Young, ?, ?, Audrey Faulkner, ?, Robinson, Hazel McMullan.
Front Row: Raymond Bruce, ? Laughlin, Rosemary Fox, Heather Martin.

Recollections by Ronnie Watt.

Ronnie Watt, son of the late Albert Watt, attended Edwards School in the late forties and has been living in Australia for over thirty years. He sent some of his memories of his school days:

"I remember some of the teachers- the lay out of the original school and grounds plus the surrounding area, eg the old forge at the junction of the Lurganbuoy Road and the School Road, that is the road into the school past Kane's house. After Jim Sloan and Mr Sterritt retired Mr Tom Riddall and Mr McIlgorm arrived to take over the reins. Both were very sports conscious and Edwards fielded both soccer and cricket teams against Sion Mills, St. Pat's, Drumquin and Erganagh schools.

The dining room at the school was the Nissan hut between the play shed and the school. It was an air cadet centre filled with treasures to be pilfered!!! Later on, the dining room was on the Eastern wing near the Hospital Road. As I was a prefect we had to assist with serving the meals, which meant extra servings to the prefects!!

The boiler room was under the building approximately half way along and it was coke/coal fired.

The toilet blocks were opposite the triangle and near the entrances for both boys and girls, which were at the back of the school. Beyond the toilets was the Nissan hut that belonged to the air cadets, (way before my time) and this was a veritable treasure trove for the boys--- a lot of stuff was taken for our "gangs". Beyond the hut was a large tarmac area for play, which had the play shelter at the end backing on to the hospital. The grounds at that stage were not very well maintained and were covered with brambles etc. When I came back on my first trip I was very surprised to see how much land had been cleared, and the amount of ground in the school area. On the west side of the school there was the woodwork room, which was used by Mr Sterritt.

The only houses in the area were Breezemount Park and that was the group facing the Lurganbuoy Road. The second development happened shortly after I left. Apart from Emery's cottages there were no other homes on that side of the road. Trimble's had a field with a vegetable garden and a hot house and the rest was vacant land right up to the reservoir. There used to be a forge at the corner of the Lurganbuoy Road and the School Road and this was the only building on that side of the road until Kanes built. We would call into the forge and watch the horses being shod.

John Watt (brother) and I used to have races at lunch time, (12.30 pm, that time always sticks in my mind) from school down to the Diamond—one would go down via the back of the Breezemount Houses and come out in the Cow Market near John Forbes' house, and the other would go via Hospital Road near Mitchell's. Again at that time Mitchell's was the only place in Hospital Road.

We never had any computers etc in school—we only had a radio that was in the Headmaster's class and we listened to plays and English lessons. I was a prefect at school but I was not perfect and I remember I embarrassed Mrs B. Pollock when she was a trainee by winking at her when an Inspector was assessing her teaching!!!

Sister Erica of the Community of the Resurrection.

On scanning the above headline readers might well be forgiven for thinking that our material had somehow become mixed up with an article for a religious sect! But this is truly not the case, as the lady referred to was indeed Dorothy Elizabeth Whitcroft, daughter of Mr William Whitcroft, a well-known teacher in Gortnagross School.

She was born in Aghalunny in 1913, one of a family of eight; Tom, Nora, Vera, Fred, Sydney, Dorothy, Cecil and Victor, and was known as Dolly at home. She went to Gortnagross School and later transferred to Edwards School and Mr Burnside prepared her for entrance to Trinity College, Dublin, from which she graduated in 1931. From there she went to the Church of England Teachers' Training College in Derby where she subsequently taught.

In 1943 she married the Rev. Eric Whitehouse and moved to Sutton Coldfield, near Birmingham. Sadly her husband died shortly after their marriage and Dolly decided to continue his work as a Missionary in Africa. She joined the Community of the Resurrection and became an Anglican nun, adopting the name Erica, in memory of her late husband.

As Sister Erica she was sent to teach in Rhodesia, Zambia and the Republic of South Africa. Following her retirement from teaching she went to live with the Community in Grahamstown and apart from being given leave to work in East Belfast during the "troubles" and two brief visits to her family, she spent fifty four years in South Africa.

Her family were concerned about her safety and well-being but were reassured on her return visits that she was doing the right thing. After forty-five years in Africa she wrote, " I certainly would not have missed being a Sister. There is a great sense of freedom and security when one knows one is where God wants us to be."

After teaching she was given the job of Sacristan in the Community until she developed Alzheimer's Disease and she passed away in Grahamstown, South Africa on 17th February 2005.

The above article was taken from a tribute to Sister Erica, written by her surviving brother Victor and sister Nora.

Edwards School

Fifty years have passed from my school days at Edwards and it is a great privilege and a very rare event that one ever gets the opportunity to reminisce about a period of your life which is so easy to forget. Without any shadow of a doubt these ten years would have been the most important in my life. Every facet of life was taught to us and, although at Grammar School and Universities they were done differently, it was at Edwards School that we learnt all our reading, writing and maths that would carry us through life. The teachers were the most dedicated and patient people I have ever encountered in my life. Unfortunately some of them have passed on and we are unable to pass on our great feelings of gratitude to them personally. Where in the world would anybody have met a kinder person on their first day at school than Miss Elliott? She made the classroom a new 'home from home'. Mrs McNutt (nee Scott) was the charming lady who taught me to write in the second year and her kindness and patience will never be forgotten. The third class was in the capable hands of Miss Millar and my fourth class was the lovely and gentle Miss Patrick who helped us all so much. With the arrival of Mr. Tom Riddall and Mr. McIlgorm the school really came to life for me with the introduction of football in the Winter and that 'strange' game of cricket in the Summer. Cricket was a very rare thing about Castlederg, but with some expert coaching from these teachers we soon had a nucleus of a useful team. Imagine the excitement in the school when Mr. McIlgorm announced that we were going to play the 'mighty Sion Mills' which was the strongest village at that time in North West. At ten years of age to play at the Holm Field it was like some young footballer playing at Wembly. Thanks to some great bowling from Derrick Semple we had the mighty Sion Mills tottering on 31 for 7 wickets when the rain came on. If we had beaten them it would have been on par with Ireland beating the West Indies thirty years later at the same venue. Mr Riddall helped us immensely with the football team. We had some wonderful players who went on to play some top levels of football. For me personally it was an honour to do goalkeeper against the famous Alan Hunter of Sion Mills who went on to play for Northern Ireland over fifty times. It was with great sadness that after I sat the 11-Plus exam (which I passed, and if this isn't a tribute to the teachers, nothing is) I had to leave Edwards School and go to Strabane Grammar. At eleven years old when you leave one school to go to a bigger one, it was to me just the same as finding out the truth about 'Santa Claus'. A part of me remains to this day at the Old Edwards School and nothing in the world will ever take these wonderful memories from me. Thanks for everything.

Geoff Huey

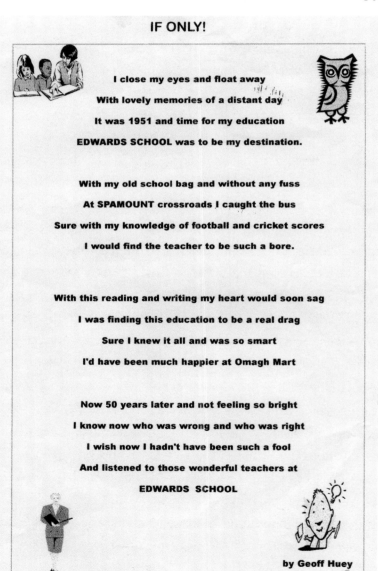

IF ONLY!

I close my eyes and float away
With lovely memories of a distant day
It was 1951 and time for my education
EDWARDS SCHOOL was to be my destination.

With my old school bag and without any fuss
At SPAMOUNT crossroads I caught the bus
Sure with my knowledge of football and cricket scores
I would find the teacher to be such a bore.

With this reading and writing my heart would soon sag
I was finding this education to be a real drag
Sure I knew it all and was so smart
I'd have been much happier at Omagh Mart

Now 50 years later and not feeling so bright
I know now who was wrong and who was right
I wish now I hadn't have been such a fool
And listened to those wonderful teachers at
EDWARDS SCHOOL

by Geoff Huey

A Headmaster's Memories.

Edwards P.S. Castlederg Cricket XI 1957
N. Gilchrist, R. Lindsay, D. Semple, K. Robb, B. Wilson, J. Emery, V. Porter,
J. Forbes, N. Lindsay, D. Baxter, A. Baxter.

My experience as a pupil at Edwards Primary School was like many others—a happy and enjoyable one. In my case this was because of my involvement in sport—playing cricket with a bat and tennis ball in the playground before the start of school and playing organised football after school. My interest in these two sports has lasted for many years since then. My football hero was Harry Gregg who did goals for Manchester United. It was no surprise then that I was the school goalkeeper and I remember vividly playing against other teams like Sion Mills.

Perhaps then it is easy to understand why I missed out on the 11 + exam--- there was little time to study. Nevertheless this had a profound effect on me. I can recall that sense of failure on the day that the results came out. It seemed to be the custom at that time to follow the postman on his rounds, with that special letter! If you passed the exam you followed the others with the postman. If not, you stayed inside, well out of the way.

I despised this type of humiliation and I was determined to succeed despite this. I was also determined to play whatever role I could to help provide the best opportunities for so-called failures both in terms of education and facilities. I am now in the privileged position as Principal, hopefully going some way to achieve this.

It is strange to think that after so many years I am still attending Edwards Primary School, not as a pupil, but as a Governor. As such, I am delighted to see Edwards P.S. going from strength to strength in a brand new school. I wish all associated with this fine school every success in the future.

Desie Williamson.

Edwards P.S. Castlederg Football Team 1959
Back Row: Sydney Irwin, Desie Williamson, Eric Robinson, Harold Montgomery,
David McKeown, Charles Bogle.
Front Row: James Simms, Ken Hanna, John Chambers, Andy Gordon, Ken Lindsay.

My Memories.

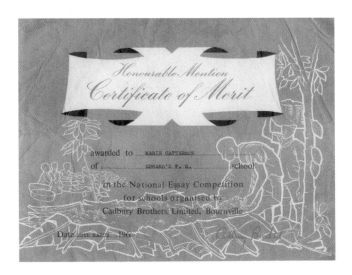

I have many assorted memories of my time at Edwards P.S. I will always remember Mr Riddall, the Headmaster. He was a brilliant teacher, very sharp, but very fair. He took cricket after school for the boys and sometimes during school as well. Other teachers I remember were Mrs McCrea, Mr Strong and Miss Elliott. She was sharp, but very good. When I was in her class I entered a National essay competition for Cadbury's Chocolate. Someone from Cadbury's had come to the school and gave a talk, promoting milk, and then we were asked to write an essay. I won the competition, much to my surprise, and I got a certificate, which my mum proudly framed and put up on the wall, and lots of chocolate goodies. There was also something small for the whole school. This was in the early sixties and from then on Miss Elliott sent me a card every Christmas.

There wasn't much variety in the type of lessons then. We seemed to have lots of writing and sums. Trips were very rare, maybe to Baronscourt Forest on one occasion.

We had milk to drink every day and a small bottle of juice about once a fortnight. There were outside toilets and trips out to them were regarded as a bit of casual freedom and we met and had conversations with the other girls.

Sports Day was eagerly awaited and when the lawnmower cut the grass you knew that it wasn't far away! We loved the free ice cream and it was a fun day, free from lessons for us! We were only allowed down to the Sports Field to practise a short time before the event and that was the only time we went down there.

I have very happy memories of my school days and it is strange to think the school is no longer on the hill! I hope all the boys and girls in the new school will enjoy their school days as much as I did.

By Marie Buchanan (nee Catterson)

Marcella Robinson
- From Edwards Primary School to Castlederg High School

Yes, as you can imagine from the title, I haven't been far!! However. I will start my biographical trip by sharing my very fond memories of my time at Edward's Primary School.

I remember playing the lead parts in a number of pantomimes along with Keith Kerrigan, for example, the 'King and Queen of France' and 'Mr and Mrs Billy Goat Gruff. I also remember the times that I 'thought' I was a comedian when I use to imitate certain characters like Margaret Thatcher and Jimmy Cricket. I remember vividly how I use to imitate Canon Quill and his very fine singing voice by singing 'He touched Me' and the principal at that time, Mr. Riddall, decided to tape me. If I wasn't singing, I was playing football or playing some kind of sport and I particularly remember wanting to play with the boys more as I just thought the girls were not up to the same standard when it came to sport!! (what a "Tom Boy").! I always regarded 'Sports Day' as a very important day; it was an opportunity for me to show off my talents. Does anybody remember those little coloured badges for coming 1st, 2nd or 3rd? Well, it was like winning a pot of gold when you won several of them!

For some reason I remember playing Mr Orr a game or two of short tennis in the assembly hall, and the reason, I suppose, I remember this is — because it was a big thing when you could beat the Headmaster!

Finally, I was in P7 and found myself at night doing fifty 'structured reasoning' questions in preparation for the 11 plus exam. Then I got my results, and at that time it was graded in numbers from 1-4 (I think). I was set on going to Castlederg High School until I received a '1' in my test along with 4 others (if I remember correctly 22 pupils did the 11 plus that year; 5 of us got a '1' and if my memory serves me right, 15 got a '2'). As a result of this I decided to go to Strabane Grammar School. Again, I excelled at sport and music, for example, I remember on a number of occasions competing in the Ulster Schools Championships and later - getting through to the All-Ireland Schools Championships 3 times, winning a bronze medal in the shot-put. There were atheletic coaches there who wanted me to go to Belfast once a week to train, but I declined, because at that time I was in the middle of GCSE's.

I also won 'Best Athelete' overall twice and was captain of the hockey team. I sang solos at the annual Christmas services, Easter services and many other important events. Apart from music and sport, I wasn't really interested in anything else at school!

After my time at Grammar school, I headed off to Belfast, to the University of Ulster, Jordanstown, to do a Foundation Studies course in Music (surprise, surprise!). While there, I was like the big fish in the sea, singing many solos with the University of Ulster orchestra and choir.

I completed the foundation course with 'commendation' which led me to being offered a place on their music degree course, but I had other ideas. I remember reading through a careers book and I just happened to open it at a page which described a music degree being offered in the Conservatory of Music, Dublin with particular emphasis on performance, (well I thought this was a sign!). So, I got the CAO application form to apply to Universities in the Republic of Ireland and off it went. I later received word that I had been offered an audition.

During the audition I remember forgetting the words of one of my songs and I thought I had surely blown it all now. Well, I will never forget it when the first thing the lady on the panel said to me was, 'We would love to have you'! She then proceeded to tell me that all I had to do now was to sit two written exams.

Off I went to Dublin again and completed the two exams, thinking I definitely won't get an offer now! Later I received word that I had been accepted. I was now in the dilemma of deciding whether to go to the Conservatory of Music in Dublin for a 4 year degree program or to stay in Belfast at the University of Ulster, Jordanstown, for a 3 year program.

I remember asking my singing teacher at Jordanstown what would she do if she was in my shoes, and she said to me that she didn't want me to leave the University of Ulster, Jordanstown, but felt that I would learn and benefit much more from going to the Conservatory of Music. And so I took her advice.

Off I went to Dublin and what a tremendous journey I experienced within those four years, (I had definitely made the right decision).

During my time there my oratorio (music based on biblical text) performances

434

included Bach's Cantatas 10, 61, 62 and 182 under the direction of Dr. Andrew Megill from Westminster College, New Jersey, USA; Handel's Messiah at Trinity College, Dublin; Mozart's Requiem, at St.Anne's Church, Dawson St. Dublin; and Vivaldi's Gloria in D, performed with the University of Dublin Choral Society. Other performances included Sally in the one act opera A Hand of Bridge by Samuel Barber, which was under the direction of the famous Irish mezzo-soprano, Dr. Bernadette Greevy, held in the National Concert Hall; mezzo-soprano in the contemporary one-act opera Hot Food with Strangers by Marian Ingoldsby. I was also a member of the chorus of 'Opera Ireland' in two of their productions, 'Don Carld and 'Carmen', which were held in the Gaiety Theatre.

Other achievements include being selected twice to go to Brussels on an International Opera Summer School for 2 weeks in August 2001 and 2002. From that experience I was offered the chance to lead the chorus in the opera. La Turandot, by Puccini, in Kuala Lumpur, Malaysia, but unfortunately due to health reasons at the time I had to decline.

I enjoyed many masterclasses with people like Bernadette Greevy, Sarah Walker (teacher at the Guildhall School of Music, London), Loh Slew Tuan, Robert Alderson (teacher in the Royal Northern College of Music, Manchester) and Vera Roza (who was a teacher to Dame Kiri Te Kanawa).

During my college years I was also very fortunate to go as a leader with the Ulster Project from 1999-2002.

After I finished my degree I decided to stay on in Dublin and to continue singing. I was offered a job in a private school called St.Columba's, Rathfarnham, to teach singing. Unfortunately, my time there was cut short as I had to come home before Christmas for surgery.

In 2003 I decided to do my Postgraduate Certificate in Education at the University of Ulster, Coleraine, and after that year I came home again to take up a teaching post in Castlederg High School- almost like a round trip"!

I would like to take this opportunity to thank Mrs Hazel McCay for giving me this opportunity to tell you my story. I would also like to wish the new Edwards Primary School God's richest blessing.

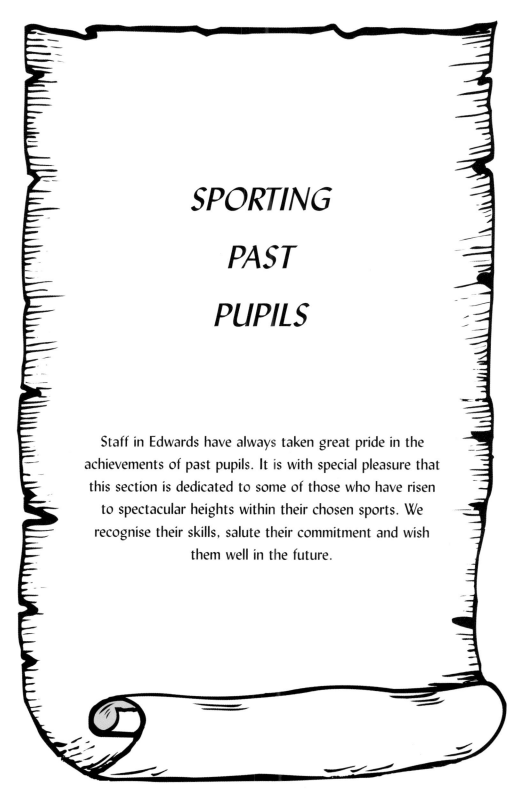

SPORTING

PAST

PUPILS

Staff in Edwards have always taken great pride in the achievements of past pupils. It is with special pleasure that this section is dedicated to some of those who have risen to spectacular heights within their chosen sports. We recognise their skills, salute their commitment and wish them well in the future.

The Match.

Do you remember a match for
milligans,
Do you remember a match,
And the roars and scowls,
Of george at a foul,
And the balls that wheeze,
Through the air like bees,
And the minutes that seemed
like hours,

2.

And the cheers and jeers of Alex
at the sneers,
Who hadn't got a wink,
And whose face was like ink,
And the slither of the ball
and the thud.
Of the thud,
Of the boots to the slither or
the slither

Of Wilson gone walking stalking
Backing and talking,
Slither to the skither;
up and down,
And the slight shrill screech
of the ref,
Do yo remember a match joe
milligan,
Do you remember a match.

                                    Fred Burke.

With Compliments
Tom Reseda
March 1981

Football in Edwards.

Edwards Primary School
L-R: Mr Gowdy, Conrad Kee, Gareth Porter, Adam Lecky, David Sproule, William Gillen, David Robinson.
Front: Philip Lowry, Simon Clarke, Lee Lynch, Matthew Baskin, Emma Glenn, Mervyn Hunter.

Since the days when football took over from gardening as a major feature of the school curriculum, it has been paramount in the minds of many pupils. Mr Gowdy, who has been in charge of this area for many years, reflected on the past:

Thursday afternoons will be remembered by many boys because of football practice. A football match played against friends on the Edwards pitch was the highlight of the week for boys who played soccer. It was also a great opportunity for teachers and pupils to mix in a less formal setting.

Soccer was also the vehicle used by Edwards and St. Patrick's P.S. Castlederg to develop community relations. A very successful six a side competition ran through the late seventies and into the eighties. Mr Brian Baxter and myself organised the annual competition, with the idea being to have three players from each school in one team. The wider community was also involved in the competition as rural schools were included. Pupils in Years 5, 6, and 7 were matched together and teams were named after famous English football teams. A knockout competition eliminated teams until one side emerged triumphant. The final featured the winning town team against the winning country team.

Competitive matches against other schools formed a part of the memories of school soccer. St Patrick's P.S. always proved to be good opponents and every game was a close affair. These competitive games were gradually replaced by the afore mentioned six a side competition. A number of schools from neighbouring towns such as Omagh, Strabane and Sion Mills, played against us and our pitch became the Old Trafford of Castlederg.

The most exacting competition to participate in was the Walker's Primary Schools Soccer Competition. Edwards P.S. qualified for the regional finals in 2000 and 2001.

In 2000 the team met and beat St Malachi's P.S. Belfast, Magherafelt P.S., and St. Mary's Portaferry, on the way to the final, in which they were drawn against Steelstown P.S. Londonderry. After a scoreless draw they were unfortunately beaten 3-2 on penalties.

In 2001 they defeated St Mary's P.S. Strabane, St Mary's Cloghcor, Glebe P.S. and St. Columbcille's. P.S. Omagh. The team travelled to Antrim Forum for the final but were beaten by Finaghy P.S. in a closely contested game and were awarded an all-red football strip. The Edwards' teams were very proud of their fine achievements in being runners-up in Northern Ireland competitions.

One of the most satisfying experiences from a soccer perspective is to see past pupils continuing to play and enjoy the sport. Edwards past pupils contribute to the local Derg View side and Management, and their recent successes have been outstanding. The icing on the cake has been to see other past pupils play for the Irish league sides and some have gained Northern Irish International schoolboy caps.

Some of those who have achieved notable successes are listed below;

Adrian Lecky, N.I. cap.

John Sproule, Omagh Town.

Gareth Sproule, Omagh Town / Portadown.

Richard Clarke, Portadown, N.I. cap.

Andrew Crawford, Omagh Town, Linfield, Newry City.

Harold Baxter, Derry City.

Alan Love, U 16 & U18 & U19 N.I. Schoolboys, Dungannon Swifts, Hearts

Richard Clarke, Omagh Town, Newry City, N.I. cap.

David Kee, Sheffield Wednesday.

We are extremely proud of every one of them and what they have achieved.

More recently girls have shown greater interest in soccer, wanting to play and indeed referee games, like our own past pupil, Clare Noble, who is an International Referee and has blown her whistle in many local, Irish League and International matches.

The first female pupil to play on the Edwards School team was Shirley McCay, who has retained her interest in football by playing with Omagh Cossacks, but is better known for her local and International hockey commitments.

Edwards P.S. Football Team 1998 - 1999
Back Row L-R: Philip Lowry, Lee Lynch, Richard Irwin, Mr Gowdy, Adam Lecky, Shirley McCay
Front Row L-R: Gareth Porter, Stephen Baxter, David Kee, Dean Forsythe,
John Montgomery, Ian Burke, Thomas Irwin.

Edwards P.E. School Football XI, 1964

Back Row: William Robinson, Alan Coulter, John Wilson, Leslie Armstrong,
Ernie Sproule, William McMullan.
Front Row: Sammy Milligan, Billy Loughlin, Norman Coulter, Will Cather, John Fulton.

Edwards Football Team 1967 - 68

Pictured Back Row: L-R: K. Johnston, K Kane, W. Sproule, A McNutt, G McNutt, T. Ballintyne.
Front Row: L-R: H. Irwin, B. Clarke, D. Clarke, R. Kane, F. Kane.

442

Edwards P.S. 1970
Mr K. Wilson, Richard Kane, David Buchanan, Bert Gilchrist,
Sammy Milligan, David Oliver, Freddie Sproule, Stephen Catterson.
Robert Robinson, Gordon Wilson, Trevor Harron, Robert Oliver, Jim Loughlin.

Edwards P.S. 1989
Mr Gowdy, Nigel Young, Andrew Crawford, Alan Loughlin, Mark Gillen, Barrett Young,
Mark Farley, Nicholas Graham, Neil Coulter, Clyde Vaughan, Timothy Woods,
Andrew Manson, Gareth Sproule, Richard Clarke

Edwards P.S. 1991 - 1992
Karl McGowan, John Mitchell, Clive McGowan, Ryan Campbell, Timothy McCallan, Gareth Timothy Monteith, Stephen Stewart, Bert Heron, Gary Clarke, Stephen Clarke, Alan Love.

Edwards P.S. 1995
Richard Lecky, Mark Speer, James Milligan, Gary Loughlin, Andrew Clarke, Trevor Irwin, Twain Forsythe, Gareth Waugh, Jonathan McCaskie, Steven Campbell, Jason Scott, Richard Clarke.

Edwards P.S. 2002
Matthew Clarke, Stephen Galbraith, David Robinson, Emma Glenn, Christopher Barclay,
Ashley Lowry, Shane Wauchope, Daryl Pearson, Wilfred Pak, Ryan Burke, Matthew Gordon,
Adam Lecky, Nathan Robb, Stephen Williamson

Successful Footballer Reflects.

Footballing Friends - Old Boys of Edwards P.S.
L - R: Richard Clarke, Richard Clarke, Andrew Crawford, Gareth Sproule

Andrew Crawford began school in 1981, starting his elementary career with Mrs Bratton trying to coax him to leave his mum and that school wasn't such a bad place. As time went on, he settled down and in his last few years he began to play football, a sport that fully involves him up to this day. Andrew enjoyed the lighthearted games at lunchtime and the after-school coaching provided by Mr Gowdy.

Realising the young talent, Mr Gowdy soon had Andrew as a regular on the school team. He loved the six-a-side competitions, usually playing in goals but one of the best occasions he recalls, was the memorable game against the local High School First Years, who went down an admirable 10-0 to a delighted Edwards team!

Leaving Edwards at eleven, Andrew went to Castlederg High School, where he was further supported by Mr James Ireland. There were plenty of friendly games sprinkled with a few competitive matches and for six years Andrew enjoyed the pace of life in the High School.

On leaving the safe haven of school, he entered the world of work, starting an apprenticeship with C. A. Anderson in Omagh. This lasted for a year and gave him a firm grounding in the hardware trade as well as preparing him for life in the family business.

He continued to play football with local side, Killen Rangers, where he was skilful in defence. One of the best memories of his teenage years and the time spent with Killen was winning the Youth League. Recognising his talent and seeing potential for greater things to come, Robert Buchannan recommended a move to Glenavon. At sixteen Andrew made the move, supported by Robert, who was to act as chauffeur during his times travelling to the club. Manager, Jackie Delaney, was pleased to nurture Andrew's obvious skills. While playing at the higher level of the Senior Reserve, Andrew broadened his experiences and was provided with opportunities to meet the challenge of better players and stiffer opposition. His skills steadily improved and he enjoyed playing with Glenavon, but he couldn't drive and was still heavily dependent on Robert to take him to training and matches. While he was deeply indebted to him, Andrew felt he could not impose upon him any longer and decided after four years to return home and play once more with Killen Rangers.

Following the spell at home, the starlet once again had itchy feet and decided to join Limavady United. This was his first experience of playing with a team in the Senior League and provided many useful learning opportunities. The Manager was Jimmy Calvin and he encouraged his young prodigy, sharpening his skills and techniques as he played in the competitive games. It was a truly memorable time for Andrew, who scored ten goals and saw the team end the season as runners-up in the League.

Following that success, Andrew again decided to drop a pace and returned to Killen for a season. He liked the more casual play without the ever-present pressure to perform, which was part of life in the fast lane of Senior League.

Meantime, a scout watching the talented young player in action, invited him to play for Portadown, which he decided would be a good opportunity to stretch his wings......or his legs!! Not for the first time he found himself involved in the busy training and playing schedule of a First Team and working with Manager

Ronnie McFaul proved difficult. Disillusioned with Senior games he "packed it in" and once more returned to his happy hunting ground in Killen.

Roy McCready, at that time Manager of Omagh Town, heard of his return, and invited him to come and play for the struggling team. Andrew accepted the invitation and helped to improve the fortunes of the underdogs. The team went from strength to strength and Andrew speaks fondly of his four years playing at St Julian's Road. On one occasion they reached the semi-final of the League and Irish Cup. They finished fourth and earned a place in the Inter-Toto Cup, which was played in Belarus.

This was a most interesting and enjoyable trip. The team flew from Shannon to Minsk, the capital city, where the host Club met them. They stayed in a pleasant hotel equipped with all mod cons, but they also saw the harsher side of life when the team took them to visit an orphanage. They were shocked and greatly moved by its primitive, dirty conditions. Returning to play they had a memorable game and finished with a credible 0-0 draw.

During his time in Omagh, Linfield twice approached Andrew, but his loyalty to his home team made him refuse. However, on the third request he decided to give Linfield a chance. Manager, David Jeffrey, was a force to be reckoned with. He was truly professional and expected nothing less than total commitment from his players. The Club was very well organised. Training took place on Tuesday and Thursday nights from seven until nine thirty with matches every Saturday. Personal fitness was seen as crucial and players were expected to keep improving. There was a strong emphasis on healthy eating and a good diet. Team talks by the Manager boosted the mental attitudes and encouraged the players to be totally focussed on their games.

The "Big Two" Derby---between Linfield and Glentoran--- to the uninitiated, is an amazing occasion. Andrew was fortunate to play in two such matches. Stepping out onto the pitch at Windsor Park was almost overwhelming---the sheer size of the crowd and the noise of the roaring fans, 16,000 in total, were enough to take a player's breath away. However, according to Andrew, once the ball starts to roll, the mind becomes focussed and you don't hear the crowd. With total modesty he reveals that he was in the winning side at one of those finals, and it is something he will never forget.

Going to Norway, in July 2003, to play with Linfield in the Champions League, was a tremendous experience for the young player from Killen Rangers. 6000 spectators watched the match and although they were beaten 1-0, they had a wonderful time and appreciated the lovely country and the kind people they met. As an up and coming player, Andrew greatly valued the high level of support and encouragement that he received at Linfield. He paid sincere tribute to Manager David Jeffrey who was always professional and treated his players with great respect.

The next change in Andrew's football career came in January 2005, when Roy McCready, then Manager of Newry City, and his previous boss at Omagh Town, enquired about purchasing him. Note, it was no longer a case of just deciding to go; Andrew was worth money and negotiations had to take place between the team managers and their Boards. A fee was agreed and the ruling body, the Irish Football Association, sanctioned the transfer. He began playing with Newry in January 2005 and is still there. Since November 2005 Paul Millar has been Manager and Andrew is finding this move to be a pleasurable and beneficial experience.

The team has very good facilities and although they have not won any major trophies, they are steadily improving. The main drawback, as anyone travelling from the West of the Province knows, is the amount of time spent on the road. Andrew travels to Newry twice weekly for training and joins the team on Saturday for matches.

Looking back over his twelve-year career Andrew has had some very special moments. He recalls scoring the winning goal in an Omagh versus Linfield match, which Omagh won; a very sweet moment indeed.

Another memorable goal was scored by the talented forward in a semi-final match between Omagh and Glentoran. Unfortunately, Glentoran won!

There is little free time in Andrew's busy life. He helps to run the family business, greatly supported by his mother and father.

Occasionally, he joins the Manchester United Supporters Club and travels to Old Trafford to watch his heroes play. He likes to spectate at European games and particularly enjoys matches between old rivals-- Liverpool and Man. United.

One of his greatest heroes has to be Eric Cantona, a player every schoolboy wants to emulate. Andrew admires the style, poise and fantastic skill of the former Manchester United player. He also paid tribute to the late George Best, the greatest player to come from Northern Ireland. Andrew once met him at a Summer School, when Best presented the prizes.

To relax, Andrew admits that he has taken up the odd round of golf, but finds it harder than football! He loves foreign travel, particularly going to Portugal. He has been there for European Championship matches between England and Germany and had a wonderful time.

On the domestic front, Andrew married Diane Halkyard from Omagh on July 18th 2005. They are happily settled in Castlederg and he still has to travel to Newry to play football.

Although most of his career to date has been injury-free, at present he is suffering from ligament damage in his ankle and is out of action for what he hopes will be a short time.

He looks back with disbelief at how fast the past sixteen years have gone, but for the foreseeable future Andrew wishes to continue playing football and maybe when the best of his competitive days are over, he hopes to be able to give something back to the game by coaching younger players. However, we haven't heard the last of this young Edwards star!

Memories of Edwards by Adam Lyons

Adam began his Primary School life in Edwards in 1982, when he entered Mrs Bratton's class as a lively four year old. One of his strongest memories is that of the beloved caretaker, Sammy Reid, pretending to shake his hand so hard and fast that it was going to drop off!! He says this is "followed closely with always standing outside the Headmaster's office." He failed to remember just why that was!!!

Although Adam says he did not go on to great academic achievements, he has attained a lot in his short life to date and he went on to detail some of his accomplishments.

He feels that at Edwards he found his love for sport and competition. He learned how to achieve goals, as he recalled that his first serious goal in life was to win the long distance race on Sports Day. This began for him the strong desire to race Motocross, not locally or nationally, but at World level-- and nothing was going to stop the young Adam pursuing this dream.

Also very intense in his memories are the school plays. In P7 he remembers playing the lead role as Father Bear in Goldilocks and the Three Bears with Clare Noble being Mother Bear. He says they had some great laughs and indeed thinks he "should have pursued an acting career".... but then on hindsight...maybe not!!

In his last year at Edwards, Adam began to compete in schoolboy Motocross events. He took part in races all over Ireland and won twice at Irish level. One of his best years had to be 1994 when he won the British Championship...not bad for a young schoolboy from Castlederg!! At this stage the winnings were only trophies and Adam required a lot of support from his parents to compete at such a level.

Turning into adult level in 1995 brought stiffer competition but the intrepid Adam was not deterred. For seven years he had no major wins but was always to be found near the top. As he found his racing feet, his best accomplishment was to be awarded second place in the Irish Adult Championship in1995. This was enough to spur him on to greater glory, so he turned professional in 1997. He moved to Kettering in North Hamptonshire and signed up for the Italian team, T.M. Racing. They sponsored his bike but he was unpaid, meaning that he had to live on small gleanings from winning races.

His wins did not go unnoticed and in 1999 he signed up with Honda U.K. and had his first signed contract. On a Honda 125cc bike, he competed in British and World Championships, cataloguing trips to France, Portugal, Spain, Holland, Croatia, the Czech Republic, Slovenia and Germany. He also ventured to America, to Kissimmee in Florida, where for a full season he raced at Ocala. Now while this sounds glamorous, Adam assures us that it wasn't and he spent a lot of time living out of suitcases.

The following season he competed for Kawasaki U.K. and again he was on the British and World Tours circuit. The firm paid for wages, travel and accommodation and life appeared to be going well for Adam. However this was not to be the case for long and he remembers this season, not for wins, but for major injuries and two operations that set him back for months. As the number one rider, Adam was under a great deal of pressure to win and he felt the bikes he rode were not large enough and were not capable of bringing about the successes that the firm was demanding. The season abruptly ended for him in San Merino with a horrific thumb injury, which Adam blithely describes as the thumb bone having been torn from his hand, resulting in severe ligament damage. He was flown home to Bath for major surgery involving pins being inserted in his thumb and the ligaments being magically sutured in place. The brave Adam made a full, if painful, recovery and returned to France to compete in the final race of the season, representing Ireland at Motocross des Nations. After the poor year, he was very pleased to finish in twentieth position and see Ireland placed twelfth out of the thirty countries that took part.

He left Kawasaki U.K. in 2000 and returned in 2001 to the Italian firm, T.M.

Racing.

Due to his poor standing as a result of his injuries he was only able to race for that season in Britain and Ireland. The Foot and Mouth epidemic also affected racing and with so few races being held, the team decided that he should race in Pesero, forty kilometres south of Rimini, in Italy, where he competed in the Italian Championships. He took part in the first three rounds and by then the season had begun at home, so he returned to racing in Britain and Ireland. Lying in third place in the British Championship and leading the Irish Championship, Adam felt victory was within sight until unfortunately he came off the bike, broke his wrist and dislocated two bones in his hand. Back again he went to see his friend, the surgeon in Bath, and following two more hours of surgery, he was out of action for the rest of the season.

Undaunted, Adam recovered yet again and continued his career with the Italian team and raced in the British Championship. Progress was fine until the final round, when he was leading the race, only to come off the bike in a sensational accident, was hit by several riders, breaking four ribs and puncturing a lung.

Lucky to be alive, he was rushed to Telford Hospital where he remained for four days. Hugely disappointed, but glad to be alive, Adam finished the season in sixth place in Britain and won the Irish Championship.

Further changes evolved in 2003 when he signed for Suzuki G.B. Still at the same level of racing, Adam's goal was to return to World Championship level and he felt fit enough to fulfil his dream. But the combination was not a happy one and due to disagreements within the team, Adam left and went to Yamaha U.K. who had an injured rider and a berth available. This was to lead to happy working conditions and Adam felt they were "probably the best team I have ever ridden for." He finished fourth in the British Championships, was taken to three rounds of the World Championships in Germany, Sweden and Holland. Fortunately he avoided further injury and proceeded to win the British Indoor Supercross that year. It is said that success breeds success and so it was for Adam. He was a member of the highest ever-placed Irish team in Motocross des Nations, finishing a very creditable seventh.

With that feather in his cap, he then went on to race in 2004 for K.T.M., an Austrian company, and he rode for the Irish team. But again he was beset by injuries and did not enjoy the success he was seeking. He missed one round and was out for two weeks, due to breaking a bone in his hand.

However, he struggled bravely on, in the hope that things could only get better. He felt there was an improvement as he was leading the home series and had reached the final round. But lady luck deserted him again in the final round on the final day when once again he parted from his bike and dislocated his shoulder bone. Of all his injuries, Adam describes this as the most excruciatingly painful he has ever attained and it rendered him out of action for five weeks. The pain was coupled with the major disappointment of being unable to represent Ireland in Holland in October 2004. Altogether it was a season he wanted to forget.

In typical Adam fashion and with youthful zest he spent the winter preparing to progress to World level and when he took time out to see me in Edwards, he had just been to Germany to sign up with Sarholz Honda and will be based in Lommel in Belgium, racing for the German team. We wish him every success in this new venture.

Reflecting on his wonderful, but dangerous, career so far, Adam puts his success down to belief in his own ability. His ambition now is to finish among the top fifteen riders in the world and he hints that there may only be another four or five years left for him to attain that position. It is our sincere hope that he will indeed make it and in that time be free from injuries and enjoy the triumph he deserves.

Richard Clarke

Richard Clarke proudly displays his Irish Cup Winners Medal.

Looking back at my time as a pupil at Edwards Primary School I was probably not the best at schoolwork and homework but I enjoyed my time there and have fond memories of my teachers then, some of whom are still teaching there today! The best times for me were Sports Days and when Mr. Gowdy took us for football for the school team. Living close to the school I spent many happy evenings playing football on the school football pitch where the new school is now built. After leaving Edwards I went on to Strabane Grammar and whilst there I was selected for Northern Ireland Schools Under 15 football team. I then represented the international team at Under 16, Under 18 and Under 21 Levels which has meant winning caps against many countries around Europe and travelling around these countries, which was a wonderful experience. I currently play for Portadown Football Club in the Irish Premier League. I signed for them at 15 and have worked my way through the Youth and Reserve teams to reach the First team. I have been at the club for ten years now and during this time I have enjoyed great team success, with winning the Irish League title in 2002 and Irish Cup in 1999 being the highlights. I have also played in two Irish Cup Finals at Windsor Park. I was named N.I Football Writers Young Player of the Year in 1999, which was a great honour. Wishing Edwards Primary School well on the move to their wonderful new school!

Richard Clarke

My Memories

Clare Noble P 1/2

I cannot remember my first day at Edwards Primary School, Castlederg, however my mum tells me that I created quite a scene crying. Thankfully that was short lived and the following years spent at Edwards were a lot more pleasant.

One figure will always stick in my mind--- the then caretaker Sammy Reid; he was always on hand at break time and dinner times to give you a piggyback or "swizz", or perhaps just help with a simple task like tying a shoelace. Looking back now, I remember at Christmas, our whole class was taken to see Santa. I remember Santa lifting me up and me sitting on his knee and kissing him; I don't remember this, but my mum tells me that later that evening at home I told her Santa was just like Sammy; little did I know that at that time that Sammy was indeed Santa.

I remember the previous principal Mr Tom Riddall; when I heard that he was retiring I went home from school that evening in an awful tearful state (I think I may have been about six years old), and telling my mum that I would not be going back to school any more, because he would not be there and I had known him all my life.

The school play was always an eventful time of year. I remember playing an angel at a Christmas play, but as I entered into the senior classes at school the plays were great fun, luckily I had the ability to land many of the lead roles, they were great fun, not to mention the time out of class to practise!!

I am the first person to admit that I was a bit of a tomboy at school. I always wanted to play football with the boys and I remember some of them were not too impressed with me playing, but they didn't have much choice. I don't think that the skill element was up to much but the fun element was without doubt there.

I left Edwards Primary School in 1989 and I moved to Castlederg High School where I followed my keen interest in sports. I tried my hand at all sports available, taking my place in as many school teams as I possibly could. I continued my studies at Omagh College and finally at Buckinghamshire College, London, were I studied for a degree in Sports and Leisure Management and then finally a Masters in sports. While at college I played soccer and hockey and was active in the college athletics team.

Clare Noble receiving her Referee's Medal at the Milk Cup Tournament.

When I returned home to Castlederg I still remained very active, playing soccer for a local ladies team and I also joined Castlederg Gaelic Ladies team, although I still felt that I was without a challenge. It was when I was reading the local newspaper that I saw an advert for a referees' beginners course – that was in October 2000, so I thought I would give it a try. I went along, started refereeing and I have never looked back since. Being a female referee in what is certainly a male dominated sport has certainly been a challenge, but a role I take much pride in living up to. Refereeing has taken me on a whirlwind of a journey from youth games, women's games, men's games, youth tournaments, International appointments and duty, and Irish league appointments. The future is bright for me in refereeing and I am willing to aim for the top.

So from humble beginnings playing football with the boys in the playground of Edwards Primary School, where I clearly developed the love for the game, I have travelled the whole of Northern Ireland and England, refereeing for soccer teams of all ages, genders and backgrounds and hope to continue, all for the love of the game and the love of sport, which I believe developed at a very early age whilst playing football in the school playground at Edwards.

Thank you. Clare Noble.

Andrew Watt

Andrew Watt with his school Rugby Team

My fondest memory of Edwards School has always been my sporting school life, even when I was in the classroom I was basically counting down the minutes until lunch time to get outside to play football, and when I wasn't doing that, I was pestering Mr Gowdy to left me update the football leagues tables on his classroom cupboard door, or help him organise the school teams, or his annual interschool football competition. I guess, I, like a few others, had a different perspective on Edwards, being a teacher's son. When everyone else went home for the day I was still walking about the school, talking/bothering the staff or dragging my brother into the school hall to kick a ball around, while waiting for mum to finish work. Through this I guess I was able to get to know the other side of the teachers, which most pupils didn't, as I knew each teacher better than most and saw the full role of a teacher's job and even at a young age it planted the seed for a career in education. Since I left Edwards PS my sporting interest changed from a love of playing football to a love of playing rugby when I joined Omagh Academy. I wonder what Mr Gowdy thought at the tme?. At Omagh Academy I was privileged enough to be 1st XV Captain in my final year as well as being selected to represent Ulster Schools U18, one of my biggest playing achievements. When I left Northern Ireland to go to University I attended Manchester Metropolitan University to study to become a PE teacher and during that time I played for Waterloo RUFC in the English National Division 1. When I left Manchester, I took up my first and current teaching post at King Edward VII and Queen Mary School in Lytham St Anne's, Lancashire, where I am now Director of Rugby. I am currently playing at my local club Fylde in Division 3. Along side this role, I also am in charge of coaching the Lancashire schools representative U15 and U16 rugby teams, and through this I have achieved my biggest coaching sporting achievement so far at my tender age when my Lancashire Schools U15 team was crowned the English RFU National Champions 2005.

My Memories of Edwards Primary School.

Boo Bear Christmas Pantomime 1992.
L - R: Roberta Allen, Lisa Clarke, Lynette Kerrigan, Wendy Loughlin, Stephen Clarke,
Wendy McCay, Lyndsey McDougall, Naomi Forbes.

I have fond memories of my time at primary school. Edwards was a great school, with great people and a great atmosphere. It gave me a fantastic start in life and started me on the road to where I am today. For me the primary years are crucial. Coming from a sports background, I hope that the Government soon realises the importance of P.E. in primary schools. The reality is that P.E. specialists would be the answer to all their obesity concerns. Prevention rather than cure, as they say!

The highlight of my time at Edwards had to be my involvement in the Christmas Pantomimes. I've been Boo Bear, Old King Cole and the Stage Manager in The Seven Dwarfs... loving them all, even if I was dressed in tights a few times! To this day I fail to understand how I learned the lines. But when I think of the organisation and the endless work of the teachers involved, I begin to realise why such events were so successful!!

Other memories include watercress sandwiches, having grown the watercress in class and the singing of that unforgettable song-
"Supercalifragilisticexpialadocious!!"

And when it comes to wet break or lunch times, I remember sitting in a classroom, and exchanging crisps. This involved each person having a packet of crisps and exchanging on request, so that we could try different combinations.... "Crisp-burgers"

On the subject of food, that brings me to my favourite dessert, cornflake squares and custard.... I can taste them already!! With that in the belly it was always time for football! In the playground this was highly competitive, with Mr Gowdy having appointed Alan Love and myself as team captains.

When it came to sport Mr Gowdy was the driving force within the school. We always had full Sports Days. I remember the classes meeting on the playground and then parading down to the sports field behind a ringing bell. Then we would take our seats, not only awaiting the opening event, but also the arrival of the ice-cream van!

Inside the classroom I was a real chatterbox and I sometimes got into trouble for speaking out of turn! Nevertheless, not all my talking was negative, as it enabled our class to "twist the arm" of a few cover teachers into allowing us to play with the Lego rather than doing any written work!!

Nevertheless, such talking in the form of questioning enabled me to gain a firm understanding in all subjects as I moved through Primary School and into Secondary School. I attended Omagh Academy...another exceptional school. In my time there I achieved 10 GCSE's and 3 A Levels. In addition I captained rugby at all levels within the school and was Head Boy in my final year. From the Academy I progressed onto third level education at The University of Ulster, Jordanstown, reading Sport, Exercise and Leisure. I graduated in the summer of 2005, with First Class Honours and I was delighted to be awarded Student of the Year. I have since entered a PGCE course at the University, specialising in Physical Education.

I am privileged to have been given the opportunity to reflect upon my primary years, and may I take this opportunity to thank everyone at Edwards Primary School for all they have done, not only for me, but also for all the children that have passed through the doors. I close with a firm belief that the school will go from strength to strength in the years to come.

Stephen Clarke.

Richard The Second: Another Football Legend!!

Under-21 international

Castlederg's Clarke finds the net for Northern Ireland

by Chris Caldwell

FORMER Omagh Town FC captain, Richard Clarke, made a decisive impact on Northern Ireland under-21s tour of Israel last week.

The 20-year-old Newry City midfielder from Castlederg made his international debut when the under-21s secured a famous 1-0 win over the home side, thanks to Nottingham Forest's and the under-21s captain, Sammy Clingen, scoring after just 14 seconds.

Having performed well during the first game, Clarke was again selected in the second match.

On home on Friday morning, Clarke told of his delight at getting his first caps, and that all important first goal: "I was in the squad last year but didn't get on the pitch.

"This year I played in midfield, and we kept the ball well. They were a good side but they had little to offer up front, so we were fairly comfortable. It was great to get playing this time and score. The right winger cut inside and played the ball over the top and I just volleyed it home."

In domestic football the talented midfielder is positive Newry City can push on from their current mid-table position in the Irish Premier League: "Things are going well at the minute at Newry, we've got a good squad."

On a personal level, he is still hopeful of the possibility of a move to a cross-channel club: "Last Christmas I was supposed to go to Hibs for a trial, but because I had so much work to do for my course it was put off, but we'll see what happens. Hopefully I have plenty of time."

Another talented youngster from west of the Bann, Kyle Lafferty, was also selected for the Northern Ireland squad to travel to Israel, but disappointingly for the Kesh teenager, an injury sustained during Darlington's scoreless draw at Boston United the Saturday before, meant he was unable to join up with the squad.

Currently the striker is back at Burnley to receive treatment and it is hoped he will return to action soon.

Former Omagh Town captain, Richard Clarke, who scored the winning goal for Northern Ireland's under-21s on Wednesday last in their 1-0 victory over Israel in Nazareth. The Castlederg native, currently with Newry City, played in both of Northern Ireland's 1-0 wins over their hosts in Israel last week. AN0799CC

only his second international appearance it was the University of Ulster, Jordanstown, sports studies student, who popped up with the winning goal as Northern Ireland secured a second successive 1-0 win, this time in Nazareth.

Speaking on his return

Extract from Tyrone Constitution Febraury 2006

464

I am sure it is seldom that a school can boast of three super footballers with the same surname, but Edwards has passed through its sporting ranks, two Richard Clarkes and one Stephen Clarke, all of them with magic talents in football! Richard Clarke of Strabane Road, Castlederg, is the youngest of the trio and in his short lifetime he has notched up an incredible number of admirable achievements. He began the first stage of his education in Edwards, where he was an affable youngster who loved to join in any of the sports activities on offer. He was always found on the playground in the early morning, enjoying football before classes, and again at lunchtime, and of course he seldom missed the Thursday evening practice sessions. Like many others, he began playing for Edwards football team and the good grounding in skills and techniques prepared him for play with Dergview at Under 12, 13, 15, 16 and 18. He then progressed to play for Dergview at Senior level and had one season with Killen Rangers. With such talent it wasn't long before he moved further up the ladder of success and he signed for Omagh Town Football Club in 2001, at the age of 16. For a young boy these were exciting times and he made his debut for the Omagh first team in August 2002 in a match against well-known League leaders Linfield. His impressive talent eventually led to him becoming the Omagh skipper. Still only a schoolboy, Richard went forward for trials to represent his country and was awarded with two Northern Ireland caps in the 2002-2003 and 2003-2004 seasons. Having completed his secondary level education at Castlederg High School, where he gained an impressive 3 A levels, Richard went on to pursue Sports Studies at The University of Ulster at Jordanstown. His remarkable talent has also been recognised by the University as he has been given honours as a present scholar, for football. He has toured China with the University of Ulster team, visiting Beijing and playing in front of a crowd of 12,000 people. The team won 3-0 and he was proud to have scored the first goal. As a student with exceptional ability he was chosen to travel to Turkey, representing Great Britain at the World Student Games. He also participated for County Tyrone in the 2002 Milk Cup Competition, one that has helped many of the country's finest young players establish themselves in the world of international football. As local journalist and Derg View player, Tommy Nethery writes, "The prestigious Milk Cup has provided a fantastic stage and shop window for the cream of the crop in the six counties, a number of our outstanding talents going on to establish full-time professional careers across the channel." Fitting well into the "cream of the crop" category, Richard moved to his present club, Newry City, in 2004, and is still playing in the top flight Carnegie Irish League. In addition to his busy schedule of matches, he has twice-weekly training on Tuesday and Thursday nights, studies at the University and despite a very limited social life, he has continued to successfully play in the Northern Ireland Under 20 Milk Cup Squad! Always in the eye of the selectors, he once again found himself chosen to represent Northern Ireland in the Under 21 team. His finest achievement to date came in February 2006 when on tour with the team, he scored his first international goal in Israel. He describes it as a fantastic unforgettable moment. (See the article from The Tyrone Constitution.) He played in the historic town of Nazareth and was delighted to score a goal and be elected "Man of the Match" by his manager, Roy Millar. Richard admits he never has a spare second and he is now preparing for an Easter trip to Switzerland. Meantime, he is striving to complete his degree in Sports Studies in 2007 and aspires in future to move to a cross-channel club.

Edwards PS:

Judith Lyons

The old saying that 'your school days are the best days of your life, is one which I definitely believe in, and I think my days at Edwards contributed greatly to this. Although I'm not sure I had the same feeling when I joined back in September 1987! My earliest memories of Edwards are of the huge painting easels and the play kitchen, judging by my culinary skill today, I don't think I spent very long in there! I think my favourite memory is of sports day. I remember walking down to the field carrying my chair with the rest of my classmates, hoping that I would win a badge or two, hopefully maybe more! Edwards gave me the chance to develop a passion for sport, one which I have carried with me right to the present day where I am currently in my final year at Heriot-Watt University in Edinburgh. In fact I am even studying Sport and Exercise Science! After leaving Edwards I joined Omagh Academy and here I fell in love with one particular sport. Hockey. My time in Omagh was spent doing some studying and playing a lot of Hockey. In my 1st year I was asked to note down what I wanted to achieve during my time at the Academy. I clearly remember my top choice which was to gain a place in the 1st XI hockey team. I achieved this in my 5th year, which was the year when we reached the final of the Belfast Telegraph Schools Cup. Unfortunately we didn't lift the cup but it was an experience that I will never forget. During that year I also had the honour of captaining the under 16 WELB squad. This stood me in good stead as in my final year at Omagh I was privileged enough to be made captain of the 1st XI team, during this time we made it to the semi-final of the schools cup and had a tour to Barcelona. During school I also was a member of Omagh Ladies Hockey Club 1st XI and enjoyed playing senior level hockey. After leaving the Academy I joined Heriot-Watt University to study for a BSc Hons in Sport and Exercise Science with Management. My love for hockey carried on right through university, where I have played for the 1s XI throughout and have enjoyed a tour to Barbados. However, in 2003 I decided to diversify into a completely different type of sport, motorsport! I applied for a competition called Formula Woman, which aimed to launch the 1st ever, all women racing championship for novices. After a written application, in which I was 1 of 10,000, I got the opportunity to attend the preliminary knockout round for Northern Ireland applicants at Kirkistown. Here 130 women including myself were put through fitness, reaction, general knowledge, media interview and driving ability tests. At the end of the day 20 girls were eliminated and the remaining 110 would have to wait to find out if they were through. 2 months later I found out that I had made it to the final 50, and that I was the only applicant who had made it through from Northern Ireland. The final 50 were then issued with a 12-week fitness plan and were advised to follow it in preparation for the elimination camp. In March 2004 I attended the elimination camp at Cadwell Park, Lincolnshire, England. During the week we faced fitness, driving, media and psychological tests, all of which were closely watched by ITV cameras for the reality T.V show that was to show the entire UK our progress including the highs and the lows. After facing a simulated helicopter crash I felt like I could face any challenge that was thrown at me, and during the week there were several. However the final selection, where we found out who had made it into the final 16 and would be racing in the Mazda Rx8 championship, proved to be the biggest heart stopping moment of all. I had to wait for what felt like a lifetime to hear I had got the 16th place. After that we were given an Mx5 road car for 4 months and trained to become proper racing drivers. The standard was high, with the 16 including a British Airways pilot and RAF jet pilot; being a student seemed pretty dull! The championship contained 7 rounds, around England and Scotland, and provided a lot of drama, which was to be expected when you let 16 women behind the wheel of a 240 bhp car!! This drama gained ratings of over 2 million people for the show. In the end I finished 10th, an achievement which was summed up by Carsport as 10th out of 10,000 and one which I am extremely proud of. After my degree, I am hoping to progress further in motorsport and I think my father is too! It seems a long time since I sat in the tiny chairs in Edwards primary school but looking back, I have to smile, even about the time I was a football fairy in the school play!! Thanks for that and all the memories!

Judith Lyons

My Memories of Edwards Primary School

Shirley McCay in Edwards Football Team Strip

I started Edwards Primary School in 1992 and one of my earliest memories was the excitement of getting to paint with Mrs Bratton in P1, along with causing havoc in the water tray and sand tray! I took part in Nativities, unfortunately not being chosen for the leading role of Mary! However, little did I know that an Angel was in fact a vital link in the birth of Jesus! I have also been in plays, which involved rubbing noses as an Eskimo and being an Indian in the Black-Foot Tribe. Despite the lack of Oscar nominations, these were great fun and always the source of many a giggle, with frantic waves to the mums and dads in the audience, a prominent feature.

I recall getting in trouble with the Headmaster for running on the grass, which is ill advised when your mother is a teacher at the school. Word soon spreads at Edwards! My mischievous behaviour was also highlighted when my best friend, Kathryn Bratton and I, locked Miss Douglas in her classroom when we were in P3.

The sight of her, in her room, and the keys in the door, provided too good an opportunity to miss! We left chuckling proudly at our latest prank, whilst Miss Douglas had to knock on the door until Mr Woods set her free!

Kathryn and I both had parents who taught at the school; so most afternoons were spent either in the sports hall or wandering around looking for some mischief to get up to!

The main things about Edwards that I most enjoyed were the sports and practical activities, and it is no coincidence that I remember little of my education and a lot of my sports! From a young age, I loved football and used to envy the boys who played at break and dinner every day. However, this jealousy proved to be short-lived as I plucked up the courage to ask if I could play. Although the source of some resentment from some who thought football was solely "for boys," the majority were more than happy to let me join in. I enjoyed this very much, and think I hold the record for eating my dinner in the shortest time, simply in the rush to get outside! Mr Gowdy was in charge of the football, and I was the first girl at Edwards to gain a place on the team. I also recall Mrs Graham taking a group of us after school for hockey on the tarmac so it is clear that I have her to thank for where I am today!

Shirley McCay

470

After taking the 11+ in P7, I went to Omagh Academy and at the moment I am studying for A-levels in Biology, English and Home Economics. I have continued my interest in sport into Secondary School and when available, play football with Omagh Cossacks and I am the captain of the school First XI hockey team. I play for Omagh Ladies Senior League One and I have also represented Ulster and Ireland in hockey at Under 16 and Under 18 level. This year I have been accorded the great honour of being captain of the Irish Under 18 team and feel proud to have "answered Ireland's call!"

Playing for my province and country has resulted in many memorable experiences, including trips to Waterford, Galway, Bristol, Manchester, Barcelona in Spain, Rotterdam in Holland, and Krakow in Poland to compete in various competitions. The highlight of my experiences was the trip to Poland with the Irish under 18 team in 2005, where we finished fourth in the European Championships. I have made many friends and in the future hope to continue playing hockey and pursue a career in sport at the University of Ulster. I have many happy memories of my time at Edwards Primary School. It is a wonderful school, with wonderful teachers and definitely will remain in my memories for the rest of my life.

Shirley McCay

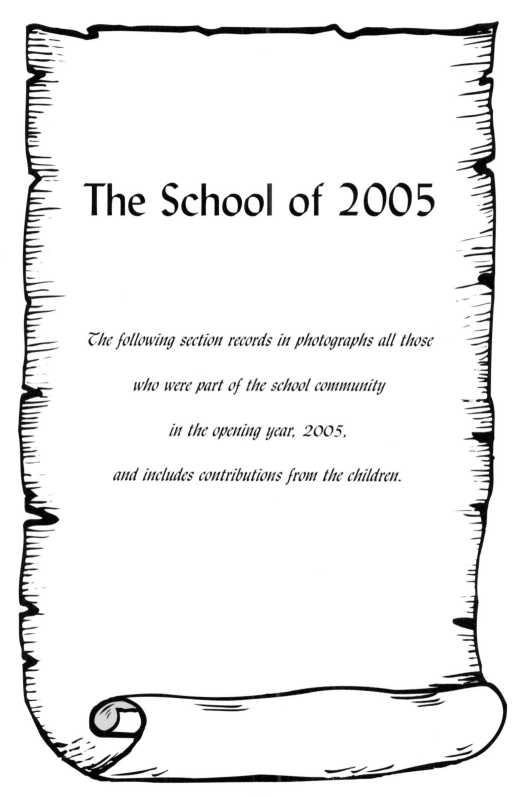

The School of 2005

The following section records in photographs all those

who were part of the school community

in the opening year, 2005,

and includes contributions from the children.

Nursery

Back row: Miss M. Young, Jake Leitch, Reece Loughlin, Simon Thompson, Jamie Harpur, Rachel Hamilton, Luke McKane, Mrs P. Bratton.
Middle Row: Adam Young, Tori McCrea, Holly Patterson, Craig Reid, Shannon McCain, Danielle Watson, Ian Bacciochi, Emma Scott.
Front Row: Ryan McCreery, Stephanie Catterson, Emma Elliott, Courtney Reid, David Hall, Chelsea Harron, Adam Clarke, Georgia Clarke.

What we do in nursery

474

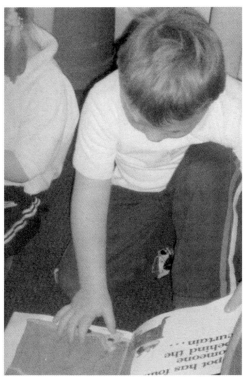

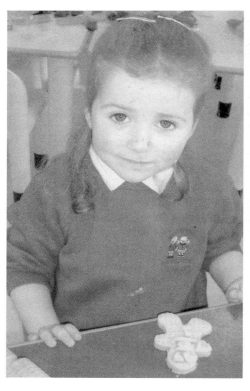
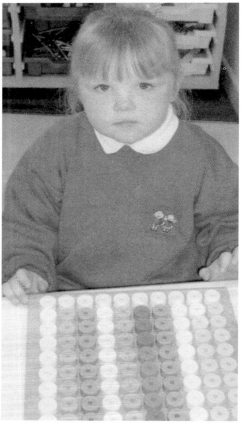

476

Special Unit 1

Back Row: Miss E. McKane, Mrs S Sproule, Jason Kilpatrick, Lee Duddy, Mark Hamilton, Drew Carruthers, Matthew Dowdalls, Mrs M E Watt.
Front Row: Matthew McCrory, Andrew Baird, Shane Wilson, Peter Clarke, Kevin Cassidy.

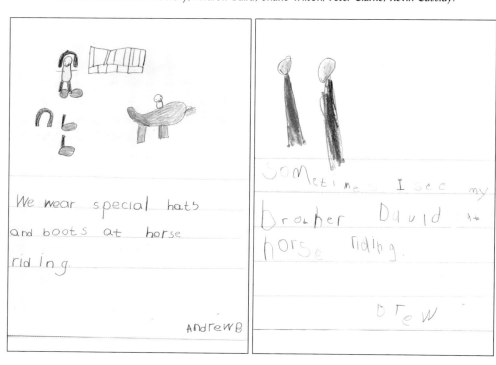

We wear special hats and boots at horse riding.

AndrewB

Sometimes I see my brother David at horse riding.

Drew

I Was riding on Nellie
We Wore our neW jumpers.

Jason

We wore our
new jumpers ot
horse riding.

Kevin

I like going horse
riding.
I like Nota.

Lee

We Wore our new
JumPers to horse riding.

Mark

Our new jumpers
for horse riding are
yellow.

Matthew

Dont look behind
when you are
riding a horse.
matthew mccrory

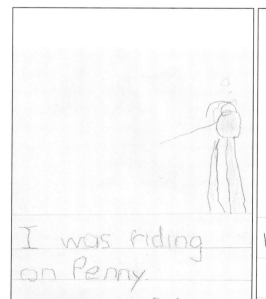

I was riding
on Penny.

Peter

Shane

We go horse riding
in Omagh.

Special Unit 2

Back Row: Mrs P Quigley, Lee Willliamson, Chloe Hyndman, Ashley Love,
Shanna Patton, Paula Frize, Mrs G McKinley.
Front Row: Matthew Kilpatrick, Alan Harron, Steven Gailey, Vicky Humphrey, Vivienne Wilkinson.

From Old to New

E – End of old Edwards School,
D – December was our month to move.
W – What to pack and what to dump,
A – A lot of crates arrived to be filled.
R – Room 9 was our old classroom,
D – Diggers came and tumbled it down,
S – SU 2 is where we are now.

S – Such long corridors we have to walk,
C – Carpets on floors, no more scraping chairs,
H – Heating panels high up in the roof.
O – Out goes the old blackboard, in with new white,
O – Our new classroom is colourful and bright.
L – Leaving was sad, but now that we're settled we all feel glad.

SU 2
Year 7
Alan Harron, Ashely Love, Shanna Patton, Vivien Wilkinson
Year 6
Chloe Hyndman, Matthew Kilpatrick, Lee Williamson, Paula Frize
Year 5
Steven Gailey, Vicky Humphrey

Year 1

Back Row: Mrs A. McCreery, Mrs K. Cowan, Taylor Gailey, Emma Keatley,
Emma Reid, Sophie Galbraith, Jacob Kerrigan, Kennedy Hill, Miss J. Douglas.
Middle Row: Gareth Hamilton, Emma Kerrigan, Rachel Maxwell, Ian Boyd,
Dillon Wilson, Scott Monaghan, Jayne Young.
Front Row: Scott Montgomery, Leah Fyffe, Luke Willliamson, Jamie Reid,
Kyle Harpur, Hannah Thompson, Kerri Hunter, Alannah Harpur.

New Things

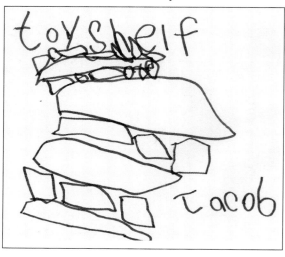

speakers

ScottM

sink

Kyle

yellow chairs

Alannah.H.

Sand tray

Emma K

long display
board

Hannah

toys

Dillon

storage unit

Jamie

telephone

Emma

486

Whiteboard

Scott

paper drawer

gargth

screen

Lean

counters

Taylor

library book stand

Kennedy

Store

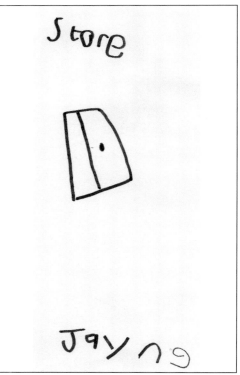

Jayng

water trot

Rachel

blue desks

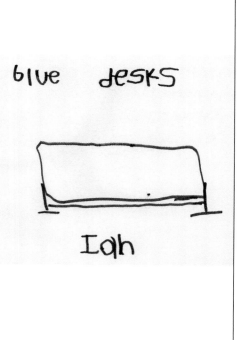

Iah

488

big book stand

Sophie

big window

Kerri

library bench

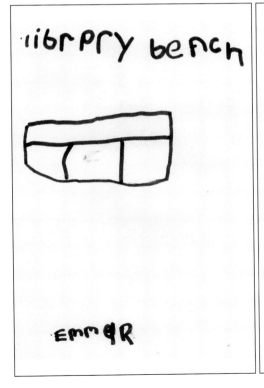

EmmaR

blue carpet

Lyla

Year 2

Back Row: Molly Finlay, Mark Keatley, Gary Barclay, Ryan Maxwell, Claire Harpur, Chelsea Gillen, Stuart Sproule.
Middle Row: Miss C. Davis, Richard Humphrey, Amy Kyle, Aimee Faulkner, Mark Harron, Stuart Mortland, Hayden Doherty, Nigel Hemphill, Mrs C. Hawkes.
Front Row: Susanne Dinsmore, Malcom Gordon, Sarah Wallace, Stephen Milligan, Emma Harpur, Holly Johnston, Heather Kerrigan, Katie Dunlop, Clarice Harron.

Our Sound Walk by Year 2.

Suzanne Dinsmore : We went round the whole school. We heard humming of the computer and we heard a dog barking.

Aimee Faulkner : We heard Miss Douglas teaching her class. We heard cats and dogs.

Hayden Doherty : We heard footsteps and we heard a ball.

Sarah Wallace : We went for a sound walk and we heard a car and a ball.

Clarice Harron : We walked past the whole school and I heard a girl coughing.

Emma Caldwell: We went round the whole school and we heard a door closing and a person sneezed.

Steven Milligan : We walked round the school and we heard the digger and the birds.

Emma Harpur : We heard the birds and footsteps.

Nigel Hemphill : I heard lots of birds singing. I like the sound of birds, they go tweet-tweet!!

Heather Kerrigan : We heard a car driving. We heard a digger outside in the playground.

Malcolm Gordon : We heard the teacher and the computer.

Claire Harpur : We went outside to hear something. We heard the boys and girls playing with the balls.

Mark Harron : We heard people up the corridor. We saw people walking out of a car.

Amy Kyle : I heard birds singing, a person sneezing and dogs barking. I liked it, it was good.

Chelsea Gillen : We heard a door closing, footsteps. Miss Douglas and somebody sneezed.

Mark Keatley : On our sound walk we heard a teacher and a computer.

Gary Barclay : We heard a digger, the digger was digging a hole.

Stuart Sproule : We heard Miss Douglas talking to her children.

Hollie Johnston : We heard a teacher and the computer.

Stuart Mortland : We went past the whole school. I heard a van and a door.

Richard Humphrey : On our sound walk we heard a teacher and the computer.

Ryan Maxwell: We heard Miss Douglas, a door closing, birds singing and a car.

Ryan Glenn : I heard a car.

Katie Dunlop : On our sound walk we heard a teacher and the computer.

Molly Finlay : I can hear the dogs barking and the birds singing.

Clarice Harron

Our Sound Walk

Steven Milligan

Our Sound Walk

Mark H

Marie Harron

Our Sound Walk

Mark K

Mark Keatley

Our Sound Walk

Chelsea   Gillen

Our Sound Walk

Miss Morrow

Molly   Finlay

Our Sound Walk

Malcolm   Gordon

Our Sound Walk

Katja
Katie Dunlop

Our Sound Walk

Our Sound Walk

Nigel Hemphill

Our Sound Walk

RYAN MAXWELL

dark King

bam

B Bo

Our Sound Walk

Amy

mrs mckinley

Our Sound Walk

Hayden

digger

dog.

bird.

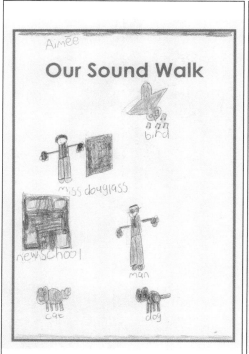

Aimee

Our Sound Walk

bird

miss douglass

new school

man

cat   dog

Emma Harper

Our Sound Walk

birds

zzzzzzz

dog

Computer

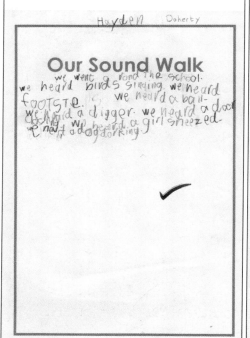

Hayden   Doherty

Our Sound Walk

we went a rond the school.
we heard birds singing. we heard
footste... we heard a ball...
we heard a digger. we heard a door
locking. we heard a girl sneezed.
e next we heard a dog barking.

✓

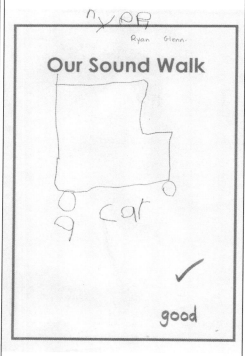

nxRA
Ryan Glenn.

Our Sound Walk

a cat

✓

good

Year 3

Back Row: Miss Z Johnston, Mrs I Forbes, Philip Clarke, Chloe Gannon, Ethan Finlay, Andrew Clarke, Stuart Harpur, Clive Hawkes, Neil Robinson, Stacey Johnston, Miss N. Moore.
Middle Row: Aaron McKane, Carly-Leigh Breydin, Rachel Irwin, Danielle Kincaid, David McCreery, Tristan Hamilton, Lochlan Dunlop, Thomas Baird, Amber Hemphill.
Front Row: Samuel Hunter, Peter Wallace, Paul Bacciochi, Gavin Deery, Blake Patterson, Jamie Parker, Craig Scott, Taylor Young.

My New Classroom in Edwards Primary School

We have a new computer in our new classroom. I have a new seat. My teacher Miss Moore has got a bookcase. We have yellow walls and pale walls. Miss Moore got a new telephone and new cupboards.

Year 3

My New Classroom in Edwards Primary School

We have to use a white board. We have yellow chairs and blue tables and nice curtains. They are more doors and they are a telephone. In

Samantha Kerrigan   Year 3

My thoughts and feelings about my new classroom

we are beside the play
ground. we have yellow
chairs and blue tables
and i love the classroom
i Like the coloures in the
classroom and the
projector is the best becouse
its batter becouse we dont have
to set on the floor.

Chloe Gannon **Year 3**

My Old Classroom in Edwards Primary School

In the old classroom there
were brown tables and brown
curtains. We had a black t v
we had steel cupboards. There
was a blackboard that went
up and down. There was
cushians in the Library to
sit on

Thomas Reid **Year 3**

My Old Classroom in Edwards Primary School

In our old Classroom
there were brown tables
and green chairs. We had a
blackboard that rolld up and
down. We had steel cupboards
that squeeked when we
opened it.

Clive Hawkes **Year 3**

My thoughts and feelings about my new classroom

I like my new classroom
because you dought don't have to
get out of your seat to
whatch the projector. The boys
just have to go out of
the classroom to get to
the toilets. I like the
new library and the
new library books.

Jamie Parker **Year 3**

My thoughts and feelings about my new classroom

I like the projector because anybody can see it and we dont have to go down on the floor. I like the both of the schools because they are nis. I didnt like the old curtans in the old clssroom because they where bad looking.

Blake patterson   **Year 3**

My thoughts and feelings about my new classroom

I like the projector because You do not have to Sit down on the floor I like the library because You dont have to Sit on the cushlans in the ad school

Neil Robinson   **Year 3**

My Old Classroom in Edwards Primary School

In our old classroom we had a big steel cupboard behind our door that we come in and out of. Beside a window we had a sink to wash your hands. We had a board that rolled up and down.

Gavin Deery   **Year 3**

My New Classroom in Edwards Primary School

My new classroom has blue tables. We have yellow chairs. We have new books. There is no chalkboard. We has a white board. There is blve carpet.

David mccrory   **Year 3**

498

My New Classroom in Edwards Primary School

My classroom has a new
White board
There is no chalk board the doors
are colourful. I sit on a nice
yellow chair. We have a Projector
to watch the tv. miss moore
has a telephone.

Andrew Clarke   **Year 3**

My New Classroom in Edwards Primary School

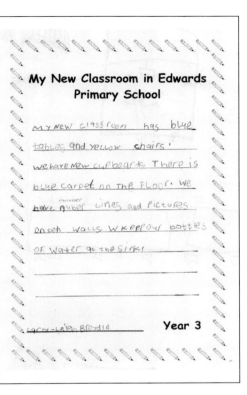

My New classroom has blue
tables and yellow chairs.
we have new cupboards. There is
blue carpet on The Floor. We
have number Lines and Pictures
on the walls we keep ow bottles
of Water at the sink.

Carly-Leigh Breslin   **Year 3**

Memories of my old school classroom

I remember that
myold classroom
was dirty and
rusty I hadto walk
along way to get
to the toilet.

Ethan Finlay   **Year 3**

Memories of my old school classroom

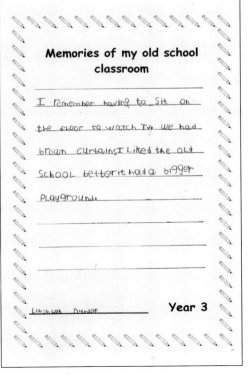

I remember having to sit on
the floor to watch Tv. we had
brown curtains I Liked the old
school better it had a bigger
playground.

Lachlan Dunlop   **Year 3**

499

Memories of my old school classroom

I remember that I made flags we had a travel agency in our room. We had a hospital in our class room I remember that I painted a christmas decorations.

Paul   **Year 3**

Memories of my old school classroom

we had brown tables and it had green chairs we had a old tv and we had vinyl on the floor and we had steel cupboards and a blan board we had to sit on cushions in the library and we had one door.

Danielle Kincaid   **Year 3**

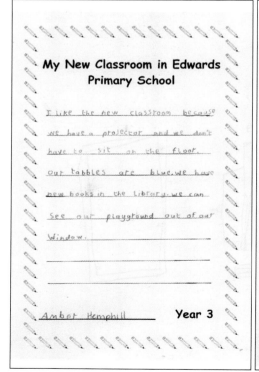

My New Classroom in Edwards Primary School

I like the new classroom because we have a projector and we don't have to sit on the floor. our tabbles are blue. we have new books in the library. we can see our playground out of our window.

Amber Hemphill   **Year 3**

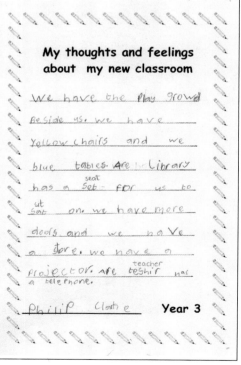

My thoughts and feelings about my new classroom

We have the play growd Beside us. we have yellow chairs and we blue tables. Are library has a seb seat for us to sit on. we have more doors and we have a store. we have a projector. Are teacher teshir has a telephone.

Philip Clothe   **Year 3**

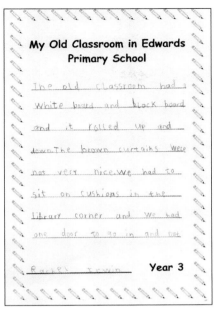

My Old Classroom in Edwards Primary School

The old classroom had a
white board and black board
and it rolled up and
down. The brown curtains were
not very nice. We had to
sit on cushions in the
library corner and we had
one door to go in and out

Rachel Irwin   **Year 3**

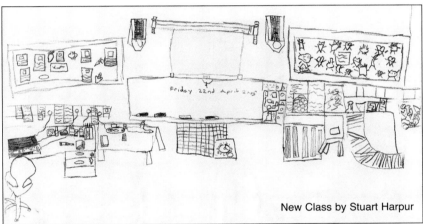

New Class by Stuart Harpur

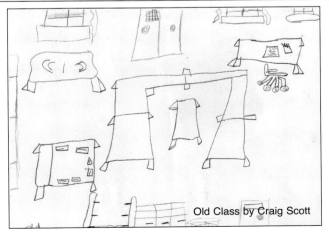

Old Class by Craig Scott

501

Our New Classroom by Year 3

Aaron McKane : Miss Moore got a new telephone and new cupboards.

Amber Hemphill: I like the new classroom because we have a projector and we don't have to sit on the floor.

Samantha Kerrigan : We have yellow chairs and blue tables and nice curtains.

David McCreery : We have new books. There is no chalkboard. We have a whiteboard.

Andrew Clarke : The doors are colourful and I sit on a nice yellow chair.

Carly- Leigh Breydin : We have number lines and pictures on the walls. We keep bottles of water at the sink.

Memories Of My Old Classroom.

Ethan Finlay : I remember I had to walk a long way to get to the toilet.

Lachlan Dunlop : I liked the old school better; it had a bigger playground.

Danielle Kincaid : We had vinyl on the floor and steel cupboards and a blackboard.

Paul Bacchiochi : I remember we had a hospital in our classroom. I made flags and we had a travel agency in our room.

Samuel Hunter : There was one door in the old classroom. There were curtains.

Stacey Johnston : I was playing with Samuel and he was cheating all the time.

Gavin Deery : In our old classroom beside a window we had a sink to wash you hands and we had a board that rolled up and down.

Peter Wallace : We had one door and we had cushions in the library.

Rachel Irwin : In our old classroom the brown curtains were not very nice.

Clive Hawkes : We had a steel cupboard that squeaked when we opened it.

Thomas Baird : There were brown tables and brown curtains.

Taylor Young : In the old Year 3 classroom the blackboard was at the top of the class. The room was filled with desks where the pupils sat. The teacher's desk was beside the window.

Thoughts and Feelings About My New Classroom.

Philip Clarke : We have the playground beside us. Our library has a seat for us to sit on.

Chloe Gannon : I love the classroom. I like the colours and the projector is the best because we don't have to sit on the floor.

Tristan Hamilton : I like our new classroom because there is lots of new stuff in it.

Jamie Parker : The boys just have to go out of the classroom to get to the new toilets.

Neil Robinson : I like the library because you don't have to sit on cushions like you did in the old school.

Blake Patterson : I didn't like the curtains in the old classroom because they were bad looking.

Year 4

Back Row: Shannon Watson, Emily Maxwell, Alex Harpur, Olivia Keatley.
Middle Row: Mrs J Sproule, Jane Condy, Shirley Love, Hannah Hawkes,
Scott Gordon, Samuel Keatley, Chloe Hall, Mrs H Graham.
Front Row: Martin Baird, Shirley Harpur, Leigha Kane, Adam Bustard, Leah Lowry, Alan Boyd.

I have blue eyes and short blonde hair. I have two older sisters. I have no brothers. I play with my sisters sometimes. I play football with my friends. I always score three goals. I like watching Kids TV. My favourite is Zoey 101 My favourite subject in school is Art and Craft. I am a happy boy My name is Kyle Duncan

I am 135 cm tall and my weight is 30kg. I am the youngest in my family. I like dying my hair blue. I like going on my mini moto. My favourite subject in school is science. I love going to rallies with my dad. My favourite hobby is cars. My best friends are Alan, Scott, Adrian and Alan. I am in year4 and my name is Adam Bustard.

They are five people in my family and I am the oldest. I have one sister and one brother. I have blue eyes and long black hair. I am learning to play the piano . I am 141cm tall . My favourite subject in school is art .My friends are Shirley Harpur, Hannah, and Leah .I am Olivia Keatley.

I have short hair and blue eyes and big teeth and floppy ears. I like going swimming on a Monday . I have got 12 freckles on My face. I have a small nose. I like getting my hair cut very short. I have three brothers. My mum says I am helpful sometimes. I am a happy boy. My height is 140 cm. My favourite subject at school is art and craft. I have 6 people in my family. My friends are Alan, Adam and Adrian. I am Scott Gordon

I have blue eyes and oily skin and I have to get cream on. I have ginger hair but I have no freckles. I am 7 years old. I am in Year 4. I have three sisters. There are six people in my family. I am the youngest in my family. My sister, Andrea is the oldest. Emma is the second oldest. My favourite subject is Art. I am a happy girl. My best friends are Scott, Shirley and Emily. My name is Lynsay Glenn.

I have green eyes and short ginger hair. My height is 1m 28cm. I have freckles on my face. There are six people in my family. I have two sisters and one brother. I am the oldest. I am 8 years old and I am in year 4. I think I am a happy boy. My best friend is Samuel; I like playing catchers with Samuel. My favourite subject is art. I like going to the swimming pool on Tuesday's after school. My name is Martin Baird.

My name is Adrian Humphrey.
I have short black hair.
I have blue eyes.
I am 130 cm tall and I weigh 27 kgs.
I like playing in clubs.
My dad does lots of jobs.
My friend is Scott.

I have long hair and green eyes and two big teeth. I have brownish black hair. My height is 127 cm. I like going to the swimming pool on Saturday and the cinema My favourite movie was Racing strips. I like playing with my ball against the wall by my self at home. I have one sister and four bothers. My favourite games are racing and catchers. My favourite subject is pe.
Who am I
My name is Shirley harpur.

I have short brown hair, and blue eyes. I like going swimming on Thursday. My favourite game is dodge ball. I play dodge ball with my sister .There is four people in my family. I have one sister no brothers. I am in year 4. My best friends are Leah, Emily, Jane, Shannon and Lynsay. Who am I Shirley love.

I am 8 years old and I have three sisters and one brother. I have brown hair and blue eyes. I have freckles on my face and some on my arms. There are seven people in my family altogether. I like going to the swimming pool with my mummy and daddy. My mum said I can be helpful sometimes I can be naughty when my brother Ryan annoys me. My favourite subject in school is art. My friends are Shirley Lindsay and Chloe. My name is Emily Maxwell.

I have brown hair and blue eyes. I have one sister called Danielle. I am the oldest. My favourite subject in school is number work. I like to go swimming on Saturdays with my dad. My best friends are Jane, Scott and Leah. My name is Shannon Watson.

I have long brown hair and green eyes. I have two sisters older than me and two brothers younger than me. My brothers always annoy me. My friends are Shannon, Hannah, Jane, Martin and Leah. My favourite work is my time book. I like playing catcher and rounders. My name is Leigha Kane.

I have blue eyes . I have green glasses. I have short brown hair. My height is 137 cm. I have an older brother and sister. I am the youngest in the family. I like playing football with my brother and working on the farm with my daddy. My favourite subject is PE. My friends are Scott and Alex.
    My name is Samuel Keatley

I have brown hair and blue eyes. I am in year 4. I have 2 brothers in school. I like playing foot ball and tennis. I am 141 cm tall. My favourite subject in school is art and craft. My favourite work is Times tables . My friends are Adam and Scott. My name is Alan Boyd .

506

I have brown eyes and my hair is long and black. I have one brother. His name is Alexander . My best friend is Shannon and Leah, Hannah and Shirley Harpur and Shirley love . My favourite game is catchers. My favourite subject in school is art. My favourite colour is pink. My favourite clothes is a blue T-shirt and a stripy skirt .I have four in my family altogether. I am a happy girl. My name is Jane Condy.

I have long, curly, brown hair and big dark brown eyes. I weigh 30 kg. My height is 133 cm. I have four best friends. Their names are Shirley Harpur, Hannah Hawkes Hannah Crawford Olivia Keatley. Three of them go to this school and we are all in year 4. When we go outside we play together. My favourite subject is math.

Who am I? I am Leah Lowry.

I have hazel eyes and long blonde hair. I am eight years old. I have one brother his name is David. I am the oldest. There are four people in my family. My favourite subject at school is PE and I enjoy Clubs on a Monday. My friends are Emily, Jane and Shannon. My name is Chloe Hall.

I am a boy. I am tractor mad. I have brown eyes and short hair. I am 8 years old. I am good at playing football. I can drive the tractor when my dad is in beside me. I have three brothers and two sisters. My favourite games are football, basketball, swimming and rugby. My name is Alex Harpur.

I have hazel eyes. I have long dark blonde hair. My height is 1m 33cm .I like to go swimming with my brother, mum and dad . I play the piano. I did an exam and got 86 marks which is an Honours certificate. My brother is the youngest and I am the oldest. There are four people in my family. My favourite subject in school is maths. I have four best friends. Their names are Jane, Leah ,Shirely H and Olivia .I am a happy Person .My name is Hannah Hawkes .

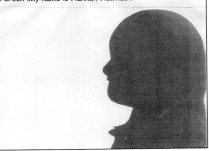

Year 5

Back Row: Brett Wallace, Charlene Hemphill, Justin Bogle, Zoe Deery, Ivan Reid.
Middle Row: Leowna Gillespie, David Harpur, Jordan Pearson, Abigail Clarke,
Nadine Doherty, Gemma Hamilton, Mrs J. A Warnock.
Front Row: Alistair Reid, Travis Glenn, Gary Hunter, John Pak, Richard Dunlop,
Danni Strawford, Andrew Catterson

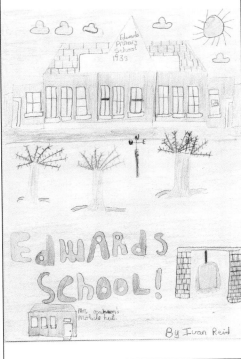

EDWARDS

EDWARDS BADGE

EDWARDS SCHOOL CASTLEDERG

Jordan Pearson

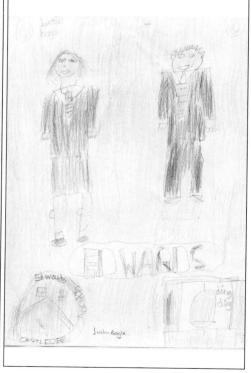

EDWARDS

EDWARDS SCHOOL CASTLEDERG

Justin Bogle.

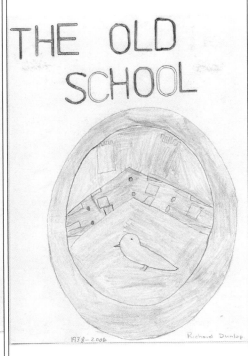

Year 6

Back Row: Yvonne Luk, Amy Semple, Leanne Lindsay, Hannah Gowdy, Kirsty Gillespie, Cathy Keatley, Adam McGrath, Caroline Irwin, Miss C Roke.

Middle Row: Heather Sproule, Julie-Ann Sproule, Elliott Hill, Dean Irvine, Travis Gordon, Adam Catterson.

Front Row: Gareth Williamson, Andrew Hamilton, Jake Scott, Wendy Forbes, Gemma Kennedy, Joseph Caldwell, Aisling Dunlop.

Gossip about our friends

Heather is kind and always would help you. She is a super friend. She has blue eyes.

She is my best friend.

Aisling is my best friend also. She has thin brown hair and is thin.

Jake is a fast runner and has brown hair. Jake likes football.

Andrew has blonde hair and is a fast runner.

Cathy is kind, helpful and she is a good friend.

By Wendy Forbes.

Amy is very funny and likes doing maths.

Travis is a fast runner.

Cathy is good at English and is a good friend.

Hannah is a good artist and so is Yvonne.

Dean likes playing football with his friends.

By Caroline Irwin.

Joseph and Gareth like writing stories.

Cathy is a friendly person.

Hannah is a great artist.

Leeanne is a very kind person and she is friendly.

Elliott has brown spiky hair.

By Yvonne Luk.

Jake likes building huts and spying. He also is my best friend.

Dean likes playing football. He has orange hair and freckles on his face.

Heather has long hair and her friends are called Aisling and Cathy.

Hannah likes playing football and she is smart.

By Travis Gordon.

Heather is funny and she likes dancing.

Hannah likes football and her favourite team is Man. United.

Aisling has long hair and is a good singer.

Amy is funny and has brown hair.

Cathy is tall and is a good friend.

By Julie-Ann Sproule.

Travis is a good football player.

Dean is good at games.

Andrew is a fast runner.

Wendy is fast at maths.

Heather is good at English.

By Jake Scott.

Elliott Hill was my first friend and great at it.

Travis Gordon is great at football.

Gareth Williamson is great at chatting but a good friend.

Yvonne is a very good girl and good at maths.

Joseph Caldwell is good to me and has a great imagination.

By Adam Catterson.

Hannah Gowdy is a smart girl who is my best friend.

Travis Gordon can be stubborn and crabit at times.

Yvonne Luk likes Maths but she doesn't really likes rugby.

Elliott Hill would be a bit silly and bad tempered, if you tease him.

Ashling Dunlop is a good friend and she is really funny.

By Kirsty Gillespie.

Julie-Ann has dark brown hair and brown eyes. She is also kind and jolly.

Travis has light brown hair and blue eyes. He also has a best friend called Jake. He is very sporty.

Cathy is my best friend. She wears glasses and has dark brown hair.

Joseph has light brown hair and he is from England.

Yvonne is from China (Hong Kong). She has black hair and was a lot of help when we were doing our Chinese New Year booklet.

By Heather Sproule.

Leanne Lindsay is a very helpful girl and she loves playing her game boy.

Gemma Kennedy is a good friend and she has a lot of cousins.

Yvonne Luk is a genius at maths and is fast at her work.

Jake Scott is a very good friend and has got quicker at his work.

Travis Gordon has girls who like him. He plays a lot of football and he likes rugby.

By Amy Semple.

Aisling is a very good friend and is funny.

Yvonne is also a good friend but does not like any sports.

Amy is very good at football and is brilliant at keeping secrets.

Travis is a good sports player and a good runner.

Jake is always very sleepy but outside he is active.

By Leeanne Lindsay.

Adam is good at Pokemon games.

Gareth and I are like a pair of granddads together.

Elliott is a fast runner.

Hannah is very smart.

Dean plays for the school rugby team.

By Joseph Caldwell.

Wendy is a fabulous dresser.

Hannah is smart.

Gemma is a fun friend.

Joseph is a chatterbox.

Adam Mc Grath has a lot of dyes in his hair.

By Aisling Dunlop.

Joseph is my friend from England.

Gareth is okay at tag-rugby.

Adam is one of my best friends.

Yvonne is really good at math.

Travis puts hair gel on.

By Elliott Hill.

Jake is the quickest runner in the class.

Joseph is a chatterbox.

Travis is the best footballer in the class.

Andrew is the third quickest in the class.

Dean has ginger hair.

By Adam McGrath.

Amy is my friend because she is funny and she is a fast runner. She is also intelligent.

Travis is a fast runner and good at football. He is a bit funny and he tells good jokes.

Heather is funny, good at telling stories and she's not cheeky. She has good fashion sense and is beautiful.

Jake is a fast runner and he is funny. He is good at football and he is a bit silly.

Wendy is funny, fun and kind. She is a fast runner and is a hard worker in class.

By Gemma Kennedy.

Travis is a fast runner and a classy footballer.

Yvonne is an excellent artist.

Jake is a good friend.

Leeanne is a very helpful girl.

Hannah is very smart.

By Dean Irvin.

Julie-Ann is always kind and helpful.

Aisling has lovely green eyes.

Wendy has nice ginger hair.

Dean is a good footballer.

Jake has brown hair.

Heather is a good friend.

By Cathy Keatley.

Lee Williamson is a good football player and is up for trying new things.

Joseph Caldwell, Elliott Hill and Adam Catterson are my best friends and we are always making new games.

Hannah Gowdy is smart.

By Gareth Williamson.

Travis is a good football player.

Dean is fast.

Jake knows how to be a good friend.

Hannah is smart.

Amy is funny.

By Andrew Hamilton.

Kirsty is a tomboy and loves playing football. She is a bit like Mr Bumps; she is always bumping into things and falling.

Yvonne Luk comes from China. She has no brothers and no sisters. Her Auntie and Uncle own a restaurant. She is also good at drawing.

Julie-Ann Sproule has six members in her family. She has two brothers and one sister. She lives on a farm and has a dog-called Bobby.

Elliott Hill has three friends. Gareth, Adam C. and Joseph. He has a brother called Carson.

Travis Gordon lives in my park. He loves football. He supports Man. U. He has three brothers and is also on the school rugby team.

By Hannah Gowdy.

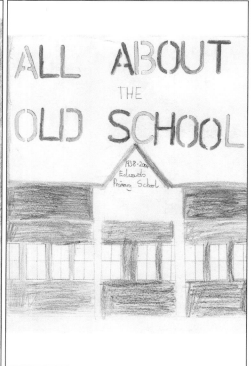

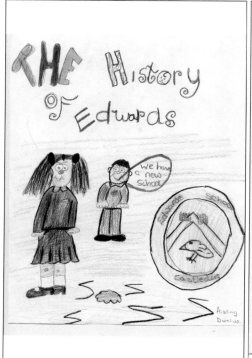

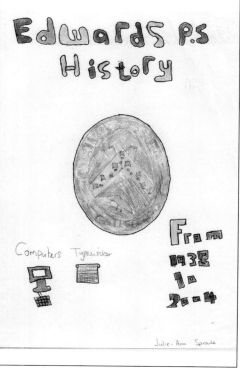

Our old school features!

Leeanne's English book Yr 6 Miss Robb

School Badge

EDWARDS SCHOOL
CASTLE DER

BY Leeanne Lindsay.

1938-2006
EDWARDS SCHOOL
CASTLE DER

Mr Cawley Teacher for year

Miss Robb teacher for year 6

Mrs McLay Teacher for year 5

Mrs Graham teacher for year 4

Miss Moore Teacher for year 3

Miss Brown teacher for year 2

Miss Douglas Teacher for year 1

Kirsty Gillespie

The Old Edwards Primary School

1938
EDWARDS PUBLIC ELEMENTARY SCHOOL

Yvonne Luk

THE OLD SCHOOL

EDWARDS SCHOOL
CASTLE DER

Wendy Forbes

519

THE school Badge

EDWARDS SCHOOL

CAStLEDERG

Heather Sprowle

1938-2005

EDWARDS No.1

EDWARDS SCHOOL CASTLEDERG

THE OLD SCHOOL

1938 EDWARDS PUBLIC Elementary School

Adam Catterson

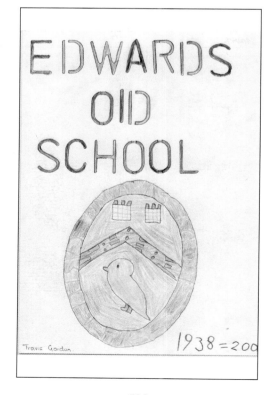

EDWARDS OID SCHOOL

Travis Gordon

1938=200

Year 7

Back Row: Ashley Duncan, Victoria Maxwell, Cheryl Hamilton, Heather Hunter, Serena Gillespie, Shannon Carruthers.

Middle Row: Mr I Gowdy, Lee Thompson, Candice Cathers, Robert Keatley, Jamie Fyffe, Darren Scott, Denver Lecky, Mark Robinson, Emma Kane.

Front Row: Glenn Sproule, Nathan Milligan, Jamie Strawford, Jacqueline Hunter, Sophie Harpur, Trudy Johnston, Elizabeth Willliamson, Nicole Kee.

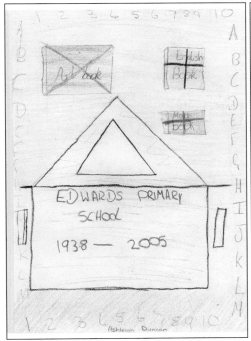

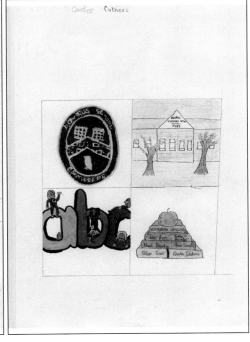

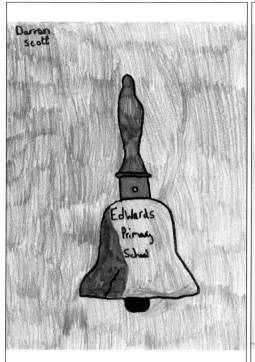

Glen Sproule   Glen S

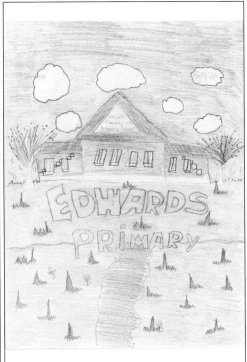

Lee Thompson

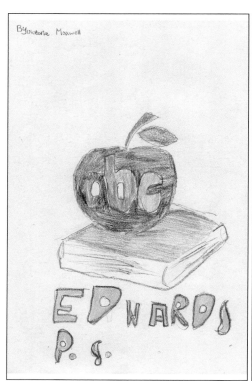

By Victoria Maxwell

EDWARDS
P. S.

A is for apple   B is for book

C is for children   D is for dinner

Sophie Harper

Nathan Milligan

Edwards Primary School

123
ABC

Robert Keatley

EDWARDS P.S

HISTORY

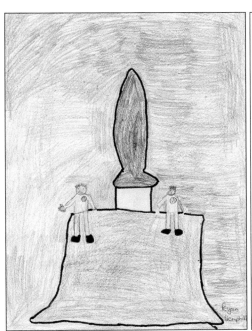

What Is Yellow?

As yellow as the sun,
On a warm summer's day.
As yellow as a banana I eat,
When I play.
Yellow is the colour of
Bart Simpson's family.
Yellow is the lemon,
That grows on a tree.
As yellow as the ball,
The boys left outside.
And yellow is the moon,
That can so highly glide.
Yellow is friendly, old
Winnie the Pooh.
And my sunglasses
Which I look through.

By Heather Hunter.

What Is Pink?

Pink is the colour of strawberry ice cream,
Pink is the dress on which sequins make gleam.
Pink is the colour of a beautiful rose,
Pink is the colour of a cold, frozen nose.

Pink is the colour of big rosy cheeks,
Pink isn't the colour of a child that is weak.
Pink are the marshmallows in my hot chocolate drinks,
Pink are my toes when I'm off the ice-rink.

Pink is the colour of my bedroom walls,
Pink is the colour of my knees when I fall,
Pink is the colour of my friends pencil case,
Pink is the colour of a flower's pretty face.

By Sophie Harpur

What is Purple?

Purple is regal and royal,
It's the velvet on the seat of the throne.
And the colour of the crown.
But it can also be hurt,
Lies, misfortune and turmoil.
Purple is a sweet smelling violet,
Lavender and lilac.
It's like a floating candle with a flame,
Or the feeling inside when your lame.
The colour of the bags under your eyes,
When you tell the teacher the
'When I went to bed' lies.
Purple is the colour of sympathy,
Or the mystery of telepathy.
Purple is the colour of thought,
Purple is a colour I like a lot.

Candice Cathers.

Football Team '05

Back Row: Glen Sproule, Nathan Milligan, Robert Keatley, Darren Scott,
Kirsty Gillespie, Heather Hunter, Mark Robinson.
Front Row: Elizabeth Williamson, Trudy Johnston, Travis Gordon, Denver Lecky,
Alan Harron, Yvonne Luk, Hannah Gowdy.

School Band '05

Back Row: Elizabeth Williamson, Robert Keatley, Heather Hunter, Sophie Harpur.
Front Row: Gary Hunter, Zoe Deery, Abigail Clarke, Candice Cathers, Emma Kane, Hannah Gowdy.

Tag Rugby Team

Back Row: Travis Gordon, Elizabeth Williamson, Caroline Irwin, Darren Scott,
Nathan Milligan, Mark Robinson.
Front Row: Dean Irvine, Wendy Forbes, Lee Williamson, Denver Lecky, Glen Sproule, Andrew Hamilton.

The Rugby team took part in a World Nations Fancy
Dress Competition. Our players dressed as Fijians
and won 3rd place.

Our Rugby Report

On Thursday 14th April, some of Edwards made an early start and headed to Belfast (The Dub) to compete in a rugby tournament, after qualifying to represent the Omagh area.

The rugby team was a mixture of P7 and P6 boys and girls. The team took along the rest of the P6 class as supporters.

All the rugby teams there had to dress up. Some dressed as Scotland, Japan, England and France. Our team dressed up as Fiji. The boys wore grass skirts and the girls wore long coloured skirts. Our team won third place in the fancy dress competition.

While the team changed into their kit the supporters practised their chants. Our team played three matches against Killoween, St Treas and Ballyclare. There were no winners because it was a fun day.

When the matches were over we had our lunch on the grass and watched a few games of rugby. A friendly dog came over to join us and ate Caroline's sandwiches.

At the end everyone was given a bottle of coke and then we headed home. We all had great fun.

By Year 6

Teaching Staff

Back Row: Miss J Douglas, Mrs H McCay, Mrs H Robinson, Miss C Roke, Mrs J A Warnock, Miss N Moore, Miss L Morrow, Mrs C Hawkes.
Front Row: Mrs H Graham, Mrs P Bratton, Mr A S Orr, Mr I Gowdy, Mrs M E Watt, Mrs G McKinley.

Classroom Assistants/Secretary

Back Row: Mrs P Quigley, Mrs I Forbes, Mrs J Sproule, Miss Z Johnston, Mrs A McCreery, Miss C Davis, Miss Y Donnell
Front Row: Miss E McKane, Mrs K Cowan, Mrs S Sproule, Miss M Young, Mrs E Walls

Kitchen Staff

Back Row: Mrs L Gilchrist, Mrs C Clarke, Mrs M Cassidy
Front Row: Mrs H Keatley, Mrs A M Meehan, Mrs M Burke

Domestic Staff

Mrs J Bogle, Mrs T Wilson, Mr B Gilchrist, Mrs G Glass

Appendix 1.

The Manor of Hastings was the huge estate that was bought by Hugh Edwards from Lucy, Countess of Huntington, and wife of Ferdinand, Lord Hastings. This appendix puts the size of the estate in context and shows the townlands included. The following details are recorded in Griffiths Valuation 1860, almost two hundred years after the purchase and they show the landowner at that time and the amount of land in acres, roods and perches.

Owner: Henry Lighton.

Golan (Adams and Hunter)
Knockbrack
Drumnabey
Spamount
Upper third
Carrickadartans
Castlebane
Cavan
Pollyarnon
Carrickaness
Cornashesk

12 townlands: 3303 acres, 3 roods, and 25 perches.

Owner: Henry Echlin (Kilmore Lodge)

Kilmore (Robinson and Irvine)
Kirlish
Carony
Drumnaforbe
Gortahar
Carrickamulkin

6 townlands : 3372 acres, 1 rood and 10 perches.

Owner: The Honourable A. G. Stuart.

Binnawooda
Lisleen
Shanog
Coolcreaghy

4 townlands: 1082 acres, 3 roods and 15 perches.

Owner: George T. Spillier

Blackhill
Clare Upper
Claremore
Ardbarron (Upper and Lower)
Lettercarn
Bolaght
Aghakinmart (Langfield)
Bullock Park
Aghadulla Harpur (Dromore Parish)
Badoney

11 townlands: 3604 acres, 1 rood 38 perches.

Owner: Sir James Stronge (Bart)

Scralea
Leitrim
Aghnahoo
Bomacatall (Upper and Lower)
Learmore
3 Ganvaghans- Kyle, Semple and Hemphill
Drumbarley

Drumrawn

Leganvey

Coolkeeragh

Dressogue

Cloghog (Upper and Lower)

Aghaleague

Culbuck

Tarlim

Coolnagard

Sedenam

Rylands

About four of the latter townlands were outside the original Davies estate.

23 townlands : 8057 acres and 22 perches.

Owner : The Earl of Castlestewart

Garvetagh (Upper and Lower)

Coolnacrunaght

Kilreal Lower

Altgolan

Killen Near

Killen Far

Mournebeg

Lislaird

Common

Mullinabreen

Ardarver

Maghernageeragh

Edenashanlaght

Tullyard

Coolavannagh

Garvagh

Garvagh Blane

Garvagh Billans

Laghtmorris

Laghtfoggy

Carndreen

Carracoghan

Creduff

Drumquin
Drumgallan
Castlesessiagh
Castlegore
Creevy (Upper and Lower)

30 townlands: 12,068 acres, 3 roods and 25 perches.

Owner : Representatives of Alex Colhoun Strabane.

Meenclogher
Aghamore
Meencarriga
Drummahon

4 townlands: 1626 acres, 3 roods and 3 perches.

Owner: Sir Robert Ferguson

First Corgary
Second Corgary
Third Corgary
Fourth Corgary (Meenaclough)
Fifth Corgary
Sixth Corgary (Craw)
Mullaghfamore
Tullycar
Altamullan
Aghyaran
Clagernagh
Carrickaholton
Aghascrebagh
Lisnacloon

Dreenan
Legatonegan
Kilclean
Dartans
Drumhonish (Drumquin)
Drumhonish (Langfield)
Unshinagh
Churchtown (Castlederg)
Craigmonaghan (Nelson)
Craigmonaghan (Funston)

Castlederg Church Lands by Lease :   Berrysfort
                                       Ballylennon (Scott)
                                       Ballylenon (Mercer)
                                       Bridgetown

28 townlands : 12,823 acres, 2 roods and 17 perches

The total amount of these eight estates is 42,636 acres and 10 perches, which is approximately the amount of land that was granted in 1609 at the time of the Plantation to Sir John Davies. Following his death in 1626 his daughter Lucy inherited this estate and then she sold it to Hugh Edwards who was supposed to have brought gold over from London to pay for it.

Appendix 2

Local clergy, members of the community and past Headmasters have served over the years on the School Management Committee or Board of Governors and have had an invaluable role in ensuring the satisfactory running of the school. There have been many changes in personnel but the following lists record the Governors at strategic times in the life of the school.

The first named school governors were:_

> Rev. Canon Thomas Olphert (Parish of Urney)
> Mr John Herdman J.P.
> Mr William King-Edwards
> Mr William Gamble
> Mr Andrew Gailey
> The Minister of the Parish of Derg and the Ministers of the Presbyterian Congregations of First and Second Castlederg were also to be Governors, but were not named.

1938:

> Rev. Canon Macourt (Chairman)
> Rev. A.W. McFarlane M.A. (Vice Chairman)
> Rev. W.G.M. Thompson B.A B.D.
> Rev. R.J. Black
> Mr James F. Gamble J.P. M.P.
> Mr W.J. Trimble
> Mr Charles Hamilton
> Mr W.J. Harron
> Mr John J. Mitchell
> Mr Samuel Robinson (Snr.)
> Mr Robert Waugh
> Mr I.B. Wilson
> Mr James G. Sloan (Hon Sec. and Principal)

1978:   Rev. Canon A.H. Northridge M.A. (Chairman)
Rev. W.J. Patterson B.Sc. (Vice Chairman)
Rev. J. Brookes
Miss G. Elliott
Dr. M. Brown
Miss K. Ogilvie
Mr H. Trimble
Mr E.C. H. Young
Mr T.F. Riddall (Hon Sec.and Principal)

2005:   Dr J.M. Brown (Chairman)
Mr D. Williamson (Vice Chairman)
Mr R. J. Montgomery
Mr T.A. Kerrigan
Mr R. Loughlin
Mr J. K. Walls
Mrs A. Hunter
Mrs G. McKinley
Mr I. Clarke
Mr A.S. Orr (Hon Sec and Principal)

Appendix 3

The following table shows all the P.R.O.N.I. documents and their reference numbers:

DOCUMENT	TITLE
D/7/1	Education Sources for Co. Tyrone.
	1835 Release of Site for Poor Boys.
D/8/1	1839 Contract for Building Edwards Charity School
D/1813/9	Files re School improvement grants - Tyrone
ED/27/83	Edwards School Endowments Scheme 1893-1943
Fin/18/5/39	Papers Re Endowed School 1922 - 1963
FIN/18/5/102	Papers Re Endowed School 1922 - 1963
ED/13/1/1699	Building of New P.E.S. 1932-1938
ED/6/1/6/1	Co Tyrone National Schools Register 1
ED/6/1/6/2	Co Tyrone National Schools Register 2
ED/6/1/6/3	Co Tyrone National Schools Register 3
SCH/1124/1/1	National School Register 1864-1909 Vol 1
SCH/1124/1/2	National School Register 1891-1926 Vol 2
SCH/1124/1/3	National School Register 1904-1953 Vol 3
SCH/1124/1/4	National School Register 1920-1954 Vol 4
SCH/1124/5/1	1875-1954 Insp' Observation Book - Boys School
SCH/1124/2/2	1893-1927 Insp' Observation Book - Girls School
D/1618/2/9	Marriage Settlement Robt Stewart / Mgt Edwards
D/1618/2/17	Lease and Deed of Mortgage
D/1618/2/13	Bill of Exchange Peter Pellisier
D/1618/2/19	Will of Thomas Edwards 1721
D/1618/2/22	Marriage Settlement Eleanor Stuart/P. Pelisier
D/1618/15/5/1	Bundle of Letters by Cairnes Edwards
D/3000/114/1	Genealogical Table Edwards Family
D/2547/24	Titbits Newspaper Article on Edwards
D/2547/27	Leaf from Family Bible
D/2547/4	E.H. Edwards Bill of Exchange
D/2547/25	Obituary Notice - Smythe Edwards

D/2547/30	Edwards Family Notes
D/2547/5	ADMISSION TO MURDER BY HENRY THOMAS
D/2547/6	TRIAL AND CONFESSION OF HENRY THOMAS
D/2547/3	LETTER FROM EDWARD EDWARDS- BALTIMORE
D/697/1	EDWARD EDWARDS MARRIAGE ARTICLES
D/1697/1	MARRIAGE SETTLEMENT ED EDWARDS/ JEAN ROSS
D/2547/1	EDWARD EDWARDS WILL 1777
D/847/21/1/2	WILL OF HUGH EDWARDS 1737
D847/27/7	WILL OF HUGH EDWARDS 1662
D/2547/21	LETTER RE PEDIGREE OF EDWARDS
D/2547/23	LETTER TO JOHN EDWARDS RE COAT OF ARMS
D/847//5/22A	WILL OF WILLIAM HOLMES
D/1618/15/5	CERT.OF RECEIPT OF LORD'S SUPPER 1744
D/2547/15	PRINTED NOTES ON DESCENDANTS
	OF HUGH EDWARDS
D/1618/14/11	CAIRNES FAMILY TREE
D/1618/14/11	LETTER - A. FLEMING TO LORD CASTLESTEWART
D/1618/15/5	CASE +OPINION ON ADMIN OF CAIRNES EDWARDS
D/2547/28	EDWARDS ARMORY NOTES

Appendix 4.

The following page is an extract from the Gedcom File on the Edwards family, which was kindly sent by Mr George Daniel Speer, of Brentwood, California, and is available in the school.

Descendants of Unknown Edwards

1-Unknown Edwards [4170] b. Est 1602, of a Welsh Family, who settled in the City of Londonderry, Ulster, N.Ireland
+Unknown
- 2-Hugh Edwards Sr. [1155] b. Est 1620, d. 24 Feb 1672, Castlederg, parish of SKIRTS, barony of OMAGH, Co. TYRONE, province of ULSTER
  +Margaret [1156] d. 20 Nov 1679, (Cathedral)
  - 3-Hugh Edwards Jr. [1157] b. Abt ? 1638, d. 9 Oct 1667, Derry
  - 3-Edward Edwards Sr. [1153] b. 1640, d. 23 Mar 1678, (Castlederg Church, parish of SKIRTS, barony of OMAGH, Co. TYRONE, province of ULSTER, IRELAND)
    +Mary Muncriffe [1154] d. Jan 1682, (Derry), m. 16 Jan 1667
    - 4-Hugh Edwards [1166] b. Oct 1668, d. Apr 1682, (Derry)
    - 4-Thomas Edwards [1167] b. Jan 1670, of Castlegore, d. 27 Apr 1721, (Castlederg Church, parish of SKIRTS, barony of OMAGH, Co. TYRONE, province of ULSTER, IRELAND)
      +Jane "Johanna" Cairnes [4204] b. 1680, d. 23 Sep 1719, (Castlederg Church, parish of SKIRTS, barony of OMAGH, Co. TYRONE, province of ULSTER, IRELAND), m. 13 Jul 1699, Cousins, par. David Cairnes M.P. for Derry [4198] and Margaret Edwards [1162]
      - 5-Elizabeth Edwards [4543] d. , Died in Infancy
      - 5-David Edwards [4544] d. , Died in Infancy
      - 5-Margaret Edwards [4545] b. Abt 1701, Castle Gore, Tyrone, North Ireland, d. , Stuart Hall, Tyrone, North Ireland
        +Robert Stuart [4565] b. 3 Mar 1700, of Stuart Hall, , Co. Tyrone, Ulster, Ireland, d. 2 Mar 1742, m. 1 Jun 1722, par. Andrew Stuart [4566] and Eleanor Dallway [4578]
        - 6-Andrew Thomas Stuart VI Lord Castlestuart [4567] b. 1723-29 Aug 1725, Stuart Hall, County Tyrone, North Ireland, d. 26 Aug 1809, Stewart Hall, Co. Tyrone, Ireland
          +Sarah Lill [4575] b. 15 Aug 1754, d. 11 Nov 1843, Hanover Terrace, Marylebone, London, Middlesex, England, m. 2 Aug 1782, par. Judge Godfrey Lill [5071] and Unknown
        - 6-Jane Stuart [4568] b. Abt 1727, Stuart Hall, County Tyrone, North Ireland, d. 1804, Stuart Hall, County Tyrone, North Ireland
        - 6-Cairnes Stuart [4571] b. 1738, Stuart Hall, Tyrone, North Ireland, d. 1752, Stuart Hall, Tyrone, North Ireland
        - 6-Eleanor Stuart [4570] b. <1749>, Stuart Hall, County Tyrone, North Ireland
          +Peter Pelisiere [4573] b. , of Laragh Bryan, Parish of Maynooth, Ireland, m. 1758, of Laragh Bryan, Parish of Maynooth, Kildare, Ireland, par. Rev. Abel Pelisiere [4574] and Unknown
          - 7-William St. George Pellisier [5072] b. 1775, , Co. Kings (Offaly), Lienster, Ireland, d. 1794
          - 7-Alexander Pellisier B.A. [5073] b. 1760, , Co. Kings (Offaly), Lienster, Ireland
        - 6-Olivia Stuart [4577] b. Abt 1751, Stuart Hall, County Tyrone, North Ireland, d. , Stuart Hall, Tyrone, North Ireland
        - 6-Harriet Stuart [4569] b. Abt 1753, Stuart Hall, County Tyrone, North Ireland
          +Sir. James Hamilton [4572] b. Abt 1745, Woodbrook, County Tyrone, North Ireland
      - 5-Hugh Edwards [4546] b. Abt 1700, Castlegore, d. 24 Oct 1737, Castlederg Church, parish of SKIRTS, barony of OMAGH, Co. TYRONE, province of ULSTER, IRELAND
        +Ann Mervyn [4553] , par. .....?..... Mervynne [4554] and Unknown
        - 6-Olivia Edwards Countess of Rosse [4556] b. , Castlegore, Co. Tyrone, Ireland, d. 11 Apr 1820
          +Richard Parsons 2nd Earl of Rosse [4561] b. Abt 1716, d. 27 Aug 1764, m. 16 Feb 1754, par. Richard Parsons 1st Earl of Rosse [4595] and Mary Paulett [4596]
          +Captain John Bateman [4562] b. , , Co. West Meath, m. 7 Oct 1770, 2nd Husband, par. Rowland Bateman Esq. [4597] and Elizabeth Colthurst [4598]

Produced by: George Daniel Speer Sr., 460 Ellisa Lane, Brentwood, California, USA, 94513, 925-634-8821, genealogy@speer.org, speer.org

30 Jun 2006